THE STRAIGHT DETROIT

AMERICA'S PREMIER LEGACY CITY

FIRST EDITION

Edited by Jeffrey T. Horner

Wayne State University

Bassim Hamadeh, CEO and Publisher
Kassie Graves, Director of Acquisitions and Sales
Jamie Giganti, Senior Managing Editor
Miguel Macias, Senior Graphic Designer
Jennifer Codner, Acquisitions Editor
Michelle Piehl, Project Editor
Alexa Lucido, Licensing Coordinator
Berenice Quirino, Associate Production Editor

Cover image copyright© 2016 iStockphoto LP/mysticenergy.

Printed in the United States of America

ISBN: 978-1-5165-1270-6 (pbk) / 978-1-5165-1271-3 (br)

 cognella® | ACADEMIC PUBLISHING

For Jill, Audrey and Melody

ACKNOWLEDGEMENTS

In practice, a book has many authors and editors, but only enough room on the cover and spine for one or two names. A book's acknowledgement page offers the opportunity to recognize those who worked with, inspired, and tolerated the named author. Here goes:

The team at Cognella Academic Publishing made the process as smooth as possible. Michelle Piehl, the project editor, has been unfailingly professional, prompt, and patient with me as I slogged through details and edits, and I didn't always turn things around to her as soon as promised. Alright, rarely were things turned around to her as promised, but never did she express frustration or exasperation with my loose deadlines. If I'm ever fortunate enough to publish with Cognella again, my first condition will be to have Michelle as my project editor. Sorry, Michelle.

Dani Skeen was similarly patient and professional when awaiting my feedback on her promotional copy for the text. Dani, I only hope that the time I took to get it right will translate into higher sales volumes.

Jennifer Codner, acquisitions editor, was my first contact with Cognella, and set the tone for all to come in terms of work and responsibilities in a conference call with Michelle that answered all of my questions and concerns without me having to ask. I had a wonderful lunch with her during her visit to campus, as she was remarkably classy, gracious, and interesting in discussing the publishing business.

I was greatly impressed with the work of Miguel Macias, senior graphic designer, who chose a cover image for the preliminary edition that I still marvel at for its austere beauty. I hope it has been retained for this first edition. If not, I assure you he came up with something better.

Berenice Quirino, associate production editor, seemed to suffer me gladly as I sent her partially-approved copyedits of essays and sections, when all she had wanted was fully-approved ones.

To the anonymous copyeditor, you are not paid enough money. Ask your direct supervisor to approve my suggested changes now.

Deep gratitude goes to former students Marissa Mewitz and Emily Smith for allowing me to use their coursework essays here. And my most heartfelt gratitude is extended to Gary Sands and Joel Stone for their original contributions that have greatly improved this work.

Thanks also to my colleague Avis Vidal, whose conversation with other Cognella authors at a conference provided the inspiration to take on this project.

Thanks also to my wife Jill, who too many times after a long day at work had to reach for the Excedrin because I needed her assistance with sentence or paragraph structure. Jill, what's a gender-neutral word for wingman?

Last, this book would not have been possible without my fabulous Wayne State University students, about whom I could write a text-length manuscript on their rich and oftentimes challenging lives. Just like this great city itself.

CONTENTS

PREFACE

Choosing relevant and appropriate readings for an introductory anthology is a painstaking task. Making vivid the facets of a subject of study in order to orient the reader to the essence of the whole not only involves careful selection of salient works but also requires a knack for storytelling. These challenges seem all the more daunting when Detroit is the subject. Detroit, as asserted by urban scholar George Galster, is a palimpsest of generational experiences, ethnicities, races, and classes. Not surprisingly, it has produced a canon of first-rate scholarship and literature to draw from.

But first some backstory: Having taught thousands of students in urban studies and Detroit-related courses, the editors of this work found it increasingly necessary to aggregate Detroit scholarship into a single work. Assigning one or two books on the city didn't capture everything that needed to be captured, and distributing individual works piecemeal to students had become onerous and time-consuming. So it was with an eye toward convenience for future students and instructors that we approached a respected publisher about producing an anthologized text for classroom use.

The intent of this book is to provide a set of in-depth perspectives on the city, including important historic events and economic, social, political, and cultural considerations that have shaped the city and continue to do so. While some of the essays included here have overlapping themes, each essay stands on its own as a unique work of explication. In addition, the concluding section contains essays that look to the future of what is referred to as America's twentieth-century city.

The reading selections herein were chosen as much for their exposition of Detroit as for their scholarly rigor. To the extent that there is a common theme running through Detroit scholarship, it would likely be the experiences of newcomers, including early French settlers, eighteenth-century British occupiers, nineteenth-century European settlers, twentieth-century African American job-seekers, and labor unions (and the turf wars of this last group, throughout the city and shop floors), to name a few. Accordingly, these perspectives and more are offered by a very wide-ranging set of authors from various racial and ethnic backgrounds and academic and cultural disciplines.

Lastly, it must be stressed that omission of important works on Detroit is in no way related to any judgment of their quality. Indeed, many excellent works on the city were not included for two reasons: availability and space. Despite these constraints, we hope that those included here will serve as a reference text both for student and for casual readers, and as a convenient repository for Detroit scholars.

INTRODUCTION

There is an easily overlooked marker lying flush with the pavement in Downtown Detroit's Campus Martius Park. The Point of Origin, a six-foot granite monolith lying beneath, was the original monument used as the basis for survey boundaries throughout the city after the devastating fire of 1805. What the Greenwich meridian is to standard time zones on Earth, the Point of Origin is to the city's Mile Road and north–south road systems. Absent the fire, it probably would not have existed, as pre-fire rights-of-way would very likely have shaped Detroit's built environment.

Also born of the fire was the city motto: *Speramus Meliora—Resurget Cineribus*, or "We hope for better things; it shall arise from the ashes." Adorning the phrase on the City Seal are two female figures, one forlorn and beholden to an engraving of flaming buildings, the other presenting a shining city on a hill. While proverbial phoenixes have indeed risen since the fire, Detroit is noteworthy among cities as being a place that has had more than its share of urban disasters and upheaval, with recovery outcomes often falling far short of those made possible by the Point of Origin.

As illustrated on the City Seal, Detroit is nothing if not a place of stark and sometimes shocking contrasts. This could be said of any major city, but the starkness and contrasts seem to project with a sharper focus here than in other developed cities. While feedback loops of journalistic convention play a part in this, there is little doubt that the city's present fortunes, good and bad, are the result of local, national, and international forces that both elevated the city to urban grandeur and lowered it to an exemplar of urban dysfunction.

America's twentieth-century city, perhaps like no other major city in the world, has experienced dizzying heights, breathtaking lows, and betrayed remarkable contrasts. Here are just a few:

- From Native American paths, to the first mile of paved concrete road in the United States; and from a comprehensive public rail transit system, to one of the most poorly served sets of transit users in large American cities.
- From the nickname "The Paris of the Midwest," to a punch line of urban deprivation and decay. From a nineteenth-century melting pot of Irish, German, Italian, and Polish immigrants, to the most segregated metro area in the country by the twenty-first century.
- From a populist reformer mayor and governor-elect, to another imprisoned—receiving a record sentence for an elected official—for corruption and racketeering.
- From the welcome granted to a soft-spoken black doctor and his family when he moved to an all-white neighborhood, to the welcome accorded the Holy See two generations later.
- From a Ku Klux Klan–supported mayor, to the first public recitation of the "I Have a Dream" speech of an Atlanta minister at a then-record attendance Civil Rights march.
- From a venerated sports franchise whose second-greatest player was the first inducted into the Baseball Hall of Fame, to a wait-until-next-year professional football team.
- From a world-renowned soul and gospel recording artist who got started singing in her father's church choir, to the godfather of punk who got started with a drum kit in his parents' mobile home. From the son of a suburban auto dealer who melded country and rap music into superstardom, to a Midtown ascetic (famous around the world, but not in Detroit) who will one day become the city's most musically talented mayor.
- From early blues artists who toiled in factories by day and played by night, to the Movement Festival.
- From the center of major religious faiths, including African Methodist Episcopalians, Baptists, other Protestants, Catholics and Muslims, to abandoned Nike missile silos.
- From the manicured estates and magnificent park in the city's most exclusive neighborhood, to the soot-dusted homes and industrial landscapes of the city's southwest.
- From a tallest-in-the-world train station, to an abandoned urban monadnock.
- From the former Big Three automakers once enjoying over ninety percent domestic market share, to bankruptcy for two of them. From having the highest rate of single-family home ownership in a major American city, to having one of the highest percentages of abandoned land in a major American city.
- From finishing second in international competition for the Summer Olympic Games, to deadly urban riots at the height of two wars.
- Walls, real and otherwise, seeking to partition those of differing races.
- Black Bottom, before and after urban renewal.
- Detroit Public Schools, formerly an illicit destination for suburban students seeking a higher-quality public education, eventually hemorrhaging students to the suburbs, and being taken over by the state. Twice.
- From Tom's Tavern, to the London Chop House. From all-night raves in the Bankle Building, to the intimacy of a crowded table at Baker's Keyboard Lounge. From the Purple Gang

selling booze in alleys, to the Goodfellows selling newspapers in the streets. From feather bowling, to fowling.

- From the weed-strewn former site of the country's second state fair, to the crown jewel of Belle Isle. From Detroit diamonds, to Shinola watches. From the Vega, to the Volt.
- From the Model T plant, to the Ford Rouge plant. From the imposing Renaissance Center, to a banal gas station in its shadow.
- From the Battle of the Overpass, to UAW membership reaching 1.5 million forty years later. From the home of 125 auto companies, to just two assembly plants in the city proper.
- From the rapidly gentrifying central business district, to blocks and sometimes entire neighborhoods seemingly beyond hope.

Detroit's contrasts also seep into the everyday for those not familiar with the city.

- An amalgam of Bauhaus, Modern, Classic, and Gothic architectural styles visible from an editor's office on a university campus; and a diverse, vigorous hybrid of students in the university classroom.
- Jarring changes of scenery over the course of a block or two, and nine-lane, mostly empty surface streets.
- Breathtaking concentrations of wealth in suburbs and distant exurbs in contrast to a redeveloping downtown and neighborhoods.

All of these studies in contrasts are worthy of scholarly explication. Indeed, many have already been so covered. What follows here is compiled scholarship that seeks to dig deeper into many of these paradoxes of Detroit, sketch out the rudiments of where the city has been, identify root causes of major twentieth-century problems, and predict where Detroit is headed under its present condition.

While no singular work can capture all of Detroit's fame, infamy, and historic perspectives (although Peter Gavrilovich's and Bill McGraw's *The Detroit Almanac* comes close), *The Straight Detroit* attempts to offer deep insights from selected Detroit scholars on events and conditions in the city—capturing, at least in part, the causes giving rise to the contrasts and conflicts in this great city.

SECTION I

READINGS

HISTORICAL PERSPECTIVES

INTRODUCTION

Our introduction to Detroit's history opens with a comprehensive, sweeping essay by **Joel Stone**, published for the first time here, and sets the table by presenting a broad, most up-to-date historical outline of the city in one work. **Susan Villerot** offers an historical essay on the experiences of one of the three Native American tribes in southeast Michigan, the Potawatomi. Elijah Brush, a "Transnational American" and the second lawyer admitted to practice law in the Michigan Territory, is profiled by **Sharon Tevis Finch**. Section I closes with an essay by **Melvin Holli** on the trials of Hazen Pingree, Detroit's reformer mayor.

1

Detroit History

JOEL STONE

Among the oldest cities in the United States, Detroit is recognized worldwide for its engineering and manufacturing prowess, particularly in the realm of automobiles, trucks, and military vehicles. The Motown Sound is easily attributable to the Motor City, and a significant number of local artists—musicians, writers, actors, architects, and visualists—have made their mark on the world. Like many large metropolitan areas, Detroiters are a demographically diverse group, rich with over sixty ethnic populations. For the most part, they live in vibrant neighborhoods that reflect class and cultural similarities.

Detroit's primary products—automobiles, engineering, and music—are rich with tradition, innovation, design acumen, and an international reach. The auto and defense industries have cyclical histories that have experienced tremendous booms and historic busts. Detroit residents—natives, transplants, and corporate nomads (many who stay)—are resilient in the challenges, and they embrace the legacy of opportunity. Detroiters, like the folks in many industrial cities, are tough.

The city is situated along a strait known as the Detroit River, and enjoys a temperate northern climate. Four seasons rotate around moderately warm summers and cold, but not brutal, winters. Spring and autumn are vibrant. Hundreds of lakes, large and small, enhance the regional lifestyle, allowing residents to enjoy a wide range of water-related activities. The bounty of local agriculture, hunting, and fishing has attracted humans to this area for thousands of years.

Concentrated evidence of permanent settlement in the Detroit area has been found near the present site of Historic Fort Wayne, a couple of miles downstream from the current city center. People with ties to the Cahokian culture, which thrived near today's St. Louis, Missouri, were sufficiently settled along the strait to create several large burial mounds (Cahokian peoples are often referred to as "mound builders.") Unfortunately, in preparing the land for later farming and industry, later inhabitants destroyed all of the mounds except one. Material from within the remaining mound has been dated to approximately 800–1,000 years ago.

The prehistoric record, until the late seventeenth century, is thin. Stone tools found regionally indicate that humans continued to visit the area, but nothing has been revealed to indicate permanent villages or towns. It isn't until the arrival of Europeans that we gain a clearer picture of activity along the strait.

French explorers entered the Great Lakes region in the early 1600s via the northern Ottawa–French River route, and they established small settlements from Georgian Bay to the western end of Lake Superior. The native Anishinabek eagerly traded animal skins for metal tools—pots, axes, firearms, knives—and a thriving fur trade developed. To the south, British adventurers pushed into the colonial hinterland west of the Hudson River and Ohio Country, engaging people of the Iroquois nations in a similar commerce. Just as the French and the British were old rivals, so the Anishinabek and Iroquois had long battled over territory and resources in the Great Lakes region. The area along the strait—south of one group and north of the other—became a neutral zone—or in the words of historian Richard White, a middle ground.[1]

At the turn of the eighteenth century, the French commander of Fort de Buade, the primary Great Lakes outpost located at St. Ignace, petitioned the crown for permission to relocate the troops and traders under his command to a more strategic southerly position. With the king's permission, Antoine de la Mothe (Laumet) Cadillac established a small fortification called Fort Pontchartrain on a bend in *le Détroit*—French for "the strait"—in 1701. As governor of what was essentially a new colony, Cadillac was responsible for managing and defending the lands and resources in the region, a situation frowned upon by rival elites in Québec and Montreal. He invited farmers and traders to join this new venture, with modest success. He also invited the native clans from St. Ignace to join him along the strait, and he welcomed new villages of Potawatomi, Odawa, Ojibway, and Huron/Wyandotte.[2]

Cadillac's tenure was brief. His strict managerial style was attacked by both his tenants and his political enemies. In 1710, he was reassigned to the Louisiana territory. A succession of governors was able to grow the village slowly, but failures in French colonial policy and the collapse of the fur trade stalled expansion. Detroit was lost to the British in 1760 during the global conflict known variously as the French and Indian War, the Great War for Empire, or the Seven Years' War.[3]

Although it was under British administration, Detroit remained a French town. The region's non-native population was about 900; during fishing season the native population could swell to six times that many. Most of the merchants remaining within the fort, and nearly all of the farm families were French. The farms, spreading along both sides of the strait and Lake St. Clair to the northeast, were narrow plots 200–300 feet wide and 2–3 miles deep. This arrangement of "ribbon farms" gave each landowners access to the waterway, land for tillage, woods for fuel, and close proximity to neighbors, which promoted social engagement and frontier security. French remained the most common language on the streets of Detroit into the early nineteenth century.

Relations between the northern native groups, long allied with Paris, and the new government were often strained. In 1763, a pan-Indian alliance led by the Odawa chief Pontiac attacked all the British forts in the region, with the intent of halting European encroachment. Fort Detroit was one of two that didn't succumb—a setback for Pontiac, who was directing that assault and was left with an untenable siege. Setting the tone for the next several decades of diplomacy, ill feelings were ameliorated only by the advance of the new American nation—a new common enemy.

During the American Revolutionary War, Detroit became a staging area for British military raids into Ohio Country. With gradual advances by the colonial secessionists, the British retrenched and constructed a significant star fort, named Fort Lernoult for its chief engineer. The number of troops stationed on the strait varied by season, swelling from a few hundred to several thousand. Curiously, while the war officially ended in 1783, making Detroit an American town, the British did not leave for thirteen years. The new government in New York did not have the resources to remove them, so British officials, ostensibly operating from the Upper Canada town of Sandwich (today Windsor) across the water, continued to maintain law and order in Detroit. It wasn't until after an American victory at the Battle of Fallen Timbers in Ohio Country that the British moved their operations to Fort Amherstburg (today Fort Malden) at the mouth of the Detroit River.

The American flag first flew over Detroit on July 11, 1796. Such was the makeup of the population that when five trustees were chosen for the town's new government, three were French-born, one was British, and only one was an American. The French generally recognized the American government and sought American citizenship. British residents, allowed to stay for a few transitional years, were divided; many became American citizens, while others moved their assets across the Detroit River to Upper Canada (today Ontario).

Within the United States, Detroit was part of the Northwest Territories, an area that eventually became the states of Ohio, Indiana, Illinois, Michigan, and Wisconsin. Formation of Michigan Territory in 1805 brought appointment of territorial governor William Hull and justice Augustus Woodward. These dignitaries, along with official federal administration, arrived in Detroit just days after a catastrophic fire destroyed the entire village. Only one storehouse remained, but the conflagration spared the fort and surrounding farms and caused only two injuries. An additional blessing was the opportunity to plan the town anew, and replace century-old wooden buildings on a modern streetscape. The layout of the city center—a melding of plans drawn by both Hull and Woodward—was established by 1825, and it remains much the same today.[4]

Another military conflict—the War of 1812, again between Great Britain and the United States—affected the fortunes of early Detroit. The war was initiated by navy vessels on the Atlantic, but the terrestrial war began and ended in the Detroit River region. Prior to the declaration of war, militia out of Fort Detroit dragged cannon down to Spring Wells and began bombarding the opposite shore. With the commencement of hostilities, Hull—an aging hero of the American Revolution, pressed into service once again—invaded Upper Canada. He established a base and advanced on the undermanned Fort Amherstburg, before retrenching in Sandwich and eventually withdrawing his forces to Detroit. Within a short time, British reinforcements—regular, militia and native—under General Isaac Brock arrived and counterattacked, easily taking Detroit. It remained in British control until after the Battle of Lake Erie, an American naval victory that turned the tide in the Northwest. An army under American general William Harrison chased British forces out of Detroit and nearby Upper Canada, remaining in occupation until nearly half a year after the war was officially over in 1815—the last remnants of an unnecessary war.

Fortunes in Detroit changed quickly following the war. Improved transportation options in the form of canals, steamboats, coaches, and eventually railroads facilitated the influx of "Yankee-Yorkers"—eastern businessmen and farmers anxious to open new lands. Turmoil in Europe, particularly the Germanic states and Ireland, prompted a wave of immigration into the Great Lakes region. Detroit's position at the center of that waterway system allowed it to welcome many of those immigrants and to sell supplies to others moving farther west. It also positioned the city well in such industries as shipping, iron work, and agriculture.

Detroit was the seat of government in Michigan Territory, and it remained the capitol into the early years of statehood, granted by Congress in 1837. During this period, many of the institutions instrumental to developing the frontier were established, including courts, tax systems, land surveys, transportation, and public schools. Locally, Detroiters improved one of the earliest public water systems in the nation. When Michigan became a state, Detroit was a thriving metropolis that boasted two newspapers, a public museum and library, eight religious congregations, six schools, three seminaries for women, and the twenty-year-old University of Michigan. The town had over five hundred buildings, including several banks, hotels, dry goods houses, and offices for dozens of lawyers, doctors, and dentists. Nearly one hundred ships, both steam and sail, were registered at Detroit.[5]

In 1830, Detroit had a population of over two thousand. By 1840 that figure was over nine thousand, and it would double each decade through 1870. Dwellings and businesses spread east and west along the river, and eventually crept northward along Woodward Avenue, Griswold, State, Wayne, Randolph, and other arteries inland. Four stage coach lines radiated from the city center; the busy westbound routes were gradually replaced by railroads, with through service established to Chicago in 1852. Travel eastward was facilitated by steamships to Buffalo, and further eastward by rail or canal through the Mohawk Valley to Albany, New York. Ohio canals eased travel southward into the Ohio River system, and eventually to the Mississippi River. Excursions northward to other towns around the Great Lakes were handled by an impressive fleet of paddle wheelers and schooners. Trade with the Michigan interior relied on rivers, short-lived canal projects, and a gradual expansion of roads—often toll roads—and turnpikes.

In the period prior to the American Civil War, Detroit played an important role in the travel of escaped slaves to freedom. Initially, the flow came from Upper Canada (later Canada West, 1841–1867), into Michigan Territory. In the pre-statehood period, many Detroiters owned slaves, as did their counterparts on the other side of the river. As laws changed, this practice died out, and Detroit's population of African American freemen—about 5 percent of the total in 1830—lived in relative prosperity.[6] Because of Detroit's position as a transportation hub and its proximity to British territory, the city became a major transit point on the Underground Railroad, an informal network of routes and safe houses used by people fleeing captivity on the northern fringes of slaveholding states. Tens of thousands of runaways founded welcoming communities in the rich farmland that is today southwest Ontario.

While an active cadre of Detroiters, both black and white, supported this activity and identified as abolitionists, a strong States Rights contingent led by politician Lewis Cass, and encouraged by the *Detroit Free Press*'s editorial vitriol, backed southern slaveholders. The city, and particularly Detroit's black neighborhoods, suffered through three deadly and destructive fugitive slave riots as a direct result of local involvement in the Underground Railroad traffic.[7]

By the Civil War, Detroit had grown to over forty-five thousand residents. It was no longer the largest city on the Great Lakes; Chicago had exploded to more than twice that number. While residents were divided regarding slavery, they united around preservation of the Union. Detroit was among the first western cities to rush troops to eastern battlefields. Soldiers from Michigan were among those who halted early Confederate military success and prevented capture of Washington, DC. By the end of the war, over 80,000 Michiganders, a majority from the state's southeast, had served the Union Army, including 1,387 African Americans.[8]

About this time, commercial interests began exploiting the mineral wealth of the Lake Superior region, particularly copper and iron ores, as well various aggregates and coal further south.

Important to the war effort, and to post-war development, was the growth of Detroit area metal-working facilities. There were several iron blast furnaces and one brass foundry, as well as seven copper smelters; copper was the most valuable industry in town. There was a prosperous shipyard with a dry dock, eight tanneries, and a dozen furniture makers. Smaller businesses made clothing, firearms, musical instruments, confections—everything you'd imagine in a growing city.

Shipping entrepreneur Eber Brock Ward gambled on a process developed by Kentuckian William Kelly. In 1864, Ward's Eureka Iron Works in Wyandotte became the first place on the continent to "blow" pneumatically produced commercial steel, a process eventually named for Englishman Henry Bessemer. With this new technology, Detroit became a leading producer of steel railroad rails, railcar wheels, and finished rolling stock. In addition, three iron stove manufacturers combined to make Detroit the stove capitol of the world. Regional shipyards were responsible for more vessel launches than any other location on the Great Lakes.

Lumber harvesting started soon after the war, and it grew to spectacular proportions within a dozen years. Detroit's location in the middle of the region, and demands of the wave of migrants settling the northwest, allowed the city to become a magnet for manufacturing capital. Much of the money was generated locally from the managers of successful real estate, shipping, mining, and lumber fortunes. A significant portion flowed from investors to the east, as far away as London and Amsterdam. With investment opportunities west of the Mississippi River limited— except perhaps the California gold bubble—the Old Northwest Territory was hot property, and Detroiters took advantage of that.

While strong in heavy industry, Detroit manufacturers showed equal leadership in industries such as pharmaceuticals, musical and mechanical instruments, chemicals, agriculture, marketing, publishing, tourism, and electrical innovation. Parke-Davis Co., Burroughs, Eureka, Ferry Seed, Remick Music, Detroit & Cleveland Navigation, R. L. Polk, and the Detroit Photographic Company all represented the biggest and best in their fields. And in Detroit, there was competition; other major pharmaceutical companies, other electronics firms, other shipping giants. Those named were just the biggest.

Prosperity generated by this commerce both supported and inspired Detroit's cultural development. Antebellum structures were gradually replaced by grand new homes and commercial edifices. Residents watched substantial new buildings—a city hall, court house, and post office—rise near beautiful churches, museums, and theaters. Athletic organizations, like bicycle and yacht clubs, constructed impressive clubhouses. The Harmonie Club, a German men's singing and social institution, built two impressive structures. The City of Detroit Parks and Boulevards Department developed a plan that included a ring road called Grand Boulevard; city parks, large and small; and the purchase and development of Belle Isle, then 720 acres of swampy farmland in the middle of the Detroit River on the outskirts of town. Within a decade, the lagoons and vistas on Belle Isle were the envy of other cities. By the close of the century, Detroit's twenty-eight square miles included 1,200 acres—almost 2 square miles—of parklands.

In the final two decades of the nineteenth century, the city grew from just over 100,000 inhabitants to over a quarter million. The most sizable ethnic groups were Germans—who experienced a fresh influx in the 1880s—Canadians, and Poles, but included significant Lebanese, Serbian, Russian and Hungarian populations. Well over 10 percent of the population were non–English speakers, the highest percentage in the nation. Detroit was a town where simple jobs were plentiful and paid well. Most were repetitive. Some were dangerous. But they could be very remunerative and socially uplifting. Detroit also challenged emerging engineering and marketing minds, rewarded innovation, and attracted great talent.

Detroit entered the twentieth century with a diverse and strong economic base; a talented, educated workforce (the least unionized in the nation); a healthy and efficient transportation system; and the look of prosperity. Elements of the frontier town were still visible in older merchant blocks and alleys, but in the next two decades that would change. In Detroit, the coming of the automobile changed everything.

The first gasoline-powered buggy motored around the city center on a spring evening in 1896. In the driver's seat was Charles Brady King, guiding the four-cylinder powered wagon, and accompanied by a young mechanical genius named Oliver Barthel. Behind them on a bicycle pedaled thirty-three-year-old Henry Ford, five years King's senior. Like many Americans, King had been inspired by 1893 Columbian Exposition in Chicago. He was there to display and sell a revolutionary pneumatic "jack" hammer he had designed, but also investigated the Grand Rapids, Michigan-made Sintz gasoline engine and the Duryea Brother's brand new self-propelled vehicle. Three years later, the King car featured a modified Sintz engine and bore some resemblance to the Duryea wagon.

Besides designing and manufacturing mechanical tools like the jack hammer, King ran a small boat yard that built gasoline-powered yachts. Along with Ora Mulford and William Pungs, he invested in the Michigan Yacht and Power Company, which made thousands of recreational crafts—from rowboats to yachts—and purchased Sintz Marine Motors manufacturing. In the automobile world, King went to work for Ransom Olds, and later the Northern Manufacturing Company, developing dozens of innovations before starting his own company in 1910. The King Car "Eight" featured a reliable eight-cylinder engine and left-hand steering, the only such vehicle displayed at the 1912 New York Auto Show. Soon afterward, King left the company, which was eventually absorbed by Studebaker.

King's young career typified much of what went on in the early automobile business. Detroit's capital was diversified, and so were the men who managed it. For instance, Mulford was primarily an advertising mogul, pioneering streetcar placards and directing advertising campaigns for Ford and Packard. He later developed Sintz Marine Engines into Gray Marine Engine Company. Barthel was in demand for anything sporting a gasoline engine, including cars, outboard motors, boats, and airplanes—all markets in which Detroit had a preeminent position.

Pungs was a principal in the Pungs-Finch Auto & Gas Engine Company.[9] Curiously, by 1910 Pungs-Finch, makers of beautiful, powerful touring vehicles, was out of business; 1912 claimed E-M-F Company, and Lozier Motor Company was gone by 1915. And yet in that year, the Detroit City Directory lists over forty companies making automobiles. Another seventy companies are listed as suppliers. By 1915, Detroit had become the automobile capital of the world.

Within a decade, many pioneer auto companies had succumbed to intense competition or merger frenzy. Competitively, a 1912 Lozier tourer cost eight times as much as a Ford Model T tourer. Lozier lost its chief designer, William Chandler, who started his own company in 1913 selling quality cars for half the price. William C. Durant formed General Motors (GM) in 1915 and drew many companies into the corporation; some survived—Buick, Fisher, Cadillac, Oldsmobile—and some were eliminated—Scripps-Booth and Cartercar, among others. Walter Chrysler, after departing GM as director of Buick, acquired Maxwell Motor Co. in 1920—which had been Thomas, then Chalmers. He renamed it in 1925, added the Plymouth and DeSoto badges, and purchased the remains of the Dodge Brothers Company.

Hudson Motors, on the city's east side, was launched by a local department store entrepreneur in 1909; with innovation and styling, it survived to become part of American Motors in the 1950s. Its Essex and Terraplane badges kept Hudson Motors, almost forgotten today, among the industry leaders in nationwide sales. Packard Motors was one of several companies, founded elsewhere, that moved to Detroit. In 1903, Henry Joy brought the luxury carmaker from Warren, Ohio, into a revolutionary Albert Kahn–designed factory, where it thrived until 1956.

Henry Ford, who had been developing cars in fits and starts, also employed Kahn to construct a plant on farmland north of Detroit. The assembly system integrated into the vast Highland Park plant allowed the Ford Motor Company to manufacture an unprecedented number of vehicles, and in turn to offer its workers an unheard-of wage. Within a few years, Ford had outgrown that facility and had begun building along the Rouge River in suburban Dearborn.

In these two decades, automobile companies had grown from a few to many, and then consolidated into a powerful few. This activity was not without consequences. In the first place, it distracted from all the other activity in town. Much like a gold rush, building automobiles became the focus of nearly every aspect of Detroit's business, society, and entertainment. Secondly, the explosion of available capital allowed the city to grow out and up at an incredible pace. Finally, such success had an effect on all segments of the economy—both good and bad.

In the first instance, automobiles became quickly linked to many people's livelihood, and good factory wages were sought after and fought over. With the standard of living on the rise, and the price of cars falling, even those of moderate means could own a car. Automobile clubs became popular, as did wardrobes for travelling. Instead of steamship cruises or river resorts, automobile camping became the favored vacation opportunity. The Good Roads Movement was co-opted from the last century's bicyclists, and became a rallying cry for auto enthusiasts eager to see America.

Fortunes were won and lost, and often won again. Speculators met in the local hotels, restaurants, and clubs to gauge the markets and explore new directions. Manufacturing was red hot, but so was the real estate market. The city center was so crowded with elegant new skyscrapers that General Motors and the Fisher Brothers chose to develop a "New Center" of town three miles north of the river. Between these was planned a new Cultural Center—for museums, libraries, colleges, and a growing medical center. Many of Detroit's iconic buildings were built during the booming days of the 1920s, including the Union Guardian Building, the Fisher Building, and the Detroit Institute of Arts.

Between 1900 and 1930, Detroit's population grew fivefold, from about 300 thousand to 1.5 million. On a national scale, it went from thirteenth in size in 1900 to fourth in 1920. The initial labor demands of the auto companies were addressed by immigrants from Eastern Europe and Mediterranean countries. After the quotas imposed by the federal Immigration Act of 1924, the auto companies recruited in the southern states: whites from the middle states and mountain regions, and blacks from the Deep South. To accommodate the influx of new residents, new neighborhoods radiated out along the city's main arteries. Detroit's footprint on Wayne County grew from 28 square miles to 138 square miles between 1900 and 1930. New hotels, apartments, and duplexes flourished, and mile after mile of single family homes expanded the metropolis.

Some of the consequences of this boom were positive: beautiful buildings blossomed across the region. Some consequences were mixed: the incredible cost of expanding infrastructure meant that unemployment was low. Some consequences were bad: with unemployment low and auto wages high, many of Detroit's industries—both manufacturing and service—had trouble retaining employees. Traditional shippers, both steamships and rail, had trouble competing with trucks and semitrailers. And then there was Prohibition.

Prohibition, the national experiment in the restriction of alcohol consumption, began in 1920. While popular in rural areas, temperance was a tough sell in urban spots. The southwest side of Michigan was staunchly German and Dutch Reformed, and highly supportive of this initiative. The southeast side was more homogenous: French, Scot, Irish, German, Polish, Italian, Russian—all culturally less opposed to alcohol. With the near proximity of Canada and its more liberal alcohol policies, Detroiters were in a position to defy the law. And they did—for a handsome profit. At the height of alcohol trafficking, it was the second largest industry in the Detroit. Under-resourced, law enforcement was unable to put up more than token resistance. Estimates suggest that 70 percent of Canada's alcohol transfers to the United States came in through the Detroit River Region, including towns along the St. Clair River and Lake St. Clair. Figures suggest that law enforcement deterred only 5 percent of the business.[10]

For many reasons, Detroit became a very popular destination for conventions and conferences. Hotels, movie, dancing, and music venues thrived alongside an estimated twenty-five thousand "blind pigs" or "joints" or "speakeasies"—essentially, unlicensed bars or gambling spots. Nearby resorts offered an open tap to those with means. Gradually, control of beer and whiskey distribution shifted from neighborhood gangs to organized crime. Gambling, mostly in the form of "numbers" or lottery rackets, was rife in the auto plants. This diversification of income was fortuitous when the Depression came.

Detroit had suffered through at least six national recessions starting in 1837, with varying degrees of pain. The Wall Street crash in October 1929 hit hard. Now a "one industry" town, Detroit felt the collapse of automobile sales within the year. Ford, which nearly hit the "two million sold" mark in 1923 (1,831,128), sold only 210,000 units nine years later. A lack of manufacturing diversity meant that the unemployment rate reached 30 percent in 1932; over 50 percent for those in the poorest neighborhoods.[11]

Auto sales began to pick up five years later, and soon afterward the specter of war in Europe shifted the focus of American manufacturing to munitions and ordnance. By 1940, Detroit resources focused on applying its manufacturing might to sating the military hunger of our European and Asian allies. Before the war was over, 30 percent of everything our allies consumed was generated by Detroit firms; this was 20 percent of total Allied war production, including our GIs' (soldiers') needs. Anything that had wheels—jeeps, trucks, tanks, bombers—was directed through the Pentagon's satellite location in the Guardian Building. Detroit was a key cog in President Franklin D. Roosevelt's "Arsenal of Democracy," and industrial innovations developed by local firms saved the government billions of dollars.[12]

The ramifications of this unprecedented escalation in manufacturing were numerous. Manufacturing contracts flowed into the city, and unemployment dropped to pre-Depression levels. Established companies like Ford, Chrysler, and Kahn built largest-in-the-world assembly, aircraft, and tank factories on farmland beyond the city limits, even across state lines. In a period during which one in five Americans moved to aid the war effort, Detroit needed applicants for jobs left vacant when local men joined the military. Engineers and efficiency experts were prized, but so were reliable assembly-line workers. Nontraditional workers, like women and people with physical challenges, were introduced to the factory floor. With European migration halted, recruiters returned to the South for workers, and many came. They brought with them rich cultural traditions—some tuneful and flavorful, and some confrontational and toxic. Blended with the inherited prejudices among the dozens of European groups—by nationality, religion, or politics—Detroit's melting pot was boiling.

Overcrowding during World War II occurred in schools and hospitals, stores and theaters, on streetcars and busses, and most critically, in housing. Competition for jobs was crucial, and when African Americans were integrated onto the shop floor, there were walkouts that closed entire plants. During this period, the United Automobile Workers (UAW) union established itself as an ally of blacks in auto jobs, helping to reduce segregation in Detroit industry. When African Americans tried to move into new housing—neighborhoods built on the outskirts of a rapidly expanding city, to accommodate war workers—it took a significant police presence to stifle aggressive opposition from the white community.

On a hot summer afternoon in 1943, racial animosities roiled into a major riot. The riot was brief but deadly; in three days, thirty-four people died. Confrontation was quelled with the arrival of federal troops. These tensions, coupled with growing labor strife and wildcat strikes, made it look like Roosevelt's armament train might derail. However, the majority of Detroiters remained focused and overcame the many adversities. Volunteers manned Civil Defense posts, catered to troops at train stations, provided daycare for working families, monitored ration programs, and lived by the slogan "Use it up, wear it out, make it do, or do without." In 1945, Detroit joined the rest of America in celebrating the end of armed conflict in Europe and the Pacific.

The effects of World War II on southeast Michigan cannot be understated. The explosion of manufacturing pulled Detroit industries out of the Great Depression, but in many cases it provided false hope. Those industries and companies that were weak before the war generally failed afterward, including shipbuilding, steamship tourism, and several automakers, including powerhouses Packard and Hudson. Labor union ascendancy caused the remaining companies to strategically distribute new plants out of the region. Aircraft and munitions production, which local manufacturers seemed to have mastered in short order, virtually disappeared; only military vehicle development remains today.

Perhaps the most notable effects of the war in southeast Michigan were on the physical and demographic landscape itself. Modern, efficient manufacturing systems required single-level facilities to be built where land was cheap, far beyond the city limits. Multistory factories in the heart of the city were left abandoned, highly visible citadels of a former era. The deindustrialization of Detroit saw the most valued and agile members of the employment pool follow jobs to suburban location or to other states, leaving behind the poorest and least-trained workers. New highways—an innovation of wartime Detroit—spread weblike from the city, further draining the core and disrupting the unity of traditional neighborhoods. The steady loss of taxpaying companies and residents continued for six decades, affecting the maintenance of city infrastructure and the delivery of basic services. Those who remained either couldn't afford to leave, or couldn't imagine living anywhere else—Detroit was home.

By the 1960s, the cumulative effects of a century of heavy industry on a region of over two million inhabitants came to a crisis point. Detroit's municipal water system, dating to 1824, did not include an adequate sewage treatment plant until 1940, severely affecting local waterways. Industrial effluvia in the lower Rouge River, a tributary running through the Ford plant, caused the water to catch fire several times beginning in the 1930s. The local fishery, which collapsed from overharvesting by 1925, had no chance of recovery in the face of dredged spawning grounds and an array of toxic chemicals and heavy metals pushed downstream from both Detroit and Windsor. A reversal of one hundred years of abuse began in the 1940s, but it would not see significant progress until the 1970s.

The post-war period was not all dire in Detroit. Returning service personnel contributed to the nationwide baby boom, and the local schools—considered among the best in the nation—were again crowded. In 1950, the city's population swelled to 1.85 million, now fifth largest in the country. New products—plastics, alloys, electronics—and techniques developed for military use were reengineered by the automobile companies to create dramatically redesigned cars. Effects of the "jet age" were seen in the sculpted grills, wrap-around windshields, plastic bodies, and tailfins of classic 1950s Detroit automobiles. For another decade, nearly every vehicle in North America was produced by the Big Three—Chrysler, Ford, and GM. The dominance of the monopoly gave Detroiters, from line workers to company presidents, a swagger and pride. This attitude extended to the many ancillary industries that thrived in the region, including advertising, marketing and sales, film production, exhibition design and fabrication, architecture, law, insurance, and investment banking. Power lunches were consumed at some of the finest restaurants in the country.

Culturally, Detroit experienced a post-war rebirth. Artists and architects whose modernist styles were highly in vogue included Carl Milles, Marshall Fredericks, Minuro Yamasaki, and Eero Saarinen. The Detroit Symphony Orchestra under conductor Paul Paray was heard over radios nationwide on the Ford Sunday Evening Hour. Country music, popular with southern transplants, was broadcast on powerful WJR-AM. Progressive jazz styles like bebop were heard in dozens of clubs and show bars, played by the likes of locals Tommy Flanagan, Yusef Lateef, and the Jones brothers Hank, Thad, and Elvin. Ethnic ensembles kept Old World traditions alive. Small recording studios and independent record labels turned out rock and roll, doo-wop, blues, and rhythm and blues product.

It was in this milieu that Motown Records was hatched, growing from a kitchen table investment to an international industry leader and Motor City ambassador. Besides its iconic dance and soul music, Detroit also became known for the hard-driving rock and roll of Bob Seger, industrial proto-punk from Iggy Pop, glam-rock innovations from Alice Cooper, the garage sound of bands like the MC5—and many more. There was a grit and honesty about music in Detroit that often defied the status quo, typical of trends in the 1960s. It was an era of stark contrasts, and Detroit had plenty of those.

The broad artistic spectrum is easily attributable to the diverse cultures in the area. As mentioned earlier, these groups gravitated to neighborhoods evincing class and cultural similarities, increasingly located in near-ring suburbs around Detroit. This tendency—intentional or not—made the region among the most racially polarized in the country. Restrictive real estate covenants and redlining practices of the Federal Housing Administration kept low-income people—mostly blacks—in densely populated ghettos. While these strictures were gradually dismantled by the courts and the forces of urban renewal, de facto segregation of neighborhoods—and by extension education and employment—remained the rule. If blacks and poor whites needed reminding of their place in Detroit's hierarchy, the police department was well-drilled in "get-tough" policies and protocols.[13]

Political elements within the city sought to maintain the status quo, but coming into the 1960s their influence waned and was replaced by Democratic progressivism in the person of Mayor Jerome Cavanagh. Within a few years, this thirty-two-year-old had instituted integration and crime prevention reforms that caused *Time* magazine to dub Detroit the "Model City." In 1963, President John F. Kennedy named Detroit the US candidate for the 1968 Summer Olympics. Mexico City prevailed in the voting.

Unfortunately, a mid-decade downturn in auto sales increased unemployment in 1967 to 4.5 percent in the region, to 6.2 percent in Detroit, and to an estimated 30 percent in the poorer neighborhoods. Incidents of petty crime increased throughout the city, resulting in a near-unanimous call for better policing. "Better" was translated as "stronger," inflaming the black community where efforts were concentrated.

The reaction, which occurred during a long, hot summer week in 1967, is regarded by some as a riot and by others as a rebellion. As in over 160 towns and cities across American (but unlike earlier Detroit uprisings), this disturbance generally involved neighborhood people looting and burning neighborhood stores and homes. Government response at most levels was confused. Vandals and victims were black and white. Official fatalities were forty-three, with about seven hundred injured, and seven thousand arrested. This represented the largest such event in US history, and it exacerbated existing trends; business evacuation continued, the flight of Detroiters—both white and black—to the suburbs increased, and poverty steadily grew.

Changes were put into operation that helped stabilize the city and established some semblance of normalcy. Within days of the federal troops leaving, influential leaders from industry, the community, and city government came together to form the New Detroit Committee. Catholic activists, focused on job training, created Focus: HOPE for areas of greatest poverty. Grass roots organizations in the black community generated several initiatives aimed at creating economic and cultural self- sufficiency at the neighborhood level.

A real morale booster for the whole city (and arguably the state) came in the form of a World Series win by the Detroit Tigers in 1968. Within a few years, civic boosters and moneyed interests began working to save several historic structures, including the Fox and Gem theaters and Orchestra Hall. Henry Ford II worked with Detroit's first black mayor, Coleman A. Young, to plan an impressive new skyscraper on the riverfront, to be called the Renaissance Center—an unapologetic nod to hopes for a revitalized city center.

Coleman Young's election as mayor in 1973 set a new tone for politics in the region. An ardent advocate for labor and citizen rights, Young moved quickly to bring diversity to Detroit city government. A plain-spoken and aggressive politician, he never hesitated to face off with suburban antagonists, but he was also effective at creating coalitions with regional business elites. For four decades, Detroit government, and to some extent Wayne County government, increasingly reflected the majority population of the city, which by the turn of the millennium was 85 percent African American.

There were significant bumps in the road, created by political and economic events in an international market. Changes in oil politics and pricing in the 1970s made efficient foreign vehicles more attractive to American consumers. Detroit's monopoly on North American auto production came to an end, and the Big Three struggled through the 1980s to make their products competitive and to ride out a worldwide recession.

To many Detroiters, the closing of J. L. Hudson's iconic Downtown department store—once the second largest in the nation and the tallest in the world—in 1983 marked the end of an era. Most of the familiar haberdashers and ladies stores, most of the coffee shops and restaurants, and most of the respectable hotels had preceded Hudson's departure. But a few remained: Henry the Hatter's, the Cadillac Hotel (under various ownerships), the shops of Greektown and Trapper's Alley, the Anchor Bar, Mario's, Lafayette Coney Island, Baker's Keyboard Lounge, Abick's. And new ones joined them, repurposing older buildings: Floods, the Majestic complex, Adler Schnee, and Emily's, whose "Say Nice Things About Detroit" campaign was everywhere. Gradually, investments from key community organizations—universities, healthcare, business, civic, and philanthropic—helped stabilize portions of the city center and Midtown, and turned the tide.

This was the period—the last two decades of the twentieth century—when Motown Records left for Los Angeles and Detroit's two major newspapers merged—at the time a landmark legal ruling. Downtown occupancy continued to fade, as it did in nearly every neighborhood. However, these were also the years that produced a hybrid electronic music dubbed Detroit Techno, the stylings of Kid Rock, and Eminem's rap. The beloved Tiger Stadium baseball park closed, but Comerica Park opened to acclaim. The Detroit Lions brought football back to Detroit at the new Ford Field.

Along with the rest of the nation, Detroiters struggled to cope with the events of September 11, 2001. Detroit was home to the largest regional Arabic-speaking population in the nation, and there were—and continue to be—struggles with religion and race. Perhaps more seriously than elsewhere in America, Detroit was hit hard by the Great Recession, which began in 2008 and forced GM and Chrysler into bankruptcy. Chrysler, which was acquired by the German firm

Daimler-Benz for a short time in the 1990s, became a part of Fiat of Italy in 2014, leaving Detroit with only two locally owned auto companies.

The recession and internal corruption also took a toll on the city government, and in 2013 the State of Michigan took control of the city. Detroit declared bankruptcy—the largest American city to do so to that point—and worked through an eighteen-month restructuring.

Offering hope for coming decades is the gradual diversification of industry within the city, favoring the technology sector, and a dramatic rebirth of the city's core. Reflecting the rejuvenation taking place downtown is the revitalization of natural habitats in the area. The fishery has rebounded beyond expectations, beavers again inhabit local waterways, over three hundred years since the city's founding, Detroit remains one of the continent's premier international ports.

Detroit has repeatedly honored its motto, "We rise from the ashes and hope for better things." There is no reason to think that that will change.

NOTES

1. Richard White, *The Middle Ground: Indians, Empires, and Republics in the Great Lakes Region, 1650–1815* (Williamsburg, VA: Omohundro Institute of Early American History and Culture, 1991).
2. For more information about the French period in Detroit, see Clarence Burton, *The City of Detroit Michigan*, Vols. 1–3 (Altenmünster, Ger.: Jazzybee Verlag, 2017), originally published by S. J. Clarke in 1922.
3. For more information about Detroit during the British and early American periods, see Burton. Also see Denver Brunsman and Joel Stone, eds., *Revolutionary Detroit: Portraits in Political and Cultural Change, 1760–1805* Detroit: Detroit Historical Society, 2009).
4. For more information about Detroit during the early American period, see Burton. Also see Denver Brunsman, Joel Stone, and Douglas D. Fisher, eds., *Border Crossings: The Detroit River Region in the War of 1812* (Detroit: Detroit Historical Society, 2012).
5. *Directory of the City of Detroit, … for the Year 1837* (Detroit: Julius P. Bolivar MacCabe, 1837).
6. The United Kingdom of Great Britain and Ireland outlawed slavery throughout its realms in 1833. The United States let individual states retain or outlaw the practice through the 1860s. Slavery was outlawed in the Northwest Ordinance in 1787, but the ordinance allowed existing owners to retain possession for a specified period. Slavery was always illegal in Michigan, but residents had to comply with various federal laws regarding the capture and return of fugitive slaves.
7. For more information about slavery and the Underground Railroad in Detroit, see Bill McGraw and Roy Finkenbine's chapters in Joel Stone, eds., *Detroit 1967: Origins, Impacts, Legacies* (Detroit: Wayne State University Press, 2017).
8. For further reading about Detroit during the Civil War, consult Paul Taylor, *Old Slow Town: Detroit during the Civil War* (Detroit: Wayne State University Press, 2013).
9. The rich history of early automobile manufacturing is told in numerous volumes. An interesting exploration of automobile and powerboat development, which took place simultaneously in Detroit, is told in Michael

Dixon, *Motormen and Yachting: The Waterfront Heritage of the Automobile Industry* (Grosse Pointe, MI: Mervue Publications, 2005).

10. Philip Mason's *Rum Running and the Roaring Twenties* (Detroit: Wayne State University Press, 1995) is a well-researched and accessible book about Detroit during Prohibition.

11. For information about the development of labor unions in Detroit, see Steve Babson, *Working Detroit* (New York: Adama, 1986).

12. There are a number of volumes addressing Detroit during World War II, including books by Charles K. Hyde (Wayne State University Press), Gregory Sumner (History Press), and A. J. Baime (Houghton Mifflin Harcourt).

13. For more information about policing practices and statistics during this period, see the chapter by Alex Elkins in *Detroit 1967.*

2

Potawatomi Indians of Detroit

SUSAN VILLEROT

None of Detroit's cultural and ethnic groups experienced more tumultuous changes during the revolutionary era than its Indian population. Whereas the French and British had to negotiate formal and informal settlement terms with one another after 1760, and both had to adapt to the American takeover of 1796, Detroit's three main Indian groups—the Ottawa, Wyandot, and Potawatomi—had to endure three different imperial regimes within two generations. This essay explores how one of these groups, the Potawatomi, responded to Detroit's many political and cultural changes in the second half of the eighteenth century. The Potawatomis did everything possible to adapt and survive, even leaving their homes to become pioneers of new lands.[1]

Before European contact, the Potawatomis were part of an alliance with Ojibwas and Ottawas known as the "People of the Three Fires." Their legend holds that the tribes originated on the Atlantic Ocean, migrated west to escape death and disease, and stopped once reaching the upper Great Lakes region. According to anthropologist James Clifton, the first "unmistakable evidence of the existence of the Potawatomi dates to 1634 but was not recorded until six years later."[2] In 1640, the Jesuit priest Father Le Jeune wrote about French explorer Jean Nicolet and his encounter with Potawatomis during his travels on the Great Lakes from Sault Ste. Marie to Green Bay. It is still not clear whether they originally lived on the east or west coast of Lake Michigan. One thing that has remained constant throughout the tribe's recorded history is its name, under various spellings. The earliest references to the Potawatomis indicate that they viewed themselves as one people, in various geographical locations. Clifton and others suggest that the Potawatomis made decisions that affected more than one village as a larger unified group, not as separate communities.[3]

European colonialism fractured this cultural and political unity. The Potawatomis became French allies, active traders, and warriors of the *pays d'en haut* (the "upper country") from the early days of New France. They fought alongside the French throughout the colonial era until the end of the Seven Years' War. Their reputation as the "most favored tribe" of the French

Susan Villerot, "The Potawatomi Indians of Detroit: Great Lakes Pioneers," *Revolutionary Detroit*, ed. Denver Brunsman and Joel Stone, pp. 59-63. Copyright © 2009 by Susan Villerot. Reprinted with permission automatically put them at odds with the British, but it also allowed them to play the European powers off each other to sweeten trading and diplomatic terms. The Potawatomi people spread across the western reaches of New France, an area now represented by Michigan, Wisconsin, and Illinois. By the American revolutionary era, Potawatomis identified themselves more closely with their immediate village than with the larger Potawatomi "nation." Their interests, economies, and alliances were intertwined with European society—a major cultural shift for a group that once had such a close and interdependent society.[4]

The Potawatomis helped to develop Detroit. In 1701, the French colonial official Antoine Laumet de La Mothe, Sieur de Cadillac, built a new fort along the Detroit River. His original expedition from Montreal included Frenchmen and Native Americans. Although their tribal identity is unknown, the Indians were probably from the Montreal area. Through correspondence with Jesuit missionaries at Michilimackinac, Cadillac also invited multiple Indian groups to settle at Fort Pontchartrain. Within several years, Potawatomis joined thousands of other Indians in the Detroit area.[5]

Living just south of the fort, the Potawatomis became essential allies in making Detroit a center of the Great Lakes fur trade. The historian John Bowes identifies the Potawatomis and other Indian groups in the Old Northwest as both "exiles" and "pioneers." They served as frontiersmen in their own right and paved the way for white settlers in uncharted western territories in the nineteenth century. Yet this role as pioneers began almost a century earlier in the Potawatomis' move south to Detroit. They helped to make the area a desirable colonial territory.[6]

As French allies, the Potawatomis lamented Britain's victory in the Seven Years' War. In 1763, therefore, they eagerly joined Pontiac's pan-Indian alliance to remove the British from former French forts, including Detroit. Although the rebellion failed, there were positive consequences for Native Americans. The British realized that regional Indian groups were worthy opponents and that they were better off keeping the peace. Detroit's British administration resumed the custom of gift-giving that was so prevalent under the French, and increasingly monitored local fur traders to ensure fairness and integrity. Additionally, the Proclamation of 1763 established a boundary to protect Indian territory and keep American colonists from expanding farther west.[7]

As Great Lakes Indians grew accustomed to their new alliance with the British, the American Revolutionary War began, and the larger Potawatomi community fractured again. Potawatomis split their support for Britain and the United States according to existing geographical divisions. The Detroit Potawatomis supported Britain throughout the war, while other groups from Illinois and Wisconsin sided with the Americans. Potawatomis at St. Joseph on southern Lake Michigan were pulled in both directions before ultimately joining British attempts to curb American expansion. The impact of European war and geopolitics had once again reached the Indian village level.[8]

Like the majority of Detroit's inhabitants, the Potawatomis remained loyal to the British even after America achieved its independence. Most Indian groups strongly opposed American western encroachment, and the Potawatomis did not resign themselves to U.S. sovereignty until after General Anthony Wayne's victory at Fallen Timbers in 1794 and the subsequent Treaty of

Greenville in 1795. The battle came after nearly ten years of fighting between Americans and Native Americans, backed by the British, for control of Ohio Country and the upper Great Lakes region. Unlike previous encounters, Indians were greatly outnumbered by American forces at Fallen Timbers, and sought refuge from the British at nearby Fort Miami (today Maumee, Ohio). The British locked the fort's gates to avoid a larger conflict with the Americans, thereby diminishing their long period of influence with local Native Americans.[9]

During this time, many Potawatomis had already left Detroit, and others were in the process of transferring their land holdings along the Detroit River and Lake Erie to private investors. One such investor was Robert Navarre, the royal notary in Detroit under the French who held similar positions with the British and early American governments. He established and maintained good relations with local Indians; the Potawatomis sold him a parcel of land along the river in 1771. They stipulated that the land be for personal use and that Navarre or his sons could build a house and farm the land. The Potawatomis also expected that Navarre maintain their burial ground, which was located on the property. The deed was signed by several Potawatomis using totems as their signatures. The exact number of Potawatomis in British Detroit was not known, but a rash of similar land sales beginning in the 1770s decreased their population even before Fallen Timbers.[10]

The Potawatomis left by a combination of compulsion and their own volition, as both exiles and pioneers. Increased numbers of white settlers at Detroit pushed the Potawatomis off their land while also giving them a financial opportunity. In 1757, several hundred Europeans lived in and around the fort at Detroit. By 1780, there were roughly 2,100 settlers. And by 1796, there were about 2,600 Europeans of various backgrounds living in the Detroit area. Of this population, a growing number were farmers, and the gradual expansion gave the Potawatomis a market for their land. They took advantage of the situation, and moved farther west to keep distance from the settlers.[11]

The Potawatomis lost the rest of their land in the Detroit area through deceitful land dealings and treaties. The United States competed with avaricious British and American land speculators for prime tracts in the Old Northwest. In September 1795, General Wayne described the treaty negotiations at Greenville and complained that speculators had kept Indians in the "Vicinity of Detroit and Raisin River," including the Potawatomis, "in a state of intoxication for many weeks whilst purchasing their lands for the most trifling Consideration."[12] Wayne and other U.S. representatives were frustrated because they wanted the same land for their new government. Eventually, they succeeded. Between the Treaty of Greenville in 1795 and the 1807 Treaty of Detroit, the Potawatomis, Ottawas, and Wyandots ceded all their remaining land in the lower peninsula of Michigan to the United States.[13]

Political changes in the Great Lakes region in the latter half of the eighteenth century had a disastrous effect on Detroit's Native American population. In the case of the Potawatomis and other Indian groups, there was little chance to eliminate British and, later, American influence after Pontiac's defeat in 1765. The Potawatomis adapted creatively to their situation, however, by selling land and moving west as white settlers increasingly migrated to the Detroit area. The Indians showed determination to choose where they lived, before wars and treaties forced their hand. Decades before the Indian Removal Act of 1830, most Detroit Potawatomis had already been pushed toward Lake Michigan. Ultimately, they were relocated west of the Mississippi River. These early inhabitants of Detroit remained pioneers, venturing west toward another new home.[14]

NOTES

1. Studies on the Potawatomis at Detroit are limited. Most works focus on them after they moved to Illinois, Kansas, and eventually Oklahoma. For the Potawatomis in Michigan, see James A. Clifton, George L. Cornell, and James M. McClurken, *People of the Three Fires: The Ottawa, Potawatomi and Ojibway of Michigan* (Grand Rapids: The Michigan Indian Press, 1986). For general overviews of the Potawatomis, see James A. Clifton, *The Prairie People: Continuity and Change in Potawatomi Indian Culture, 1665–1965* (Lawrence: Regents Press of Kansas, 1977), and R. David Edmunds, *The Potawatomis: Keepers of the Fire* (Norman: University of Oklahoma Press, 1978). See Richard White, *The Middle Ground: Indians Empires, and Republics in the Great Lakes Region, 1650–1815* (New York: Cambridge University Press, 1991), for relationships between Europeans and Indians in the Great Lakes region.
2. Clifton, *Prairie People*, 11.
3. Clifton, Cornell, and McClurken, v, 50; Edmunds, 58; White, 101; William Warren, *History of the Ojibway People* (St. Paul: Minnesota Historical Society, 1984), 80–82.
4. Clifton, Cornell, and McClurken, 51.
5. *City of Detroit*, 1:84; Clifton, Cornell, and McClurken, 16; Clifton, *Prairie People*, 86. For Cadillac's correspondence with the Jesuits and early descriptions of Detroit, see *MPHC*, 33:107–51.
6. John Bowes, *Exiles and Pioneers: Eastern Indians in the Trans-Mississippi West* (New York: Cambridge University Press, 2007). Bowes also cites the Shawnees, Delawares, and Wyandots as unintentional trailblazers in the western expansion of the United States.
7. Gregory Evans Dowd, *War under Heaven: Pontiac, the Indian Nations, and the British Empire* (Baltimore: Johns Hopkins University Press, 2002), 177–80; White, 308; Clifton, Cornell, and McClurken, 54.
8. Colin G. Calloway, *The American Revolution in Indian Country: Crisis and Diversity in Native American Communities* (New York: Cambridge University Press, 1995), 41.
9. Clifton, Cornell, and McClurken, 55; Edmunds, 130–32. See also the letters from Anthony Wayne to Henry Knox and Timothy Pickering, in *Anthony Wayne, a Name in Arms: Soldier, Diplomat, Defender of Expansion Westward of a Nation*, ed. Richard C. Knopf (Westport, CT: Greenwood, 1960), 352, 379, 384, 389, 427, 461.
10. Deed signed by thirteen Potawatomi Indians on May 26, 1771, Robert Navarre Papers, BHC. For additional land sales by the Potawatomis before 1795, see the following deeds in BHC: Deed signed by eighteen Potawatomi chiefs on July 6, 1776, giving Alexander and William Macomb Grosse Ile, Macomb Family Papers; Deed signed January 6, 1777, Chene Family Papers; Deed signed July 26, 1780, Harold E. Stoll Papers; Deed signed July 28,

1780, John Askin Papers; and Deed signed July 8, 1785, Campau Family Papers. For the sale of Grosse Ile, see also the essay in this volume by Cathryn Eccleston.

11. Donna Valley Russell, ed., *Michigan Censuses 1710–1830, under the French, British, and Americans* (Detroit: Detroit Society for Genealogical Research, 1982), 19–74; David Poremba, ed., *Detroit in its World Setting: A Three Hundred Year Chronology, 1701–2001* (Detroit: Wayne State University Press, 2001), 38; Anthony Wayne to Timothy Pickering, September 20, 1795, in Knopf, cd., 461.

12. Anthony Wayne to Timothy Pickering, September 20, 1795, in Knopf, ed., 461.

13. "Treaty of Greenville 1795," The Avalon Project: Documents in Law, History and Diplomacy, Yale Law School, http://avalon.law.yale.edu (accessed July 22, 2009); George E. Fay, ed., *Treaties, Land Cessions, and Other U.S. Congressional Documents Relative to American Indians Tribes* (Greeley: University of Northern Colorado, 1971), 22. The 1807 Treaty of Detroit was formally known as the "Treaty with the Ottawa, etc." and was written and agreed upon on November 17, 1807, and proclaimed on January 27, 1808. For additional cases of land speculation, see the essays in this volume by Alexandria Reid, Kimberly Steele, and Douglas D. Fisher.

14. Potawatomi Indians today live primarily in Oklahoma and Kansas. For Oklahoma, see Citizen Potawatomi Nation, www.pbpindiantribe.org (accessed July 22, 2009). For Kansas, see Prairie Band Potawatomi Nation, www.pbpmdiantnbc.com (accessed July 22, 2009). There are also still Potawatomis living in Michigan. According to a report in 2000, the Huron Potawatomi Reservation had only eleven registered members, but the Pokagon Band of Potawatomi Reservation, which borders Michigan and Indiana, had 35,415 residents. See "Population of Indian Reservations, Trust Lands and Tribal Statistical Areas in Michigan, 2000," www.michigan.gov/documents/indiancountry_31994_7.pdf (accessed July 22, 2009).

3

Elijah Brush, Transnational American

SHARON TEVIS FINCH

Elijah Brush, Died Dec. 14, 1814. Aet. 42.
Loyal Soldier, Eloquent Advocate,
Loving Husband, Devoted Father
At Thy Hearthside Unforgotten Ever
—gravestone, Elmwood Cemetery, Detroit, lot 73A

In 1798, a young lawyer named Elijah Brush arrived in Detroit. Twenty-six years old, born in Bennington, Vermont, educated at Dartmouth, Brush was one of the first American pioneers in the Detroit River region, a true transnational American. Brush epitomized these earliest American migrants who came to seek their fortunes in a place that had until lately been only a small fur-trading *entrepot* and French agricultural settlement—a far outpost of the British and French empires, a primitive frontier of European civilization. There were only five hundred European descendants in Detroit in 1796, when the Americans assumed control from the British. They lived side-by-side, sometimes uneasily, with hundreds of Native Americans who still clung to their lands. Brush came to this multicultural frontier environment and thrived because he was willing to shed the traditional habits of the East Coast, ready to flex and grow with his new country.[1]

Portrait of Colonel Elijah Brush
Artist unknown, c. 1812. Oil on canvas
Detroit Historical Society Collection.

What did this young man do in Detroit in the fifteen years before his untimely death? He developed a successful law practice, was on the cutting edge of every public matter, was elected a trustee of the town of Detroit in 1803, was appointed the second mayor of the newly

Sharon Tevis Finch, "Elijah Brush, Transnational American," *Border Crossings: The Detroit River Region in the War of 1812,* ed. Denver Brunsman and Joel Stone, pp. 49-61. Copyright © 2012 by Sharon Tevis Finch. Reprinted with permission.

25

incorporated city of Detroit in 1806, was appointed the second treasurer of the territory of Michigan in 1806, served as the second attorney general of the territory during the period from 1808 to 1813, led local militias, helped mobilize the troops before the War of 1812 when General William Hull was absent, and served as commander of Detroit under Hull during the invasion of Upper Canada and occupation of Sandwich in July and August 1812. The significance of his accomplishments is concealed within this listing. In essence, he wove the vividly separate threads of his environment into a masterful tapestry of interculturalism—a microcosm of the new America.

Behind Brush's public persona and accomplishments lay a rich personal life with deep roots in the Detroit River region. He and his wife created a transnational space for themselves and their descendants. In 1802, Brush married Adelaide Askin, daughter of John Askin and Marie Archange Barthe Askin. John Askin was a leading British trader, merchant, and landowner in the Detroit River region. His first wife was Indian; his second was French. Foreshadowing his son-in-law Elijah, Askin had married out of his cultural background, wedding the daughter of one of the most land-rich men in the area. This acceptance of cross-cultural marriage was common in the region, starting when the French *coureur de bois* (fur traders) cohabitated with Indian women and fathered their *métis* children. Adelaide Brush spoke and wrote French as easily as English, and all her letters to her *"chere mere"* Archange were in French, as were those of her sisters. Elijah and Adelaide had four children who lived to adulthood, Edmund Askin, Charles Reuben, John Alfred, and Archange (known as Samantha or Sumantha). Two children who perished in early childhood, Charles Brush and John Askin Brush, are buried on the family plot in Detroit's historic Elmwood Cemetery with the rest of the family. Adelaide, called "Alice" or "Allice" by her family in letters, remained close to her parents, despite their removal to Sandwich in Upper Canada in 1802. Elijah thereafter conducted Askin's business on the American side of the Detroit River.

Brush's life was a living illustration of how the region and its border operated. Until the British turnover of Detroit in 1796, there was effectively no border to local residents. The new political division of the Detroit River region did not affect the lifestyles of its inhabitants, who were intermarried, interrelated, intercultural, and international. When the border was affirmed, most became transnational figures, moving easily back and forth across the river both by private craft and ferry. Letters from Elijah Brush, John Askin, and many others demonstrate the fluidity and porousness of this border, as they referred to trips to the other national territory simply as "coming over" and "going over."[2]

However, the growing political tensions between Britain and the United States before the War of 1812 turned that porous border into a barrier that limited free association and trade for both sides. In 1807, when relations were strained, Askin wrote to his friend and business associate Isaac Todd in Montreal that he was unable to get to "the other side" for some weeks and could not "until the present disturbance ... blows Over."[3] When war finally broke out in 1812, it caused many families, including Askin's, to divide not only geographically and nationalistically, but also in battle. Every young male in the Askin family except Brush fought on the British side. Brush fought as an officer on the American side. This painful result of the heightened recognition of the border is one of the reasons why the historian Alan Taylor calls this conflict a *civil war*.[4]

Askin respected Brush from the start. In an early estimation, Askin wrote, "My daughter Alice married to Mr. Brush—a lawyer who has a good deal of practice and well liked." To another associate, Askin beamed, "[Brush] bids fair to be an able Lawyer has considerable practice is sober and industrious therefore I believe Allice has made a good choice."[5] Throughout the years, Askin continued to describe Elijah in glowing terms—as a "warm hearted fellow," "as kind & friendly a man, as ever was"—and commended "the goodness of Mr. Brush's heart, & good I believe it to be."[6] Askin also apprenticed his son Alexander to read law with Elijah, remarking, "I believe Mr. Brush's professional knowledge at least equal to any lawyer we have."[7]

In 1806, Brush bought the Askin farm in Detroit. It was important to both the Askins and the Brushes that the farm stay in the family, since it had been purchased from Askin's father-in-law, Charles Andrew Barthe, a French *habitant* settler. Brush's title was only fourth in line from the original land grant from the king of France. The agreement was that Brush would make payments upon a debt to Askin's creditors in Montreal, Todd and James McGill, until he could pay off the purchase price. Brush also bought other lands from Todd and McGill on credit. However, times were tough before the war, and Brush was soon unable to marshal funds in Detroit or sell enough property to make timely payments. Askin reassured Todd and McGill repeatedly that Brush would pay his debts when he could. In October 1808, Askin wrote to Todd: "Mr. Brush is certainly a regular, industrious, sober man, and except in improvements is by no means extravagant for a man who *earns so much by his profession*."[8] At the time, there was little specie available on the frontier. This deficiency in available cash is one reason the 1806 Detroit Bank scheme was so popular and why Brush subscribed for one hundred shares of the fraudulent institution. Brush was not alone in being taken in by eastern "sharpies." Many leading residents of Michigan Territory fell for the scam, including Governor Hull and Judge Augustus B. Woodward.[9]

Brush worked hard to support his family and pay his debts. He was the second lawyer admitted to practice in the Michigan territorial Supreme Court and had a busy private legal practice, in addition to his public work as attorney general representing the territorial government. Brush was in court almost daily, appearing on nearly every page of the territory's early court records.[10]

His most famous cases are the two Michigan "slave cases" in 1807 that set the legal standard for slavery in the Northwest Territory. Although he held slaves—according to one account, up to twenty at a time—Brush, like any good lawyer, could serve on either side of a case. He represented both slaves and owners in the landmark cases. In one, he championed the black Denison family of Detroit, some of whom were already free, in their lawsuit to have their still-enslaved adult children declared free. The law was clearly against Brush, and he lost the case; the Northwest Ordinance of 1787 banned new cases of slavery, but did not provide the authority to manumit existing slaves. In the second case, the same judge, Woodward, declared that blacks who were legally enslaved in Upper Canada but managed to escape to the United States could not be extradited to their Canadian masters. Doing so violated the provision in the Northwest Ordinance that barred new cases of slavery in the territory. Moreover, British law did not accord such a return to American slave owners. In this case, Brush represented the British-Canadian slaveholder James Pattinson, who was married to Adelaide's sister. In each instance, there was a happy ending for the slaves. The Denisons crossed the river to Upper Canada where they could not be extradited to the United States, lived with the Askins and worked for the family's friends. They remained in Canada for years, eventually returning to the U.S. without challenge after the War of 1812. The Pattinson slaves, meanwhile, remained in Michigan Territory, where they could not be extradited to Upper Canada. Together, the cases, particularly the Pattinson decision, made slavery untenable in the Detroit River region.[11]

The slave cases were representative of the multicultural and transnational character of Brush's business and legal affairs. In July 1805, he went on a trip as Askin's agent to represent Indian chiefs in their sales of tribal lands to Americans, a scheme the scholar Milo Quaife called "the Cuyahoga Dream." Askin was to receive a percentage of the Indians' profits. Brush wrote to Askin that he had returned exhausted from his trip and would "come over" later to report in depth on how an American Indian agent would not cooperate in letting the Indian chiefs negotiate away their lands. At the end of the letter, Brush lightened the tone by wishing "to beg Some Cellery plants from Mrs. Askin as many as She can well Spare."[12]

Beyond his public affairs, this domestic detail highlights the essential qualities of Brush's life as a transnational American. Consumer goods and household necessities were in short supply on the Detroit frontier. Throughout their correspondence, Brush was called upon by Askin to secure and bring an assortment of household items across the river: tea, grapevines, a dining room table (which had to be built), boots (which took months and almost got lost in transit), and "shoes for Mrs. Askin." Not only merchandise went across the river. The custom before the war was to send letters to Canadians in care of Detroit residents who would then deliver them across the river, since the official international post had not developed. Endorsements on many letters show this forwarding chain.[13]

Within the Askin family, Brush participated in a larger regional trade of various domestic goods and foodstuffs. John Askin Jr., the firstborn child of John Sr.'s Indian wife, also participated in the network from his post as an interpreter and storekeeper on St. Joseph Island, a British, possession in northern Lake Huron near Fort Mackinac. John Jr. often asked his father to send household necessities such as apple trees and onion plants from the Detroit River region, and he shipped British merchandise southward. As the relationship between Britain and the United States hardened before the war, numerous trade restrictions were put in place—including an American embargo on British goods. Although British-American trade was illegal, it went on briskly in the northern borderlands, far from Detroit. John Jr. explained smuggling methods in 1808 in a note that also expressed frustration with Brush:

Brush disappointed me. he was to have sent me a Barrl of Cyder if not two. he could as well Smuggle Cyder to our side as wine to his. If he had sent it to Makina addressed to Doct[or] Mitchel & wrote the Doct[or] that it was intended for me it would have been in my store House long ago. We have a method in this Quarter, unknown below how to import & export into the U.S. Per the *Nancy* you'll receive a keg of Sugar marked in your Name which I send you & one keg mark'd P address'd to your Care which is intended for Mrs. Peltier & Several things which are intended as addressed in a Bundles marked in your Name[.][14]

During the war, restrictions on travel, shipping, and communication in the Detroit River region, once so easily navigated, increased. After the Americans occupied Amherstburg in late September 1813, John Jr., a militia officer in the British-held Mackinac region, feared that his letters home would be intercepted and John Sr. would be accused of illicit correspondence with the enemy army.[15]

Brush's transnational family and business activities did not keep him from being a committed American citizen. Indeed, he was a civic force, an advocate for the causes and people of Detroit. In 1805, Brush was appointed one of two fire inspectors for the town. He was frequently in the lead on writing petitions about public matters. After the calamitous fire of 1805 destroyed Detroit, he joined James May and John Anderson in writing to President Thomas Jefferson for assistance. The following year, the French inhabitants of the "Potawatomi Coast," downriver from Detroit, petitioned (in French) for tax relief; they asked that Brush be on the supervising committee. In 1811, Brush reported to the judges of Michigan Territory on the handling of financial matters. On the eve of the War of 1812, Brush and other community leaders marshaled the militia. On May 8, 1812, Brush joined a subscription paying 16 shillings of his own money to purchase gunpowder for the defense of Detroit. After the town fell, the British put an occupation government in force. Brush was the first of thirty-one signatories to a petition asking Judge Woodward to stay and help them in their time of trouble. The petition explained the difference between public servants who cared and those who didn't. Brush was of the first sort, consistently at the forefront of any civic action.[16]

That civic-mindedness extended to military affairs. With the rank of colonel, he commanded the First Michigan Militia, which was charged with guarding the northern perimeter of Fort Detroit. Just after the war broke out, Brush wrote to Askin in a touching blend of formality and intimacy:

Dear Sir I am going to send my family to reside at Mr. Meldrums. I know not what maybe the destany of this country, my family are dear to my heart, will you receive some money in Keeping for them, and if so, would you prefer to have it in bills on our Government, or Cincinnati Bank notes as to specle there is none here. Adieu and may God bless you E. Brush If at any time hereafter you think proper to send for Alice & the children, they will go over.

The letter shows the fluidity of the river region, where one could just "go over," and Brush could expect his wife and children to safely cross in wartime. Adelaide and the couple's children likely spent the opening of the British occupation with the family of Detroit merchant George Meldrum, as Elijah had arranged; they may have also "gone over" at different times to stay with her parents in Sandwich.[17]

After Hull surrendered Michigan Territory in August 1812, Brush, as the acting commander of Fort Detroit, unhappily signed the capitulation document. The responsibility, along with his transnational family background, perhaps explains the rumors that soon circulated that Brush was complicit in the surrender. Immediately after the capitulation, Brush wrote to Askin asking for a copy of these charges so that he could respond, saying that he wanted "an opportunity to contradict any representations derogatory to my character." An eyewitness later recalled Brush's "anger and chagrin" at the hoisting of the white flag over Fort Detroit.[18]

Although Brush was critical of Hull's leadership and benefited from his family ties with Askin, he was no traitor. Days before the surrender, the colonel was a co-signer, with several other officers, of a letter to Ohio Governor Return Jonathan Meigs Jr. warning of Hull's weakness and asking for a new commander. There are conflicting accounts of what happened to Brush after the British victory. The strongest evidence suggests that the British held him as a prisoner for a brief period at Fort George on the Niagara front before paroling him from Kingston to the U.S., perhaps as a result of assistance from his father-in-law.[19]

By early November 1812, Brush had returned to the Detroit area. In a letter to his children, John Askin reported, "We hear Every two or three days from Mr. Brush & Allice who with their dear Children are all well."[20] In January 1813, Brush and other community leaders performed a dramatic act of citizenship by attempting to get permission from British Colonel Henry Procter to ransom American captives who were being held by Britain's Indian allies following the battles at the River Raisin. Procter offered to pay $5 a head for the captives, while the Indians received up to $80 from inhabitants on both sides of the river. He was so displeased with the pressure by the American group that he banished all twenty-nine of them in early February 1813—Brush's second exile of the war. He did not return to his home and family in Detroit until the British occupation ended following the American victory in the Battle of Lake Erie on September 10, 1813. A few months after his return, Brush died.[21]

A faithful soldier, a colonel in the Michigan territorial militia and the Legionary Corps (a branch of the militia), Brush died from a disease contracted during the war. A cholera-like illness raged through Detroit soon after the British occupation ended in September 1813. Nearly 1,300 military personnel fell ill, of whom as many as 800 died. The epidemic was so severe that the city ran out of coffins, and a mass grave of soldiers was created at the present intersection of Washington Boulevard and Michigan Avenue in downtown Detroit. Unlike many, Brush did have a coffin and a gravestone, but his stone today incorrectly marks the date of his death as December 14, 1814 (see epitaph at the opening of this essay). Letters indicate that Brush died at the height of the epidemic a year earlier, on or around December 14, 1813. In February 1814,

Askin's longtime business partner Isaac Todd offered his condolences on "the loss … I am told [of] Mr. Brush."[22]

Brush's probate estate file valued his personal property at $2,666.66. In five pages of elaborate script, a man's life is laid out—the pioneer scarcity, the intellectual quotient, the measure of the man. This inventory graphically demonstrates the simplicity of life in Detroit at the time of the War of 1812. Brush was a successful attorney, a landowner, and a community leader, yet his material goods were few, with the striking exception of his books, his professional stock in trade. Accounts owed to him totaled $7,337.94 1/2, illustrating the difficulty everyone had in paying their debts when there was little money in circulation. Adelaide stated that the family had $500 cash on hand when Brush died, which was soon spent on family necessities.[23]

Even in death, Brush was a transnational figure. He left Adelaide a life estate in his property, to devolve equally to their four children. This meant she could occupy and use the property as she saw fit, but could not sell or encumber the real estate. Brush also designated Adelaide as his executrix—the person who would officially handle his estate. The totality of this legal arrangement reflected the gender attitudes of multiple cultures in the Detroit River region. There was the British method of leaving the estate to the children, with the wife holding dominion until her death. There was the French approach of treating the wife as a business partner, by making her the executrix and not tying up the estate during her lifetime, as the British might have done. And, finally, there was the American style of treating all children equally, regardless of gender or birth order. Adelaide, as executrix of his will, faithfully pursued the estate claims and ensured the family's financial stability after Elijah's death, assisted by their son Edmund, also a lawyer. This property, the Brush Farm, became some of the most valuable in Detroit. It enveloped much of the eastern portion of what became the downtown area and was kept in one piece for a long time by Edmund. Rather than sell portions of the property, he used what was dubbed the "Brush lease." A long-term lease was offered at a low rate, with the lessee or tenant to pay all of the real estate taxes and other assessments. Eventually, the portion near present-day Comerica Park and the Detroit Medical Center was subdivided into an area of luxurious Victorian mansions known as Brush Park.[24]

Elijah Brush could not have foreseen the rich future for Detroit and his family when he wrote, "I know not what maybe the destany of this country," shortly before his beloved town fell. His short life in Detroit bore out its pioneer promise of building a new and successful territory, one that mixed old and new cultures. He was a natural border crosser, moving with ease through the region's multicultural population and across its porous border. He strung together the diverse threads of Native Americans, French inhabitants, British subjects, African Americans, and other American settlers. He was both a true transnational figure and a true American.

NOTES

1. There are only short biographical portraits of Elijah Brush, all of which contain some inconsistencies no incorrect information. See *Askin Papers,* 1:15, 207 n48; *City of Detroit,* 2:1361; Silas Farmer, *The History of Detroit and Michigan: Or the Metropolis Illustrated* (Detroit: S. Farmer, 1890), 1031; and Judy Jacobson, *Detroit River Connections: Historical and Biographical Sketches of the Eastern Great Lakes Border Region* (Baltimore: Clearfield, 1994), 59–63. For Detroit at the time of Brush's arrival, see Frederick C. Bald, *Detroit's First American Decade, 1796–1805* (Ann Arbor: University of Michigan Press, 1948).

2. For the border after the American Revolution, see Denver Brunsman and Joel Stone, eds., *Revolutionary Detroit: Portraits in Political and Cultural Change, 1760–1805* (Detroit: Detroit Historical Society, 2009). For descriptions of crossing the border, see *Askin Papers,* 2:531–63, 570–71, 581, 600, 729, 769.

3. John Askin to Isaac Todd, September 4, 1807, in *Askin Palters,* 2:571.

4. Alan Taylor, *The Civil War of 1812: American Citizens, British Subjects, Irish Rebels, & Indian Allies* (New York: Knopf, 2010). For the participation of the extended Askin family in the war, see the essay in this volume by Timothy Marks.

5. John Askin to Isaac Todd, February 23, 1802, in *Askin Papers,* 2:370 ("My daughter"); John Askin to Robert Hamilton, April 8, 1802, in *Askin Papers,* 2:374 ("[Brush] bids fair").

6. John Askin Sr. to John Askin Jr., July 5, 1809, in *Askin Papers,* 2:627 ("warm hearted"); John Askin to James McGill, July 17, 1812, in *Askin Papers,* 2:709 ("as kind"); John Askin Sr. to John Askin Jr., July 5, 1809, in *Askin Papers,* 2:641 ("the goodness").

7. John Askin to Isaac Todd and James McGill, March 25, 1807, in *Askin Papers,* 2:546. Apprenticeship to a practicing lawyer was the law school of the time. Alexander Askin later removed himself and his legal studies across the river, since he did not intend to practice in the U.S. and Upper Canadian law required a five-year apprenticeship in the province. The decision provides another example of the border's new importance. Alexander Askin to Charles Askin, April 28, 1808, in *Askin Papers,* 2:600.

8. John Askin to Isaac Todd, October 8, 1808, in *Askin Papers,* 2:612.

9. For an example of the lack of currency in trade, see Joseph Guy to John Askin, June 26,1806, in *Askin Papers,* 2:525. For the Detroit Bank, see *City of Detroit,* 1:622–27; "The Detroit Bank," in *MPHC,* 8:571–78; and the essay in this volume by John Paris.

10. See the first two volumes of *Transactions of the Supreme Court of the Territory of Michigan,* ed. William W. Blume, 6 vols. (Ann Arbor: University of Michigan Press, 1935–40).

11. For records in the slave cases, see *Transactions of the Supreme* Court, 1:87–88, 414–18; and "Relative to the Subject of Slavery," in *MPHC,* 12:11–22. For the impact of the cases on slavery in the Detroit River region, see Gregory Wigmore, "Before the Railroad: From Slavery to Freedom in the Canadian American Borderland," *Journal of American History* 98 (2011): 437–54; and the essay in this volume by Charlie Keller.

12. Elijah Brush to John Askin, July 8, 1805, in *Askin Papers,* 2:471–72; 472 (quote).

13. For references to different items to be secured and transported, see *Askin Papers,* 2:475, 480, 583, 606, 677 ("shoes").

14. John Askin Jr. to John Askin Sr., June 17, 1808, in *Askin Papers,* 2:606.

15. John Askin Jr. to John Askin Sr., May 1, 1815, in *Askin Papers,* 2:780.

16. Bald, 237; "Memorial of Elijah Brush, James May and John Anderson to the President of the United States" [1805 or 1806], in *MPHC,* 8:549–53; "Subscription to Raise Powder. 1812," in *MPHC,* 8:620; "Address of the Citizens of Detroit to A.B. Woodward" (January 6, 1813), in *MPHC,* 36:271.

17. Elijah Brush to John Askin, August 11, 1812, in *Askin Papers,* 2:729. The Meldrum farm was just east of what is now Mt. Elliot Street on Detroit's near east side, coincidentally the eastern boundary of Elmwood Cemetery. For George Meldrum, see Charles Wilson Goode, "Meldrum & Park: Commerce, Society, and Loyalty in Frontier Detroit," in *Revolutionary Detroit,* 133–39.

18. Elijah Brush to John Askin, September [?], 1812, in *Askin Papers,* 2:730; "Shubael Conant," in *MPHC,* 28;631. For the fall of Detroit, see Taylor, 164–65; and Anthony J. Yanik, *The fall and Recapture of Detroit in the War of 1812: In Defense of William Hull* (Detroit: Wayne State University Press, 2011), 93–102.

19. For internal opposition to Hull, see *City of Detroit,* 2:1035–36; and Yanik, 81–82. For Brush's release, see Mr. Scott to Colonel Gardner October 8, 1813, in *MPHC,* 15:406. Several sources mistakenly state that Brush was paroled to Ohio and never returned home. The error has possibly resulted from confusing Elijah with another Brush in the northwest theater, Captain Henry Brush from Chillicothe, Ohio. Henry Brush brought reinforcements to the River Raisin at the time of the capitulation. He refused to surrender and went back to Ohio.

20. John Askin Sr. to his children, November 12, 1813, in *Askin Papers,* 2:773.

21. *City of Detroit,* 2:1042. For the aftermath of the massacre, see also the essays in this volume by Carly Campbell and Scott A. Jankowski.

22. Isaac Todd to John Askin, February 3, 1814, in *Askin Papers,* 2:776. For reasons unclear, Clarence M. Burton recorded Brush's death as April 1, 1814 (*City of Detroit,* 2:1361), a mistake duplicated in *Askin Papers,* 1:207 n48. The editor, Milo M. Quaife, later corrected the error *(Askin Papers,* 2:370 n6). For Askin's illness, see John Anderson to Solomon Sibley, December 6, 1813, in Clarence M. Burton, *History of Detroit, 1780 to 1850: Financial and Commercial* (Detroit: Burton, 1917), 63. This work lists Brush's death as December 14, 1813 (65), which is consistent with the timing of Brush's illness and the closest approximation that we have. Writing to Solomon Sibley on December 31, 1813, Benjamin Chittenden reported on Brush's recent illness and death (Box 37, Solomon Sibley Papers, BHC). For the epidemic that likely look Brush's life, see *City of Detroit,* 2:1050; and the historical marker at the mass grave site (www.hmdb.org/marker.asg?marker=21745, accessed August 5, 2012). Brush was first buried on family land before he was finally laid to rest in Elmwood Cemetery on November 14, 1849. The error on his gravestone could be due to a mistake when the stone was prepared after the tumult of the war and epidemic. It is also possible that a new gravestone was made around the time of his body's removal to Elmwood. I thank Michael Shukwit of Elmwood Cemetery for graciously assisting me with its archives.

23. The Wayne County Probate Court files of Elijah and Adelaide Brush are found on microfilm in the Archives of Michigan, Lansing. Elijah Brush, File 108, Roll 6616.28. Adelaide Brush, File 3100, Roll 6660. I thank the archivists at the Archives of Michigan for their unstinting personal assistance.

The Apprenticeship: Good Government Mayor

MELVIN HOLLI

During his four terms as mayor, Hazen S. Pingree met many of the problems common to municipalities of his day, and with energy and originality he brought Detroit to prominence among American cities. Yet his first year as mayor in 1890 was a poor, if not deceptive, indication that a social reformer would emerge in 1892 and 1893. Initially committed to a businessman's concept of good municipal government, Pingree first followed a course which other mayors before him had taken and which had done little to change conditions in urban America.

During his first administration, Pingree rooted out dishonesty and inefficiency in a fashion that excited civic uplifters. Pingree struck at what he conceived to be the causes of corruption as ruthlessly and effectively as had any of the "good government" mayors of Eastern cities. Paring away inefficiency, he brought the power of his administration to bear upon crooked contractors, bad workmanship, and the lax policies of municipal departments. Pingree's approach to urban problems also had much in common with the mugwump tradition which sought to upgrade the quality of public service and to lower its cost by the creation of systems which brought in honest and able municipal employees.

Hazen S. Pingree's inaugural message, delivered before the common council on January 14, 1890, dealt with the paving problem. Approaching the problem as a businessman would, Pingree pointed out that Detroit had invested its money badly in 130 miles of wooden block pavements which had been laid on a sand and loam base. He observed that Detroit had spent more than one-half million dollars on Jefferson and Woodward Avenues, two of the city's main thoroughfares, during the previous sixteen years, but that these pavements still remained in poor condition. To lay a pavement of cut stone or asphalt would have required a greater capital outlay, he conceded, but the return would have been worth it. For good pavements would have provided a solid foundation ready for inexpensive resurfacing. The Mayor also asked for better street cleaning and requested that the city "keep apace with private enterprise" by buying "improved machinery." Nothing contributed "so much to the prosperity of a city as well paved streets," concluded Pingree.[1]

Pingree's assessment was correct. The city's streets were, indeed, in such wretched condition that the Detroit *Journal* described them as "150 miles of rotting, rutted, lumpy, dilapidated paving...." The cedar blocks were often set afloat by spring rains or driven deeply into the mud by heavy traffic. During the summer dry season dust storms accompanied every breeze that cooled the city. On streets where the blocks were still on the surface, the resins and pitches that oozed from the cedar frequently caught fire from carelessly discarded cigar butts. Such streets were also difficult to clean, and the sandy loam base prevented drainage and created unsanitary pools of water. Local historian George B. Catlin reported that Detroit was one of the worst paved cities of its size in the country when Pingree assumed office in 1890.[2]

Such inferior pavements in a city of 200,000 people were undoubtedly due in part to public inertia. Also responsible, however, was a group of unprogressive contractors who had failed to equip themselves to handle modern road surfacing and who preferred to hire low-priced unskilled labor to dump blocks and mud on the streets. Although the contractors lacked the skills and equipment to do modern paving, their collusion with the Democratic party was usually adequate to overcome their technological shortcomings. According to the Detroit *Journal,* the contractors' "combine" paid 10 per cent to the Democratic bloc in the city council to keep out low-priced, modern macadam men. Theft and shabby workmanship also played their part. Two foremen for the Talbott Company testified later that they had been paid bonuses by their employer to cut corners and violate city specifications. "I frankly confess I take all the advantage of the city I can on contracts," said a company foreman. Although Pingree's predecessor had broken up the "combine" in 1889 and secured indictments against several leading Democratic councilmen, including Chris Jacob, witnesses had the unnerving habit of disappearing, and prosecution was seldom successful. It was widely believed that the old Irish hangers-on such as councilmen Robert H. Murphy and William O'Regan and Board of Public Works Commissioner James Hanley were deeply implicated with the paving "combine," and their consistent opposition to better pavements in 1890 and 1891 lent credibility to the charge.[3]

Pingree scored his first victory for good streets in May, 1890, when the council adopted some of his paving specifications, including concrete foundations for a few of the heavily-trafficked thoroughfares. In June he pushed an ordinance through the council which authorized concrete foundations and hard-road surfaces for Jefferson and Lafayette Avenues, which serviced two wealthy neighborhoods. During 1892 he secured measures which improved the city's major arteries and obtained brick surfacing for Gratiot Avenue and asphalt for Woodward Avenue. Anxious to complete his program, Pingree, over the protest of churchmen, ordered the contractors to work seven days a week in 1892 because he believed that hard-surfaced streets were an important health measure which would eliminate pools of stagnant water and debris, which spread disease. Distressed by the city's constant surveillance of the private contractors to force them to fulfill obligations, Pingree demanded that security bonds be posted. He also asked Detroit to establish a municipal paving department.[4]

In July, 1893, the Mayor made a major advance when the council accepted the principle that concrete road beds, when economically feasible, would be a routine part of Detroit's future paving policies. In 1893, only Buffalo had more asphalt-pavement mileage than Detroit. Two years later, the Detroit *Journal* declared that Detroit's streets were in better condition than those of any city of comparable size in the country. The Mayor's constant attention to street improvements brought Detroit to the front rank of well-paved cities of the United States.[5]

The same pattern of Democratic collusion with corrupt contractors emerged in the sewer scandal of 1890, and revealed how common graft had become under the old urban order. In March, Pingree ordered an engineering investigation of Detroit's sewage system, which disclosed that many of die recently constructed mains and lines were rotting and crumbling. To win council backing for his improvement program, Pingree led a group of aldermen into the sewers, where they saw concrete as soft as mush, bricks that had fallen out of place, mortar that crumbled with the touch of the hand, water and mud cascading through the walls, and obstructions which backed up the effluence. Although some of the blame lay with faulty craftsmanship, Pingree placed the major responsibility on the city's cement supplier, who had furnished an unsuitable, low-quality product.[6] To end such abuses of the public interest, Pingree established an informal research bureau and converted his office into a concrete testing laboratory filled with jars and bottles of sand and various brands of cement, water, and pressure gauges. Every test of tensile strength of the brand of cement which had been sold to the city showed that it lacked the required hydraulic properties and firmness. Pingree roared his disapproval as the inferior product cracked before the gauges could even register, whereas the Portland and Louisville brands withstood forty pounds of pressure. The supplier of inferior cement threatened to sue Pingree, but his case collapsed when a hardened sample of his cement was presented to an alderman at a public hearing, and he crumbled the sample with his bare hands. A former employee of the supplier testified that floor sweepings which had leaked from other bags had been sold to the Board of Public Works and that the company had a general policy of "short weighting" the city.[7]

Democratic Commissioner James Hanley of the Board of Public Works tried to defend his purchase of inferior workmanship and supplies, but Pingree had already outflanked him with the appointment of two businesslike G.O.P. commissioners who brought an end to Hanley's lax policies. The new Board dropped the cement company from its list of suppliers, established stiffer standards for purchasing, and solicited out-of-town bidders, thus abolishing the inefficient localism which was a part of the Democratic business and political philosophy. To eliminate some of the shabby workmanship that flourished under the patronage system, the Board began purchasing a vitreous, precast pipe to replace sewer masonry for the smaller lateral lines. Even so, in August, 1892, two sewer contractors attempted to bribe the G.O.P. council for several contracts. They were assured by the Pingree administration that competitive bidding and good workmanship were the only requirements for city work. The rational order of the business world had triumphed over the casual corruption of the old Democratic sewer and paving "combines" by 1892.[8]

In another scandal, involving the school board, Pingree moved vigorously to eliminate a long tradition of corruption and collusion. The board, elected on a ward basis, had long been either a nursery for the politically ambitious or a pasture for marginal businessmen who hoped to recoup their private losses at public expense. "Scarcely a session passes that something is not done which has the odor of 'boodle' about it," said the Detroit *Journal.* Pingree was especially irked that the school board awarded lucrative contracts at secret sessions, because of loose budgetary controls, and that the board did not act as a city-wide agent to plan intelligently for Detroit's educational needs. In 1893, hoping to centralize planning and eliminate some of the worst abuses of localism, Pingree secured die enactment of a state law that authorized the Mayor to veto board expenditures. Pingree's goal was not budget cutting but an efficient utilization of the money available for education.[9]

The Mayor's veto power over money measures was, however, inadequate to reform the school board, for the board chose to ignore the state law and reverted to its old patterns of defiance and questionable dealing. Finally, on August 15, 1894, Pingree exposed the corruption and rooted out some of the most dishonest members of the board. "It was like a scene from a melodrama or a page from a sensational novel," reported the Detroit *Evening News,* "for such things happen often on the stage but seldom in real life." At a meeting of the board, Pingree announced: "There are quite a number of the members of this board who are going to jail tonight." He called upon the dishonest schoolmen, as yet unnamed, to resign and to save the city from disgrace. When Pingree was met with stony silence and then opposition, he pealed off the names of the corrupt in slow cadence, repeating the charges clearly and deliberately while issuing warrants. Then he called in police officers from the wings to arrest four board members. When the indicted chairman of the school real-estate committee called Pingree a liar, die Mayor ordered: "Officer, take this man to jail," and a squad of policemen closed in. Pingree then proceeded with his indictment, asserting: "Why, actually members of this board have sold themselves out regularly to this and that and the other contractor. It is frightful. And it made no difference. After they had been bought they frequently sold themselves again, and left the parties they first sold to."[10]

In court it was disclosed that Pingree, determined to leave no loopholes open, had employed several private detectives. They worked in co-operation with a school furniture salesman who had been informed by several board members that a personal payoff would be the price of a contract with the Detroit public schools. The salesman met with the ring in a local hotel room, which Pingree's detectives had rigged in advance for observation. A stenographer recorded the conversation. The salesman led the schoolmen through their usual performance, in which they demanded their bribes and seriously incriminated themselves.[11]

Armed with a dossier of solid evidence, Pingree brought the corrupt board members to trial. Two were sentenced to prison, one jumped his bail bond and fled the state, and the fourth member secured an acquittal. The exposure did indeed shake the town, as Pingree had predicted, and ended one of the long-enduring corrupt practices in Detroit.[12]

During his first term Pingree also attempted to eliminate inefficiency and waste by a number of economy measures. In refusing payment of a personal liability claim against Detroit, Pingree maintained that the city should contest all such cases in court not only to save money but also to force the public attorneys to earn their keep by defending the interests of the city. When the municipal clerks asked for overtime pay to prepare the tax rolls, Pingree vetoed the proposal and asserted that the clerks, who then worked a six-hour day, deserved no additional compensation. The Mayor hoped to plug the continual leaks in the treasury which drained away public resources with needless extras. In turning down a pay raise for the election inspectors, Pingree claimed that their unsatisfactory services did not justify an increase. A pork barrel measure to add to the number of city attendants on Belle Isle Bridge was quashed by Pingree because it provided "for too many high priced employees who would be more ornamental than useful." "Our first duty ... as representatives of the taxpayers of the city of Detroit is to carefully guard their interests," Pingree said, "How can Detroit taxpayers and business men compete—as they have to—with Chicago taxpayers and business men when compelled to pay from 40 to 100 per cent more for having the same things done?"[13]

The answer of the first Pingree administration reflected the nostrums of an earlier generation of business-minded reformers: eliminate the hacks who were nursed at the "political teat" in the interests of the merit system. The Mayor prodded the garbage inspectors to perform more efficiently, pressed for measures to reduce the pay of sidewalk inspectors, wanted to do away with the gas inspectors who performed few useful functions, strove to eliminate the surfeit of city hall janitors who were political appointees, tried to check the idleness of municipal clerks, and attempted to force public employees to put in a full day's work. Although he opposed the eight-hour day for city laborers (who averaged ten hours) in 1891 because he felt that it would infringe upon their liberty of contract, Pingree supported an eight-hour day for janitors with the hope that they might be induced to work more than their customary four- to six-hour day.[14]

The first Pingree administration had aimed at modifying and improving the mechanisms of municipal government in an effort to make them work as the city charter had intended. Pingree had injected large doses of efficiency into the old system and had tried to scrap many of the agencies whose contribution to good government was questionable. Not only had the Mayor rooted out dishonesty, but he had also worked hard to eliminate the worst excesses of localism and particularism: Pingree had attempted both formally by charter reform and informally by the use of patronage power to centralize administrative and municipal control and to focus power in the office of the mayor. It was clearly an attempt to incorporate the best features of the business world into municipal administration. Responsible, efficient, and clean government had been the goal of countless "reform" mayors; and, in this respect, Pingree's crusade for a better Detroit possessed few features that could not be found within the business-inspired reform movements in other cities.

The prelude to Pingree's concern with the larger social question of transportation came in his struggle to lower ferry rates. Pingree was convinced that the high cost of a ferry ride from Detroit across the Detroit River to Belle Isle Park prevented citizens from enjoying this refreshing respite. When the Mayor threatened to revoke the ferry company's license or to purchase a publicly owned fleet, the company dropped its rates from ten cents to five cents, and a new licensee took over the operation. During the fracas, Pingree examined city-owned water frontage and found that free public access had been blocked by private businesses that had encroached upon municipal property and deprived citizens of their right to the Detroit River at eighteen public landings. Pingree began clearing away the dock areas and winning back for the public free access to water and recreation.[15]

In 1892 Pingree also inaugurated a campaign to eliminate the toll gates which stood astride the city's five main thoroughfares and which levied tribute on two-thirds of the traffic coming into Detroit. The toll roads were in wretched condition because their owners had failed to comply with charter provisions requiring repair and maintenance. Even after the city had repaired and paved the main thoroughfares, some of the plank road companies exercised their ancient charter rights and continued to charge a toll on them for incoming traffic within one-half mile of the city hall. Few escaped the "blackmailing toll-gate," as Pingree called it, for even the Board of Public Works' teamsters had to pay tribute when driving on city streets to the water works. Pingree called the toll roads a "relic of barbarism" and charged that their owners were guilty of legalized robbery. All the Pingree administration's attempts at legislative and legal redress failed, however, for the courts upheld the property rights of the charter holders. Pingree made several attempts to buy out the charters at reasonable prices, but he was rebuffed by the road companies which demanded exorbitant payment. Also opposing the Mayor were a few of the old ward-bound councilmen of narrow vision, but he had little difficulty in lining up votes for the necessary appropriations.[16]

Still it required coercion and harassment of the rawest form to force the owners to sell or even to cooperate. Strathearn Hendrie, one of the principal owners of the Jefferson Avenue gate, obtained a court injunction which temporarily stopped the city from paving Detroit's main northeast highway, Jefferson Avenue. Furious with these "leeches on the municipality," Pingree advised citizens to refuse to pay tolls on the grounds that the plank road charters were forfeit because of gross negligence. "If they won't get out the people should organize and drive them out," said the Mayor. Despairing of legal and reasonable remedies, Pingree struck at Hendrie, the toughest of the toll road curmudgeons, and built what became known as the Pingree by-pass around Hendrie's Jefferson Avenue gate. When Hendrie remained obstinate even though vehicles now could pass the gate without paying, Pingree pushed a 60-foot wide macadamized road up to and around the toll house, which was left stranded in the middle of the road. Hendrie then applied for another injunction, but the court ruled that his company owned only the 16-foot strip in the center, and thus his tolls were uncollectable on 44 feet of outside lanes on Jefferson Avenue. The toll companies, having learned the lesson, sold out to Detroit on reasonable terms.

By the middle of 1896, every toll company had been ousted from within the city limits. "Now we can drive over our streets feeling that we are free men," declared Pingree.[17]

The struggle for lower ferry rates and a free road system presaged Pingree's concern with the larger question of urban transportation. Pingree was beginning to realize that the social needs of urban Detroiters could not be met by simply tinkering with the machinery of municipal government and wiping out corruption with a Calvinistic zeal.

NOTES

1. *Journal of the Common Council,* 1890 (Detroit, 1891), pp. 1–2.

2. Detroit *Journal:* May 2, June 3, 1890, Pingree Scrapbook (hereafter, P.S.); *Journal of the Common Council,* 1891 (Detroit, 1892), p. 5; Norman Beasley and George W. Stark, *Made in Detroit* (New York, 1957), p. 22; George B. Catlin, *The Story of Detroit* (Detroit, 1926), pp. 593, 598.

3. Detroit *Journal:* April 25, 1890; May 1, 2, 1890; Detroit *Evening News:* April 25, 29, 1890; January 11, 1897, P.S.; Catlin, *The Story of Detroit,* p. 593.

4. Detroit *Journal:* May 29, 1890; June 11, 1890; July 27, 1892; Detroit *Free Press:* June 4, 1890; June 8, 1892; Detroit *Evening News:* June 16, 1892; September 26, 1892; December 21, 1892; July 5, 1893, P.S.; *Journal of the Common Council,* 1890, pp. 131–36.

5. Detroit *Journal:* August 12, 1896, P.S.; *Twentieth Annual Report of the Board of Public Works, 1893–94* (Detroit, 1894), p. 8; Edward W. Bemis, "Detroit's Efforts to Own Her Street Railways," *Municipal Affairs,* III (September, 1899), 473.

6. Detroit *Tribune:* March 26, 1890; May 22, 1890; Detroit *Evening News:* May 22, 1890, P.S.; *Journal of the Common Council,* 1890, pp. 122–23.

7. Detroit *Free Press:* March 28, 1890; Detroit *Tribune:* April 24, 1890; May 23, 1890, P.S.

8. Detroit *Tribune:* March 29, 1890; February 4, 16, 1892; Detroit *Journal:* August 12, 1892, P.S.

9. Detroit *Journal:* March 25, 1892; Detroit *Tribune:* January 14, 1893; May 26, 1893, P.S.

10. Pingree quoted in Detroit *Tribune:* August 16, 1894; Detroit *Evening News:* August 16, 1894, P.S.; "Hazen S. Pingree, Mayor, Etc. v. The Board of Education of the City of Detroit," 94 *Michigan,* 404–8.

11. Hazen S. Pingree, *Facts and Opinions* (Detroit, 1895), pp. 201–2.

12. Detroit *Journal:* October 19, 1894; June 13, 1895; October 2, 1896, P.S.

13. *Journal of the Common Council,* 1890, pp. 395, 539, 667, 839, 860.

14. Unidentified newspaper clipping, P.S., March-April, 1892; Detroit *Tribune:* February 18, 1891; Detroit *Evening News:* December 8, 1892; Detroit *Free Press:* February 20, 24, 28, 1892; April 5, 1893, P.S.

15. Detroit *Tribune:* May 27, 1891; June 20, 1891, P.S.; *Journal of the Common Council,* 1891, pp. 6, 410, 522.

16. Lansing *State Affairs,* December 13, 1893; *Journal of the Common Council,* 1893, pp. 774–75; *ibid.,* 1895, p. 435; John C. Lodge, I *Remember Detroit* (Detroit, 1949), p. 65.

17. Pingree quoted in Detroit *Evening News:* April 10, 1895; July 31, 1896; *Journal of the Common Council,* 1893, p. 774; Detroit *Free Press:* June 22, 1894; September 1, 1895, P.S.; *Journal of the Common Council,* 1894, p. 4; *ibid.,* 1895, p. 1459; *ibid.,* 1897, p. 12.

SECTION II

READINGS

INDUSTRIAL DECLINE AND LABOR

INTRODUCTION

Detroit's industrial past is examined at its organizational roots in an essay from **Thomas Sugrue's** renowned book on the causes of Detroit's decline, followed by **Bryan Jones and Lynn Bachelor's** exploration of local political economy from a chapter in their classic work. The section closes with a penetrating essay by **Sumit Chaudhury and Hansa Iyengyar** on the role played by the Big Three automakers in Detroit's demise.

1

The Damning Mark of False Prosperities: The Deindustrialization of Detroit

THOMAS J. SUGRUE

Obsolescence is the very hallmark of progress.
—Henry Ford II (1955)

Unemployment is not a crime. It is a social ill full of hardships, set-backs, anxieties, needs and sacrifices which would he landed under any other circumstances. It is truly the weakest spot in Democracy's armor, the likely erosion point in the social structure, and the damning mark of false unstable or lopsided prosperities.
—William Wakeham (1951)

The; intersection of Grand Boulevard, John R Street, and the Milwaukee and Junction Railroad, just four miles north of downtown Detroit, seemed the heartbeat of the industrial metropolis in the 1940s. Within a two-square-mile area extending along the Grand Trunk and Michigan Central railroads was one of the most remarkable concentrations of industry in the United States. To the north was Detroit's second largest automobile factory. Dodge Main, which employed over thirty-five thousand workers in a five-story factory building with over 4.5 million square feet of floor space. Studebaker had a plant at the corner of Piquette Avenue and Brush where it produced its luxury sedans. Just to the north, on Russell Street, was a cavernous redbrick building that housed Murray Auto Body, a major independent producer of automobile chassis. Packard Motors produced cars in a sprawling ninety-five-building complex that extended for nearly a mile along East Grand Boulevard. At shift change time, the area came to a virtual standstill, as cars, buses, and pedestrians clogged the streets. The whole area was often covered in a grayish haze, a murky combination of pollutants from the factories and car exhaust. Even at night the area bustled, as the factory windows emitted an eerie "blue-green glow," and echoed with the "screams and clank of the machinery."[1]

By the late 1950s, this industrial landscape had become almost unrecognizable. The Milwaukee-Junction area was hard hit by layoffs and plant closings. Murray Auto Body, Packard, and Studebaker shut down between 1953 and 1957. Dodge Main cut its work force by several thousand in the late 1950s. The shells of several empty multistory factories stood as cavernous hulks on the horizon, unobscured by smoke and haze on all but the foggiest days. Dozens of taverns and restaurants that had catered to workers were boarded up. And the neighborhoods surrounding the plants, which had housed thousands of industrial workers, had quickly become run-down. Property values fell, because plant closings deprived the small frame houses on the East Side of their only real advantage, their proximity to the workplace. Their largely white residents followed the flight of jobs to suburban and exurban areas. Traffic on the new Chrysler and Ford Freeways whisked past the former plants, the drivers oblivious to the blighted landscape around them. Similar rotting industrial areas could be found throughout the city, most notably on the city's far East Side, near Connor Road between Gratiot and Jefferson, where Mack, Briggs, Hudson, and Motor Products plants had closed. Even the area around the enormous Ford River Rouge plant lost some of its luster, as whole sections of the plant were modernized and thousands of workers who had patronized local stores, bars, and restaurants were laid off or transferred.

The 1950s marked a decisive turning point in the development of the city—a systematic restructuring of the local economy from which the city never fully recovered. Detroit's economy experienced enormous fluctuations in the 1950s. Between 1949 and 1960, the city suffered four major recessions. Because the auto industry was tremendously sensitive to shifts in consumer demand it weathered recessions badly. The unpredictability of demand for automobiles, especially in times of economic uncertainty, had serious ramifications for Detroit's working class. A slight shift in interest rates or a small drop in car sales resulted in immediate layoffs.[2] That the auto industry' was especially vulnerable to economic vagaries was, however, nothing new. What was new in the 1950s was that auto manufacturers and suppliers permanently reduced their Detroit-area work forces, closed plants, and relocated to other parts of the country.

Looking out onto the city in 1952, social welfare worker Mary Jorgensen observed that "Detroit is in the doldrums." But what she observed, unknowing, were the first signs of long-term economic problems that beset Detroit, not just a momentary economic lull. More important than the periodic downswings that plagued the city's economy was the beginning of a long-term and steady decline in manufacturing employment that affected Detroit and almost all other major northeastern and Midwestern industrial cities. Between 1947 and 1963, Detroit lost 134,000 manufacturing jobs, while its population of working-aged men and women actually increased. Workers who had enjoyed a modicum of stability in the boom years of the 1940s suffered repeated bouts of unemployment in the 1950s. Laid-off workers were also consumers whose loss of buying power rippled through out the city's economy, affecting local businesses from department stores and groceries to restaurants and bowling alleys. The growing gap between job seekers and job opportunities would have profound ramifications in subsequent decades.[3]

CAPITAL MOBILITY

The transformation of Detroit's economy in the 1950s is best understood from a long-term perspective. Throughout the nineteenth and early twentieth centuries, American industry followed a pattern of centralization. Considerations of topography, access to transportation routes (either water or railroad), and the availability of raw materials determined plant location. The process of deindustrialization—the closing, downsizing, and relocation of plants and sometimes whole industries—accelerated throughout the twentieth century. Advances in communication and transportation, the transformation of industrial technology, the acceleration of regional and international economic competition, and the expansion of industry in low-wage regions, especially the South, reshaped the geography of American industrial cities. Beginning with the New Deal, the federal government channeled a disproportionate amount of resources to the South, culminating in the Sunbelt-dominated military-industrial complex of the Cold War era. Postwar highway construction, spurred by state and local expressway initiatives in the 1940s, and federally funded highway construction after 1956, made central industrial location less necessary by facilitating the distribution of goods over longer distances. Companies also moved to gain access to markets in other sections of the country, especially rapidly growing areas like California and the urban West.[4]

The forces of capital mobility reshaped the landscape of industrial America. New factories appeared on rural hillsides, in former cornfields, and in cleared forests, and the shells of old manufacturing buildings loomed over towns and cities that were depopulated when businesses relocated production in more profitable places. In the 1920s, New England textile towns were ravaged by the flight of mills to the Piedmont South, presaging similar shifts of capital that would transform much of the industrial North later in the century. By midcentury, what had been a trickle of manufacturing jobs out of the industrial heartland became a flood. In the 1950s, the flight of industry and the loss of jobs reconfigured the landscape of the most prominent industrial cities across the region that came to be known as the Rust Belt. Detroit, Chicago, New York. Pittsburgh, Philadelphia, Baltimore, Trenton, Boston, Buffalo, and St. Louis all lost hundreds of thousands of manufacturing jobs beginning in the 1950s, as firms reduced employment in center-city plants, replaced workers with new automated technology, and constructed new facilities in suburban and semirural areas, in medium-sized cities, often in less industrialized states or regions, and even in other countries.[5]

Automobile manufacturers were in the vanguard of corporate decentralization. The growth of a national and international market for automobiles led firms like Ford and General Motors to construct plants throughout the country. Technological advances, especially in transportation, made industrial decentralization possible. Yet decentralization was not simply a response to the inexorable demands of the market, it was an outgrowth of the social relations of production itself. Decentralization was an effective means for employers to control increasing labor costs and weaken powerful trade unions. The deconcentration of plants gave employers the upper hand during periods of labor unrest. General Motors, the first firm to deconcentrate production on a wide scale, built new plants in the 1930s in rural parts of the country, as a means of reducing wages and inhibiting union militancy in manufacturing cities like Detroit, Pontiac, and Flint, where most of its facilities had been located. The early decentralization experiments had little impact on Detroit. The city's share of national automobile production remained large throughout the first half of the twentieth century. But the pre-World War II decentralization efforts foreshadowed the auto industry's aggressive efforts to deconcentrate production and reduce its Detroit workforce after World War II.[6]

In the late 1940s and 1950s, Detroit's economy began to feel the effects of the mobility of the Big Three automobile manufacturers—Ford, General Motors, and, to a lesser extent, Chrysler. Between 1946 and 1956, General Motors spent $3.4 billion on new plants and facilities. Equally ambitious in its restructuring plans was Ford, which made aggressive decentralization the central part of its postwar corporate policy. From the end of World War II through 1957, Ford alone spent over $2.5 billion nationwide on a program of plant expansion. Chrysler, whose finances for capital expansion were small compared to its rivals, still spent $700 million on plant expansion in the same period.[7] Between 1947 and 1958, the Big Three built twenty-five new plants in the metropolitan Detroit area, all of them in suburban communities, most more than fifteen miles from the center city.[8] The lion's share of new plants, or "runaway shops," as Detroiters called them, however, went to small- and medium-sized cities in the Midwest, like Lima, Lorain, and Walton Hills, Ohio; Kokomo and Indianapolis, Indiana; and to the South and West, especially California.[9] In 1950, 56 percent of all automobile employment in the United States was in Michigan; by 1960, that figure had fallen to 40 percent.[10] As they expanded in other regions of the country, the major automotive producers reduced employment in their older Detroit-area plants.

A major reason that employers cited for the construction of new plants outside Detroit was the lack of available land for expansion. With new assembly-line technology, auto companies found the multistory plants of the 1910s and 1920s outdated. A few plants in the 1930s, and all new postwar auto plants, were built on one level. As more workers commuted to their jobs by car (71 percent of manufacturing employees in 1955 went to work by private car), firms also looked for large sites to accommodate massive parking lots. In addition, after World War II, Detroit lacked large sites with railroad frontage. A 1951 survey found only 367.5 acres of undeveloped land adjacent to railroad lines. The land was scattered about in 36 parcels, the largest site covering only 54 acres. The entire stretch of land abutting the Detroit Terminal railroad between Highland Park and Dearborn was fully developed; the Wabash Railroad line had only 48.5 acres of undeveloped frontage on the East Side and only 2.1 acres on the West Side. These small sites were simply insufficient for any large-scale factory construction. As a 1956 report noted, expanding firms could find "elbow room" only in the outlying fringe areas."[11]

First to follow the auto industry out of the city were auto-related industries, in particular machine tool manufacturers, metalworking firms, and parts manufacturers. Between 1950 and 1956, 124 manufacturing firms located on the green fields of Detroit's suburbs; 55 of them had moved out of Detroit. Leading the flight were metals-related firms' manufacturers of metal-working tools, wire, stampings, and dyes. These small plants (most with between eight and fifty workers) employed about 20 percent of Detroit-area workers in 1950, forming the second largest category of employment in the city after automobile production. It is impossible to calculate the number of metal and auto parts firms that moved outside the Detroit metropolitan area altogether, but undoubtedly many followed auto plants to their new locations in other parts of the country. The mobility of large auto producers and small firms alike reconfigured Detroit's industrial landscape, leaving empty factories and vacant lots behind, and bringing runaway shops to areas that just a few years earlier had been farms.[12]

Yet it was not foreordained that the auto companies would construct single-story automobile plants and downsize or abandon their older multistory factory complexes, nor was it inevitable that smaller machine tool and parts firms would prefer plants in outlying areas. The assumption that companies in the postwar period had no choice but to move to sprawling suburban and rural sites, surrounded by acres of parking lots and manicured lawns, is wrongly based in an a historical argument about the inevitability and neutrality of technological decisions. Industrial location policy was not a neutral response to market forces or an inexorable consequence of economic progress. Corporations made decisions about plant location and employment policy in a specific political, cultural, and institutional context, in the case of postwar Detroit in the aftermath of the rise of a powerful union movement and in the midst of a shop-floor struggle over work rules and worker control.[11]

AUTOMATION

The most important force that restructured Detroit's economy after World War II was the advent of new automated processes in the automobile, auto parts, and machine tool industries. In the late 1940s and 1950s, many Detroit industries, ranging from major automobile manufacturers to small tool and die firms, embraced automation. Automation had roots in earlier technological innovations in the automobile industry: it was the most refined application of the Fordist system of production.[14] In the wake of the long General Motors strike of 1946, GM began to experiment with labor-reducing machinery in its Flint Buick plant. Ford, however, led the automotive industry in experimentation with automation. In 1947, Ford set up an "Automation Department" to direct the reorganization of its manufacturing operations; its competitors and many other industries followed suit over the next fifteen years.

Automation offered two major benefits to manufacturers: it promised both to increase output and to reduce labor costs. Chrysler executive Harry R. Bentley described the purpose of automation as the "optimum use of machines to produce high-volume, high-quality products at the lowest possible cost." Although automation's advocates exaggerated its utility and underestimated its costs, automation sometimes did have dramatic effects. Before the introduction of automated engine production at Ford's Cleveland plant, it look 117 workers lo produce 154 engine blocks per hour; after automation the same output required a mere 41 workers.[15]

Industrialists touted automation as a way to improve working conditions and workers' standard of living. Del S. Harder, a Ford vice president and Detroit's most energetic proponent of automation, argued that "the era of automation is nothing more than a continuation of the industrial revolution which greatly increased our national wealth … and helped bring about the highest standard of living in the world." In Harder's view, automation would improve working conditions, reduce hours, and improve workplace safety. It was simply "a better way to do the job."[16]

Certainly automated production replaced some of the more dangerous and onerous factory jobs. At Ford, automation eliminated "mankilling," a task that demanded high speed and involved tremendous risk. "Mankilling" required a worker to remove hot coil springs from a coiling machine, lift them to chest height, turn around, and lower them into a quench tank, all within several seconds. In Ford's stamping plants, new machines loaded and unloaded presses, another relatively slow, unsafe, and physically demanding job before automation. Here automation offered real benefits to workers.[17]

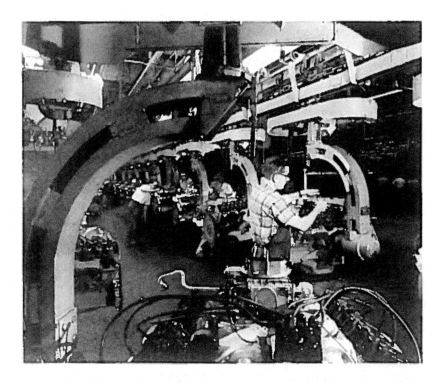

Figure 1.1: When Ford introduced automated assembly lines in its newly opened Lima Ohio plant in 1954, it relocated production from the River Rouge plant, displacing hundreds of Detroit workers. Lima was typical of towns that attracted relocating industry in the 1950s. It was small and overwhelmingly white.

Despite these occasional benefits, automation was primarily a weapon in the employers' antilabor arsenal. Through automation, employers attempted to reassert control over the industrial process, chipping away at the control over production that workers had gained through intricately negotiated work rules. Manufacturers hoped that self-regulating, computerized machinery would eliminate worker-led slowdowns, soldiering, and sabotage on the line. Contended one of automation's advocates: "'Changing times have raised the idea around Detroit" that in the future, industrialists would look to "how to get the most out of machines rather than how to get the most out of people. Personnel men of the future, they say, may be automation experts." Automation would lower the risk "of considerable damage to parts through worker carelessness." Automation also provided engineers and plant managers a seemingly foolproof way to reduce industry's dependence on labor and reduce labor costs. Above all, automation counteracted the "increasing cost of labor … given a sharp hike by recent Reuther assistance."[18]

Corporate leaders bluntly stated that automation would ensure that they retained the upper hand in labor-management relations. Only a little more than a decade after the emergence of the UAW, in a period of tremendous labor strength, automation was a formidable tool for management. A manager in the newly automated Ford engine plant in Cleveland reminded UAW President Walter Reuther that "you are going to have trouble collecting union dues from all of these machines."[19] The reduction of the work force in certain plants after the introduction of automation eviscerated some of the most powerful bastions of labor activism.

Automation had a devastating impact on the work force at the Ford River Rouge plant. Rouge workers were represented by UAW Local 600, one of the most militant in the industry. The plant was also the largest employer of blacks in the Detroit area, and throughout the 1940s, a majority of black workers there consistently supported the left-wing caucus of the UAW. Slowdowns or wildcat strikes at the Rouge could paralyze Ford production nationwide. In key sections of the plant, like the Motor and Plastics buildings, workers had gained a great degree of control over production through a mix of custom and work rules. Ford officials, hoping to weaken union strength on the shop floor, targeted the Rouge for automation. In 1950, Rouge workers assembled all Ford and Mercury engines; by 1954, Ford had shifted all engine production to the new automated Cleveland plant. Rouge workers with seniority were transferred to Cleveland or to the new Dearborn Engine Plant that built engines for Lincolns. Stamping, machine casting, forging, steel production, glassmaking, and dozens of other operations were shilled from the Rouge to new Ford plants throughout the 1950s.[20] As a result, employment at the Rouge fell from 85,000 in 1945, lo 54,000 in 1954, to only 30,000 in 1960.[21]

In the early, experimental stages of automation, the Big Three auto companies set up sections of new plants whose processes paralleled those at already existing plants. They compared productivity at old and new plants, and either modernized or closed older plants to increase productive capacity, or used the threat of a plant closing to prod workers to speed up production. New automated plants often replaced part or all of the production at existing facilities and eliminated whole job classifications. In Ford's first heavily automated plant, the Buffalo Stamping Plant, "workers were chiefly inspectors." Ford officials found that productivity at the older Dearborn stamping plant lagged behind Buffalo, and proceeded to automate Dearborn and reduce its work force. Ford further automated and decentralized stamping, opening a new Chicago plant in 1956, where company officials cut the number of job classifications by more than two hundred. The decentralization and automation of Ford stamping eliminated thousands of jobs, and weakened union shop floor control.[22]

Automation had its most far-reaching consequences in engine production, one of the most labor-intensive jobs in the auto industry before the 1950s. In 1951, Ford shifted a large part of its engine production from the Motor Building in the Rouge Complex to its new highly mechanized Cleveland plant and its new Dearborn plant. In the process, Ford eliminated close to three thousand jobs at the Rouge. By 1953, the Cleveland and Dearborn plants were running parallel production. Where 950 workers made piston connecting rods at the Rouge, they were replaced by two units of 146 workers each at Cleveland and Dearborn, resulting in a net loss of 804 jobs in the Detroit area. In addition, Ford paid its new Cleveland workers an average of eleven cents less per hour than at Dearborn. A similar pattern followed in every engine-related job. The hemorrhage of jobs continued in 1953 and 1955, when Ford announced the construction of new engine production facilities at Brookpark Village, Ohio, and in Lima, Ohio."[23]

The effects of automation on job opportunities in communities like Detroit were a well-guarded corporate secret. Responding to labor union criticism of automation, employers downplayed the possibility of significant job loss. When Ford began automating and decentralizing the Rouge plant, John Bugas, Ford's vice president for industrial relations, told workers that they had nothing to fear. "I do not believe," wrote Bugas in 1950, "that the over-all reduction in employees in the Rouge operations resulting from the building of new facilities will be substantial." Ford labor relations official Manton Cummins dismissed claims that automation led to job loss as a union-led "scare campaign." Yet the only detailed statistics on automation and its effects on employment, a UAW-sponsored study of Ford from 1950 to 1953, indicated a net loss of 4,185 jobs in the first years of industrial restructuring (Table 1.1).[24]

In the first flush of automation campaigns, industry publications like *Automation* magazine argued that automation reduced labor costs, but by the mid-1950s, they seldom raised labor as a rationale, because automation's effect on jobs had become a sensitive political issue. Instead, the magazine's editors went on the defensive against charges that automation led to job loss. In February 1960, for example, the magazine noted that "lest anyone be deluded into thinking of [the Plymouth Detroit assembly plant] as a workerless automaton, it should be reported that this place employs in excess of 5,000 people."[25]

Corporate leaders expressed unbounded optimism about automation. "Obsolescence is the very hallmark of progress," argued Henry Ford II, in a 1955 address. Technological change brought with it short term hardship, but long term gain. "The faster we obsolete products, machines, and antiquated, costly means of working, the faster we raise our living standards and our national wealth." Ford recognized that "In some areas where industries have been partly obsoleted whole

Table 1.1 Automation-Related Job Loss at Detroit-Area Ford Plants, 1951–1953

	Job Loss
Engine Division (Rouge)	1,727
Gear and Axle (Rouge)	231
Crankshaft (Motor Building, Rouge)	18
Piston (Motor Building, Rouge)	575
Frame and Cold Header Unit (Rouge)	531
Plastic Unit (Rouge)	30
Dearborn Stamping	940
Highland Park	85
Mound Road Plant	48
TOTAL	4,185

Source: J. O'Rourke, Memo on Automation in Ford Plants, January 31, 1957, UAW-RD, Box 65.

communities may suffer real hardship." In his view, such suffering was inevitable, for there would be "no direct way I can imagine to avoid by private means the dislocations that come from technological obsolescence."[26]

General Motors Vice President Louis Seaton was even more sanguine than Ford, but more disingenuous. He railed against the belief that automation "is a grim reaper of jobs" and noted that General Motors employment had gone up since the introduction of automation. He was quick to cite national-level statistics, but made no reference to the local consequences of GM modernization. Interestingly, he advocated early retirement as "one means of cushioning the effect of reduced employment," and noted that thousands of workers had retired under the "flexible retirement age provision" of the GM pension plan.[27]

The UAW, for the most part, worried about automation only insofar as it affected employment levels nationwide. National-level data gave little reason for concern. In the 1950s, there was little evidence to show that the number of auto industry jobs nationwide would fall because of automation. Some economists argued that over the long run, the introduction of automated processes would increase jobs nationwide. Aggregate employment statistics, however, masked profound local variation. Local economies in places like Detroit reeled from the consequences of automation-caused plant closings or work force reductions. Walter Reuther and other UAW officials initially expressed some concern about the effects of automation on employment and union strength in industrial cities, but for the most part they poured their energy into cushioning the effects of layoffs through extended unemployment benefits, improved pension plans, and preferential hiring plans for displaced workers. Labor leaders also became staunch advocates of government funding for education and retraining programs to prepare workers for new automated jobs. Contract provisions guaranteed that workers who lost their jobs because of automation would be protected by seniority and transferred to other jobs. Their programs offered remedies for the symptoms of automation, rather than grappling with the root causes of unemployment.[28] While transfer guarantees mitigated the effects of displacement in the auto industry for workers with seniority, the introduction of automated processes led to "silent firing," a term that referred to the unheralded reduction of entry-level auto industry jobs in Detroit. Silent firing aroused little controversy, but it cut into the pool of available unskilled and semiskilled jobs in the city, and, over the long run, weakened union strength in what had been a union stronghold.[29]

Detroit's workers bore the burden of technological changes in the 1950s. Automation had two other important consequences for the Detroit-area labor market. First, it gave a competitive advantage to General Motors and Ford, which hurt Chrysler and destroyed the independent automobile manufacturers in the city. Second, it led auto companies to take on productive capacities formerly left to independent manufacturers, driving many parts suppliers out of business and further reducing Detroit's employment base. Automation affected virtually every sector of the city's economy, reshaping Detroit's industrial labor market, and unleashing forces whose destructive powers no one—industrialists and workers alike—could fully anticipate.

CHRYSLER, THE INDEPENDENT AUTO PRODUCERS, AND SUPPLIERS

Advances in productive technology brought disproportionate benefits to two of the Big Three manufacturers. The third, Chrysler, attempted to follow its competitors' lead in automating and decentralizing its production facilities. At the flagship Dodge Main plant, new technologies reduced employment in the paint shop by nearly twenty-five hundred; in body assembly by twenty-one hundred; and on the motor line by eleven hundred. Before automation in the late 1950s, the Plymouth Detroit assembly plant on Lynch Road produced 180 cars per hour on two assembly lines. With the introduction of labor-saving technology, one newly automated line at the old Plymouth plant turned out 60 cars per hour, while "Other assembly plants in dispersed geographical locations make up the difference in schedule and produce closer to the marketplace." Engine production, which had occupied 25 percent of the floor space at the Plymouth Detroit plant, was shifted to the new Trenton Engine Plant, in a suburb south or Detroit.[30]

Despite its efforts, Chrysler Corporation spent far less on automation and decentralization than its competitors in the 1950s. Because of poor management, the company lacked the funds to invest in new development. The result was two-edged. Chrysler jobs stayed in Detroit to a much greater extent than Ford and General Motors jobs; in fact by 1960, Chrysler was Detroit's largest employer. But the company struggled to remain economically viable. It speeded up production dramatically in the late 1950s, laid off thousands of workers, and relentlessly used overtime to increase output without dramatically increasing labor costs. As a result, Chrysler employment plummeted. During the recession of 1958, the number of Chrysler production workers bottomed out at 59,440, nearly half of the number employed in the peak year of 1950.[31]

The scramble to automate production crushed independent auto manufacturers. Automated machinery was very costly, requiring massive capital investments. As Ford and General Motors engaged in an intense battle for market share in the early 1950s, their technological innovations, productivity, and profits far surpassed those of smaller firms like Nash, Hudson, Willys, Kaiser-Frazer, Studebaker, and Packard. Big Three sales bit into the independents' already small niche in the automotive market—their combined market share fell from 18 percent in 1948 to 4 percent in 1955.[32] In the 1950s, in their drive to remain competitive with the Big Three, independent producers began to invest heavily in automation. Unlike General Motors or Ford, however, they were poorly capitalized and struggled to remain profitable while retooling their plants. Typical was Packard, which cut employment in its Detroit plant from 16,000 to 4,000 between 1952 and 1956 to remain competitive. Packard merged with Studebaker in 1954, and its Detroit plant closed in 1956, leaving the 4,000 remaining workers, most of whom were over forty years old, unemployed.[33] Hudson Motors followed a similar route. At its peak in 1950, Hudson employed 25,330 workers in its two outdated Detroit plants. Those jobs soon disappeared. The new conglomerate American Motors, which absorbed Hudson, removed all production from Detroit between 1954 and 1957. As a fitting coda to its troubled history, the Hudson plant on Jefferson and Connor was torn down and replaced by a parking lot in July 1959.[34]

Corporate restructuring bad its most dramatic consequences in smaller manufacturing concerns around Detroit. In the mid-1950s, Ford, Chrysler, and General Motors began to produce auto bodies and other parts in integrated, automated facilities, rather than relying on independent suppliers. Three independent car body and parts manufacturers, all based in Detroit, closed in the mid-1950s. In 1953. Briggs Auto Body was absorbed by Chrysler Corporation. In 1954, another major independent, Murray Auto Body, closed its doors permanently. And in 1956, Motor Products shut its Mack Avenue plant after Chrysler took over its stamping business. In three years, over ten thousand workers were displaced in these three closings alone.[35]

The case of Murray Auto Body starkly revealed the combined impact of automation, decentralization, and plant closings. In 1947, Ford employed 13,000 workers in its stamping division and contracted parts from Murray, a nearby supplier which employed 5,000 workers. In the early 1950s, Ford took over all stamping production. Murray lost its contract and closed its plant in 1954; its 5,000 workers lost their jobs. Ford, following the policy of decentralization, reduced employment in its Dearborn stamping operation to 6,000 workers, and shifted most of its production to two new stamping plants which employed 7,000 workers elsewhere in the Midwest. In the process of reorganization, Detroit lost 11,000 jobs and one manufacturer.[36]

Equally striking was the decline in peripheral manufacturing jobs in Detroit. Detroit's nonautomotive manufacturers averaged only 140 employees per plant at the end of World War II.[37] These plants, manufacturers of machine tools, wire, castings, stampings, and other metal products, were subject to violent cyclical fluctuations related to automotive production.

Figure 1.2: Two of the several plants that closed on Detroit's East side in the 1950s were the Motor Products and Briggs plants. Altogether, the East Side lost more than seventy-thousand jobs between 1954 and 1960.

As larger better-capitalized machine tool plants were automated, many small companies failed. And although the automobile companies continued to rely on an extensive network of independent suppliers, automation and the integration of parts production also decimated many of Detroit's "one-cylinder" manufacturing companies. Ford, for example, took over production of forgings, axles, wheels, stampings, and other parts formerly provided by outside suppliers, crippling many independent firms.[38] General Motors also shifted parts production from independent suppliers, largely based in the Detroit area, to its own new parts plants in Ohio and Illinois.[39] Firms such as Bolm Aluminum, Falls Spring and Wire, F.L. Jacobs, Thompson Products, Richard Brothers, and Federal Mogul shut down their Detroit operations in the mid-1950s. Several thousand employees of these smaller firms, unlike workers with seniority in the Big Three who had the option to be transferred when displaced by automation, entered the ranks of the unemployed.[40]

COSTS: LABOR AND TAXES

Automation was not the only force contributing to job loss in Detroit. Smaller firms that did not automate production or suffer automation-related job losses still fled the city in increasing numbers in the 1950s. Labor relations were especially important in motivating firms to relocate outside of Detroit, or to expand facilities outside of the city. Employers left industrial centers with high labor costs for regions where they could exploit cheap, nonunion labor. One such firm, Ex-Cell-O, a major machine tool manufacturer, built six new plants in rural Indiana and Ohio in the 1950s, and none in metropolitan Detroit. Ex-Cell-O's president, H. G. Bixby, argued in 1960 that the reason for the failure of firms like his to expand in metropolitan Detroit was that "there was something seriously wrong with our business climate," Bixby blamed union activity for the flight of industry from Detroit. The "militant and venomous attitude toward industry has and will continue to limit job opportunity.... Industries, like people, will not go where they are insulted and vilified daily. If Michigan labor union leadership is seriously interested in job opportunity for their members, they must change their attitude from one of conflict to one of cooperation with industry."[41] Forty-nine percent of Michigan industrialists interviewed in 1961 felt that "the labor situation" was worse in 1960 than it had been ten years earlier.[42]

Wage costs were also an important consideration in plant location, especially, for small firms. From the 1950s through the 1970s, high wage costs ranked first in small manufacturers' complaints about the Detroit business climate. One small industrialist lamented that "the unions are so strong that they have more influence than they should have. Make unreasonable demands and get them." In his words, "Unions have killed a lot of small industries. They raise union rates. This means costs go up and then prices have to go up. Then a small firm cannot compete. And that is the end." One small Michigan firm opened a new plant in Alabama, citing "labor demands" and the "wage rate" as reasons for leaving Detroit.[43] Fruehauf Trailer also moved out of Detroit to cut labor costs. In 1950, it laid off its thirty-five hundred Detroit workers, and opened a new plant in Avon Lakes, Ohio, where it reduced the workforce to twenty-five hundred, imposed higher production quotas, and cut wages by 25 cents an hour.[44]

Tax rates also ranked as a major factor in plant location policy, although corporate leaders exaggerated the effect of the tax burden on their operations. In 1954, *The Detroiter*, the organ of the Detroit Chamber of Commerce, stated that the "excessive burden of taxation on inventories is an important factor in causing the location of new plants outside the Detroit city limits."[45] Ex-Cell-O's Bixby also complained of the high taxes in metropolitan Detroit. In 1957, General Motors cited tax increases as a rationale for halting expansion in Michigan. And in 1959, Chrysler Vice-President W. C. Newberg warned that taxes "dictate some decisions about plant location and hinted that in the absence of a "fair and even distribution of property taxes," Chrysler might leave Detroit.[46] One industrialist worried that his firm paid "three and four times the amount of taxes per net worth that our competitors are paying in Ohio, Pennsylvania, Illinois, California." Detroit's real and personal property taxes were particularly galling to members of the city's business community.[47]

Detroit officials were responsive to fears of high property taxes: Detroit did not increase its property tax levy between 1948 and 1958. But business leaders, tempted by lower tax rates in nonmetropolitan areas, frequently used the threat of mobility to push for changes in tax laws favorable to industry. In the meantime, the flight of industry diminished Detroit's tax base. Runaway shops took with them tax revenue essential to the provision of city services, and the city was forced to rely on state and federal aid, running up a growing deficit. City officials, discouraged by threatened business flight, attempted to maintain a tax structure favorable to businesses by keeping property taxes low and shifting the burden to income earners, who faced a 1 percent levy beginning in 1962. With an aging infrastructure, an enormous school district, an expensive city-funded social welfare program, and a growing population of poor people, Detroit could not reduce its taxes to the level of its small-town and rural competitors.[48]

Neighboring states took advantage of the plight of Detroit and other large cities and encouraged panic over urban tax rates; many held out the promise of low business taxes as a lure to Michigan firms who wanted to cut overhead costs. Some state chambers of commerce and economic development officials placed advertisements in trade publications trumpeting their favorable tax climates. According to Bixby, Detroit taxes "were 2⅓ times as high as the state and local taxes per plant in Ohio, and 1¾ high as in Indiana."[49] The combination of low taxes and low-wage labor markets lured firms away from Detroit to small towns throughout the Midwest and South.

FEDERAL POLICY AND DECENTRALIZATION

The federal government also actively encouraged industrial deconcentration. Beginning during World War II, it fostered military-industrial development in suburban areas at the expense of center cities, in part as a precaution in case of air attack. Firms also frequently took advantage of federal largesse to subsidize new plant construction on green-field sites. The Chrysler Warren Tank Plant, built in 1941 in an undeveloped suburban area fifteen miles north of downtown Detroit, and the enormous Willow Run aircraft complex, constructed in 1942 on over fifteen hundred acres of rural land twenty-five miles west of the city, stood as models to postwar industrial planners.[50]

Government support for industrial decentralization went even further during the Korean War and afterward. During the Korean War buildup, for example, only 7.5 percent of $353 million allocated for the purchase of equipment and new plant construction in metropolitan Detroit went to firms located within the city of Detroit; 92.5 percent of the funding went to "out lying parts of the region.[51] In addition, the Department of Defense also pioneered a "parallel plant" policy, building new defense plants outside of traditional industrial centers that duplicated existing production.[52] Chrysler shifted tank engine production to New Orleans and tank production to Newark, Delaware. Ford, which had constructed aircraft engines in Detroit during World War II, shifted production to sites in Chicago and Missouri. And Cadillac began the manufacture of light tanks in Cleveland.[53]

The growing power of Sun Belt politicians in Congress further diminished Detroit's share of the massive federal defense budget. By the end of the Korean War, the northeastern and Midwestern share of the Cold War defense budget had shrunk greatly. Southern members of Congress, many heading influential committees, steered federal military spending toward their home states. Between 1951 and 1960, the South's share of the national defense budget doubled. Even more impressive was the impact of defense dollars on the West. California was the major beneficiary of defense spending. In 1951, it was awarded 13.2 percent of national defense contract dollars; by 1958, its share was 21.4 percent. Detroit and other industrial centers in the Northeast and Midwest, all of which had benefited from the flow of defense dollars during the 1940s, suffered the effects of the Pentagon-financed development of the Sun Belt.[54]

The major automobile manufacturers also contributed to the loss of defense contracts in the immediate postwar years. They quickly reconverted plants from defense to civilian production, in anticipation of high demand for cars after the war, while manufacturers in other regions positioned themselves for continued military research and development and defense production. The result was the Detroit area did not attract new high-technology aircraft and electronics manufacturers that benefited from government largesse during the Cold War.[55]

Detroit, the World War II "arsenal of democracy," had become, in the words of a critic of defense policy, a "ghost arsenal"[56] In 1954 alone, the Detroit area lost nearly 56,000 defense jobs; it lost another 26,000 between 1955 and 1957. By 1957, only 33,000 workers in all of metropolitan Detroit worked in defense industries. At a time when the national military-industrial complex was growing by leaps and bounds, Detroit's share of Defense Department contracts shrunk rapidly. The loss of defense jobs in the city occurred simultaneously with the decline in employment in other industries. Detroit's loss of defense jobs only added to its already deep economic troubles.[57]

The movement of firms out of the city, whether spurred by government subsidies or by market considerations, created a spatial mismatch between urban African Americans and jobs. Persistent housing discrimination combined with job flight to worsen the plight of urban blacks. The mismatch was not as perfect as many theorists have contended; some large suburban plants, as we have seen, did hire blacks. But most smaller firms did not. Tool and die companies that located in the all-white suburbs north of Detroit, for example, tended to rely on local contacts to find new employees. The gap between black workers and job opportunity grew the further firms moved from the metropolitan area. And increasingly firms, from automobile manufacturers to parts suppliers, relocated in small towns and rural areas with minuscule black populations. Firms that moved to the South seldom broke Jim Crow customs, offering the lion's share of their jobs to white workers. Discrimination combined with nonmetropolitan industrialization to limit black economic opportunity.[58]

OVERTIME

Automation and decentralization combined with a third industrial change that reduced the size of Detroit's work force: the increasing use of overtime. Beginning in the mid-1950s, employers began to favor the use of overtime in lieu of hiring additional workers. In January 1954, Ford's decision to put all workers in its Lincoln-Mercury plants on fifty-four-hour weeks made the daily papers. The use of overtime was not unprecedented, but it had generally been restricted to model changeover season, at the end of the summer when plants needed to be retooled quickly for the production of a new year of cars. Ford's overtime announcement attracted attention because it came in the middle of a production year, and was controversial because at that time more than 107,000 Detroit workers were unemployed.[59]

The use of overtime became even more common as the decade went on. Between 1958 and 1962, UAW workers put in between 2.3 and 4 hours of overtime per week over the course of the year. UAW economists estimated that 37,600 additional workers could have been employed over that period if overtime were abolished. By 1965, overtime was fully entrenched as a labor policy, in the auto industry and in most other American manufacturing enterprises. That year, the average manufacturing worker put in 3.5 hours of overtime per week and the average auto worker put in 5.9 hours of overtime.[60] In the late 1950s and early 1960s, managers in the auto industry increased output by putting whole plants on periods of sustained overtime. Some plants went on fifty-eight-hour-per-week schedules for three-month periods. In one plant, managers scheduled at least forty-eight hours of work for the entire work force for fifty-six of eighty consecutive weeks.[61]

Overtime was one of few management strategies that appealed both to many workers and to corporate accountants. Overtime allowed managers to reduce the costs of hiring and training new workers, as well as benefits packages, while maintaining high production levels. It also diluted union strength by reducing membership. Union leaders argued, quite plausibly, that overtime reduced the size of the labor force and added to the ranks of the unemployed. Corporate leaders, however, rejoined that because "the unemployed are, *on the average* less qualified than those who are employed," the abolition of overtime "will not necessarily shift the margin of employability for those out of work."[62]

If union leadership saw the dangers of overtime, not all rank and file members did. Many workers supported overtime, for the reason described by John Kenneth Galbraith, that overtime ended "the barbarous uniformity of the weekly wage" premised on the belief that "all families have the same tastes, needs."[63] Overtime was appealing because it offered workers the rare opportunity to increase their wages substantially, given the barriers within plants that prevented workers from moving to higher-paying jobs. Moreover, overtime provided workers with extra pay which offered a hedge against the frequent layoffs that plagued the automobile industry, especially in the 1950s. Workers occasionally went on wildcat strikes to protest what they considered to be the unequal assignment of overtime In 1955, when the Ford Livonia Transmission Plant gave eight hours of overtime to its Saturday afternoon shift workers, 150 final assembly workers who were not assigned overtime walked out in protest.[64] Employers also used the prospect of overtime pay as a lure to prospective workers. Advertisements for tool and die jobs in Detroit papers frequently mentioned the availability of overtime work. On the other hand, because it was usually mandatory, overtime was often unpopular, especially among younger workers. Those who had no desire to work nine- to twelve-hour days were involuntarily subject to grueling hours and pressure to keep productivity high.[65]

INDUSTRIAL JOB LOSS AND ECONOMIC DISTRESS

Detroit seemed to embody American confidence and affluence in the aftermath of the triumph of World War II, but just when the city's boosters proclaimed an industrial rebirth, the destructive forces of industrial capital ism began the process of economic corrosion that made Detroit the epitome of the Rust Belt. Between 1948 and 1967, Detroit lost nearly 130,000 manufacturing jobs. The number of manufacturing jobs fell by almost half in the 1950s (Table 1.2). The trend of job loss continued through the next four decades, mitigated only slightly by the temporary boom in the local economy and in automobile production from 1964 through 1969. Bolstered by the views of postwar social scientists who emphasized American affluence, the perception of Detroit's decline lagged far behind reality. While social scientists were writing of Detroit as the home of the "embourgeoised" auto worker, the face of industrial Detroit was being transformed by enormous economic upheavals. A growing number of Detroit residents joined the ranks of "displaced workers," dislocated by industrial changes and trapped in the declining metropolis.

The restructuring of Detroit's industrial economy diminished opportunity for several segments of the Detroit work force. First, the loss of manufacturing jobs removed a rung of the ladder of economic opportunity for the poorest workers, especially those with little education and few skills. The testimony of workers who lost their jobs when Detroit's Packard plant shut its doors in 1956 revealed the high costs of industrial decline. "I felt like some one had bit me with a sledge hammer," stated one worker. Recalled a stock-handier with twelve years seniority: "It was such a shock ... I had been there so long.... They just threw us out and didn't say nothing ... they just threw us out on the street." A worker with thirty years of seniority perhaps best summed up the effects of plant closings in the 1950s: "It hit and hit hard, hit the man who was a common assembler the hardest."[66]

In the aftermath of the wartime and postwar boom, the bust of the 1950s was devastating. The city's economy had seemed dynamic and unstoppable, insatiable in its demand for labor. Making the process all the more traumatic, layoffs and plant closings were unpredictable.

Table 1.2 Decline in Manufacturing Employment in Detroit, 1917–1977

	1947	1954	1958	1963	1967	1972	1977
Manufacturing Firms	3,272	3,453	3,363	3,370	2,947	2,398	1,954
Total Manufacturing Employment[a]	338.4	296.5	204.4	200.6	209.7	180.4	153.3
Total Production Employment[a]	281.5	232.3	145.1	141.4	149.6	125.8	107.5

Source: U.S. Department of Commerce, Bureau of the Census, *City mid County Data Books* (Washington, D.C.: U.S. Government Printing Office, 1949, 1956, 1962, 1967. 1972, 1977, 1983).

[a]In thousands.

Seemingly secure jobs could be eliminated without notice when a plant automated. Events in the 1950s reminded workers that even the factory buildings that seemed like permanent landmarks on Detroit's skyline were mortal. Bustling plants were abandoned and boarded up as companies moved production outside the city or went out of business. In the midst of celebratory descriptions of national prosperity, as pundits spoke of embourgeoisement, the gap between rhetoric and reality grew.

If many workers were affected in some way by changes in the city's economy, blacks bore the brunt of restructuring. Persistent racial discrimination magnified the effects of deindustrialization on blacks. Data from the 1960 census make clear the disparate impact of automation and labor market constriction on African American workers. Across the city, 15.9 percent of blacks, but only 5.8 percent of whites were out of work. In the motor vehicle industry, the black-white gap was even greater. 19.7 percent of black auto workers were unemployed, compared to only 5.8 percent of whites. Discrimination and deindustrialization proved to be a lethal combination for blacks. Seniority protected some black workers from permanent layoffs, but it disproportionately benefited while workers. Blacks had not gained footholds in most plants until after 1943—most were hired in the late 1940s and early 1950s, well alter large numbers of white workers had established themselves in Detroit's industries. Thus they were less likely to have accumulated enough seniority to protect their jobs. And because blacks were concentrated in unskilled, dangerous jobs—precisely those affected by automation—they often found that their job classifications had been eliminated altogether.[67]

By the early 1960s, observers noted that a seemingly permanent class of underemployed and jobless blacks had emerged, a group that came to be called the "long-term unemployed." In 1962, the editors of the *Michigan Labor Market Letter* looked back at the troubled 1950s. The last decade, they noted, had been marked by "significant and sometimes violent changes in our economy." They looked with chagrin on the "creation of a very large and alarmingly consistent list of long-term unemployed." Each year from 1956 to 1962, state officials ranked Detroit as an area of "substantial labor surplus." While black and white workers alike suffered from economic dislocations, black workers faced a particularly gloomy future. Overrepresented in Detroit's labor surplus were two groups of African American workers: older, unskilled workers and youth.[68]

The most poignant stories of unemployment and dislocation involved older workers, those who had seniority at plants that had closed down altogether, or those who did not have enough seniority to qualify for a transfer to new jobs. They often had years of experience working in heavy industry, but few skills easily transferable to other jobs. The experience of older black workers was somewhat worse than that of older whites. A survey of workers unemployed when Detroit's Packard plant closed in 1956 found that black workers suffered longer bouts of unemployment (thirteen months compared to ten for whites; 38 percent unemployed for more than nineteen months compared to 26 percent for whites). Blacks also took more substantial pay cuts than whites when reemployed.[69] When Murray Auto Body closed in 1954, 76 percent of black employees surveyed exhausted their unemployment benefits, compared to only 27 percent of whites. Those blacks who found new employment went "to an average of twice as many places to find work as the sample as a whole," and suffered a wage drop twice that of reemployed white workers.[70]

Less visible, but even more momentous than the emergence of a pool of unemployed older, disproportionately black workers, was the dramatic reduction of entry-level jobs. As a committee investigating the city's labor market in the late 1950s noted, "the real loss comes not so much in lay-offs as in a falling off in the number of new hires." As manufacturing industries restructured, decentralized, and cut back plant work forces, experienced workers protected by seniority moved into jobs that would have earlier been filled by recent migrants to the city and young workers entering the work force for the first time.[71] Firms that were decentralizing and automating saved costs by relying on trained, experienced workers. Whenever possible, employers tried

Figure 1.3: The enormous Packard plant on East Grand Boulevard closed in 1956. By the early 1960s, the Packard complex had become a while elephant, and its machinery, furniture, and equipment were offered for auction.

to minimize the union backlash against automation and decentralization by reducing employment through attrition and curbs on new hiring, instead of layoffs. Responding to workers' fears of job loss at the River Rouge plant, Ford managers noted that a reduction of the labor force "can be handled by the simple expedient of not hiring new employees rather than laying off older ones."[72]

The decline in the number of entry-level manufacturing jobs disproportionately affected black migrants and black youth. Black migrants were less likely in the 1950s to find entry-level jobs in manufacturing that had provided security and relatively good pay to their predecessors in the 1940s. Detroit's pool of manufacturing jobs decreased at the same time that the population of working-age black adults continued to rise. In 1959, the *Detroit News* noted that "Too many Negro families who have moved here to work in the automobile plants are now unemployed. For

Table 1.3 Percentage of Men between Ages 15 and 29 Not in Labor Force, Detroit, 1960

Age	White	Nonwhite
15	76.3	76.2
16	56.6	77.7
17	42.3	61.6
18	15.0	41.0
19	8.9	35.3
20	7.8	24.9
21–22	4.9	20.5
23–24	3.4	12.5
25–29	2.3	10.1

Source: Detroit Metropolitan Area Employment by Age, Sex, Color, and Residence, copy in DNAACP, Part II, Box 10, Folder 10–5, ALUA. Those in school are not included in the figures.

most there are no prospects of jobs. Many are unemployable and either illiterate or nearly so." They had followed the path of migration to the North, with expectations of entry-level industrial work that required few skills—the sort of work that had attracted blacks to the North since the beginning of the Great Migration. But all too often, upon arrival in Detroit, they found that factories simply were not hiring new workers. "There is little hope for them to regain employment," Urban League vocational counselors reported. "There will be very few employment opportunities open to these people."[73]

The combination of discrimination and deindustrialization weighed most heavily on the job opportunities of young African American men. Young workers, especially those who had no postsecondary education, found that the entry-level operative jobs that had been open to their fathers or older siblings in the 1940s and early 1950s were gone. The most dramatic evidence of the impact of industrial changes on young black workers was the enormous gap between black and white youth who had no attachment to the labor market (Table 1.3). The exclusion of a generation of young men from the work force, at a vital time in their emergence as adults, prevented them from gaining the experience, connections, and skills that would open opportunities in later years. It also confirmed their suspicions that they were entrapped in an economic and political system that confined them to the very bottom. By the end of the 1950s, more and more black job seekers, reported the Urban League, were demoralized, "developing patterns of boredom and hopelessness with the present state of affairs." The anger and despair that prevailed among the young, at a time of national promise and prosperity, would explode on Detroit's streets in the 1960s.[74]

Only fifteen years after World War II, Detroit's landscape was dominated by rotting bulks of factory buildings, closed and abandoned, surrounded by blocks of boarded up-stores and restaurants. Older neighborhoods, whose streets were lined with the proud homes that middle-class and working-class Detroiters had constructed in the late nineteenth and early twentieth centuries, were now pockmarked with the shells of burned-out and empty buildings, lying among rubbish-strewn vacant lots. Deteriorating housing and abandoned storefronts were but signs of the profound social and economic changes that were reshaping the metropolis.

The effects of the loss of industry and of jobs rippled throughout the local economy. Over a million square feet of space in seven inner-city factories were vacant in 1956; over 9.9 million square feet of factory space were idle in the entire city in 1957.[75] The area worst bit by the industrial changes of the 1950s was Detroit's East Side. The Michigan Employment Security Commission reported that its Connor Road office (which served all of Detroit's East Side south of

Figure 1.4: The flight of industry, the loss population, and the decline of Detroit's economy in the postwar period devastated the city's numerous commercial strips. Unrented stores were often abandoned and vandalized, scarring the city's landscape.

the Ford Freeway) had been the state's busiest. Serving an area with twenty-three plants and 102,967 workers in March of 1953, the MESC office had processed thousands of orders for firms seeking employees. The situation had changed drastically by 1960. Between 1953 and 1960, the area had lost ten plants and 71,137 jobs. Seven plants had closed altogether, two had moved to the suburbs, and one had moved out of Michigan altogether. The MESC office reported that in the depressed economic climate of the late 1950s "an order for 25 [job placements] creates excitement." The East Side, once the epicenter of the auto industry, had become "an economic slum" in the course of a decade.[76]

Detroit's East Side was devastated by the sudden loss of its manufacturing base. Local stores that had relied on the business of regularly employed factory workers suffered. In 1957, the mile-long strip of East Jefferson between Connor and Alter Roads on the city's far East Side had

Table 1.4 Building Permits Issued for Factories and Shops, Detroit, 1951–1963

1951	148	1958	31
1952	106	1959	35
1953	124	1960	29
1954	72	1961	24
1955	91	1962	16
1956	86	1963	14
1957	49		

Source: Comprehensive Division, Detroit City Plan Commission, March 10, 1964. City Plan Commission Papers, Box 3, Folder: Interoffice Memos, February 1961–December 1964.

forty-six vacant stores. Similar decline beset other former industrial sections of the city. By 1961, a survey of twenty-five miles of commercial streets in Detroit showed a vacancy rate of over 11 percent. The inner core of the city (within a three-mile radius of downtown) had a vacancy rate of 22 percent. Business districts adjoining former industrial areas were especially hard hit. Detroit's suburbs, by contrast, had only a 4 percent commercial vacancy rate.[77] Most indicative of the city's deteriorating economic health, the number of shops and factories constructed or modified in Detroit fell tenfold between 1951 and 1963 (Table 1.4).

Not only commercial construction was hurt by the devastation of the city 's industrial economy. The stunted labor market made homeownership in the city all the more insecure. Workers who managed to hold onto their well-paying, unionized, industrial-sector jobs were able to achieve a level of comfort that few of their blue-collar counterparts in the American past had been able to achieve. They became homeowners. But a growing number of workers found that the status that they had achieved as propertyholders was extremely tenuous. Again African Americans suffered disproportionately. As more blacks found well-paying work in the city's primary industrial sector in the 1940s and 1950s, they bought homes in unprecedented numbers. But because they were at great risk of layoffs and unemployment, their hold on property was all the more precarious.

The process of industrial decline had other far-reaching consequences. It imperiled Detroit's fiscal base. As jobs left the city, so too did white workers with the means to move to suburbs or small towns where factories relocated. Wealthier whites also followed investments outward. As a result, Detroit's population began an unbroken downward fall in the 1950s. As Detroit's population shrank, it also grew poorer and blacker. Increasingly, the city became the home for the dispossessed, those marginalized in the housing market, in greater peril of unemployment, most subject to the vagaries of a troubled economy.

The 1940s had been a rare window of opportunity for blue-collar workers in Detroit, especially for African Americans. During World War II, the number of entry-level jobs in manufacturing grew

Table 1.5 Joblessness in Detroit, 1950–1980 (percent)

	1950	1960	1970	1980
All Workers Unemployed[a]	7.5	7.6	6.9	11.7
Not in Labor Force[b]	16.5	19.5	26.7	37.9
Not Working[c]	22.8	25.7	32.6	45.1
Blacks Unemployed[a]	11.8	18.2	9.8	22.5
Blacks not in Labor Force[b]	18.7	23.3	25.4	43.9
Blacks Not Working[c]	28.3	37.2	32.7	56.4

Sources: Author's calculations from U.S. Department of Commerce, Bureau of the Census, *Census of Population, 1950* (Washington, D.C.: U.S. Government Printing Office, 1952), vol. 2, part 22, Tables 35, 36; *1960*, PC1–24C, Tables 73, 77; *1970*, PC1-C4, Tables 85, 92; *1980*, PC80–1-C24, Tables 120, 134.

[a]Includes all males over fourteen who were in the civilian labor force and seeking work for 1950 and 1960; sixteen years and older in the civilian labor force seeking work for 1970 and 1980.

[b]Has as its denominator all males aged fourteen or older for 1950 and 1960; sixteen years and older for 1970 and 1980.

[c]Includes total unemployed plus total not in labor force divided by total working-age male population.

so fast in Detroit that discriminatory barriers lost some of their salience. Even if large segments of the Detroit labor market remained largely closed to black workers, they still found operative jobs in the automobile industry and in other related industries during the wartime and postwar boom. The decline of manufacturing in Detroit in the 1950s, however, hit black workers with real force. Rates of unemployment and joblessness in Detroit rose steadily beginning in the 1950s especially among African Americans (Table 1.5).

One of the tens of thousands of Detroiters who entered the ranks of the jobless was Tecumseh Haines. A metal polisher, Haines had survived temporary layoffs and managed to hold onto his job until 1959, when he was laid off indefinitely. Like most black workers, Haines held one of the auto industry's less desirable jobs, one that paid him only eighty-nine dollars a week. However difficult, the job had seemed secure. At age thirty-four, married, with one child, one of the nearly 20 percent of blacks who was unemployed in 1960, Haines looked for another job. His persistence and resourcefulness paid off. He eventually found employment as a bottle washer at a fruit products factory, although at sixty-three dollars per week he took a substantial pay cut. After he had been employed in his new job for ten months, the fruit company cut its work force, and Haines, a new employee with no seniority, found himself unemployed again.[78]

Haines shared the experience of employment and unemployment in Detroit in the late 1950s and early 1960s with a lot of other workers, both black and white. But the differences between Haines and his white coworkers outweighed the similarities. In the heady days of the early 1950s, when Haines was in his early twenties and planned to start a family, a job at an auto plant was his ticket to upward mobility. Thrown out of work in the late 1950s, he had few options. The best opportunities for semiskilled workers were in the small Midwestern towns and suburbs where many automobile plants and suppliers had relocated. But such places were generally inhospitable to blacks. Following the migration of jobs to the South was even less appealing an option. And based on his experiences in Detroit, he probably felt that he could expect little more in another major city. Whatever became of Tecumseh Haines, his choices were few.[79]

In the eyes of many at the time, and of most commentators since, the 1950s was a decade of prosperity. The decade was the era of the embourgeoised auto worker, the "golden age of capitalism," the era of affluence. In the corporate boom of the decade, some workers did indeed attain the dream of economic security and employment stability. But the forces unleashed by automation, decentralization, and relocation wrecked many workers' lives. Another displaced worker, William Wakeham, worked in one of the most unpleasant jobs in the Ford River Rouge complex, the core room of the iron foundry. Foundry work, relegated largely to blacks, was unbearably hot and dangerous, but it provided a steady wage and secure employment for Wakeham and his coworkers. In 1951, however, Ford eliminated its foundry, laying off thousands of workers. To add insult to injury, when Ford opened a new "specialized foundry," it replaced former foundry workers with "special workers," mostly whites, who had been transferred from other plants. Wakeham lashed out against the inequities of the economic changes that left him unemployed and would provide fewer and fewer opportunities for his children and grandchildren. "Unemployment is not a crime," he wrote. "It is a social ill full of hardships, set-backs, anxieties, needs and sacrifices which would be lauded under any other circumstances. It is truly the weakest spot in Democracy's armor, the likely erosion point in the social structure, and the damning mark of false, unstable or lopsided prosperities." No words could better describe the failed promise of postwar Detroit.[80]

NOTES

Parts of chapters 5 and 6 appeared "'Forget about Your Inalienable Right to Work': Deindustrialization and Its Discontents at Ford, 1950–1953," *International Labor and Working-Class History* 48 (Fall 1995): 112–30. Reprinted with the permission of International Labor and Working-Class History, Inc.

1. For descriptions of plants, see *Michigan: A Guide to the Wolverine State*, Work Projects Administration American Guide Series (New York: Oxford University Press, 1941), 234, 277–78, 286–87. Seventy-six tons of soot and ash per square mile fell each year in the inner-city section of Detroit bounded by Grand Boulevard and the Detroit River. James Sweinhart, "What Detroit's Slums Cost Its Taxpayers," (Detroit: Detroit News Reprints, 1946), 9, CHPC, Box 73, Folder: Racial Relations. Quotes from Gloria Whelan, "The First City," *Michigan Quarterly Review* 25 (1986): 184.
2. On fluctuations in the Detroit economy, see G. Walter Woodworth, *The Detroit Money Market, 1934–1955*, Michigan Business Studies, vol. 12, no. 4 (Ann Arbor: Bureau of Business Research, School of Business Administration, University of Michigan, 1956), 14–17.

3. Mary West Jorgensen, "A Profile of Detroit," January 1952, DUL, Box 21, Folder 21–17. On job loss in other major industrial cities, see Appendix A. For a snapshot of industrial problems in other cities in the 1950s, see Irving Bernstein, *Promises Kept John F. Kennedy's New Frontier* (New York: Oxford University Press, 1991), 160–67. The history of deindustrialization after World War II has yet to be written. But glimpses of the overall pattern in other cities can be found in: "Deindustrialization: A Panel Discussion," *Pennsylvania History* 58 (1991): 181–211; John T. Cumbler, *A Social History of Economic Decline: Business, Politics, and Work in Trenton* (New Brunswick, N.J., Rutgers University Press, 1989); Irwin Marcus, "The Deindustrialization of Homestead: A Case Study, 1959–1984," *Pennsylvania History* 52 (1985) 162–82; Gary Gerstle, *Working-Class Americanism: A History of Labor in a Textile City, 1920–1960* (Cambridge: Cambridge University Press, 1989), 320–28; Ronald Schatz, *The Electrical Workers:* A *History of Labor at General Electric and Westinghouse* (Urbana: University of Illinois Press, 1983), 232–36. Not all northern cities experienced economic decline in the postwar years. Indianapolis, for example, grew during the postwar years. See Robert G. Barrows, "Indianapolis: Silver Buckle on the Rustbelt," in *Snowbelt Cities: Metropolitan Politics in the Northeast and Midwest since World War II,* ed. Richard M. Bernard (Bloomington: Indiana University Press, 1990), 137–57.

4. For an overview see Bruce Schulman, *From Cotton Belt to Sunbelt: Federal Policy, Economic Development and the Transformation of the South, 1938–1980* (New York: Oxford University Press, 1991). See also Ann Markusen, Peter Hall, Scott Campbell, and Sabina Deitrick, *The Rise of the Gunbelt: The Military Remapping of Industrial America* (New York: Oxford University Press, 1991); Roger Lotchin, *Fortress California 1910– 1961: From Warfare to Welfare* (New York: Oxford University Press, 1992); Roger Lotchin, ed., *The Martial Metropolis: U.S. Cities in Peace and War* (New York: Praeger, 1984).

5. For a general overview, see Thomas J. Sugrue, "The Structures of Urban Poverty: The Reorganization of Space and Work in Three Periods of American History," in *The "Underclass" Debate: Views from History,* ed. Michael B. Katz (Princeton, N.J.: Princeton University Press, 1993), 85–117; David M. Gordon, "Capitalist Development and the History of American Cities," in *Marxism and the Metropolis: New Perspectives in Urban Political Economy,* ed. William K. Tabb and Larry Sawers (New York: Oxford University Press, 1978), 25–63. For a discussion of these processes, see Eva Mueller, Arnold Wilken, and Margaret Wood, *Location Decisions and Industrial Mobility in Michigan, 1961* (Ann Arbor: Institute for Social Research, University of Michigan, 1961), 5–6.

6. Douglas Reynolds, "Engines of Struggle: Technology, Skill, and Unionization at General Motors, 1930–1940," *Michigan Historical Review* 15 (1989): 79–81, 91–92.

7. Detroit Metropolitan Area Regional Planning Commission, "Location of Industrial Plants," 16, SEMCOG, Box 9.

8. On plant deconcentration in the 1940s and 1950s, see Detroit Metropolitan Area Regional Planning Commission, "Location of Automotive Plants," Michigan P-1 (G) Project Completion Report, 1955–56, 18, SEMCOG, Box 9. For a general survey of Detroit's industrial patterns, see Robert Sinclair, *The Face of Detroit: A Spatial Synthesis* (Detroit: Department of Geography, Wayne State University, 1972), 36–11.

9. "Location of Automotive Plants," 17; untitled memo with list of auto plants constructed since 1949, in UAW-RD, Box 76, Folder 5; for a discussion of similar patterns in the 1970s and 1980s, see Barry Bluestone and Bennett Harrison, *The Deindustrialization of America: Plant Closings, Community Abandonment, and the Dismantling of Basic Industry* (New York: Basic Books, 1982), 166–68, 170–78.

10. Mueller et al., *Location Decisions,* 53.

11. "Available Industrial Properties Adjacent to Railroads, City of Detroit," February 1, 1951, in Mayor's Papers (1951), Box 2; on commuting patterns, see Detroit Metropolitan Area Regional Planning Commission, "Home Location Patterns of Industrial Workers in the Detroit Region," December 1955, copy in Department of Labor Library', Washington, D.C. Harold Black, "Detroit: A Case Study in Industrial Problems of a Central City," *Land Economics* 34 (1958): 218–26; "Report of a Survey by a Special Committee of the Michigan Chapter of the Society of Industrial Realtors on Trends in Industrial Location," 1956, p. 2, copy in VF—Pre 1960s, Box 18, Folder: Industries, location of, 1950s.

12. Detroit Metropolitan Area Regional Planning Commission, *The Manufacturing Economy of the Detroit Region,* Part I Revised, (March 1950), 15; Detroit Metropolitan Area Regional Planning Commission, *Recent Growth and Trends in Manufacturing in the Detroit Region* (1956), 2–3, 10 (both in Department of Labor Library, Washington, D.C.)

13. See for example, Paul E. Peterson, "Introduction: Technology, Race, and Urban Policy," in *The New Urban Reality*, ed. Paid E. Peterson (Washington, D.C.: The Brookings Institution, 1985), 1–29. A powerful rejoinder is David F. Noble, *Forces of Production: A Social History of Industrial Automation* (New York: Knopf, 1984). For a general discussion of regional industrial decline, see George Sternlieb and James W. Hughes, eds., *Post-Industrial America: Metropolitan Decline and Inter-Regional Job Shifts* (New Brunswick, N.J.: Rutgers University, Center for Urban Policy Research, 1975); John Kasarda, "Urban Industrial Transition and the Underclass," *Annals of the American Academy of Political and Social* Science 501 (January 1989): 26–47.

14. See statement of D. J. Davis, Ford vice president for Manufacturing, U.S. Congress, Joint Committee on the Economic Report, Subcommittee on Economic Stabilization, *Hearings on Automation and Technological Change,* 84th Congress, 1st Session, October 1955, 53 (hereafter referred to as *Automation Hearings).* On the roots of automation, see Stephen Meyer, "The Persistence of Fordism: Workers and Technology in the American Automobile Industry," in *On the Line: Essays in the History of Autowork,* ed. Nelson Lichtenstein and Stephen Meyer (Urbana: University of Illinois Press, 1989), esp. 86–93.

15. Quoted in James C. Keebler, "Working Automation," *Automation* 3 (January 1957): 29.

16. Harder quoted in Floyd G. Lawrence, "Union Belabors Automation," ibid., 2 (May 1955): 22; For further discussion of employers' defense of automation, see Ronald Edsforth, "Why Automation Didn't Shorten the Work Week: The Politics of Work Time in the Automobile Industry," in *Autowork,* ed. Robert Asher and Ronald Edsforth (Albany: State University of New York Press, 1995), 165–67.

17. James C. Keebler, "Another Milestone Passed," ibid., 5 (February 1959): 26.

18. Floyd G. Lawrence, "Progress With Ideas," ibid., 2 (July 1955): 23, For a discussion of automation and workers' control in other industries, see Noble, *Forces of Production.*

19. Reuther testimony, *Automation Hearings.* 124. For a variation on this quote, see John Barnard, *Walter Reuther and the Rise of the Auto Workers* (Boston: Little, Brown, 1983), 154. In Barnard's version, Reuther offered the acerbic response: "And not one of them buys new Ford cars either."

20. Davis statement in *Automation Hearings,* 56–57, 63; Ford Press Releases, January 18, 1950, February 26, 1950, March 30, 1952, July 7, 1954, all in UAW-RD, Box 82, Folder: Ford Motor Company Plants and Equipment. See also Nelson Lichtenstein, "Life at the Rouge: A Cycle of Workers' Control," in *Life and Labor: Dimensions of American Working-Class History,* ed. Charles Stephenson and Robert Asher (Albany: State University of New York Press, 1986), 251–53. The most comprehensive lists of Ford expansion projects are Ford Press Release,

August 20, 1957, and Memo from George Marrelli to Nelson Samp, June 13, 1957 (which includes number of employees in each plant), both in UAW-RD, Box 76, Folder 5.

21. Allan Nevins and Frank Ernest Hill, *Ford: Decline and Rebirth, 1933–1962* (New York: Scribner, 1963), 340–41; U.S. Congress, House of Representatives, *Hearings Before the Committee on Unemployment and the Impact of Automation of the Committee on Education and Labor,* 87th Congress, First Session 1961, 512; Memo, Carrol Colburn to Woody Ginsburg, "Material for NBC." March 26, 1959, UAW-RD, Box 50, Folder 13.

22. Ford press releases, August 18, 1949, July 7, 1954, June 20, 1955; Nevins and Hill, *Ford: Decline and Rebirth,* 364–65, Stephen Amberg, *The Union Inspiration in American Politics. The Autoworkers and the Making of a Liberal Industrial Order* (Philadelphia: Temple University Press, 1994), 190.

23. Ford press releases, September 3, 1953, June 14, 1955. In both. Ford stated that these new plants "will not replace any existing facilities," but merely "add to our present engine capacity." Nevins and Hill, *Ford: Decline and Rebirth,* 340, 364–65; Lichtenstein, "Life at the Rouge," 252; Memo on Automation in Ford Plants, from Jim O'Rourke to Ken Bannon, January 31, 1957, in UAW-RD, Box 65; Edward B. Shils, *Automation and Industrial Relations* (New York: Holt, Rinehart and Winston, 1963), 231.

24. John Bugas to Carl Stellato, June 7, 1950, and Manton Cummins to Carl Stellato. July 18, 1950, copies in UAW-WPR. Box 249, Folder 249–19.

25. James C. Keebler, "More Automatic Operation," *Automation* 6 (February 1960): 46.

26. *Detroit Free Press,* April 29, 1955.

27. Louis Seaton, "Expanding Employment: The Answer to Unemployment," General Motors pamphlet (c. 1959), 4, 12, in VE Pre-1960, Box 4, Folder: Employment-Unemployment 1950s.

28. See Reuther testimony, *Automation Hearings,* 97–149; Shils, *Automation and Industrial Relations,* 127–72; an optimistic view on automation, by the Dean of the University of Chicago Business School and an Eisenhower administration adviser, is W. Allen Wallis, "Some Economic Considerations," in *Automation and Technological Change,* ed. John Dunlop (Englewood Cliffs, N.J.: Prentice-Hall, 1962), 103–13. For greater detail on union responses to automation, see Chapter 6 below.

29. I borrow the term "silent firing" from Julius Rezler, *Automation and industrial Labor* (New York: Random House, 1969), 30.

30. "Displacement of Workers Increasing in Michigan," *Michigan CIO News,* June 13, 1957; Keebler, "More Automatic Operation," 44.

31. Steve Jefferys, *Management and Managed: Fifty Years of Crisis at Chrysler* (Cambridge: Cambridge University Press, 1986), 127–45.

32. Memo from Frank Winn to Marry Chester, Re: Preferential Hiring, September 11, 1956, 2, UAW-RD, Box 72, Folder 36.

33. Studebaker and Packard's combined market share fell from 6.8 percent in 1948 to 2.1 percent in 1955; ibid., 1, 3; *Michigan CIO News,* August 18, 1956; Stephen Amberg, "Triumph of Industrial Orthodoxy: The Collapse of Studebaker-Packard Corporation," in Lichtenstein and Meyer, *On the Line,* 190–218; on the effects of the Packard closing, see Michael Aiken, Louis A. Ferman, and Harold L. Sheppard. *Economic Failure, Alienation, and Extremism* (Ann Arbor: University of Michigan Press, 1968). Ninety-five percent of Packard workers at the time of closing were over forty; nearly a quarter were over sixty. The average worker had twenty-three years of seniority.

34. *Detroit Times,* June 6, 1957; Memo from Frank Winn to Harry Chester, 2; Herbert Northrup, *The Negro in the Automobile Industry,* Report No. 1, The Racial Policies of American Industry (Philadelphia: Industrial Research Unit, The Wharton School of Finance and Commerce, University of Pennsylvania, 1968), 30; *Detroit News,* July 23, 1959.

35. *Detroit Free Press,* June 4, 1954; "Summary of Changes of Chrysler Corporation," July 8, 1960, UAW-RD, Box 76, Folder 5; Steve Babson et al., *Working Detroit: The Making of a Union Town* (Detroit: Wayne State University Press, 1986), 162.

36. Harold L. Sheppard and James L. Stem, "Impact of Automation on Workers in Supplier Plants: A Case Study," (c. 1956), typescript in VF, Box 4, Folder: Employment-Unemployment 1950s; James Stern, "Facts, Fallacy, and Fantasy of Automation," in *IRRA Proceedings, 1958* (Madison, Wis.: Industrial Relations Research Association, 1959), 54.

37. "Homes and Industry" (1945), 3, UAW-RD, Box 9, Folder 9–19.

38. Detroit Metropolitan Area Regional Planning Commission, "The Changing Pattern of Manufacturing Plants and Employment, 1950–1960, in the Detroit Region," 2, SEMCOG, Box 9; Nevins and Hill, *Ford: Decline and Rebirth,* 340, 352.

39. "The Change in the Michigan Share of the UAW Membership, 1947–49 to 1955–56," 1, in UAW-RD, Box 76, Folder 5.

40. *Michigan CIO News,* November 4, 1954, June 13, 1957; *Northeast Detroiter,* February 27, 1957; Memo from Frank Winn to Henry Chester, 3.

41. H. G. Bixby, "How Shall We Produce a More Favorable Climate for Business, Industry, and Payrolls in Detroit and Michigan" (hereafter referred to as "Favorable Climate"), speech before the Economic Club of Detroit, April 18, 1960, copy in FK, Box 8, Folder 265, For an attempt to refute rationales like Bixby's, see Edward D. Wickersham, "Labor as a Factor in Plant Location in Michigan" (Ann Arbor: School of Business Administration, University of Michigan, 1957), copy in VF, Box 18, Folder: Industries, location of, 1950s.

42. Mueller et al., *Location Decisions,* 30–31.

43. Mueller et al., *Location Decisions,* 40–41.

44. "Why They Are Shifting Plants out of Detroit," *Militant,* March 27, 1950.

45. *The Detroiter,* November 15,1954.

46. *Detroit Free Press,* April 28, 1957; Bixby, "Favorable Climate"; *Detroit Free Press,* n.d. [c. 1959], clipping in UAW-PAC, Box 60, Folder 60–35.

47. Mueller et al., *Location Decisions,* 38–39.

48. *Detroit Free Press,* November 9, 1954; *Detroit News,* June 5, 1957; *Community News,* February 28, 1957; Jon C. Teaford, *The Rough Road to Renaissance: Urban Revitalization in America, 1940–1985* (Baltimore: Johns Hopkins University Press, 1990), 75–76, 140, 143–44.

49. Mueller et al., *Location Decisions,* 23–24; *Detroit Times,* June 16, 1957; Bixby, "Favorable Climate," 9. In a 1972 survey, taxes ranked second after wages on a list of reasons why Detroit firms planned to relocate outside the city. See Lewis Mandell, *Industrial Location Decisions: Detroit Compared with Atlanta and Chicago* (New York: Praeger Publishers, 1975).

50. Detroit Metropolitan Area Regional Planning Commission, "Location of Automotive Plants," 13, SEMCOG, Box 9.

51. Detroit Metropolitan Area Regional Planning Commission, "Industrial Land Use in the Detroit Region," February 1952, 2, ibid.

52. *Detroit Free Press,* July 15, 1951.

53. "Tank Output Lags Six Months," *New York Times,* January 7, 1952.

54. *Military Procurement Hearings before a Subcommittee of the Committee on Armed Services of the United States* Senate, 86th Congress, 1st Session, July 1959, 25. On the rise of the sunbelt, see also Schulman, *From Cotton Belt to Sunbelt,* 135–73. For comparisons with Detroit, see Kenneth T. Jackson, "The City Loses the Sword: The Decline of Major Military Activity in the New York Metropolitan Region," in Lotchin, *The Martial Metropolis,* 151–62; Geoffrey Rossano, "Suburbia Armed: Nassau County Development and the Rise of the Aerospace Industry," ibid., 61–87; and Martin J. Schiesl "Airplanes to Aerospace: Defense Spending and Economic Growth in the Los Angeles Region, 1945–1960," ibid., 135–49.

55. William Haber, Eugene C. McKean, and Harold C. Taylor, *The Michigan Economy: Its Potentials and Its Problems* (Kalamazoo, Mich.: The W. E. Upjohn Institute for Employment Research, 1959) 14, 17, 66. For a concise summary of the causes for the decline of Detroit as a military production center, see Markusen et al., *The Rise of the Gunbelt.* 62 -68.

56. Guy Nunn, "Detroit: Ghost Arsenal?" *New Republic,* February 4, 1952, 16–17.

57. Haber, McKean, and Taylor, *Michigan Economy,* 90–91; statewide defense manufacturing employment peaked at 220,758 in March 1953, and fell to 28,857 in January 1959. See Memo from Carrol Colburn to Woody Ginsburg, "Material for NBC," March 26, 1959, UAW-RD, Box 50, Folder 13.

58. The classic article on job mismatch (a case study of Detroit) is John F. Kain, "Housing Segregation, Negro Employment, and Metropolitan Decentralization," *Quarterly Journal of Economics* 82 (1968): 175–97. "NAACP Study Concerning Trade Union Apprenticeship," (prepared by Herbert Hill), l960, pp. 41–42, NAACP, Group III, Box A180, Folder: Labor: Apprenticeship Training; on discrimination in new General Motors plants in small-towns and suburbs in Ohio, the South and the West, see "Report of the Labor Secretary," April 1957, NAACP, Group III, Box A309, Folder. Staff Herbert Hill Reports, 1957–63; *Wall Street Journal,* October 24, 1957; Kevin Boyle, "'There Are No Union Sorrows that the Union Can't Heal': The Struggle for Racial Equality in the United Automobile Workers, 1940–1960," *Labor History* 35 (1995): 5–23.

59. *Detroit News,* January 1, 1954; Tom Kleene, "Ford Opposes Reuther Again, Sees No Cause for Gloom," *Detroit Times,* January 18, 1954.

60. *Detroit News,* October 25, 1955; *Michigan's Labor Market* 11, no. 2 (February 1950), 11; "Production Worker Overtime Hours in Manufacturing (1958–1962)," and "Overtime in Manufacturing and in the Motor Vehicle Industry, 1965," both in UAW-RD, Box 65, Folder: Auto Industry—Big Three—Workforce, Salaries, and Benefits, 1950–67.

61. Statement of Leonard Woodcock Before the General and Select Subcommittee on Labor, House Committee on Education and Labor, on H.R. 9802, March 11, 1964, 20–23, in UAW-RD, Box 65, Folder: Auto Industry—Output, 1947–64.

62. Testimony by Theodore Yntema, vice president of Ford, Statement of Auto mobile Manufacturers Association before the Joint Committee of General Subcommittee on Labor and Select Subcommittee on Labor of the Committee on Education and Labor, on H.R. 9802. "The Overtime Penalty Pay Act of 1964," February 28, 1964, 7, in UAW-RD, Box 65, Folder: Auto Industry-Output 1947–64. Emphasis in original.

63. *Galbraith quoted in William Serrin, The Company and the Union: The Civilized Relationship of the General Motors Company and the United Automobile Workers* (New York: Knopf 1973), 237.

64. *Detroit News,* April 4, 1955.

65. Auto industry leaders recognized that workers usually found overtime appealing. See Testimony by Theodore Yntema, 14–17, 19. On the barriers to occupational advancement within plants, see Eli Chinoy, *Automobile Workers and the American Dream* (New York: Random House, 1955); on the difficulties of mandatory overtime, see Dan Georgakas and Marvin Surkin, *Detroit: I Do Mind Dying: A Study in Urban Revolution* (New York: St. Martin's Press, 1975), 31, 33; for a perceptive discussion of contemporary workers' attitudes toward overtime, see Richard Feldman and Michael Betzold, eds., *End of the Line: Autoworkers and the American Dream: An Oral History* (New York: Weidenfeld and Nicolson, 1988), 283.

66. Harold L. Sheppard, Louis Ferman, and Seymour Faber, "Too Old To Work—Too Young to Retire: A Case Study of a Permanent Plant Shutdown," Report to United States Senate, Special Committee on Employment Problems, December 21, 1959 (Washington, DC.: U.S. Government Printing Office, 1960), quote on 8; pamphlet copy in VF—Pre-1960, Box 4, File: Employment—Unemployment 1950s. For a further discussion of the impact of unemployment on Packard workers, see Aiken, Ferman, and Sheppard, *Economic Failure,* esp. 30–151.

67. Figures from U.S. Department of Commerce, Bureau of the Census, *Census of Population, 1960,* PC(1)-24C (Washington, D.C.: U.S. Government Printing Office, 1962). Table 77.

68. *Michigan Labor Market Letter,* November 1962, 14, 15.

69. Sec Sheppard, Ferman, and Faber, Report to the U.S. Senate, Special Committee on Employment Problems; Michael Aiken and Louis A. Ferman, "The Social and Political Reactions of Older Negroes to Unemployment," *Phylon* 17 (1966); 333–46.

70. Sheppard and Stem, "Impact of Automation," typescript, 3, 6, VF—Pre-1960, Box 4.

71. "Youth and Automation," n.d. [c. l960], UAW-RD, Box 64, Folder: Youth.

72. Manton Cummins to Carl Stellato, July 18, 1950, in UAW-WPR, Box 249, Folder 249–19.

73. *Detroit News,* July 15, 1959; Vocational Services Monthly Report, April 1959, DUL, Box 45, Folder A9–7; see also Vocational Services Annual Report, 1959, ibid., Folder A9–8.

74. Vocational Services Department Monthly Report, April 1959, ibid., Folder A9–7.

75. Detroit City Plan Commission, *Industrial Study: A Survey of Existing Conditions at id Attitudes of Detroit's Industry* (Master Plan Technical Report, Second Series), July 1956, 46; *Detroit Times,* June 2, 1957.

76. "When People Move," DUL, Box 46, Folder A10–13; *East Side Shopper,* June 6, 1957. The case of Pittsburgh's Hazelwood neighborhood offers an interesting point of comparison. Between 1950 and 1970, the area, centered around the Jones and Loughlin steel plant, with sizable railyards and a thriving business district, lost half of its workers and 28.4 percent of its residents, and witnessed a dramatic decline in its commercial district. See Joel A. Tarr and Denise DiPasquale, "The Mill Town in the Industrial City: Pittsburgh's Hazelwood," in *Urbanism Past and Present* 13 (Winter/Spring 1982): 9–11.

77. *East Side hopper,* April 18, 1957; *Detroit News,* May 5, 1957; *Detroit Free Press,* January 18, 1961.

78. Ibid., February 29, 1961. It is not clear from the article whether or not Haines's wife worked. The average unemployed worker in Detroit in early 1961 shared much in common with Haines: male, age thirty-seven, married with one child.

79. Jacqueline Jones, "Southern Diaspora: Origins of the Northern Underclass," paper presented to the 106th Annual Meeting of the American Historical Association, Chicago, December 30, 1991, noted that small towns in Ohio and Indiana, many of which attracted auto factories and suppliers, had minuscule black populations, and remained hotbeds of hostility to blacks.

80. *Ford Facts,* December 1, 1951.

2

Detroit: Industrial Democracy or Capitalist Oligarchy?

BRYAN JONES AND LYNN BACHELOR

There was a time in which the united front was a legitimate political approach to revolution. And that meant working with all elements, including the capitalists and industrialists.
—Detroit's Mayor Coleman A. Young, 1980

"To Detroit, the Constantinople of the West." Thus a well-to-do merchant of Pontiac toasted his guests from Detroit in the 1890s.[1] And indeed, the "city of the straits," located on a narrow body of water connecting Lake Erie with Lake St. Clair and Lake Huron, resembled, geographically, the famous eastern city on the Bosporus. Like the old capital of the Roman Empire, Detroit's lifeblood was commerce. Lumber and copper from the north and foodstuffs from the fertile farms of Michigan's "Thumb" passed through its port. Manufactured goods from the East moved through, serving the farms and communities of Michigan.

Yet even then the analogy was strained. Detroit contained fewer than three hundred thousand people, while Constantinople held more than one million. New York, Philadelphia, and Chicago had decades before become national metropolises, while Detroit was still a provincial capital. More importantly, however, the relatively tranquil Detroit of the 1890s, with its tree-lined boulevards and lingering French flavor, was on the verge of undergoing perhaps the most rapid and complete change in its economic raison d'être that a modem city has ever experienced. Already Detroit had become, like Constantinople, an ethnic polyglot city, as waves of German, Irish, Italian, and, most recently, Polish, immigrants had arrived. The census of 1890 reported that only 20 percent of Detroit's two hundred thousand citizens had been born of native white parents. And industrial development had commenced; the old commercial elite was being joined by the new manufacturers. Iron, steel, tobacco and flour processing, meat packing, carriage manufacture, and machine-tool operations had been established and were growing.

The great transformation, however, was yet to occur. Within twenty short years, Detroit was transformed from a commercial city boasting a moderate manufacturing capacity into an industrial giant, the center of a vast automotive industry employing hundreds of thousands of workers and providing the livelihoods, directly or indirectly, of hundreds of thousands more.

The scope and intensity of the transformation are almost incomprehensible. In 1900, Detroit's population was 300,000; by 1930 it was 1.6 million. Transformed by the same economic forces, Flint, a provincial lumbering and carriage-building town in the Genesee valley, grew from 13,000 in 1900 to 91,600 in 1920 and to 156,500 in 1930. The demand for labor for the automobile factories spawned a vast housing market, and the city grew rapidly outward. Most building during the time was of workers' cottages and two- and three-flat buildings; this gave Detroit its characteristic industrial, sprawling appearance, in sharp contrast to the tenements of East Coast cities.

Industry itself was experiencing a great transformation. In 1905, some twenty-seven hundred factories in Michigan were granted state licenses to produce automobiles.[2] By 1920 only a handful of firms dominated the market, and by 1930 the basis structure of the automotive economy was set, with General Motors and Ford dividing the lion's share of the domestic market. Automobile manufacture had gone from a cottage industry with easy entry (an entrepreneur needed only enough capital to establish an assembly operation, relying on the well-developed supplier system to produce the components) to a tight oligarchy with the entry of new firms being virtually impossible.

MILWAUKEE JUNCTION

Typical of this new industrial order was Milwaukee Junction, where the Michigan Central Railroad joined the Detroit and Milwaukee Railroad not far from General Motors' world headquarters, which was completed in 1921. The rapid industrial expansion after 1900 forced manufacturers to search for space for their factories beyond the city's riverfront and traditional core, which was largely occupied by an earlier generation of industry: shipbuilding, stove manufacture, pharmaceuticals, and tobacco products. The search for space led northeast, to Milwaukee Junction.

During the period of great industrial expansion, the most significant industrial growth in Detroit occurred in three locations: "Outside of Ford's monumental achievements at his Highland Park plant beginning in 1910 and at the River Rouge site after 1917, the most significant industrial growth in Detroit took place in the vicinity of Milwaukee Junction."[3] The area rapidly became home to many of the early entries into the automotive-manufacturing business: Cadillac, Dodge, Studebaker, Detroit Electric, Ford, Packard, and Hupp. In addition, the three major independent producers of automotive bodies—Fisher, Murray, and Wilson—all located at Milwaukee Junction.

All seemed insignificant in comparison to the sprawling Dodge Brothers plant, built there in 1910. Designed by premier industrial architect Albert Kahn, it consisted of thirty-six separate buildings, encompassing more than five million square feet of space. It included its own foundry, powerhouse, and stamping, casting, transmission, and engine operations. The vast assembly building was four stories of bedrock-solid reinforced concrete. Employment there reached seventeen thousand by 1917 and peaked at forty thousand during World War II.

"Dodge Main" was the first major plant organized by the United Automobile Workers in 1936, and in 1937 Dodge Main's Local No. 3 was the largest local union in the country, with a membership of more than twenty-six thousand workers.[4] But if Dodge Main represented the high tide of American industrial might, it also represented the decentralization and decline of urban industrial dominance. Chrysler Corporation bought Dodge in 1928, and the manufacturing components of the operation were gradually phased out. In the 1950s the transmission line was moved to Indiana, and by the 1960s the once-mighty Dodge Main had become Hamtramck Assembly. When it closed in early 1980, Chrysler employed only three thousand workers there.[5]

SOCIAL AND POLITICAL CHANGE

The transformation in economic function brought about radical transformation of the social fabric and the political structure. Historian Oliver Zunz, basing his statement on his painstaking quantitative research of census and land-use data of 1880, 1900, and 1920, describes Detroit in the late nineteenth century, as "a multi-ethnic city, divided into a congeries of ethnic communities which were semi-autonomous." Although the native white elite dominated the commercial and industrial life of the community, the ethnic communities possessed significant cultural and economic autonomy. "Each ethnic group lived in its own section of the city, combined wealthy and less wealthy, rich and poor people, employers and employees … and the different communities lived fairly isolated from each other."[6]

Remarkably, by 1920, "that structure of multi-class ethnic communities had completely vanished."[7] Detroit had become the prototypical modern industrial city, with its population separated into two classes, increasingly antagonistic and divided over control of the means of production. The cross-class ethnic communities of the earlier era had disappeared, and Zunz reports that the only significant ethnic clusterings occurred in working-class neighborhoods. Perhaps most importantly, the plural opportunity structure of the nineteenth century, with social mobility possible within ethnic communities and in the broader community social structure, became "a single opportunity structure in the twentieth century when industry comes to dominate the whole hierarchy of work, to recognize the neighborhood, the culture, and every aspect of life."[8]

With the great industrial and social transformations came a change in the political structure. During the late 1800s and early 1900s, Detroit's government was typical of cities of the day: the mayor-council form, ward elections for the common council (an upper house, elected at large, had been abolished by the state legislature in 1887), and a thoroughly partisan style. The mayor was elected for a two-year term and sat as an ex officio member of the Board of Education, whose members were also elected from wards. The 1880s and 1890s were characterized politically by new German immigrants, who challenged the entrenched Irish in elections to the common council and for control of the local Democratic party. The pattern of alliances changed when Mayor Hazen Pingree was able to pry the German vote from the Democratic party and to build support among Poles for his brand of progressive Republicanism.[9]

The reforms by Pingree, however, failed to curb municipal abuses, which, in the early 1900s, were characterized by recurring scandals as the city government strained to cope with explosive growth and rapid social change. In 1910 the Wabash Railroad had bribed the common council's leader "Honest Tom" Glinnan and virtually every alderman in order to get a street closed for a right of way. In 1912, Henry Leland, founder of Cadillac Motor Company, and thirty-six other members of the city's Protestant elite formed the Good Citizens' League to combat the corruption. The league drew its support from the traditional anti-Catholic wing of the Republican party, but it also was strongly supported by the temperance forces.[10]

In 1918, prodded by the efforts of the Good Citizens' League, the citizens of Detroit adopted a new city charter. The charter abolished the ward system and provided for the election of a nine-member common council, to be elected at large. The Board of Education was also reformed, with seven members to be elected at large. The charter was adopted primarily to suppress ethnic divisions and to increase the power of the white Protestant elite.[11] Ironically, however, it came into effect in an urban world in which ethnic divisions were being transcended by class antagonisms. City government itself became a monolith, similar in organization to the industrial corporation.

The industrialization of Detroit spawned two other massive changes in the social organization, both of which had major political consequences. The first, the unionization of the work force, came just after the Great Depression had devastated the city. The second, the migrations of American blacks and southern whites, reestablished ethnicity as a major organizing force in political and social life. In the eyes of some observers, automotive manufacture had, by the 1960s, created a city of "race and class violence."

The massive social dislocation of the depression in Detroit may be gauged by some figures. In 1929, Ford employed over 128,000 workers in the Detroit region; by 1931 Ford employed only 37,000 workers. Between the spring and fall of 1929, General Motors cut its Pontiac work force from 29,000 to 14,000. In Flint, production dropped to one-seventh of normal.[12]

While the immediate effect of the depression was massive human suffering among industrial workers, the delayed effect was unionization. The great breakthrough for the United Automobile Workers (UAW) occurred during 1936 and 1937, when, following a series of sit-down strikes, General Motors agreed to bargain collectively. Detroit's labor force quickly became the most unionized in the country.

BLACKS IN DETROIT

Detroit had an established Negro community prior to industrialization, in part because of the city's location as a terminal on the underground railroad. But the early industrial period bypassed the black community, and between 1870 and 1910, Detroit's Negro population declined as a percentage of the population. Then, between 1910 and 1920, the black community grew sevenfold, while the while population was doubling.[13] This dramatic increase, brought about by migration from the South, was a result of Henry Ford's policies of promoting employment for blacks in his company, although he concentrated them at his massive Dearborn Rouge Complex. In 1937, 9,825 blacks worked at Rouge, about 12 percent of all workers there. In comparison, General Motors employed only 2,800 Negro workers, mostly in Flint and Pontiac, in 1941.[14]

By the early 1940s, some 100,000 Negroes resided in Detroit, 7.6 percent of the population. Both blacks and organized labor entered municipal politics in Detroit as important factors at about this time. After the race riot of 1943, Mayor Edward Jeffries attacked both blacks and labor, cleverly undermining the "united front" strategy of blacks and the UAW leadership. His overwhelming victory indicated the weakness of the influence that union leaders had on their members' votes when race became an issue. Yet the election "marked the emergence of a close political alliance between black Detroit and the UAW that would remain an important feature of Michigan's political landscape for years."[15]

The labor/black alliance gained a majority interest in the Democratic party during the late 1940s, pushing aside the party's more conservative Irish Catholic wing. But both were relatively uninfluential in municipal politics until the reform administration of Mayor Jerome Cavanaugh. Ironically, Cavanaugh was associated with the more conservative wing of the Democratic party, but he was able to overcome the business community's support of Mayor Louis Miriani and win the mayoralty election of 1963. Cavanaugh moved quickly to solidify his support among blacks and liberal whites.[16]

The relationship between blacks and predominantly white UAW leadership in union politics has been equally complex. While the vast majority of black workers have been relatively complacent in union politics, during the 1960s a strong insurgent movement developed, led by black radicals. The League of Revolutionary Black Workers strove to heighten class consciousness in Detroit factories, particularly at Dodge Main, with some success. The league died when its leadership cadre split up. Sociologist James Geschwender, in his analysis of the league, suggested that the league "is more likely to have been a significant harbinger of things to come than it is to have been a passing epiphenomenon."[17] The prophecy seems to have been hollow; unlike the Great Depression, which stimulated militant unionism in the automobile industry, the hard economic times of the late 1970s and 1980s seem to have had a chastening effect on black union insurgency.

In 1960, blacks made up 29 percent of the city's population, which was mostly concentrated in two sprawling ghettos. The improved economy of the 1960s and the intensified white flight from the city after the 1967 racial disorders meant that a far wider variety of housing was available to blacks, and by 1980, blacks were living throughout the city proper. In 1970, Detroit's population was 44 percent black; by 1980, it was 63 percent black.

In 1973, black state senator and former labor activist Coleman A. Young defeated Police Commissioner John Nichols in a bitterly fought, racially polarized election by a razor-thin margin. At the same time, a change in the city charter increased the mayor's power in making appointments and in financial affairs, simultaneously reducing the power of the common (now city) council. Armed with increased formal powers, acute political skills, and the enthusiastic support of the black community, particularly its poorest segment, Coleman A. Young has become the strongest mayor in the city's history.

Young's policies have consistently echoed three themes: increasing opportunities for blacks in the city's thoroughly reformed bureaucracies, forging linkages with private-sector elites in order to accomplish economic- development objectives, particularly in the downtown business district, and working closely with state and national officials to maximize the flow of intergovernmental funds to the city. Clearly the success of these aims depended on the cooperation of individuals outside of the city, and Mayor Young has earned a reputation as a master coalition builder. His early support of Jimmy Carter gained him a special relationship with the Carter administration. Young also had close ties with the administration of Republican Governor William Milliken, so much so that Milliken's Democratic opponent in 1978 accused Young of keeping down the Democratic vote in Detroit. Young has also worked closely with the city's business community on various civic projects.

DETROIT'S EVOLVING POWER STRUCTURE

At the turn of the century, Detroit's industrial power structure was almost exclusively white, Anglo-Saxon, and Protestant. Oliver Zunz's study of the 133 largest industrial employers in 1900 found the new industrial elite to be 71 percent Republican, 87 percent Protestant (almost all Episcopalian, Congregational, or Presbyterian), and 85 percent Anglo-Saxon. Interestingly, many had only recently settled in Detroit, and most were founders or cofounders of the manufacturing firms they headed.[18]

Although the great transformation brought about by the automobile changed the sources of wealth, it did not, it seems, change the base of this private power structure. In a study of the Detroit economic elite in the early 1970s, Lynda Ewen reported a tight-knit elite whose wealth was based on manufacturing, commerce, and banking and which was characterized by a great deal of intermarriage.[19] Neither Zunz nor Ewen, however, examined explicitly the linkages between politics and this economic elite; therefore these studies tell us little about the relationship between private elites and public power.

Other studies do, however, suggest substantial linkages; they also indicate that independent power derives from control of institutions in the public sector. Moreover, these studies provide evidence of separate constituencies and interests in the two domains. Thomas Anton and Bruce Bowen report data that suggest a pragmatic working relationship between the private and political decision makers in Detroit. In a survey of ninety-two members of the economic elite in 1975, 63 percent reported that they spent half or more of their working time on public issues. The attitudes of these individuals were characterized by pragmatism rather than ideology.[20] Anton concludes that "Detroit's concentrated and highly-organized institutional structure produces a small group of elite leaders who easily exchange information and opinions among themselves."[21]

The most interesting modern study of the Detroit power structure was conducted by the *Detroit News,* under the supervision of sociologist Charles Kadushin. The *News* assembled a list of major Detroit organizations in business, banking, government, law, community affairs, the media, religion, sports, the arts, labor, medicine, society, and wealth, and among retired executives. The top individuals in the organizations thus isolated were listed; they numbered some twelve hundred. The seventy-five individuals who appeared most often (usually across sectors) were interviewed, and an additional forty whose names were frequently mentioned by the initial seventy-five were also interviewed. The forty-seven most powerful individuals were those mentioned most frequently in a variety of circumstances.[22]

Kadushin writes that the power structure is

> composed of two groups linked by some common members. The first group is composed of the rich, the socially elite and the commercially important people of Detroit. This group includes auto magnates, former board chairmen, bank presidents, top retail merchants, heads of local utilities…. The second group is composed of people from working-class backgrounds and it holds resources not of things, but of people. Politicians, labor leaders, lawyers, ministers and other professionals form this group…. But what may be unique to Detroit is the fact that the second is also well connected to the first (or "elite") group. This is both the result and the cause of coalition policy-making in Detroit.[23]

THE AUTO INDUSTRY AND CIVIC PROJECTS

Seldom have the leaders of automobile companies taken the lead in civic affairs in Detroit, but when they do intervene, the results tend to be dramatic. Henry Leland of Cadillac spearheaded the city's municipal-reform movement, but, in general, the executives of General Motors have not been noted for their involvement in community affairs. The Ford family is much more active; it has endowed many cultural projects, in particular the symphony and the art museum.

The most spectacular civic accomplishment, however, of Henry Ford II was Renaissance Center, a hotel and office complex on the Detroit River. Ford was committed to a major project on the river, and he acted as the entrepreneur in putting together the investment package. This was not an easy matter, because most of the investors did not view the project favorably. Of the fifty-one corporations that invested in the original plan, thirty-eight had strong ties to the automobile industry.[24] Ford Motor Company itself invested one-third of the total.

More recently, General Motors, after making a corporate decision to keep its headquarters in Detroit rather than to move to New York, has committed funds to projects in the New Center area. Both commercial and residential projects have been initiated. The residential projects, which have been directed at restoring older houses and apartment buildings directly north of GM's world headquarters, met with some opposition from neighborhood groups. The city, however, has been solidly behind the project and has helped by writing applications for federal grants and by committing community-development funds to the area.

SECTORAL CENTRALIZATION

Robert Dahl, in his path-breaking study of urban power in New Haven, Connecticut, wrote: "Industrial society dispersed, it did not eradicate political inequality.... The political system of New Haven, then, is one of *dispersed inequalities*."[25]

The best evidence from the city that felt industrial transformation most strongly is contrary to this. In Detroit, rather than dispersing power by creating new forms of political resources, thus allowing new groups to gain access to the political system, industrialization swept away the variegated, diverse, small-scale social structure and replaced it with a unitary system. No longer could an individual achieve upward mobility within his ethnic community: a single system of social stratification had replaced the cross-class ethnic communities. Social cleavages were no longer rooted in ethnic diversity; class, and later class and race, were Detroit's social fissures. It became much harder for the individual entrepreneur to establish himself in the manufacturing sector; he had to join the large-scale corporation to achieve success. In government, too, a structure that reflected urban diversity had been replaced by a unitary structure. No longer could politics serve as a balancer of ethnic interests; the municipal-reform success of 1918 had ensured that.

It would be a mistake, however, to assume that industrialization had replaced pluralism with an elitism in which the economic notables dominated politics and government. Quite the contrary. By forging deep, reinforcing divisions in society, this industrial revolution had solidified power within a limited number of sectors. If industrialists were powerful because of their large-scale organizations, so was labor, whose organizational structure had to follow the contours of the oligopolistic corporate structure. Government, in the hands of individuals whose backgrounds and organizational interests not infrequently were at variance with the captains of industry, was better organized to deal with the heads of corporations than were the neighborhood-level politicians and interest groups. Power in the church was increasingly centralized, with the parish priest becoming less a neighborhood entrepreneur and more a small part of a religious bureaucracy that was organized on a metropolitan scale.

Increasingly, the important political agreements are being forged among leaders who represent a very limited number of economic and political sectors, each of which has different interests and constituencies. Business, labor, government, and, to a far lesser extent, the church: these are the participants in politics. It is a politics of large scale; it works (to the extent that it can be said to work) because leaders in each sector can impose settlements on other actors within his sector with minimal need to engage in internal bargaining. The touted "coalition building" that has occurred in Detroit is possible because only the leaders need to agree; the hierarchical arrangements within sectors negates the need for expanding the bargaining beyond the sector's leaders.

In the automotive industry, market pressures and the enormous problems of meeting federal regulatory standards have increased the tendency toward centralized decision making and policy control. Chrysler has traditionally been led by "strong-willed, authoritarian individuals, and decisions have been made by one person alone."[26] Since its founding, Ford had, until the retirement of Henry Ford II, always been headed by a member of the Ford family. As a consequence of his equity position in the company, Henry Ford II continues to wield a critical influence in corporate decisions.

At General Motors, all major policy decisions are made at central headquarters. Over the years, headquarters has assumed more of the decision-making functions in the corporation; for example, all personnel and labor-relations matters were centralized in 1937. In the past, however, the company's belief in internal competition to promote productivity allowed a considerable amount of discretion for division management. This discretion has been severely circumscribed in recent years, because of corporate standardization programs and the demands of federal regulatory standards.[27]

Similarly, union power has become increasingly centralized, with local automobile-union workers generally following policies that emanate from the United Automobile Workers' Solidarity House in Detroit. Only a national union could deal effectively with corporations as large as the automobile companies. As importantly, the modern pattern of collective bargaining became firmly established in the GM/UAW agreement of 1948. After a lengthy strike in 1945/46, both the company and the union wished to avoid another round of bitter labor strife, The agreement provided for the industry's first multiyear contract, a cost-of-living formula, agreement in principle that pay raises had to be tied to increases in productivity, and an understanding of the "private" nature of the bargaining process.[28] This contract established the unwritten norms for collective bargaining that prevail in the automobile industry, and it contributed substantially to the national, centralized power that is enjoyed by Solidarity House.

GOVERNMENTAL FRAGMENTATION

Coalition building among sector elites fails most often because government is the most fragmented sector. In 1918 there were no suburbs to speak of in Detroit. Today Detroit is home to only about 27 percent of the area's residents. The modern tendency to reimpose special agencies and districts has also affected metropolitan government (or the lack of it) in Detroit. Hence city/suburban divisions have appeared on issues of transportation, water and sewerage, taxation, and economic development.

In their study of ten cases of public decision making in the Detroit metropolis during the 1950s, Robert Mowitz and Deil Wright were most struck with the pluralistic governmental system in operation. The dispersion of governmental power into a multiplicity of general-purpose and special governmental units made the accomplishment of metropolitan goals difficult but not impossible. Indeed, when the differences of interest are negotiated to produce solutions, the resulting changes "strengthen rather than weaken the pluralistic governmental structure of the metropolis."[29] To these authors, the resulting system of fragmented public power, with negotiation and adjustment on important civic projects, implies a pluralistic power structure. "The success with which the various competing organizations and groups have prevented power from becoming concentrated in the hands of a ruling elite makes it unlikely that the pluralistic power balance will be significantly tipped in the future."[30]

While the Detroit metropolis today remains as governmentally fragmented as ever, certain changes over the last twenty-five years now operate to make metropolitan cooperation more difficult. Detroit is both poorer and blacker in relation to its suburbs than it was in 1960. Indeed, in that year, a number of Detroit neighborhoods were in the highest income quartile for the metropolis. The aggressive style of Mayor Young and the racial consciousness of suburban whites have contributed to problems in interjurisdictional cooperation. Today, the mayor of Detroit represents an entirely different constituency from the majority of his suburban counter parts, not just a different governmental jurisdiction.

The resulting governmental power configuration is both fragmented and dispersed. Local governments in the Detroit metropolis increasingly represent not just geographically distinct jurisdictional interests but critical social groupings as well. Jurisdictional boundaries today re-inforce basic social divisions more than they did a quarter of a century ago, when the city itself was more diverse. This fragmentation weakens the ability of governments to negotiate among themselves and with the representatives of the giant manufacturing corporations that dominate Detroit's economy.

SECTARCHY

This characterization of power in Detroit is admittedly based on a limited number of studies and our own nonsystematic observations. Nevertheless, none of the terms that are currently being used to describe the configurations of community power quite fit the description of sectorally organized power that we presented above. Pluralism connotes a dispersion of power and an openness to groups that fits only part of Detroit's power configuration, the governmental sector. Even this characterization may better fit relations among governments than within them. On a number of civic projects, both Mayor Young and his predecessors have been able to forge a community consensus—the Renaissance Center is the premier example.

The logic of pluralism implies that power relations are shifting and unstable, and resulting public policies follow the contours of changing political coalitions. In Detroit, power is far more structured than this. Elitism stresses stability and concentration of power, as do we, but it rel-egates the power that is rooted in elections as secondary and posits a unity of purpose among members of the elite that does not seem to be warranted in the modern industrial city.[31]

We suggest the term *sectarchy* (from the Latin *sectare,* "to cut") to describe this system of sectoral power.[32] We hesitate to propose this new term, less out of deference to current termi-nology than to the use of the related term *polyarchy* by such scholars as Robert Dahl and Charles Lindblom. Lindblom, for example, has defined polyarchy as a set of decision rules for choosing political leaders through an electoral system. He then goes on to examine the close connection between government and business in polyarchies.[33] We have substantial sympathy for this ap-proach, but we feel that it fails to capture the notion that political power is based in the sectoral organization of the political economy. Government as well as private organizations in a polyarchy bring resources to bear in politics; elections ensure that at least part of the time, elected leaders will have interests different from those of the leaders of business and labor organizations. The size and scope of modem government ensures that political leaders will have resources to pursue these interests. In Detroit, peak bargaining among sectors is quite common, and it is in this format that major decisions are made—not within the councils of government alone. The difference between this structure and elitism, pluralism, or a polyarchy that is heavily dependent on market forces (as in Lindblom's model) is striking enough that a separate term is warranted. The likelihood that it exists elsewhere strengthens the case for the proliferation of terms.

THE ORGANIZATIONAL BASES OF URBAN POWER

The nature of Detroit's sectarchy is probably best appreciated by Mayor Young among all the major actors. In an interview in early 1984 he responded to a question concerning his apparent recent failure to "build coalitions." Young responded:

> The coalition I was successful in establishing when I first became mayor pre-dated the severe economic conditions that laid siege to this city and to the auto industry. And those members of the auto industry were so damn busy fighting to keep their companies' heads above water that they didn't have time for much else. In the meantime, there was almost a complete change in leadership.
>
> I was looking at a picture in my office just the other day. It was 1976, the third year I was in office, when Jimmy Carter came through here, running for president. And there was Pete Estes from General Motors, Riccardo from Chrysler, Ford from Ford, Leonard Woodcock from the auto workers' union, Jimmy Carter, and me. I'm the only one that's left.[34]

Young equated leadership with organizational position, and indeed, the bases for power in the industrial city are organizational. When one leaves his position in the organizational structure, he leaves most of his political power behind. It is indeed these "command posts," in the words of C. Wright Mills, that confer power.[35] As Andrew Hacker has noted, "Members of [the] elite are easily replaceable; in many cases it is impossible to distinguish an officeholder from his predecessor or successor."[36] Thomas Dye has also focused on the key role of institutional position in power configurations.[37]

These key command posts, which are so important in theories about institutional elites, are in the hands of people who, because of their positions in the political and economic systems, have very different interests to pursue. Politicians hail from very different backgrounds than do businessmen, and they clash with businessmen on a number of important issues. Union leaders, who are representative of a distinct economic interest that is often different from either business or government, are nevertheless frequently consulted formally on major policy initiatives and are able to contribute to civic projects by depicting them to their members in a favorable light. Not infrequently, members of the business community themselves hold differing opinions on civic projects, with local commercial interests seeing the situation differently from the way in which multinational automobile companies and their suppliers see it. (A special case of this was Henry Ford's advocacy of the Renaissance project, with Ford, the local advocate, lobbying the other automotive companies and Ford's own suppliers directly and strongly for investment funds.) Nevertheless, on at least major issues that involve all sectors, representatives of each sector negotiate with leaders from other sectors, secure in the knowledge that they will not be undercut by intrasectorial divisiveness.

The result is either a very structured form of pluralism or a fairly open system of elite rule, depending on one's perspective. Major decisions that affect urban policy are often made in forums in which representatives of the major sectors are in direct contact with one another. Usually these forums, always bringing together representatives of government, labor, and business, are established in order to "solve problems." Examples include Detroit Renaissance, which is a group of business and government leaders that convenes to promote downtown revitalization; the Economic Alliance of Michigan, an association of business and labor that works on economic policy concerns; and New Detroit, the nation's first "urban coalition" of blacks, business, labor, and government, which was established after the 1967 civil disorders to promote black economic progress.

This pattern of sectarchy does not imply that other traditional forces in urban politics are impotent; far from it. *Within* the governmental sector, on issues of concern only to governmental officials, such groups as public-employee unions, bureaucrats, and neighborhood groups do influence city policies, and these policies are important for the development of the region. But where the sectors meet, a pattern of bargaining at the peaks emerges.

Peak bargaining does not include all urban issues; rather, it incorporates the current concerns of participants. (As one former radical organizer commented to us, "I finally see that Henry Ford doesn't care how Detroit distributes its community development block grant funds.") It is not even clear that, in the aggregate, issues that are "peak bargained" are more important than those that are handled through more traditional channels. Peak bargaining does seem to encompass expensive capital projects and issues of current high salience, however.

A major issue is whether this system of peak bargaining is biased toward the economic elite. It is possible that the sectarchy of the industrial city yields results that generally favor the upper economic strata. Clarence Stone has identified the differing bases of power of public officials and private elites and has concluded that the economic elites are disproportionately powerful because the politicians rely on them for support for public projects.[38] And Charles Lindblom points to the "privileged position" of businessmen because they provide the economic livelihood of the community.[39] Paul Peterson argues that a special relationship emerges between public and private officials when the community's export industries are involved.[40] It is exactly this issue—the relative influence of public officials and corporate leaders in real decision-making situations involving the manufacture of automobiles in Michigan—that we examine in the rest of this book.

NOTES

1. Pound, *Detroit,* p. 1.
2. *Crow, City of Flint Grows Up,* p. 52.
3. *Final Environmental Impact Statement, Central Industrial Park* (Detroit: City of Detroit Community and Economic Development Department, Dec. 1980), p. B–8
4. Ibid., p. J–2.
5. Ibid., p. B–3; see also *Profile of an Urban American City: Hamtramck, Michigan* (Detroit: League of Women Voters, 1980).
6. Oliver Zunz, "The Changing Face of Inequality: An Interview with the Author," *Detroit in Perspective* 6 (Fall 1982): 9–10; see his *The Changing Face of Inequality* (Chicago: University of Chicago Press, 1982).
7. Zunz, "Changing Face," p. 11.
8. Ibid.
9. Melvin G. Holli, *Reform in Detroit: Hazen Pingree and Urban Politics* (New York: Oxford University Press, 1969), chap, 1
10. Robert Conot, *American Odyssey* (New York: Bantam, 1975), p. 241.
11. Ibid., p. 256.
12. Joyce Shaw Peterson, "Auto Workers Confront the Depression, 1929–1933," *Detroit in Perspective* 6 (Fall 1982): 49.
13. Deskins, *Residential Mobility*, p. 32.
14. August Meier and Elliott Rudwick, *Black Detroit and the Rise of the UAW* (Oxford: Oxford University Press, 1979), pp. 6–7.
15. Ibid., p. 205.
16. A detailed examination of the Cavanaugh years may be found in Conot, *American Odyssey.*
17. James Geschwender, *Class, Race, and Worker Insurgency* (Cambridge: Cambridge University Press, 1977), p. 227; see also Dan Georgakas and Marvin Surkin, *Detroit: I Do Mind Dying* (New York: St. Martin's, 1975).
18. Zunz, *Changing Face,* pp. 203–16.
19. Lynda Ann Ewen, *Corporate Power and Urban Crisis in Detroit* (Princeton, N.J.: Princeton University Press, 1978).
20. Results are summarized in Anton, "Impact of Federal Grants on Detroit in 1978," pp. 14–15.
21. Ibid., p. 14.
22. *The Top Forty-Seven Who Make It Happen: A Study of Power* (Detroit: Detroit News, 1978).
23. Charles Kadushin, " 'Small World'—How Many Steps to the Top?" *Detroit News,* 17 Sept. 1978.
24. Andrew R. McGill and Barbara Young, "One Man Shakes a City: Henry Ford Has the Power," *Detroit News,* 8 Oct. 1978.
25. Dahl, *Who Governs?* p. 85.

26. John B. Schnapp, *Corporate Strategies of the Automotive Manufacturers* (Lexington, Mass.: Lexington Books, 1979), p. 130.

27. Ibid., pp. 146–47.

28. Alfred P. Sloan, Jr., *My Years with General Motors* (Garden City, N.Y.: Anchor, 1972), pp. 457–76.

29. Robert J. Mowitz and Deil S. Wright, *Profile of a Metropolis* (Detroit: Wayne State University Press, 1962), p. 630.

30. Ibid., p. 631.

31. J. Allen Whitt, *Urban Elites and Mass Transportation* (Princeton, N.J.: Princeton University Press, 1982), pp. 8–32.

32. If unifying Latin and Greek seems awkward, try the Greek stems alone: chotomarchy.

33. Lindblom, *Politics and Markets*.

34. "Mayor Young a Decade Later," *Detroit Free Press,* 2 Feb. 1984.

35. C. Wright Mills, *The Power Elite* (New York: Oxford University Press, 1956).

36. Andrew Hacker, "What Rules America?" *New York Review,* 1 May 1975, p. 10, quoted in Domhoff, *Who Rules America Now?* p. 217.

37. Thomas Dye, *Who's Running America?* (Englewood Cliffs, N.J.: Prentice- Hall, 1976).

38. Stone, "Systemic Power," pp. 876–990.

39. Lindblom, *Politics and Markets*.

40. Peterson, *City Limits*.

3

The Demise of Detroit: Why the Big Three Lost?

SUMIT KUMAR CHAUDHURY AND HANSA IYENGYAR

INTRODUCTION

The US automobile industry, that had long been the symbol of the US' industrial dominance had traditionally centered on Detroit's Big Three (Big Three) automobile companies—'Ford Motor Co.' (Ford), 'General Motors' (GM) and 'Chrysler Corp.' (Chrysler). All through the 1960s and 1970s, the Big Three had enjoyed unrivalled success in the US and had seldom considered the fledgling foreign companies worthy of competition. But in toasting their own success, they overlooked and underestimated their competitors, who made rapid inroads into the US market (Annexure I) with a slew of products ranging from small cars to pick-up trucks and from family sedans[1] to luxury cars[2], which were better in quality and lower in price than Detroit's offerings. By the 1980s, the Big Three automakers were facing serious problems in the form of declining sales, diminishing market share and looming financial crises, due to the increasing dominance of foreign carmakers in the US, with cars from companies like Toyota, Honda and Nissan (Japan), Hyundai (Korea) and Volkswagen, BMW and Mercedes-Benz (Germany), capturing the loyalty of the US customers.

Further, while the Big Three had left the demands of the customer unheeded and spewed out cars that did not meet the customer requirements, the foreign manufacturers had taken special care to ensure that each and every whim of the customer was catered to. This 'customer-centric' focus was one of the major reasons behind the success of the foreign companies. Besides, the 'foreign' companies were no longer viewed as foreign since most of them had set up manufacturing plants in the US by the end of the 1980s. With the threat from the competition looming large, the Big Three went on a discounting spree, selling their cars at lower prices and offering 'zero percent finance' schemes to their customers, which brought back short-lived spurts in sales but damaged the credibility of their brands. The terms of Big Three's contract with the 'United Automobile, Aerospace and Agricultural Implement Workers'[3] (UAW), led to the Big Three shouldering huge 'legacy' costs. With their new models being unable to attract the increasingly discerning customer

---

Annexure 1: Major Automobile Manufacturers in the US

BMW Group

BMW of North America has been present in the US since 1975 and owns the BMW and MINI brands. Worldwide production of the BMW Z3 roadsters and the BMW X5 Sports Activity Vehicle comes solely from the BMW Manufacturing Corp. plant located at Spartanburg, SC. The BMW US Holding Corp., the Group's headquarters for North, Central and South America, is located at Woodcliff Lake, New Jersey.

DaimlerChrysler

DaimlerChrysler is one of the world's leading automotive, transportation and services companies. Its passenger car brands include Mercedes-Benz, Chrysler, Jeep, Dodge and Smart. Commercial vehicles are produced under Mercedes-Benz, Freightliner, Sterling, Western Star, Setra, Thomas Built Buses, Orion and American LaFrance. After the November 1998 merger of Daimler-Benz, Europe's largest industrial company, and Chrysler Corporation, one of the US' most innovative automotive companies, DaimlerChrysler today has a global workforce, a global shareholder base, global brand awareness and a global outlook. DaimlerChrysler employs more than 100,000 workers across the US, and has dual headquarters in Auburn Hills, Michigan, and Stuttgart, Germany.

Ford Motor Company

Ford Motor Company is a global leader in the automotive industry, selling more than seven million vehicles annually in more than 200 markets worldwide. The company employs more than 370,000 people and has 112 wholly-owned, equity-owned and joint venture manufacturing plants in 30 countries on six continents. Ford has nine automotive brands—Ford, Lincoln, Mercury, Jaguar, Mazda, Volvo, Aston Martin, Land Rover and THINK. In the US, Ford (including Visteon, its automotive components and systems subsidiary) employs over 173,000 employees and has manufacturing and assembly facilities in 47 cities in 14 states.

General Motors

General Motors is the world's largest automotive corporation and full-line vehicle manufacturer. The company employs more than 388,000 people and works with more than 30,000 supplier companies worldwide. With brands including Chevrolet, Pontiac, Oldsmobile, Buick, Cadillac, GMC, Saturn, Saab, Opel, Vauxhall and Holden, GM has manufacturing operations in 50 countries and has a presence in more than 200 countries. GM also has technology collaborations with BMW AG of Germany and Toyota Motor Corp. of Japan, and vehicle manufacturing ventures with several automakers around the world, including Toyota, Suzuki, Shanghai Automotive Industry Corp. of China, AvtoVAZ of Russia and Renault SA of France.

Toyota

Toyota employs over 30,500 people throughout the US and Canada. Toyota currently manufactures vehicles and parts at eight North American plants, including Camry (built in Georgetown, KY) and Tundra, a new full-size truck manufactured in Princeton, IN. Toyota is developing new technologies which reduce the impact its vehicles have on the environment. One example is Prius—the world's first mass-produced hybrid vehicle. Prius achieves extraordinary fuel economy and reduces emissions by up to 90%. Toyota also is developing breakthroughs in fuel cell technology and electric vehicles. The e-commerce, CNG Camry and the RAV4-EV are examples of Toyota's ongoing research and development of alternative fuel vehicles.

Volkswagen

Founded in 1955, Volkswagen of America, Inc. is headquartered at Auburn Hills, Michigan. It is a subsidiary of Volkswagen AG, headquartered at Wolfsburg, Germany. Volkswagen of the US and its affiliates employ approximately 3,000 people in the US, and are responsible for the sale and service of Audi, Bentley, Lamborghini and Volkswagen products.

Hyundai

Established in 1967 in Korea, Hyundai initially entered the US market in 1986 and focussed on the small-car and entry-level vehicle segment and mostly imported its vehicles. Headquartered at Garden Grove, California, Hyundai Motors America has invested $1 billion in its first manufacturing plant in Montgomery, Alabama, which will be operational by 2005. Hyundai's brands include Atos, Atos Prime, Sonata, Getz, Accent, Elantra, Coupe, XG and Centennial in the passenger car segment and Santa Fe, Trajet, Galloper, H1, Terracan and Matrix in the SUV segment.

Honda

Honda started its first US plant in 1979 and since then, evolved into a company that directly employs more than 24,000 US citizens. Honda's models include the Accord Coupe and Sedan, Civic Coupe, sedan and hybrid, Civic Si, Civic GX, CR-V, Element, Odyssey, Insight, Pilot and S 200.

Compiled by the author

and the popularity of the foreign cars soaring, the Big Three had no option but to roll-out enhanced versions of their earlier and popular models as an attempt to cash in on their earlier 'glory days'. Still, the future for the 'Big Three' seemed uncertain. As Micheline Maynard, author of *'The End of Detroit'* stated in her book, "... foreign cars are not really foreign anymore. Millions of them are built in the United States every year ... If the current sales trends continue, cars and trucks from foreign-based companies could easily, some say inevitably, account for 50% of all American sales by the year 2010."

THE FALL OF THE TITANS

In the 20th century, Detroit and the Big Three were symbolic of the industrial might of the US, as they introduced the concept of mass production, were instrumental in manufacturing tanks and aircraft during World War II and were the source of employment for thousands of the US citizens after the war. Despite the existence of foreign automakers like Volkswagen (VW) in the US since the 1950s, the Big Three continued to dominate the US automobile market in the 1960s, with GM alone holding 60%[4] of the market. In the early 1970s, Detroit was the bastion of the global automobile industry and the US, with a production of 8.3 million cars, was the world's largest producer of automobiles.[5]

But Motown's[6] glory proved to be short-lived. Detroit was up against serious competition in the form of foreign manufacturers who had forayed into the US market. One of the reasons for Motown's problems was the Oil Shocks of 1973 and 1979, which resulted in an increase in the oil prices. Detroit's fuel guzzling models soon lost their popularity in the US market, with customers preferring the smaller and fuel-efficient Japanese cars. By the end of 1978, 1.5 million Japanese cars were sold, which accounted for more than half of the import sales in the US, and by the end of 1980, Japan had captured 30% of the US market, beating the US to become the world's largest manufacturer of automobiles.[7] Prompted by the increasing demand for their vehicles, companies like Honda, Nissan and Toyota set up manufacturing plants on the US soil. Annual losses at Ford for 1980 exceeded $1 billion and this jarred Motown into the realisation that the competition was getting tougher. This realisation prompted a wave of modernisation drives that saw the Big Three investing $69 billion[8] by the mid-1980s in new plants, equipment and the designing of new models. Ford hit back with new models—Ford Taurus and Mercury Sable, the products of its 'modernisation drive'.

Inspite of the Big Three revamping their product lines and coming up with efficient plants and production techniques, they lost the small-car and mid-sized sedan market to Toyota's Camry and Honda's Accord by the end of the 1980s. The 1990s saw the Korean manufacturers assuming dominance in the entry-level vehicle market. By mid-1990s, VW with the Passat and Hyundai with the Sonata, also joined the fray for a share of the sedan market and Detroit's share of the passenger car market kept decreasing (Exhibit I).

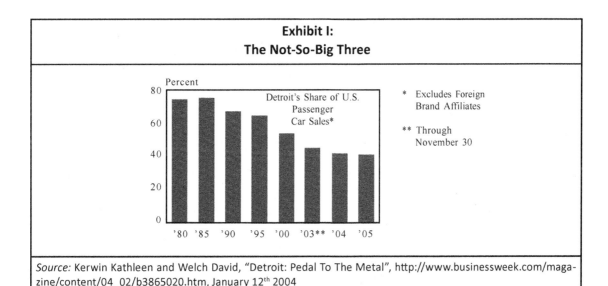

Exhibit I:
The Not-So-Big Three

Detroit's Share of U.S. Passenger Car Sales*

* Excludes Foreign Brand Affiliates

** Through November 30

Source: Kerwin Kathleen and Welch David, "Detroit: Pedal To The Metal", http://www.businessweek.com/magazine/content/04_02/b3865020.htm, January 12th 2004

To add to the woes, Detroit witnessed the luxury car segment, which it had once dominated with the Lincoln Continental and the Cadillac, captured by Toyota's Lexus, BMW and Mercedes-Benz, with more competition emerging in the form of VW's Audi, Honda's Acura and Nissan's Infiniti models. The weakening of the US economy after the Gulf War[9] resulted in compounding the Big Three's troubles and in 1991, their combined losses amounted to $7 billion. At this time, Motown discovered the latest craze of the US consumer—the Sport Utility Vehicle[10] (SUV). The Big Three started dominating the SUV market and between them held more than 90% of the SUV sales.[11] With every second car sold in the US being a SUV, Motown rode to success fuelled by the raving popularity of these bulky vehicles.

But the non-US carmakers was also fast to react. Competitors flooded the market with SUVs, minivans and crossover vehicles (a mix of passenger car and a SUV), from Toyota's RAV-4 and Lexus' LX 470 to Honda's Acura MDX and the Pilot SUV. Mercedes and BMW also entered the luxury SUV segment with the M-Class and the X5 respectively, while Porsche brought out the Cayenne and Hyundai came up with the Santa Fe. In order to boost the sales, which had sunk after the 9/11 terrorist attacks,[12] GM announced a 'zero percent finance' (interest-free loans) scheme. This kick-started a 'credit binge' in the market as Ford and Chrysler also followed suit and by mid-2002 the Big Three were offering deals worth $2,000-$3,000 per vehicle.[13] Although this resulted in a spurt in the sales, the after effects proved to be disastrous with sales dipping each time the incentives were revoked. On the other hand, the foreign companies were able to sell their vehicles at little or no discount. By 2002, the Big Three's profit margins per car had gone down drastically. For example, GM was able to make a profit of just $330 per car, while Toyota made $1,000 and Honda made $1,600.[14] By 2002, the Big Three's share of the US market was pegged at 63%, a 10%[15] decrease (from 1996), while the foreign brands made steady inroads into the passenger car segment and, between them, held 55% of the market by the end of 2003.

Commenting on the foreign invasion of the US car market, Richard Wagoner, the chief executive officer at GM, said, "Once these manufacturers establish a foothold in the US, they begin to mimic our broad product lines, eventually become accepted by the public as a 'domestic' brand, and suddenly, we lose our home-field advantage."[16]

DETROIT'S ACHILLES HEEL

Despite being the forerunners of the automobile industry in the US, Motown was unable to withstand the onslaught from the foreign competitors. Although foreign companies had been active in the US since the 1950s, they were mostly engaged in importing fully assembled vehicles. In 1958, imports constituted 8%[17] of the cars sold in the US market, with half of those being VW's Beetles. It was only in the 1970s that the foreign competitors, for the first time, began to assert themselves primarily because of their economical and fuel-efficient cars. The 1970s and 1980s saw Detroit losing the small-car market to foreign competitors, which was followed by the Big Three ceding their hold on the mid-sized sedan and the luxury car market. The SUV was the only track to profitability for the Big Three, but by 2003, the competitors had come up with their own versions of the SUV and the Big Three realised that they had lost that advantage as well. Detroit also lost its hold on the minivan[18] and in 2003, its share had fallen down from an all time high of 94% (1992) to 70% .[19] By the end of 2003, the composition of the 'US Big Three' changed

Exhibit II US Vehicle Sales (August 2003)		
Company	Units Sold	% Change (since August 2002)
GM	464,774	(-0.8%)
Ford	288,515	(-13.1%)
Toyota	200,482	(+11.4%)
Chrysler	190,388	(-6.4%)
Honda	147,253	(+11.2%)
Nissan	80,820	(+14.2%)
Hyundai	41,073	(+5.9%)
Volkswagen	32,376	(-3.5%)
BMW	23,068	(+7.2%)

Source: "Toyota wins on US car sales", http://news.bbc.co.uk/2/hi/business/3079610.stm, September 4th 2003

Exhibit III(a):
Car Market Driving Away from Big Three

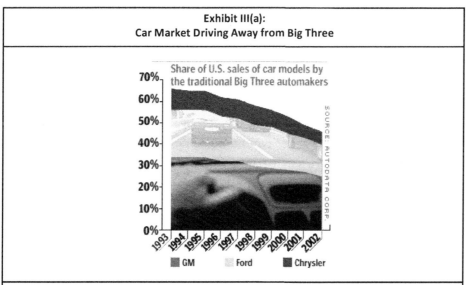

Source: Isidore Chris, "Detroit rediscovering cars", http://money.cnn.com/2003/03/11/pf/autos/ cars_comeback/index.htm, March 11th 2003

Exhibit III(b):
Big Three's Drive Away from Making Cars

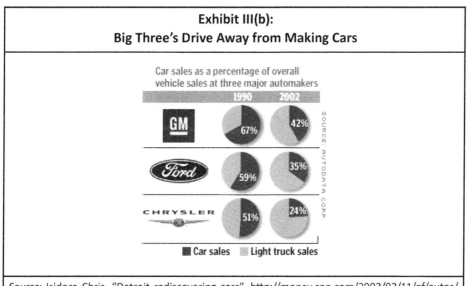

Source: Isidore Chris, "Detroit rediscovering cars", http://money.cnn.com/2003/03/11/pf/autos/ cars_comeback/index.htm, March 11th 2003

(Exhibits III (a) and III (b)) when Toyota overtook Chrysler to become the third largest producer of automobiles in the US with a market share of 11%.[20] (Exhibit II).

One of the major reasons behind the decline of Detroit was that the foreign manufacturers understood the pulse of the market. Initially, when Toyota, Honda and Hyundai entered the US, they had failed with their offerings, which were the same as their domestic models. They soon realised that their models were not able to cater to the needs of the US market and went ahead to collect information from the customers and dealers on what they really wanted. This led to the development of fuel-efficient cars that gave the foreign manufacturers a strong foothold in the US. Subsequent feedback enabled them to come up with cars that were better in quality, reliability and were spacious, apart from being affordable. The focus on customers' needs also led to the introduction of cars with new body styles and crossover vehicles that Motown had never thought of. As Joe Ivers, the auto-quality guru at 'J.D. Power and Associates', a global marketing information firm, said, "They (defects) don't reflect technical failures, but failures to satisfy the consumer. The term 'quality' has become a palette on to which people paint their own problems."[21] Even seemingly trivial issues like excessive wind noise[22], uncomfortable seats or cheap plastic dashboards became major points of consideration for the customers. The manufacturers had to constantly upgrade these features to satisfy customer demands. High quality also translated into pricing premium for the vehicle, as consumers did not mind paying slightly higher rates for a vehicle that met their requirements. Better quality also meant increase in customer loyalty and greater resale value for the car, and all these played an important role in the customer's choice of the vehicle. On the other hand, Detroit had failed to listen to the needs of the customers, which led to many a complaint and the discerning US buyers quickly shifted their loyalties. As Chrysler marketing chief, Joseph Eberhard, said, "It's like turning around an oil tanker. If you've had two bad transmissions, you're not likely to give us another chance. I can't blame you."[23]

To counter the invasion in the car segment, the Big Three focused all their energies into the light truck and SUV segments with models like the Ford's Taurus, GM's Saturn and the Mercury Sable. The 1990s was the 'decade of the SUV' and with profits margins soaring up to $15,000 a vehicle[24] on models like the Cadillac Escalade and Lincoln Navigator, Detroit had found a winner. With the new found success, Detroit once more underestimated its opposition and instead of taking steps to improve upon the production and attend to union problems at their plants, the Big Three put the problems on a back burner. As William Ford Jr., chairman of Ford, said, "We have absolute collective amnesia in this business. We can't handle success. We do our best as a company when our back is to the wall."[25] The European, Japanese and Korean companies were quick to react and they came up with an impressive line-up of their own and by 2002, they had eaten up 7% of Detroit's truck market, and for every percentage point of market share lost, Motown lost $4 billion in sales.[26] As Micheline Maynard, stated in her book, "This sense of unshaken superiority has been Detroit's most fatal flaw. For its hubris has led to blindness in the halls of the Big Three, disappointment and even a vague sense of betrayal among many American consumers ... Too many American car buyers are simply fed up with the vehicles that

Detroit has tried to peddle to them. Millions of customers, loyal to GM for generations, finally got tired of tinny doors, keys that didn't fit both the door and the trunk, and instrument panels that simply looked cheap. Despite the improvements that Detroit has made, despite all its vows and promises, the list of flaws in its cars continues to exceed that of its rivals."[27]

Apart from attractive finance schemes, GM also offered generous terms to its car rental customers like 'Enterprise' and 'Hertz', who ran rental fleets. Ford and Chrysler followed, but this move proved to be detrimental to their image. The companies soon lost respectability among the customers, as Wesley Brown, a consultant at 'Nextrend', a Los Angeles based auto consultant, said, "They've ruined the image of these brands because it's almost to the point where they're paying you to take the vehicle off the lot."[28] This also hurt the resale value of Detroit's cars. On the other hand, the foreign companies were able to sell their vehicles without having to resort to hefty discounts and financing schemes. Also, by avoiding deals with the car rental agencies, they maintained a high-quality image.

Another point in consideration was that the Japanese used a 'pull system'[29] for manufacturing and market forecast. They kept a close watch on the trends of the market and quickly adapted their vehicles to meet the demands. This was possible mainly due to the use of the 'lean'[30] model of production, which allowed them to make rapid changes to their product lines and volumes. Detroit mainly followed the mass production model, which was not as flexible and which led to the build-up of large amounts of material, work-in-process and finished vehicle inventory. These only added to the costs of the company. Further, the foreign companies preferred to set up their plants in the Southern states of the US, as they were not unionised under UAW. Detroit, on the other hand, had to take the approval of the UAW, before they planned to reduce capacity or stop production, even temporarily. A study by the 'Centre for Automotive Research', an industry analyst based at Michigan, estimated that by mid-2003, Detroit's production would exceed demand by 2.2 million vehicles[31] and their labour contracts banned plant closings and required the companies to continue paying for idle workers. They also had to bear the pension and healthcare expenses of the workers, which were as high as $1,200 per vehicle,[32] and which had to be considered before the company could calculate the profits. These expenses, coupled up with the hefty discounts offered, only worsened Motown's bottomline. For example, by 2003, GM had a pension fund shortfall of $19 billion, which was as big as its market capitalisation.[33]

With the foreign companies becoming increasingly dependent on the US market for their profits, they began to expand their production capacities and invested more into design and development of newer and better quality models. The days of Detroit's dominance were numbered, as Chrysler's chief operating officer, Wolfgang Bernhard, said, "In this kind of industry, you have a mindset to defend your core segment. But if everybody is playing offence and you're playing defence, you lose."[34] By focusing on eliminating defects in their products and waste in their production system, the foreign manufacturers were constantly able to increase the quality and reduce the price. This also enabled them to save on the costs of product withdrawals and warranty claims for the replacement of faulty parts, which was one of the areas where the Big

Three fell behind. As Ford's chief financial officer, Allan Gilmour, said, "We've got to be efficient while we're innovative. American companies haven't done a very good job of that."[35]

Micheline Maynard rightly highlighted the plight of Motown, when she stated, "Detroit's single-handed control of the American automobile industry has been lost forever. From small-cars to luxury cars, from family sedans to mini vans, vehicles made by foreign-based companies are escalating in popularity ... four out of every ten vehicles sold in the United States this year will be built by companies with foreign nameplates ... There is a strong chance that by the end of this decade (2010), at least one of the Big Three will not continue in the same form that it is in now. The dissolution of a Detroit automaker would be a tragedy for its employees and vendors. But, given the vast array of vehicles that they can choose from, consumers might not even miss one of the Big Three companies, should it disappear ... The ultimate irony of Detroit's demise is that it has been defeated by companies that did the job Detroit once did with unquestioned expertise: turn out vehicles that consumers wanted to buy and vehicles that captured their imaginations ... The great tragedy of Detroit's decade-long demise is that it is self-inflicted ..."[36]

NOTES

1. A closed-roof passenger car with four doors and a trunk for carrying cargo, or a similar two-door car with at least 33 cubic feet of rear interior space.
2. Stylish and modern cars priced above $50,000.
3. The International Union, United Automobile, Aerospace and Agricultural Implement Workers of America (UAW), one of the largest and most diverse unions in North America, has approximately 710,000 active members and over 500,000 retired members in the US, Canada and Puerto Rico.
4. Maynard Micheline, "The End of Detroit", Currency/Doubleday, 2003, page 8
5. www.aaca.org
6. Centre of the United States automobile industry; located in south-eastern Michigan on the Detroit River across from Windsor. Also used as an acronym for Detroit's auto industry collectively.
7. www.aaca.org
8. Ibid.
9. A war fought between a coalition led by the United States, to free Kuwait from Iraqi invasion in 1990–1991.
10. Large jeep-like vehicles weighing over 4300 lbs (1950 kgs).
11. "The End of Detroit", op.cit., page 17
12. The day in 2001 when Arab suicide bombers hijacked United States airliners and used them as bombs for attacking various targets and which resulted in the destruction of the World Trade Center in New York.
13. "Storm clouds over Detroit", www.economist.com, November 14th 2002
14. "Twenty years down the road", www.economist.com, September 12th 2002
15. "Storm clouds over Detroit", op.cit.
16. Muller Joann, et al., "Autos: A New Industry", http://www.businessweek.com/magazine/content/02_28/b3791001.htm, July 15th 2002
17. www.aaca.org

18. A small box-shaped passenger van which usually has removable seats and used as a family car.

19. "The End of Detroit", op.cit., page 18

20. Bremner Brian and Dawson Chester, "Can anything stop Toyota?", http://businessweek.com/magazine/content/03_46/b3858001_mz001.htm, November 17th 2003

21. Kerwin Kathleen, "When flawless isn't enough for car buyers", http://www.businessweek.com/magazine/content/03_49/b3861091.htm?chan=search, December 8th 2003

22. A whistling sound produced when a vehicle moves at high speeds.

23. "When flawless isn't enough for car buyers", op.cit.

24. "The End of Detroit", op.cit. page 17

25. "Autos: A new industry", op.cit.

26. Ibid.

27. "The End of Detroit", op.cit., page 29

28. Kerwin Kathleen, et al., "Commentary: Can Motown get out of this funk?", http://www.businessweek.com/magazine/content/03_25/b3838034.htm?chan=search, June 23rd 2003

29. The production of items only as demanded for use, or to replace those taken for use.

30. A quality management program and a way of managing the business, with an eye for continuous improvement of products and processes.

31. "Commentary: Can Motown get out of this funk?", op.cit.

32. "The End of Detroit", op.cit., page 14

33. "Extinction of the car giants", http://www.economist.com/opinion/displayStory.cfm?story_id=1842437

34. "Autos: A new industry", op.cit.

35. Ibid.

36. "The End of Detroit", op.cit., pages 8–25

SECTION III

READINGS

RACE AND POLITICS

INTRODUCTION

D etroit's tumultuous legacy of racial conflict warrants an entire section of the book. This section begins with **Sidney Fine's** exhaustive account of the events surrounding the 1967 Rebellion, followed by an essay by **Jeffrey Horner** that offers an overview of conditions for blacks leading up to the events of July 1967, and the importance of community resources in averting civil uprisings. Next, two essays by **Joe T. Darden and Richard Thomas** (from their 2013 book) cover the poor relations between blacks and the majority-white police force in the Civil Rights era, and the rise of black power in the post–Civil Rights era.

1

"They Have Lost All Control in Detroit": July 24, 1967

SIDNEY FINE

In terms of criminal offenses reported to the Detroit Police Department, the hours between midnight and 5:00 A.M. on July 24 were the most violent of the entire Detroit riot.[1] It was during these hours that Governor George Romney first contacted Washington about the possible use of federal troops. For the remainder of the day the Detroit police, the National Guard, and the State Police sought in vain to quell the escalating disturbance while, behind the scenes, Romney engaged in labyrinthine negotiations with the Johnson administration that led, eventually, to the dispatch of army paratroopers to Detroit and their deployment on the streets of the city.

The temperature soared to 90° in Detroit on July 24, and it was an uncomfortably humid, breezeless day. The police log for the five hours after midnight carried reports of "rioting, looting, ... burning," and sniping over a wide area of the city both east and west of Woodward. The spread of the riot to the lower east side led the police and the Guard to decide at 1:55 A.M. to set up a second field command post at Southeastern High School, and five minutes later Cavanagh called for a curtailment of business activity downtown that day.[2]

The Police Department's central district inspector reportedly said at 12:30 A.M. that the police were using firearms only to protect their lives and the lives of fire fighters but not to halt looting and firebombing. When Romney and Cavanagh were asked at a 3:00 A.M. press conference if police would fire at looters, Cavanagh hesitated to reply, but Romney responded, "fleeing felons are subject to being shot at." The orders to the Guard at that point were "to shoot to kill if fired upon, and to shoot any person seen looting," but Guardsmen needed permission from General Moore to fire fully automatic weapons. Later in the morning Cavanagh expressed a reluctance "to lay down [a] hard and fast rule" regarding use of firearms, saying that police officers had to use their "professional judgment" in this critical matter. Perhaps it was this that led to "the word that went through the Department," according to a reporter covering the riot, "that it was all right [for the police] to open fire." By evening the police, the Guard, and the State Police were all firing at fleeing looters.[3]

When Inspector James A. Cole arrived at noon to take charge of the Southeastern High command post, he received orders to stop the riot and enforce the law by whatever means necessary. He was not, however, briefed on any specific tactics to follow. He decided to deploy his men four to a car, four cars to a patrol unit, and to use the Guard to protect strategic points. His task was complicated by the fact that the telephones, riot guns, ammunition, helmets, and scout cars available to him were all in short supply, a problem that increasingly affected the riot control efforts of the department as a whole. Because of the shortage of weapons, the department requested police officers to use their own rifles and shotguns.[4]

At 9:28 A.M. the Seventh Precinct station came under sniper fire, and at 12:10 P.M. the police reported the situation as being "out of control" in that precinct and in the Fifth Precinct as well. Looting during the morning was described in police reports as "almost citywide." At 4:17 P.M. air intelligence reported twenty-three fires burning west of Woodward and six east of Woodward. There were rumors that rioters would make well-to-do blacks a target that night, and the Police Department advised the FBI that employers in the predominantly white northwestern part of the city were arming their employees to protect against looting. In the final two or three hours of the day sniping, whose incidence was exaggerated throughout the riot, appeared to be the major riot problem, as the police, Guardsmen, and state troopers were all reportedly pinned down by sniper fire; and two precinct stations, the Southeastern High command post, and at least three fire stations also came under attack. Tanks and armored personnel carriers rumbled through the streets to rescue law enforcement personnel reportedly immobilized by sniper fire. "It looks like Berlin in 1945," the mayor stated. By midnight, according to Hubert Locke, veteran police officers were "convinced that they were engaged in the worst urban guerrilla warfare witnessed in the United States in the twentieth century."[5]

July 24 was a day of confusion for law enforcement personnel. A rookie policeman recalled that the police were "piling in cars and patrolling up and down and up and down and hours of confusion—trained policemen—a bunch of them just doing whatever they wanted to…. We stopped lots of cars full of loot. Sometimes we took it away. Other times we arrested people. There was no reasonable approach to anything." Another police officer sent to Twelfth Street recalled that "the whole place was unbelievable. Rioters and looters, what looked like thousands, were running all over the place like they were crazy…. There was smoke and fire everywhere— burned out buildings in all directions." When a Romney aide visited police headquarters, he found "confusion throughout the building. The entire administrative apparatus of the Detroit Police Department and the city," he reported, "was in shambles."[6]

The confusion reached its height during the waning hours of July 24. A police source informed the FBI that the police and the Guard were firing at one another due to the darkness and "state of general confusion." Jimmy Breslin reported that one Guardsman was firing up a dumbwaiter shaft while a fellow Guardsman fired down the shaft. A trooper on Linwood fired his weapon at the same time as police officers in the vicinity were screaming for everyone to stop shooting. A law enforcement officer hollered that he had spotted a sniper or snipers on a roof, but a police car radio called on everyone to hold fire since the alleged snipers were State Police troopers. When an automobile came around the corner, Breslin reported, the police aimed their shotguns at it, and a black male staggered from the vehicle claiming he had been shot in the leg. He pulled down his pants to prove the point, and, despite a police order not to move, he started walking around the car, saying "Shoot me!" "The city is an asylum," Breslin concluded.[7]

The Detroit riot on July 24, like other major riots, began to take on the character of a "tandem riot." In this second phase of the riot, "control agents" responded to disorderly behavior in the streets by resorting to "official violence" against the rioters. Reinforced by the Guard and humiliated and frustrated by their "enforced passivity" and the successful challenge to their authority the previous day, the police sought to reestablish their "dominance and control" and "to teach the bastards a lesson." "The worm has turned," the executive director of Wayne County Suburban Legal Services heard a policeman say that night to a black lad riding a new bicycle. In Detroit, as in Watts and Newark, what had begun, to some degree, as a riot of blacks against police became, in some degree, "a riot of police against blacks," illustrating the point that "civil disorder is an emergent process very much dependent on the nature of the interaction between control agents and disturbance participants."[8]

The behavior of the police beginning on July 24 and their excessive use of physical force were the product of more than their desire for revenge. Working twelve-hour shifts, with scant rest between tours of duty, the police were fatigued—two police officers entered a looted furniture store at one point, rested on a sofa there, and then started chasing looters again. The police, furthermore, were "thrown off balance" by the sheer magnitude of the disorder, and they were apprehensive about the personal danger to which they were being exposed. "You're damn right I was scared," one policeman replied when asked in a later interview if he had been frightened during the riot.[9]

The "norms of [police] professionalism" were weakened, if not altogether eroded, by "the fear and rage building in those early riot hours," with the result that the racial attitudes of white police officers were increasingly expressed in behavior that would have been more restrained under normal conditions. He had not realized before, a *Detroit Free Press* reporter who covered the riot remarked, that "there are large numbers of Policemen who do not like Negroes." He heard one police officer say of blacks during the riot, "They are savages." Another *Free Press* reporter heard a policeman assert, "Those black son-of-a bitches. I'm going to get me a couple of them before this is over."[10]

Given their view of blacks as a privileged minority, it is not surprising that a sizable majority of white officers below the rank of inspector, as a survey revealed, did not see the riot as a "protest against unjust conditions" or the product of "social conditions of inequality." Like the white working-class community from which they largely came and like white police officers in other cities, white patrolmen tended to view the riot as caused by "agitators" and "conspiratorial groups," desire to get "something for nothing," "undisciplined self-interest," "lack of respect for law and order," and "temper of the times." Beliefs of this sort probably help to explain police behavior in the riot's second phase.[11]

Looking back on the "bad excesses" of some policemen during the riot, Ray Girardin explained, "Everybody's got a breaking point.... They don't resign from the human race when they join the police department. And it's a lousy job and considering their background and their training, they can blow up too.... [T]he police aren't supposed to; there [sic] not allowed to, but it's understandable that sometimes they do." The riot was surely one of those times—a black policeman, noting the conditions under which the police had been operating, recalled, "I'm black and I wanted to hit on someone by Monday, so how did they [white police] feel by Thursday?"[12]

When asked in the sample survey of 286 police officers after the riot why some police officers had treated "suspects" roughly during the riot, 53 percent of the white inspectors, 44 percent of the whites of other ranks, and 42 percent of the black officers attributed it to "stress, strain; police tense, overwrought." Only 2 percent of the white inspectors and 3 percent of other white officers were willing to admit to "personal prejudice" as the motivating factor, but 19 percent of the black police thought this the cause.[13]

The arrival of the National Guard in Detroit was followed by an escalation of the violence. The Guard's behavior, so much criticized both during and after the riot, resulted from the nature of the organization and its personnel, the lack of significant training for Guardsmen in riot-control tactics, fatigue and fear, and the manner in which the Guard was deployed. The Guardsmen were mainly high school graduates in their middle twenties who held primarily white collar or skilled jobs. A substantial majority had joined the Guard to avoid the draft. Like the National Guard elsewhere in the nation, only about 1 percent of whom were black, the Michigan Guard was essentially lily white—of the more than eight thousand Guard soldiers who served in Detroit, only forty-two were black. Judging by a postriot survey of the Second Battalion of the 182d Artillery, a Detroit unit, white Guardsmen had the same view of blacks as Detroit's white police did. When one of them was asked if the riot had changed his view of blacks, he replied, "Yes, I no longer consider Negroes civilized." Undersecretary of the Army David McGiffert concluded that the experience of the Michigan Guard in the riot confirmed that the National Guard could not "conduct civil disturbance operations in urban Negro communities without creating the impression" that it was a "discriminatory organization."[14]

"They are gutsy guys," a member of Cavanagh's staff said of the Guard during the riot, "but they have no more training for this kind of situation than a good group of Boy Scouts." The United States Army determined the basic riot training program for the Army National Guard, but it did not, as of July 1967, specify the number of hours the Guard had to devote to such training. Of the 280 hours required by the Guard training program, Michigan devoted only 6 hours to riot-control training, which was less than most states required. It appears, moreover, that officers were more likely than other ranks to receive even this minimal training. The riot training, furthermore, was largely devoted to crowd control, which was not particularly relevant to the kind of situation the Guard faced in Detroit.

Among the 405 members of the Second Battalion of the 182d Artillery who served on Twelfth Street, only 11 percent believed themselves well trained, and 31 percent claimed to have received no training at all. Governor Romney stated on July 28 that only 180 of the more than 8,000 Guardsmen then serving in Detroit had received any significant amount of training. The responsibility for this was primarily that of the army, which had been "remarkably indifferent" to the readiness of the Guard to cope with civil disorders and had been slow to react to training requirements that should have been "obvious" after the Watts riot.[15]

The Guardsmen were lacking in discipline and military appearance. When reporter William Serrin visited the Guard at its Grayling training camp just before the riot, he found that a large number of the soldiers were "sloppy in uniform and bearing" and that many were "just plain fat." In Detroit, army commanders, the police, and reporters all were troubled by Guardsmen's disregard for their weapons and their lax discipline. Guardsmen on duty were apt to sit on the sidewalk or lean against store fronts, and saluting by them was "almost nonexistent."[16]

When the Guardsmen arrived in Detroit, many of them were wearing "badly soiled" uniforms, and many needed haircuts and shaves. This was not, however, their fault. The men from Grayling had been in the field for four days and nights before leaving for Detroit, and they had not received advance notice of their new assignment. Some of them had clothes in the laundry, others had not had time to pack their belongings. They were immediately committed upon arrival in Detroit and did not have an opportunity to improve their appearance, to which the army attached so much importance.[17]

The Michigan Guardsmen were not only poorly trained; they were also, in the main, poorly led. Too many Guard officers, in the army's view, were "substandard." In Detroit, Guard commanders at the outset rarely went out into the field to circulate among their men, "staff coordination was poor[,] and staff follow-up almost nonexistent." Some officers did not know where their men were or what they were doing. Only 38 percent of the men in the Second Battalion of the 182d Artillery thought that their officers knew what was going on all the time, and 18 percent believed that their officers never knew what was happening.[18]

The equipment of the Guard left a good deal to be desired. The Guard was particularly short of radio equipment, which often required Guardsmen to position themselves near police officers so as to take advantage of the police communications system. Guardsmen occasionally had to use pay telephones to communicate! Although the Guard had sufficient weapons for each soldier, most were of World War II vintage. The Guard had the capacity to use chemical agents, but most of its training had been with "dispensers" that were effective against crowds rather than the small groups the Guard usually encountered in Detroit. The Guard, finally, did not have enough maps of the same scale for all of its commands.

The quality of the intelligence available to it handicapped the Guard during the early stages of its operation in Detroit. The collection of intelligence by the Guard was slow, and reports were often incomplete and inaccurate. Information gathered by individual Guardsmen and patrols was not reported back to headquarters in many instances, sometimes because of the shortage of radios. The Guard also lacked detailed information on the city of Detroit and the area of the city in which it was operating. Finding it difficult to assess the meaning of patrol reports, Guard headquarters relied on a "situation overlay" showing the degree of hostile action in each area that was updated every two hours during the night and every six hours during the day.[19]

In seeking to carry out their assignments in Detroit, Guardsmen, particularly at the outset of their service, suffered from both fatigue and fear. After having been on the road for most of the night, the large number of Guardsmen arriving on July 24 were almost immediately sent out into the streets, and many went for thirty hours without sleep. Since they were committed piecemeal, it was initially difficult for the Guard command to establish normal shifts of relief and rest, with the result that some Guardsmen received minimal relief from their duties during the first two or three days in Detroit. When separated from their police escorts, some Guardsmen got "lost" and could not be located for a time. A *Detroit News* reporter recalled that while he was hiding under a burned-out truck early one morning, Guardsmen pulled up in an armored personnel carrier, and one of them said, "We're lost! Can you tell us where we are? We're from Grand Rapids."

It is not surprising, furthermore, that most Guardsmen, unfamiliar with Detroit, lacking a "feel of the community," and thrust into the city in piecemeal fashion in the midst of a riot, were "scared shitless," to quote Girardin. "Take these kids out of a small town up in the sticks of Michigan," Girardin told the Kerner Commission, "and bring them into a city, straight to a congested area with all the tension and excitement going on, they did not know how to act." They became jittery and "itchy," started "seeing things," and began firing their weapons at no visible target and without regard for the safety of bystanders.[20]

The principal charge levied against Guardsmen was that they were "trigger happy." "Left in isolated locations with little or no instructions," away from their commissioned and noncommissioned officers, fatigued and frightened, and new to combat, Guardsmen fired their weapons all too frequently and without any real cause. The Department of the Army reported that the 46th Division had fired 155,576 rounds of ammunition by the morning of July 29. Although the figure is suspect, there is no doubt that Guardsmen fired their weapons at a rate that alarmed police and reporters alike. A *Free Press* reporter heard one Guardsman say to another, "I'm going to say halt and then bang, bang, bang." The second Guardsman replied, "No, that's not the way to do it. You say bang, bang, bang, halt."

Arriving in Detroit on July 23, one Guardsman remarked, "I'm gonna shoot anything that moves and that is black." A Guardsman would fire at an alleged sniper or at streetlights to protect against sniping, and other Guardsmen, hearing the shots, would nervously begin firing at "nothing in particular" in response. Sometimes Guardsmen ended up shooting at one another. One night a soldier at a Guard staging point accidentally fired his weapon, and seventy-five other Guardsmen began firing at nearby buildings to defend themselves, one of many examples of "nervous people firing answering shots for the accidental shots." Armored personnel carriers of the Guard moved through the streets spraying bullets at buildings suspected of harboring snipers—the Guard, according to an army general who served in Detroit during the riot, fired ten thousand rounds into a single building. Reporters joked that "the only thing that saved ... [them] was that the Guard couldn't hit anything." According to the deputy commander of the Army Task Force in Detroit, eight Guardsmen injured themselves or their buddies by aim less firing.[21]

At 4:20 A.M. on July 24 General Noble Moore authorized the Guard to make "straight line patrols on major thoroughfares without [an] accompanying Detroit Police officer." The 46th Division then began assigning some of its men to jeep patrols consisting of two jeeps with four men in each. Other Guardsmen were assigned to "on-call task forces" made up of fifteen soldiers and two police officers that responded to looting and other reports. Still other Guardsmen, 450 of them eventually, were assigned to protect fire fighters, two to three soldiers serving with each piece of equipment responding to a fire. The Guard used tanks and armored personnel carriers in combating alleged snipers. By 7:15 P.M. the Guard was supposedly "committed to independent action" and was no longer available for police use, but the facts appear very much otherwise, no doubt because of Guard communication problems.[22]

The 1,761 riot-oriented mobile radio messages after 11:00 A.M. on July 24 compared with 903 such messages during the same hours on July 23; and the criminal offenses reported to the Police Department increased from 777 on the riot's first day to 1,289 on the second. As in most large-scale riots, the second day of rioting exceeded the first day in its severity.[23]

Looting, reported by 9:40 A.M. to be "almost citywide," continued to be the major form of riot activity on July 24. A *Free Press* reporter viewed the looting as not just a consequence of the riot but as "the chief reason for prolonging it. It was just too sweet, too simple and too stupid not to join in," Barbara Stanton remarked. She noted that thousands of rioters were "grabbing and running in a sometimes senseless, sometimes calculated snatch at the good things of life." "They were having a hell of a time on Twelfth Street" on Monday morning, another reporter noted. The crowd, he observed, was running through the streets "picking and choosing, their faces glistening with sweat and whiskey and sometimes pure joy." "I want my size," one looter said to another in a shoe store. "Who cares what your size is," the second looter responded. "Take everything in the whole mother place." The police arrested many looters, but they could not stem the thievery. "You pick 15 up, and there's 20 more," one officer said.[24]

On July 24 Detroit faced what its fire chief called "probably the worst fire emergency ever faced by an American city in modern times." There were 617 alarms in the riot areas that day compared to the 209 alarms on July 23. Fires were "breaking out all over" on the west side and, increasingly, on the east side, as entire city blocks were damaged by fire. Fires that would normally have been fought by 150 men were now being attended by only 10 or 12 fire fighters. Chief Quinlan thought that the arsonists were employing "a divide-and-conquer-strategy. They set a fire in one area," he declared, "and when the firemen get there the guys who started them are several blocks away starting another." Some calls to the department, Quinlan believed, were "merely traps to lure the Fire Fighters into ambush to be sniped at." Arriving at a fire, firemen were sometimes pelted with rocks, bottles, and cement block and, perhaps, subjected to sniping.

Until they received Guard protection, firemen sometimes attempted to defend themselves by using the lids of garbage cans as shields.

By late Monday the nine hundred to one thousand firemen on duty, many having worked for twenty-four straight hours, were approaching exhaustion, and five of them had collapsed from heart attacks or fatigue. Thirty-five fire departments were by that time aiding the Detroit department. In a successful effort to gain control of the situation, the Detroit department decided to establish three command posts on the perimeters of the riot sectors, which enabled fire officials to assign their crews in shifts, one shift resting while the other responded to fire calls.[25]

The racial feelings that white firemen, like white policemen, might have suppressed in normal times were occasionally given expression in the strained conditions of the riot. While Guardsmen frisked two blacks on July 25, firemen observing the action shouted, "Kill the black bastards! Control those coons. Shoot 'em in the nuts!"[26]

The police made 2,931 riot-related arrests on July 24, far above the number on any other day of the disturbance.[27] Seventeen riot-related deaths resulted from the events of the day, again the largest number on any one day of the riot. Police officers shot and killed seven black looters or alleged looters, one of whom was also a suspected arsonist. Two additional black looters were killed as the result of simultaneous firing by policemen and Guardsmen. One death resulting from police action appears to have been entirely accidental—the police officer involved, who had had only five hours of sleep the night before, slipped while chasing a looter, and the officer's weapon discharged with fatal result. The officer fainted when he learned what had happened.

Quite apart from their possible role in two of the deaths already noted, Guardsmen were responsible for two additional deaths on July 24. One was a white male who was incorrectly alleged to have been a sniper and who had not received a command to halt. The other, John Leroy, was a black passenger in a car that allegedly ran a road block. It is more likely that the car stopped on command, that an unknown person then fired, and that this led to aimless firing by Guardsmen that wounded the four passengers in the car, including Leroy, who died on July 28 following abdominal surgery.[28]

Two persons, a black male and a white fireman, were accidentally killed by high tension wires on July 24.[29] White store owners shot two looters, one black and one white. Two other deaths, those of Herman Ector and Nathaniel Edmonds, led the prosecutor's office to seek war rants for murder. Ector, a thirty-year-old black male, was shot by a black private guard who was apparently displeased by something Ector had said about the guard's treatment of some looters he had seized. Although the police told the victim's brother that the unfortunate Ector had been looting, as the private guard claimed, he had done nothing of the sort. A Recorder's Court judge freed the guard following the preliminary examination. Ector's father went berserk after his son's "senseless death," locked his family in the house one day, and held the police at bay for seventeen hours.[30]

Edmonds, a twenty-three-year-old black, was shot on the porch of his aunt's home by Richard Shugar, a white who said Edmonds was a looter and who claimed self-defense. A witness at

Shugar's preliminary examination asserted that the assailant had said to Edmonds before firing, "I will paint my picture on you," and had then pulled the trigger, saying "Bam." The state brought Shugar to trial on a first-degree murder charge, a Wayne County assistant prosecutor telling the jury that the accused had gone "on a hunting expedition that ended in an execution." The all-white jury found Shugar guilty of second-degree murder.[31]

Detroit was itself a victim of the large-scale rioting of July 24, as much of the city outside the riot areas took on the character of "a ghost town." The downtown was deserted, stores, banks, and the Detroit Stock Exchange closing their doors in response to the mayor's request to curtail business that day. General Motors and Chrysler Corporation canceled their second and third shifts so that workers could observe the curfew, and there was high absenteeism during the first shift. Kroger closed all its Detroit stores, and A&P closed twenty stores in the riot areas. The public schools canceled their summer classes, and Wayne State University, the University of Detroit, Marygrove College, and Mercy College followed suit. No mail was delivered in Detroit on July 24, garbage collection was suspended, bus transportation was curtailed, and the Detroit Public Library and its branches, the Detroit Institute of Arts, and the zoo were closed. Two airlines canceled flights to Detroit, and the Detroit Tigers shifted their scheduled July 25 home game with Baltimore to that city.[32]

Detroit General Hospital, operating under a disaster plan rehearsed since World War II, looked like a military field hospital on July 24, with State Police and National Guardsmen stationed at every entrance. The number of doctors on duty rose from a normal fifty to seventy-five to two hundred. Seeking to concentrate on the numerous riot-related injuries, the hospital closed its clinics for the duration of the disturbance and moved ambulatory patients to Detroit Memorial Hospital next door.[33]

The escalation of the riot on July 24 "horrified" and "frightened" leaders of Detroit's black community. A meeting of clergymen and community leaders, most of them black, resulted in a "strong statement" condemning the riot and calling for a "strong police crackdown" but "with citizens observers present."[34] Seemingly "confused and surprised" by what was happening on the streets of Detroit, fifty Trade Union Leadership Council leaders issued a public statement that blamed the riot on a "relatively small number of hoodlums and hatemongers" whose actions were hurting "the total [black] community." Although Detroit blacks, the statement asserted, were "far from satisfied" with their conditions, they were well aware of the "substantial progress" that had been achieved. The grievances of blacks, the statement continued, were no excuse for the violence that threatened to "destroy years of effort to build a community" of which both blacks and whites could be "proud."[35]

Most of Detroit's black leaders, the police, and state and city officials concluded during the riot's second day that federal troops were needed to quell the disturbance. Since it was Romney's understanding by late on July 23 that all available law enforcement personnel had been committed to the riot and since there were "strong rumors" that the rioters were planning to invade the suburbs, the governor asked Girardin, Reuter, and Nichols to consider what additional manpower

Detroit needed. They concluded that three thousand federal troops were required. "To be on the safe side," Romney upped the figure to five thousand, Cavanagh and Davids concurring according to the governor.[36]

Cavanagh phoned Vice President Hubert Humphrey either just before midnight on July 23 or at 2:00 A.M. on July 24 to say that the situation was "getting out of hand" and to inquire about the possible deployment of federal soldiers in Detroit. A sympathetic Humphrey told Cavanagh, "If it can happen in your town, it can happen anywhere." While the mayor was speaking to the vice president, Romney entered the room. Unaware that Cavanagh was going to phone Humphrey, the governor was suspicious of the mayor's motives. Cavanagh gave Romney the phone, and he too expressed the need for federal troops. Either then or in a return call, Humphrey advised that a request for troops should be transmitted through Attorney General Ramsey Clark.[37]

Despite the recognized need for the army, there was a long delay of almost twenty-four hours before paratroopers actually appeared on the streets of Detroit. The delay was the result of a complex of factors: the uncertainty of Attorney General Clark regarding the legal requirements a state government had to meet before the president could aid it with troops; Romney's vacillation in seeking the troops; Lyndon B. Johnson's mistrust of Romney and the president's desire to make things as difficult for the governor as possible and, at the same time, to deflect any criticism from himself should the army have to be deployed in Detroit; and, finally, the coincidental war in Vietnam. If Clark had been more familiar with the history of previous federal interventions in local civil disorders, especially in Detroit in 1943, had there been a different cast of characters in the key positions in Lansing and Washington, and had there been no ongoing war in Vietnam, army paratroopers would probably have appeared on the streets of Detroit hours before they actually did, and at least some of the deaths and destruction resulting from the riot could have been averted.

There really was no excuse for responsible federal officials not to know what the law required regarding the use of federal troops in civil disorders, particularly in view of the memoranda President Roosevelt had ordered following Detroit's 1943 riot.[38] The Constitution authorized the federal government, on "application" of the legislature or governor of a state, to protect the state against "domestic violence." The applicable federal legislation, dating from 1792, used the word "request" rather than "application" and the phrase "insurrection in any State against its government" rather than "domestic violence." The statute, however, had been invoked in situations that could hardly have been called insurrections. On nineteen occasions before July 1967, the last time in Detroit's 1943 riot, the president had responded affirmatively in whole or in part to state government or District of Columbia requests for armed assistance. Some weeks before the 1967 Detroit riot the Office of Legal Counsel of the Department of Justice began assembling material on the use of federal military force in civil disturbances, but Clark's recollection is that he had not reviewed the matter "in detail." Also, during the Newark riot, which immediately preceded the Detroit riot, the Justice Department had given consideration to the use of federal troops.[39]

Romney phoned Clark at his home at 2:40 A.M. on July 24 to say that five thousand army soldiers "might" be required in Detroit if conditions did not improve. When Romney asked Clark if it was necessary for him to send a telegram asking for troops, the attorney general, who had been roused from his sleep, gave the governor to understand that an oral request for troops would be sufficient and that he was not to "worry about procedures." Romney seemed to believe and later claimed that he had asked for troops in this initial conversation with Clark, but he clearly had not. Although Clark later alleged that he had been referring only to the alerting of troops in telling Romney not to "worry about procedures," it does not appear that this is what he said to the governor. In any event, following his conversation with Romney, the attorney general called the president, who authorized the alerting of army units for possible dispatch to Detroit. Clark passed this word to Secretary of the Army Stanley Resor, who instructed Chief of Staff Harold K. Johnson to initiate the necessary planning. At 4:20 A.M. General Johnson issued "alert orders" to the 82nd Airborne at Fort Bragg, North Carolina, and the 101st Airborne at Fort Campbell, Kentucky. By 7:15 A.M. the headquarters of the XVIII Airborne Corps had developed plans to send one brigade from each division, about five thousand men in all, to Detroit.[40]

Believing, it would appear, that he had requested federal troops, Romney called a press conference following his conversation with the attorney general to announce what he had done. Although troops might not be needed, the governor asserted, the "prudent thing" under the circumstances was to ask for them. He said that he expected the troops to arrive that morning. Cavanagh also indicated at the press conference that Romney and he had made "a formal request" for troops.

In the midst of the press conference Romney was called to the phone by Clark, who now told the governor that he must submit a written request for troops and must state that there was an "insurrection" in Michigan that he could not suppress. This advice to Romney makes it evident that Clark had been referring to more than just the alerting of troops in their initial conversation. What is likely is that the attorney general, who had gone to the Department of Justice by that time, had either examined the applicable legislation or sought advice about required procedures for sending federal troops and consequently found it necessary to correct what he had originally told the governor. The attorney general, it should also be noted, used the word "insurrection" and not "domestic violence" in speaking to Romney this second time, although he later claimed otherwise. A city official told the press that Romney believed that Clark had broken his word to the governor. "I had the impression," Romney later said of the attorney general, that "he was making more of a political than a legal request everything considered."[41]

By the time Clark phoned Romney, General Johnson had contacted General Simmons and Inspector Arthur C. Sage of the Detroit Police Department, both of whom indicated that they did not believe federal troops were needed. Clark passed these views on to Romney when he called the governor away from his press conference. Returning to the press conference, Romney stated that he would confer with law enforcement officials and would reappraise the situation before making "a final and official request" for troops. Quite apart from the difficulty of predicting the course of the riot and hence the possible need for troops, Romney was undoubtedly reluctant to state categorically that he could not control the disorder, as Clark now insisted he must, lest this reflect adversely on his leadership as a state governor and presidential candidate. His legal advisor, also, informed him that if he declared that Detroit was in a state of insurrection, which it decidedly was not, this might cancel insurance policies in the riot areas.[42]

At 5:50 A.M. Resor asked Clark if he wanted the paratroopers alerted so as to be able to arrive at Selfridge Field, thirty miles from Detroit, by noon or two or three hours later. Clark replied that it was difficult to answer the question because he did not know what Romney would do and he did not want "to press" the governor. If Romney wanted the troops, Clark said, Washington "would hate to delay it very long." After Resor told him that the Associated Press had reported that Romney had withdrawn his request for troops, which overstated what Romney had said on the subject, Clark told the army secretary that he could "probably start letting down" with regard to alerting the paratroop brigades.[43]

When Romney spoke to Clark again, at 6:50 A.M., the governor reported that Simmons, whom Romney had accused of having "countermanded" the request for troops, was unable to provide assurance that the Guard could "control the whole situation." Clark's judgment was that Romney had "really worked him [Simmons] over" to get this response. Simmons, however, later said that he had not been that familiar with the situation in Detroit when he had spoken to General Johnson, which is almost certainly correct. Romney told Clark about the looting and arson in Detroit, said that the police were "picking up shortwave radio talk by a bunch of young hoodlums ... about keeping the fires going," and claimed that the damage by then was greater than it had been in Watts or any other riot. He asserted, however, that he could not state categorically either that he could control the situation or could not do so. If, however, he said, he waited until the riot was completely out of control, there would be "a much worse situation to deal with." Clark told the governor that he had a maximum of three hours to decide about federal troops if they were to arrive in Detroit before dark. He urged Romney to be "very cautious" about requesting troops because Washington had to think about trouble elsewhere in the nation also. "If we commit too much at one place too early," Clark said, "we just can't play that game."[44]

Following this third conversation with Clark, Romney and Cavanagh toured the riot areas while Romney staff members worked on drafts of a troop request. At 8:55 A.M. Romney read Clark over the phone a lengthy telegram in which the governor and Cavanagh "officially recommend[ed] the immediate deployment of federal troops into Michigan to assist state and local authorities in reestablishing law and order in ... Detroit." Romney indicated that no more than 5,800 to 6,000 men—4,000 Guardsmen, 350 to 500 State Police troopers, and 1,500 police—were available at any one time to enforce the law, that they had to "cover" a city of 139 square miles, and that many of them were overworked. He reported, however, that there was "no evidence" that Detroit was in a "state of insurrection."

Stating that Cavanagh and he believed five thousand army soldiers were needed, Romney asserted, as before, that the mayor and he were unable to "state unequivocally" that the situation could not "soon be contained," but, at the same time, they "most emphatically" could not say it would be contained "under existing circumstances." The governor correctly noted that experience had demonstrated that the second night of riots was "usually more violent" than the first and pointedly reminded Washington that the delay in sending troops to Detroit in 1943 had caused "a great deal of unnecessary bloodshed."[45]

Clark told Romney that a "recommendation" of troops was unacceptable, that he would have to "request" the soldiers in order to comply with the law. Furthermore, the attorney general pointed out, the governor had not stated that all the manpower available to the state had been fully committed nor had he categorically asserted that he could not control the disorder. Wanting to place the burden of the decision to commit troops on Washington, Romney, in asking for federal help, had substituted the word "recommend" for "request," which appeared in an earlier version of the telegram but had then been crossed out. He knew, moreover, that the Guard had not yet been fully committed to the streets of Detroit, and he remained reluctant to state that he was unable to enforce law and order in his state without the aid of the United States government.

Clark claimed a few days later that Romney had not actually asked for troops in the wire but had simply been "running some language" past the attorney general. This assertion strains credulity. Romney, for his part, complained to Cavanagh that Clark was being "unreasonable" and had switched the rules on him, presumably at the direction of the president. As to why the state had delayed its "recommendation" until 8:55 A.M., Romney lamely explained that only one slow typist had been available and had taken "an inordinately long time" to type the wire.[46]

After his conversation with Clark, Romney conferred with Simmons, Davids, Girardin, and Reuter, and all agreed on the need for federal troops. At 9:45 A.M. Romney read Clark a second telegram, addressed to the president, in which the governor and the mayor "officially request[ed] the immediate deployment of federal troops" in Michigan and stated that there was "reasonable doubt" that Cavanagh and he could "suppress the existing looting, arson and sniping" without federal aid. Wanting the troops "before nightfall," Romney stated that time "could be of the essence." Although Romney used neither the words "insurrection" nor "domestic violence," did not assert that the state had committed all its forces, and did not assert categorically that the state could not cope with the riot unaided, Clark, despite all he had earlier told the governor, now raised no objection. A few minutes later Romney sent the wire to the president, whom. Clark had already advised of its contents.[47]

It should hardly be a matter of surprise that Lyndon Johnson was keeping in close touch with developments in Detroit. The manner in which he was to respond to Romney's request for troops reflected his concern about race relations at that time of racial turbulence, the mounting criticism directed at him because of the war in Vietnam, and, not least of all, the fact that Romney was a leading contender for the 1968 Republican presidential nomination.[48]

Despite the official request for troops, the president was not immediately certain that he would comply, telling Clark that it was "60–40 for me [Johnson] to go." The president instructed Clark, in the meantime, to get the "best General possible," as well as "level-headed civilian people," for the assignment, to tell Resor "to go full speed ahead," and, if troops were to be dispatched, to use units with "as many Negroes as possible."[49]

Beginning at 10:40 A.M. Johnson met in the cabinet room with advisors and staff to decide how to respond to Romney's request. Those present were Secretary of Defense Robert McNamara; Clark; Roger Wilkins, the head of the Community Relations Service; Warren Christopher, confirmed that day as deputy attorney general; John Doar, head of the Civil Rights Division of the Justice Department; George Christian,

Tom Johnson, and Lawrence Levinson of the White House staff; and Justice Abe Fortas, the president's key advisor on the troops issue. As Wilkins recalled, Johnson was not "very charitable" in dealing with Romney's riot behavior. No doubt reflecting Clark's view that the state of affairs in Detroit was being "substantially exaggerated" by Romney, Johnson described the governor as being "a bit hysterical and substantially uninformed." Johnson assumed that Romney had been reluctant to state flatly that he could not control the situation because to have done so would have been tantamount to an "admission of failure."[50]

Johnson was exceedingly reluctant to send troops to Detroit. He was especially troubled about "the danger [of the] first picture of [a] fed'l soldier shooting [a] negro." He made it clear at the White House meeting that he did not "want hate [transferred] to LBJ and fed'l troops," which he suspected was Romney's motive in asking for the army. Johnson knew, however, that he had to respond in some fashion to the Romney request—concern, indeed, was expressed around the table about the president's delaying action while Detroit "burned." Shortly after 11:00 A.M., consequently, the president told McNamara "to prepare troops for movement," and the secretary of defense then instructed Resor "to load the troops on the aircraft." Their destination was to be Selfridge Field, and, as Johnson had stipulated, the troops were ordered to "hold there." Johnson, furthermore, wanted it understood that, if troops were deployed in Detroit, they were to "assist and support," not "supplant," local forces.[51]

As noted, Johnson was concerned about who would command the federal troops. He did not want a Douglas MacArthur type, a "hero," as the president put it, "riding ... on [a] white horse." He wanted someone, rather, who would exercise restraint, would have "a high degree of respect for human life," and "would instill great discipline in the troops," someone, in short, Johnson said, who would "know [the] party line." The army had already selected General John L. Throckmorton, commanding general of the XVIII Airborne Corps, and he fit the Johnson prescription. "A thoroughly professional, no-nonsense officer" who had served in World War II, Korea, and Vietnam and who had commanded the 82nd Airborne when it had been sent to Mississippi to protect James Meredith, Throckmorton was a person of "very good judgment" and one possessed of "courage and common sense."[52]

Mistrusting Romney, all Johnson was prepared to do in sending troops to Selfridge was to have them available should a "trusted" presidential emissary on the scene personally decide that they were needed in Detroit, regardless of what Romney said. The president had not displayed the same reluctance regarding troops in dealing with Democratic governors. Through Joseph Califano, the special assistant to the president, Johnson had offered Governor Edmund (Pat) Brown of California "all the assistance in the world" during the Watts riot; and without even waiting for a request for troops from Governor Richard Hughes of New Jersey, with whom Johnson enjoyed a "close relationship," the president had phoned, as Hughes recalled it, to ask the governor if he needed the army to quell a 1966 New Jersey disorder, and the White House, apparently, had also stood ready to provide whatever was needed to aid the state during the Newark riot. Quite apart from Johnson's misgivings about Romney, it probably did not help Michigan's cause in seeking troops that the president and Cavanagh, as already noted, had begun "to fall out somewhat" because of the mayor's opposition to the war in Vietnam and his criticism of federal spending for space exploration.[53]

The man Johnson selected to make the "on-the-spot assessment" before federal troops could actually be deployed in Detroit was Cyrus Vance, who had just resigned as deputy secretary of defense. McNamara suggested Vance for the assignment because he had dealt with racial incidents while in the Department of Defense and had also served as a troubleshooter for the president in the Dominican Republic. Clark initially opposed the choice because he thought the use of a special emissary might make it appear that the president was "trying to disassociate himself" from the trouble, because "the use of hotshots for special missions" reflected adversely on the incumbent bureaucracy, and because he feared that Vance, as a former Defense Department official, might be too inclined to recommend the use of force. Fortas, however, sided with McNamara, and the president, who had "great confidence" in Vance, endorsed the choice.[54]

When McNamara phoned Vance to ask if he would accept the Detroit assignment, he agreed to do so provided his wife could accompany him. Suffering from back trouble, Vance at the time needed assistance in putting on his socks and tying his shoes. When Vance arrived at the White House shortly after agreeing to go to Detroit, he was briefed on the riot and became aware, as he recalled, that "the political aspects" of the situation made matters "a little more difficult" than they might otherwise have been. He was informed that he was to go to Detroit as a special assistant to the secretary of defense to confer with Romney and Cavanagh and to make plans for providing them with troop support if needed. Johnson instructed Vance to take "a very hard look" at the situation before deciding if troops were needed.[55]

At the close of the discussion in the cabinet room, Johnson, in consultation with Clark and McNamara, prepared a telegram for Romney that Fortas then edited. Romney was told that since he had stated that there was "reasonable doubt" that he could "maintain law and order," the president was sending troops to Selfridge Field to be available for "immediate deployment if required" and that Vance had been directed to confer with him and "to make specific plans" for providing the state "with such support and assistance" as might be required. When Clark read the wire to Romney, the governor pronounced it "very helpful," according to the attorney general, but Romney was clearly unaware that the decision actually to deploy troops in Detroit was still open.[56]

The Vance party, which included Christopher, Doar, Wilkins, and Albert Fitt, the army's general counsel and a native Detroiter, left Washington just after noon on July 24. During the flight Vance asked members of the party, on arrival, to secure an estimate of the situation in Detroit from federal agencies in the city so that he would be able to make an informed judgment about the use of troops by early evening. The airlift of the two brigades from Fort Bragg and Fort Campbell began at about 2:00 P.M. Upon their arrival at Selfridge, Vance and Throckmorton decided to place the incoming troops on a thirty-minute alert so that they could be quickly moved into the city if needed. The two men then went to police headquarters to confer with Romney, Cavanagh, and law enforcement personnel, Throckmorton, as instructed, changing into civilian clothes for the trip.[57]

The Vance party found the scene at police headquarters "one of considerable confusion and frantic[,] exhausted men." Cavanagh and Romney seemed to Fitt to be near the "end of their physical tethers." What most "astonished" federal officials, was that although about 5,000 Guardsmen had been deployed on the streets, at least 1,900 Guardsmen were being held in reserve, and an additional 956 men were in rear detachments at Grayling or en route to Detroit. The Vance party concluded that the state had failed to take full responsibility for the riot and did not understand the importance of trying "to flood the riot-torn areas with as many law enforcement personnel as possible." "They seemed to feel," Clark recalled, "that somebody else had to take care of the situation." Vance and Throckmorton lost no time in telling Romney and Simmons to "Get them [Guardsmen] out on the streets right now." Romney's defense was that Girardin and he, while awaiting the arrival of the Vance party, had worked out plans for deploying the Guard reserve but had delayed putting the plan into effect because they expected federal authorities to federalize the Guard and then to coordinate its use with that of the army. Wilkins, however, thought that city and state officials "didn't know what to do" and "had no moves planned." "I had never seen as impotent a group of men in my life," he recalled.[58]

In briefing Vance, Cavanagh stressed the number of arrests, the number of fires in the city—"It's a great town if you're a fire buff," Christopher told Clark over the phone—and intelligence reports about likely attacks by rioters that night on the homes of middle-class blacks, who were allegedly arming themselves. When Romney urged immediate deployment of the troops, Vance, according to the governor, asked if he could say that Detroit was in a state of insurrection that he could not control. "They are still pressing me on this insurrection thing," Romney told his legal advisor. Explaining to Vance why insurance considerations prevented him from making the statement the presidential emissary appeared to desire, Romney, at the same time, said that he did not want "semantics" to prevent the entry of the federal paratroopers into the city.[59]

Since Vance insisted that he had to assess the situation and report to the president before he could decide on the use of the paratroopers, Romney and Cavanagh suggested that he tour the city. The touring party, which included Vance, Throckmorton, Doar, Romney, and Cavanagh, departed in a five-car convoy at about 5:15 P.M. and spent about two hours observing the three hardest hit riot areas. Although the party observed a good deal of damage during the tour, they saw no looting or sniping or any "undue amount of surliness," and the fires they witnessed appeared to be being brought under control. "The only incident during our tour," Vance stated, "was a flat tire." Seeking to explain what appeared to be a lull in the riot, Romney, as he recalled it, said to Vance, "Rioters gotta eat too." The Vance party came away from its tour with the distinct impression that the disorder was subsiding. This appeared to be confirmed for Vance and Throckmorton when they received a similar appraisal from federal agencies in Detroit, an appraisal, however, that was "fragmentary" and admittedly "left much to be desired."[60]

To assist Vance in judging the course of the riot, Colonel John Elder of the Vance party began to compile an incident summary based on data from a variety of sources but mainly from the police. This hastily put together document indicated a very sharp decline in incidents on July 24 as compared to July 23, especially during the late afternoon and early evening hours while Vance was trying to assess the need for federal troops. Elder's summary, for example, listed 183 incidents for the two hours of the Vance tour on July 24 as compared to 654 incidents during these same hours the day before. These figures, however, were altogether at variance with those provided in the more carefully compiled statistical report on the riot issued by the Police Department shortly after the disturbance. According to the police report, the 208 riot-related messages the police received during the two hours of the Vance tour, despite the seeming lull in the riot, compared with 132 such messages during the same hours on July 23, and the seventy-one criminal offenses reported to the police during the tour exceeded the sixty-three reported during the same two hours the day before. As a confidential FBI report indicated, the Police Department did not believe that the riot was subsiding during the time of the Vance tour.[61]

John Doar quickly came to realize that the Vance tour left a good deal to be desired as a basis for assessing the state of the riot. Doar thought that the Vance party should have flown over the riot areas or at least observed aerial photographs of the disturbance areas. Also, and more important, he concluded that the party should have visited the "lowest police command post" and questioned its commander. As it was, the Vance party passed within blocks of the Herman Keifer command post without visiting it. Vance later conceded that he probably should have spent more time with the police.[62]

Following the tour, Vance, whom Johnson had asked to call the White House with a status report every thirty minutes, informed the president that the situation appeared to be "under control," primarily because more men were patrolling the streets than on July 23.[63] After reporting to the president, Vance met with a group of black community leaders who wanted to express their views on the troops issue. Accounts of the meeting, which Damon Keith chaired, differ, but it seems certain that a majority of the black leaders—perhaps all but John Conyers and Julian Witherspoon, who feared the army presence would "inflame" the situation—favored immediate deployment of the paratroopers. Later in the evening Keith told the president's emissary that he would be personally to blame if any more deaths resulted from delay in sending in the federal troops.[64]

At a press conference following the community meeting, Vance continued to insist that the paratroopers were not needed in the city. Although he said that he did not want "to appear to be an ungrateful host" to the city's "distinguished guests," Cavanagh expressed disagreement with this judgment. Blundering and seemingly unaware of what he was saying, Romney declared that the situation had become "more hopeful" since the previous day because of the arrival of the paratroopers, the efforts of the police, the Guard, and the community as a whole, and the assistance fire departments from outside Detroit were providing the city. He indicated that it might even be possible to lift the emergency the next day. Inexplicably, Romney later maintained that these remarks "represented no modification" of his request for troops.[65]

Black community leaders were "furious" with Romney, and he was quickly made to realize that he had not expressed himself correctly at the press conference. A few minutes after the session, at about 8:30 P.M., he told Vance that he wanted the troops in the city before dark. At 9:30 he informed Vance and Throckmorton that conditions were worse than the night before. According to his own account, Romney told Vance that he realized that the fact that he, Romney, was requesting the troops was a factor in the federal government's reluctance to commit them. He wished it understood, however, that it was he who was running the "major risks" in making the request, and he wanted the troops committed whatever it might cost him politically. He told Vance, Romney stated, that he was not "going to continue being pushed around the way Clark had been pushing [him] around." The governor informed the press later that he could not say that Detroit was in a state of insurrection that he could not control, which implies that Vance was still pressing him on this point even though Clark had already accepted the governor's request for troops as meeting legal requirements.[66]

Although Vance was unpersuaded by Romney's pleas and allegedly thought that the governor was being "very cagey" about what he was willing to say, the sharply rising incident rate persuaded Vance and Throckmorton at 9:00 P.M. to move three battalions of paratroopers from Selfridge to the State Fairgrounds, close to the east side riot area. As the incident rate continued to mount and after further consultation with Throckmorton, Cavanagh, and Romney, Vance concluded at 11:00 P.M. that local law enforcement personnel could no longer contain the disorder. Reporting this to the president ten minutes later, Vance recommended, at long last, that the paratroopers be committed to the streets of Detroit.[67]

Johnson, who had been meeting in the White House from about 8:30 P.M. with members of the administration, Fortas, and J. Edgar Hoover, was following the reports coming in from Vance, the FBI, and the news media. "The atmosphere," the president recalled in his memoirs, "was heavy with tension and concern." Before the president announced a decision regarding use of the paratroopers, both Walter Reuther and the black Michigan Congressman Charles Diggs, Jr., called the White House to urge the commitment of the soldiers. At the request of Cavanagh, who claimed that Romney was still wavering with regard to troop use, Reuther telephoned Johnson to recommend deployment of the paratroopers. The president's response was that he could not do so "in good conscience" since Romney was still "vacillating." Reuther warned the president that the longer he waited, the worse the situation would be.[68]

According to a White House staffer, the Diggs call came after the president had decided to commit the troops but before he had made the decision known. Although critical of Romney, Diggs allegedly "raised hell on the phone for about ten minutes about the failure to bring in the troops" and said that "the blood was on the Administration's hands." Not trying "to be diplomatic about it," Diggs made it clear that he thought the delay in committing the troops had "some kind of political implication" since it was Romney who had requested the action. The White House thought that Diggs, who made his call public, was himself "playing politics in this to the hilt."[69]

At about the same time as Reuther phoned, Hoover told the president, "They have lost all control in Detroit. Harlem," the FBI director warned at the same time, "will break loose within thirty minutes. They plan to tear it to pieces." Harlem did not "break loose," but Vance, in effect, soon confirmed what Hoover had said about Detroit. Responding to Vance's recommendation that the paratroopers be committed, Johnson cautiously replied, "We will look at it and call you back shortly." When Throckmorton came on the phone once Johnson had decided to deploy the paratroopers, the president expressed concern about "the ground rules of engagement" and the reaction of the soldiers to sniper fire. "Well," Johnson said, "I guess it is just a matter of minutes before federal troops start shooting women and children." Tormented by repeated assertions that he was responsible for the killing of women and children in Vietnam, Johnson was troubled that his critics were "just waiting" to "charge that we cannot kill enough people in Vietnam, so we go out and shoot civilians in Detroit." This led Throckmorton to respond, "Mr. President, we will only shoot under the most severe provocations."[70]

Cautious to the end, Johnson asked Vance if Romney had declared martial law, as the president, referring to back issues of the *New York Times* as his source, incorrectly believed Governor Harry Kelly had done during the 1943 Detroit riot. "This would show," the president declared, that Romney had "taken all the steps which he can take." Before the troops were deployed, Johnson also wanted Vance to consider calling a press conference to plead for law and order, which Vance did just before midnight, and to set up loud speakers in the riot areas to "appeal to the people ... to cease and desist and obey the law," which Vance could hardly have done. Johnson also wanted Vance to inform Detroit's blacks that the paratroopers being deployed in the city were the very same soldiers who had defended black schoolchildren in Little Rock (101st Airborne) and James Meredith in Mississippi (82nd Airborne).[71]

At 11:20 P.M. President Johnson signed a proclamation ordering all persons engaged in "acts of violence" in Detroit to "cease and desist therefrom and to disperse and retire peaceably forthwith." He also issued an executive order authorizing the secretary of defense to use the armed forces of the United States to disperse the rioters and to federalize Michigan's Army National Guard and Air National Guard for the same purpose. Concerned about the long delay in responding to Romney, the White House sought to make it appear that the president had decided to commit the troops almost one hour before he actually did.[72]

Throckmorton sent reconnaissance patrols into the riot areas at about 11:30 P.M., but the main body of paratroopers did not move into the streets of Detroit until 2:30 A.M. on July 25. This was more than ten hours after the troops had begun arriving at Selfridge and seventeen and one-half hours after Romney had first recommended the action. The looting and burning had escalated in the meantime, and the death toll had mounted. Throckmorton, however, characterized the "timing" for the deployment as "just about perfect," and Vance saw no reason to second-guess his own action.[73]

Just before midnight on July 24, President Johnson, flanked by McNamara, Clark, and Hoover, addressed the nation on television. Declaring that "pillage and looting and arson have nothing to do with civil rights," Johnson asserted that the federal government would not "tolerate lawlessness" or "endure violence." With characteristic Johnson overkill, the president stated a mere six times during his seven-minute speech that he had committed federal troops because Romney could not control the situation. As Cavanagh noted, Johnson "whacked the hell out of Romney."[74]

In his memoirs, presidential aide Harry McPherson, who had prepared a draft of the speech that Johnson did not use, stated that the speech had been written by "a Washington lawyer." Actually, the speech had been written or, at least, rewritten by Justice Fortas, although he denied even having approved the speech in testifying before a Senate committee that was considering confirmation of his appointment to be chief justice of the United States Supreme Court.[75]

Cavanagh and Romney watched the president's speech together. When the address was over, a "visibly shaken" Romney, Cavanagh recalled, "walked around in circles, just mad as hell." "That isn't fair," Romney said to an aide. "Here I've been working all day and he lays it onto me like that." As Cavanagh was aware, Johnson "saw a chance to prod a pretender for the presidency ... and he did it." According to the mayor, Vance was later startled by Romney's bitter reaction to Johnson, Cavanagh claiming that when Vance mentioned the president to the governor on one occasion, he "just got livid and almost went for Vance's throat."[76]

Although both McPherson and Califano thought the Johnson speech "excessive," they had remained silent when they saw the draft of the address. McPherson thought that this was because they were intimidated by the stature and brains of Fortas. The *Detroit News* remarked that the speech was Johnson "at his worst," and the *Free Press* was critical of the "petty, irrelevant political overtones" of the address. Denying any political motivation, the White House insisted that sensitivity about the requirements of the law and a concern about setting a precedent for federal intervention explained the president's stress on the inability of local authorities to maintain law and order.[77]

Concerned about the negative reaction to Johnson's "tough" speech, Fortas advised the president on July 26 that it would now be appropriate for him to play a different role and to speak to the nation as "a teacher and moral leader, appealing for public order." Fortas suggested an address in which the president would call for "a day of reflection" on the racial crisis and urge the churches to devote themselves to prayer about the subject. Johnson delivered the suggested speech the next day.[78]

In another effort to respond to the criticism both of the president's delay in committing federal troops to Detroit and the political "overkill" of his TV address, the White House fed information to the press that placed the blame for what had happened on Romney's vacillation. A White House-inspired story that appeared in the *New York Times* on July 30 argued that the president had moved "as swiftly as possible but also as prudently as necessary." The *Times* account made the White House seem more responsive to the state's request for troops than it actually had been, ignored the different signals Romney had received from Clark, misrepresented what had transpired at the meeting of black community leaders following the Vance tour of the riot areas, and moved up the time both of Vance's recommendation that the paratroopers be deployed and Johnson's signing of the emergency proclamation. An "obviously angry" Romney struck back in a press conference the next day. Ignoring his own changes in position, Romney incorrectly asserted that, from his first phone call to Clark, he had "never ceased hounding" the attorney general and then Vance for federal troops; and he charged that "the President of the United States played politics in a period of tragedy and riot." If the paratroopers had entered the city at 6:00 or 7:00 P.M. on July 24, the governor stated, "it would have made a difference."[79]

The White House decided to have Ramsey Clark reply to Romney in a press conference on August 1, with Fortas preparing an opening statement to be used by the attorney general. Clark, "a shy person" who had not met with the press since becoming attorney general, was willing to talk to reporters on this occasion because, he recalled, he was troubled by Romney's "effort to have his fiction agreed upon." Denying that the president had asked him to hold the conference, Clark presented an account of his initial phone conversation with Romney that differed from the governor's version, recalled no dispute with Romney about the word "insurrection," and claimed, contrary to the record of his phone calls, that he had used both the words "insurrection" and "domestic violence" when he discussed the troops issue with Romney just after 5:00 A.M. on July 24. He insisted that Romney's "recommend" telegram was not intended as a request for troops, which was not Romney's understanding of the matter.[80]

On the same day as Clark's press conference Charles Bartlett authored an article in the *Washington Star* about the Romney-Johnson controversy that supported the White House version of the matter. The article, which benefited from "a long backgrounder" provided by Vance, was regarded by the White House as "the best indictment of Romney's double-talking" about the troops issue.[81] Also on that same day the White House twice phoned the assistant director of the FBI to inquire if the Bureau could obtain a tape of a Romney statement on radio and TV on the morning of July 24 purportedly showing that the governor had changed his mind about the need for troops. Hoover, who viewed the request as "fraught with political dynamite," thought it foolish to attempt to secure the tape since he assumed that the press would become aware of the action and that this would cause Romney to "pop off again." Despite Hoover's concern, the

FBI did seek to secure the reported tape but was unable to do so. If Romney or the Detroit media learned of this failed effort, they made no public mention of it.[82]

Although newsmen were given to understand following the Clark press conference that the White House would have nothing more to say on the Johnson-Romney dispute, Johnson, who found it hard to let go of a subject, "surprised" the press by returning to the controversy during an August 3 press conference. It was the Constitution, the law, and tradition that explained his action, the president said. After Johnson left the room, Vance told the assembled reporters that "there was no politics involved" in the president's actions.[83]

Johnson may have been somewhat reassured about his conflict with Romney when he received advance notice on July 31 of a Gallup presidential preference poll that had the president running five percentage points ahead of the Michigan governor. A Sindlinger poll a week later, however, indicated that 64 percent of the respondents in the nation and 79 percent in Michigan thought the president had waited too long before sending troops to Detroit. In Michigan, 64 percent thought Johnson had played politics in dealing with the troops issue, but only 35 percent of the respondents in the nation held this view.[84]

The administration's continuing concern about Romney's criticism of White House behavior became evident as it awaited the governor's testimony before the Kerner Commission on September 12, 1967. In anticipation of what Romney might say, the White House prepared to release the Vance report on the riot since, as Califano told the president, it contained factual information that the governor had "vacillated and was looking for federal help to get bailed out." When Romney defended himself before the commission, claiming that it was Clark, not he, who had changed his mind about troops and denying, in effect, that any Guardsmen had been held in reserve, the administration, "with almost frantic suddenness," released the Vance report and also had Clark issue a statement to the press rebutting what Califano considered to be the Michigan governor's "grossly distorted account." In his memoirs, the only riot Lyndon Johnson discussed was the Detroit riot. The events of July 24–28, 1967, he wrote, "will forever remain etched in my memory."[85]

Although the charges and countercharges of Romney and the Johnson administration probably contributed more to public confusion than enlightenment, it is likely that Romney gained some advantage in the dispute as the "underdog" and that Johnson came off "second best."[86] Whatever the public reaction, the essential fact is that the misunderstandings, misperceptions, and conflicting ambitions of the public officials involved delayed the deployment of federal troops in Detroit until after the riot's worst day had come to a close.

NOTES

1. [DPD] *Statistical Report on the Disorder Occurring in the City of Detroit, July 1967*, p. 32.
2. Ibid., p. 51; *NYT*, July 25, 1967; Albert Callewaert and Arthur Yim, "The Detroit Police Department and the Detroit Civil Disorder," Dec. 1967, app. A, Box 407, JPC Papers; Robert Conot, *American Odyssey* (New York: William Morrow and Co., 1974), p. 536; Hubert G. Locke, *The Detroit Riot of 1967* (Detroit: Wayne State

University Press, 1969), p. 35; Detroit Incident, Col. Davids, GR Papers, Box 319; Sequence of Events, July 24, 1967, Box 345, ibid.

3. To Director from Detroit, July 24, 1967, 1:13 A.M., 9:48 P.M., FBI-FOIA; Robert C. Cassibry Memorandum for the Record, July 24, 1967, Box 4, Office Files of James Gaither, LBJ Library; For General [Harold K.] Johnson from [Lawrence] Levinson, July 24, 1967, Box 26, HU2/ST22, ibid.; Headquarters Command Post Activity Log, Box 4, Ray Girardin Papers, Burton Historical Collection, Detroit, Michigan; *DFP,* July 25, 1967; *DN,* July 24, 1967; James Trainor tape, July 24 [1967], Box 393, JPC Papers; Callewaert and Yim, "Police Department," app. A, Box 407, ibid.; Deposition of Gene Goltz and William Serrin, Jan. 8, 1968, Series 32, Box 2, NACCD Records.

4. Callewaert and Yim, "Police Department," app. A, Box 407, JPC Papers; To Director from Detroit, July 24, 1967, 1:37 P.M., FBI-FOIA; *DFP,* July 25, 1967; Capture and Record of Civil Disorder in Detroit, July 23–July 28, 1967, Box 345, GR Papers.

5. Callewaert and Yim, "Police Department," app. A, Box 407, JPC Papers; To Director from Detroit, July 24, 1967, 9:20 P.M., 11:34 P.M., FBI-FOIA; *DFP,* July 25, 1967; *DN,* July 25, 1967; *NYT,* July 25, 1967; Sequence of Events, July 24, 1967, Box 345, GR Papers; Locke, *Detroit Riot,* pp. 40–41. The higher Locke figures for the number of police and fire facilities under attack involved some duplication.

6. *DFP,* July 23, 1972; *DN,* July 22, 1977; Capture and Record, Box 345, GR Papers.

7. To Director from Detroit, July 24, 1967, 11:34 P.M., FBI-FOIA; FBI Confidential Report, July 25, 1967, Box 32, NACCD Records; *DN,* July 25, 1967.

8. David Paul Boesel, "The Ghetto Riots 1964–1968" (Ph.D. diss., Cornell University, 1972), pp. 141–42, 145–47; Louis Goldberg, "Ghetto Riots and Others," in David Boesel and Peter H. Rossi, eds., *Cities under Siege: An Anatomy of Ghetto Riots, 1964–1968* (New York: Basic Books, 1971), p. 137; Joe R. Feagin and Harlan Hahn, *Ghetto Revolts* (New York: Macmillan Co., 1973), pp. 178–79, 191–92; Elliot D. Luby, Summary, in "Violence in the Model City: A Social Psychological Study of the Detroit Riot of 1967" [1969], pp. 13–14, Box 378, JPC Papers; Robert A. Mendelsohn, "The Police Interpretation of the Detroit Riot of 1967" [1968], pp. 34, 72, Box 30, ORA Papers; Herman Wilson memorandum to Charles E. Nelson (interview with Charles Brown), n.d., Series 59, Box 2, NACCD Records; Gary T. Marx, "Civil Disorder and the Agents of Social Control," *Journal of Social Issues* 26 (Winter 1970): 31, 42, 49, 51–52; Marx, "Two Cheers for the Riot Commission Report," *Harvard Review* 4 (Second Quarter 1968): 5.

9. *NYT,* July 25, 1967; *DFP,* July 24, 1977; Stanley Webb to Roger Wilkins, n.d., and enclosed report, Detroit Riot File, Community Relations Service, Department of Justice, FOIA; Robert Shellow et al., "The Harvest of American Racism," Nov. 1967, pp. 13–14, Series 7, Box 1, NACCD Records; Mendelsohn, "Police Interpretation," pp. 73, 81, Box 30, ORA Papers; Marx, "Civil Disorder," p. 49; Interview with Arthur Howison, July 24, 1984, p. 28, transcript in MHC.

10. Mendelsohn, "Police Interpretation," pp. 71–78, Box 30, ORA Papers; Luby, "Police and Jail Treatment of Detroit Negro Riot Arrestees" [1968], Box 427, JPC Papers; Goltz and Serrin Deposition, Series 32, Box 2, NACCD Records; *Ann Arbor News,* July 29, 1967.

11. Mendelsohn, "Police Interpretation," pp. 9, 11, 13, 19–20, 62, 65–66, Box 30, ORA Papers; Peter H. Rossi et al., "Between White and Black: The Faces of American Institutions in the Ghetto," in *Supplemental Studies for the National Advisory Commission on Civil Disorders* (Washington: GPO, 1968), p. 111.

12. Maurice Kelman and Ed Batchelor interview with Ray Girardin, Oct. 29, 1971, pp. 414–15, transcript in my possession; Detroit Information: Grant Friley, n.d., Box 81, NACCD Records.

13. Mendelsohn, "Police Interpretation," p. 80, Box 30, ORA Papers.

14. Paul Lowinger and Frida Huige, "The National Guard in the 1967 Detroit Uprisings" [1969], pp. 7, 10–11, 13, University of Michigan Law School Library, Ann Arbor, Michigan; *NYT,* Aug. 11, 1967; *DFP,* July 23, Aug. 11, 1967; *DN,* Aug. 22, 1967; Van Gordon Sauter and Burleigh Hines, *Nightmare in Detroit* (Chicago: Henry Regnery Co., 1968), p. 229. See also Goltz and Serrin Deposition, Series 32, Box 2, NACCD Records; and Special Subcommittee of the House Committee on Armed Services to Inquire into the Capability of the National Guard to Cope with Civil Disturbances, *Hearings,* 90th Cong., 1st sess., 1967, p. 5870 (hereafter *Capability Hearings).*

15. *DFP,* July 28, 30, 31, 1967; Address by Ralph E. Haines, Sept. 19, 1967, (Paul J. Scheips) Civil Disturbance File, Task Force Detroit, Center of Military History, Washington, D.C.; NACCD, Transcript of Proceedings, Aug. 11, 1967, pp. 248–56, Series 1, Box 1, NACCD Records; *Capability Hearings,* p. 5968, app. 2, p. 6287; Permanent Subcommittee on Investigations of the Senate Committee on Government Operations, *Riots, Civil and Criminal Disorders, Hearings,* 90th Cong., 2d sess., 1968, pt. 7:1505; House Committee on Armed Services, Special Subcommittee to Inquire into the Capability of the National Guard …, *Report,* 90th Cong., 1st sess., no. 36, 1967, p. 5655; James Richard Gardner, "The Civil Disturbance Mission of the Department of the Army, 1963–1973 …" (Ph.D. diss., Princeton University, 1977), p. 86; James F. Cantwell to Stanley R. Resor, July 28, 1967, Box 77, Accession 71A3073, Records of the Office of the Secretary of the Army, RG 335, Adjutant General's Office, Alexandria, Virginia; Richard Davis to Commanding General, XVIII Airborne Corps, Aug. 7, 1967, in "After Action Report," Task Force Detroit, 24 July–2 August 1967, D-3, Box 1, Records of the Michigan Department of Military Affairs, Adjutant General Division, RG 78-125, State Archives, Lansing, Michigan; Sauter and Hines, *Nightmare,* pp. 59, 226; Lowinger and Huige, "National Guard," p. 8; Conot, *Odyssey,* p. 538.

16. *DFP,* July 23, 1967; Sauter and Hines, *Nightmare,* pp. 227, 228; *Capability Hearings,* pp. 5915, 5970, 6129–31.

17. *Capability Hearings,* pp. 5915, 5965, 5967, 5971–72, 6031, 6044; Winston Wessels Field Notes, July 30, 1967, Winston Wessels Papers (copy in my possession); Davis to Commanding General, Aug. 7, 1967, in "After Action Report," D-5, Box 1, RG 78-125.

18. Sauter and Hines, *Nightmare,* pp. 225, 228; *Capability Hearings,* pp. 5970, 6122–24; Lowinger and Huige, "National Guard," p. 9.

19. *Capability Hearings,* pp. 5969, 5917–18, 5920, 6051, 6077; *DN,* Aug. 19, 1967; Davis to Commanding General, Aug. 7, 1967, D-3, 4, 5, Box 1, RG 78-125; Sauter and Hines, *Nightmare,* p. 225; Lowinger and Huige, "National Guard," p. 9; John Alfred Berendt, "From the Wonderful Men Who Gave You Kent State," *Esquire* 75 (Apr. 1971): 46; [Doar] "Lessons Learned," Box 15, Warren Christopher Papers, LBJ Library.

20. *Report of the National Advisory Commission on Civil Disorders* (Washington: GPO, 1968), p. 54; *Capability Hearings,* pp. 6031, 6041; Official Transcript of Proceedings before the NACCD, Aug. 15, 1967, pp. 474, 550, Sept. 12, 1967, pp. 909, 927, Series 1, Box 2, NACCD Records; Tom Popp Memorandum for Wilson (interview with Cecil Simmons), n.d., Series 59, Box 2, ibid.; Howard M. Dryden, "National Guard Association of Michigan," n.d., Box 3, Records of Michigan Department of Military Affairs—Public Information, RG 77-45, State Archives; Conot, *Odyssey,* p. 538; Xavier Nicholas interview with Jon Lowell, 1982, pp. 13–14, transcript in Nicholas's possession; *Christian Science Monitor,* July 27, 1967, DRSB No. 1; Garry Wills, *The Second Civil*

War (New York: New American Library, 1968), p. 50; John Hersey, *The Algiers Motel Incident* (New York: Alfred A. Knopf, 1968), p. 159; Tracy L. Clark to Commanding General, July 31, 1967, Civil Disturbance File, Task Force Detroit; *Riots, Civil and Criminal Disorders,* pt. 7:1504–5; Roger Wilkins, *A Man's Life* (New York: Simon and Schuster, 1982), p. 198.

21. *DN,* Aug. 24, 1967; Dryden, "National Guard," Box 3, RG 77-45; DA to JCS, July 29, 1967, Civil Disturbance File, Task Force Detroit; *DFP,* July 30, 1967; *Newsweek* 70 (Aug. 7, 1967): 20; Wills, *Civil War,* p. 52; Goltz and Serrin Deposition, Series 32, Box 2, NACCD Records; Deposition of Saul Friedman, Jan. 19, 1968, ibid.; Official Transcript, Aug. 15, 1967, pp. 474, 552, Series 1, Box 2, ibid.; Lowell interview, p. 15; *Christian Science Monitor,* July 27, 1967, clipping in Box 345, GR Papers; *Time* 90 (Aug. 4, 1967): 16; Oral History Interview of Jerome P. Cavanagh, Mar. 22, 1971, p. 51, LBJ Library; Frank Angelo, "Riot Coverage," n.d., Box 12, Frank Angelo Papers, MHC; *Capability Hearings,* pp. 5877, 5970; Conot, *Odyssey,* pp. 538–39; Bob Clark, "Nightmare Journey," *Ebony* 22 (Oct. 1967): 124; To Director from Detroit, July 24, 1967, 12:55 A.M.–11:31 P.M., FBI-FOIA; Paul J. Scheips phone conversation with Alexander Bolling, Apr. 30, 1967, Civil Disturbance File, Task Force Detroit; Scheips phone conversation with Charles P. Stone, May 1, 1979, ibid. Cf. Scheips phone conversation with John Throckmorton, Aug. 27, 1979, ibid.

22. Headquarters Command Post Activity Log, July 24, 1967, Box 4, Girardin Papers; Sequence of Events, July 24, 1967, Box 345, GR Papers; Levinson for Johnson, July [24], 1967, Box 26, HU2/ST22; DA/Sit Rep 1/25/0600, Box 4, Accession 71A1, RG 335; Cassibry Memorandum, July 24, 1967, Box 44, Gaither Files; Callewaert and Yim, "Police Department," app. A, Box 407, JPC Papers; Charles J. Quinlan to Mayor's Development Team (MDT), Aug. 11, 1967, Box 533, ibid.; Davis to Commanding General, Aug. 7, 1967, in "After Action Report," D-5, Box 1, RG 78-125; *Capability Hearings,* p. 5960; *DN,* July 25, 1967; Official Transcript, Aug. 15, 1967, p. 536, Series 1, Box 2, NACCD Records.

23. [DPD] *Statistical Report,* pp. 22, 23, 32, 53; *DFP,* July 30, 1967.

24. Callewaert and Yim, "Police Department," app. A, Box 407, JPC Papers; *DN,* July 25, 1967; *DFP,* July 25, 1967; *NYT,* July 25, 1967; Sequence of Events, July 24, 1967, Box 345, GR Papers.

25. Official Transcript, Aug. 15, 1967, pp. 532–35, Series 1, Box 2, NACCD Records; *DN,* July 25, 1967; *DFP,* July 25, 1967; *Riots, Civil and Criminal Disorders,* pt. 5:1262–64; Sauter and Hines, *Nightmare,* p. 59; Daniel C. Myre to Frederick Davids, Aug. 7, 1967, SP 20-762-67, State Police Records, Department of State Police, Lansing, Michigan; Quinlan to MDT, Aug. 11, 1967, Box 533, JPC Papers; Joe Lapointe, "Six Days in July," *Detroit Monthly,* July 1987, p. 65; Detroit Fire Department, Civil Disturbance, July 1967, A Partial Report, Feb. 1968, Box 5, Girardin Papers.

26. Clark, "Nightmare Journey," p. 24.

27. [DPD] *Statistical Report,* p. 13.

28. Sauter and Hines, *Nightmare,* pp. 47–52, 73–94, 104–12, 182–84; Albert Schwaller to Chief of Detectives, Oct. 26, 1967, Exhibit No. 67, Case No. 55-15-X, Records of the United States Senate, RG 46, NARA; Chronological Index, Civil Disorder, July 1967, Box 79, NACCD Records; Homicide File No. 7187, Aug. 3, 1967, ibid.; *DFP,* Aug. 25, 1967, July 24, 1977; John Doar Memorandum for Attorney General, Sept. 28, 1967, Box 29, Ramsey Clark Papers, LBJ Library. There are discrepancies in the various accounts of riot-related deaths.

29. Sauter and Hines, *Nightmare,* pp. 35–40, 52–58, 65–73; Schwaller to Chief of Detectives, Oct. 26, 1967, Case No. 55-15-X, RG 46.

30. Norton Cohen to William Cahalan, Aug. 14, 1967, Box 12, American Civil Liberties Union-Metropolitan Detroit Branch Papers (July 23, 1971), ALHUA; Bernard Dobranski Memorandum to Wilson (interview with William Cahalan), Oct. 12, 1967, Series 59, Box 2, NACCD Records; Homicide File No. 7153, Aug. 3, 1967, Box 79, ibid.

31. Sauter and Hines, *Nightmare,* pp. 94–98; Homicide File No. 7170, July 31, 1967, Box 79, NACCD Records; People of Michigan vs. Richard Paul Shugar, A139609, Preliminary Examination, Aug. 29, 1967, Detroit Recorder's Court, Detroit, Michigan; *DN,* Jan. 29, 1969.

32. *DFP,* July 25, 1967; *DN,* July 25, 1967.

33. *DFP,* July 25, 1967.

34. Ibid.; *DN,* July 25, 1967; Webb to Wilkins, n.d., and enclosed report, Detroit Riot File, Community Relations Service, FOIA; Charles S. Brown to _____, n.d., Series 45, Box 15, NACCD Records.

35. *DN,* July 25, 1967; text of statement [July 24, 1967], Box 393, JPC Papers.

36. "Detroit Riot—July 23, 1967," Box 232, GR Papers; Transcript of [Romney] Press Conference, July 31, 1967, Box 319, ibid.; Official Transcript, Sept. 12, 1967, pp. 914–15, Series 1, Box 2, NACCD Records.

37. Detroit Disturbance, Chronology of Significant Events, July 24, 1967, Box 319, GR Papers; Transcript of Press Conference, July 31, 1967, ibid.; Cavanagh interview, p. 46; Interview of George Romney, July 24, 1984, pp. 1–2, 12, transcript in MHC; Sauter and Hines, *Nightmare,* p. 35; Memo for the Record from the Vice President, July 24, 1967, Box 15, Christopher Papers; Ramsey Clark Statement, Sept. 12, 1967, Box 11, Office Files of Joseph Califano, ibid.

38. See chap. 1.

39. "Riot Control and the Use of Federal Troops," *Harvard Law Review* 81 (Jan. 1982): 638–46; Robert Griffin, "The Role of the President in Civil Disorder," Aug. 4, 1967, Box 232, GR Papers; Attorney General to Romney, Aug. 5, 1967, Box 346, ibid.; *Capability Hearings,* p. 5813; Statement of Martin F. Richman, Aug. 15, 1967, Office of Legal Counsel, Department of Justice, FOIA; Richman to Sol Lindenbaum [Aug. 8, 1967], ibid.; Oral History Interview of Warren Christopher, Oct. 31, 1968, pp. 1–2, LBJ Library; Interview with Ramsey Clark, Mar. 4, 1984, p. 1, transcript in MHC.

40. Telephone Calls of Attorney General, July 24 [1967], Box 58, Califano Files; The Detroit Riots Chronology, Box 43, Gaither Files, ibid.; Press Conference of Ramsey Clark, Aug. 1, 1967, Box 44, ibid.; Oral History Interview of Ramsey Clark, Apr. 16, 1969, pp. 7–8, ibid.; Clark interview (1984), pp. 5–6; Disturbance Chronology, July 24, 1967, Box 319, GR Papers; Transcript of Press Conference, July 31, 1967, ibid.; Trainor tape, July 24 [1967], Box 393, JPC Papers; *DN,* Aug. 4, 1967; "After Action Report," p. 2, Box 1, RG 78-125.

41. Disturbance Chronology, July 24, 1967, Box 319, GR Papers; transcript of Romney-Cavanagh press conference, July 24, 1967, ibid.; Transcript of Press Conference, July 31, 1967, ibid.; Trainor tape, July 24 [1967], Box 393, JPC Papers; Attorney General Calls, July 24 [1967], Box 58, Califano Files; *DFP,* July 30, 1967; *DN,* Aug. 4, 1967; Clark interview (1984), p. 6; Cavanagh interview, p. 46.

42. Resor-Clark telephone transcripts, July 24, 1967, Box 58, Califano Files; Attorney General Calls, July 24 [1967], ibid.; Information Brief No. 1, Army Operations Center, July 24, 1967 (0930), Box 44, Gaither Files; Clark Press Conference, Aug. 1, 1967, ibid.; Trainor tape, July 24 [1967], Box 393, JPC Papers; transcript of press conference, July 24, 1967, Box 346, GR Papers; Transcript of Press Conference, July 31, 1967, Box 319, ibid.; Robert Danhof Log, July 24, 1967, ibid.; *NYT,* July 30, 1967; *DFP,* July 30, 1967.

43. Resor-Clark transcripts, July 24, 1967, Box 58, Califano Files; Attorney General Calls, July 24 [1967], ibid.; Trainor tape, July 24 [1967], Box 393, JPC Papers; Sequence of Events, July 24, 1967, Box 345, GR Papers.

44. Attorney General Calls, July 24 [1967], Box 58, Califano Files; Resor-Clark transcripts, ibid.; *Capability Hearings,* p. 6076; Official Transcript, Sept. 12, 1967, pp. 918–19, Series 1, Box 2, NACCD Records; Transcript of Press Conference, July 31, 1967, Box 319, GR Papers.

45. Danhof Log, July 24, 1967, Box 319, GR Papers; Transcript of Press Conference, July 31, 1967, ibid.; Romney to Clark, July 24, 1967, with Remarks …, Sept. 12, 1967, ibid.

46. Attorney General Calls, July 24 [1967], Box 58, Califano Files; Clark Press Conference, Aug. 1, 1967, Box 44, Gaither Files; draft of telegram [July 24, 1967], Box 232, GR Papers; Transcript of Press Conference, July 31, 1967, Box 319, ibid.; Sauter and Hines, *Nightmare,* p. 60; Conot, *Odyssey,* p. 537.

47. Disturbance Chronology, July 24, 1967, Box 319, GR Papers; Romney to Johnson, July 24, 1967, with Remarks …, Sept. 12, 1967, ibid.; Transcript of Press Conference, July 31, 1967, ibid.; Trainor tape, July 24 [1967], Box 393, JPC Papers; Detroit Riots Chronology, Box 43, Gaither Files; Attorney General Calls, July 24 [1967], Box 58, Califano Files.

48. See the polling data in White House Name File—Romney, Box 256, LBJ Library.

49. Attorney General Calls, July 24 [1967], Box 58, Califano Files.

50. Detroit Riots Chronology, Box 43, Gaither Files; handwritten notes [July 24, 1967], Box 44, ibid.; Clark Memorandum for President, July 24, 1967, Box 71, Appointment File [Diary Backup], LBJ Library; Wilkins, *Man's Life,* p. 195.

51. Handwritten notes [July 24, 1967], Box 44, Gaither Files; Detroit Riots Chronology, Box 43, ibid.; George Christian Memorandum for President, July 24, 1967, Box 71, Appointment File [Diary Backup], LBJ Library; Lyndon Baines Johnson Diary, July 24, 1967, microfilm copy in University of Michigan Library, Ann Arbor, Michigan; Wilkins, *Man's Life,* pp. 195–96; *Washington Post,* July 30, 1967; [Brooke E. Kleber] Chronology, Detroit Civil Disturbance, July 23–Aug. 2, 1967, Civil Disturbance File, Task Force Detroit.

52. Handwritten notes [July 24, 1967], Box 44, Gaither Files; [Kleber] Chronology, Civil Disturbance File, Task Force Detroit; Christopher interview, p. 10; *DFP,* July 26, 1967; *NYT,* July 26, 1967; Sauter and Hines, *Nightmare,* p. 86; Interview with Cyrus Vance, Mar. 14, 1985, p. 4, transcript in MHC.

53. Lyndon Baines Johnson, *The Vantage Point: Perspectives on the Presidency, 1963–1969* (New York: Holt, Rinehart and Winston, 1971), p. 169; Oral History Interview of Edmund Gerald (Pat) Brown, Feb. 20, 1969, Aug. 19, 1970, p. 18, LBJ Library; Oral History Interview of Governor and Mrs. Richard Hughes, Aug. 6, 1969, p. 83, ibid.; Oral History Interview of Harry McPherson, Apr. 9, 1969, p. 19, ibid.; Paul J. Scheips and M. Warner Stark, "Use of Troops in Civil Disturbances since World War II," Supplement II (1967), p. 78. Johnson had also offered help to Acting Mayor Paul Screvane in the 1964 Harlem riot. Fred C. Shapiro and James W. Sullivan, *Race Riots: New York 1964* (New York: Thomas Y. Crowell Co., 1964), p. 182.

54. Detroit Riots Chronology, Box 43, Gaither Files; Tom Johnson Memorandum for President, July 24, 1967, Box 71, Appointment File [Diary Backup]; Christian Memorandum for President, July 24, 1967, ibid.; LBJ Diary, July 24, 1967; Johnson, *Vantage Point,* p. 169; *DFP,* July 30, 1967; Oral History Interview of Albert Fitt, Oct. 25, 29, 1968, p. 24, LBJ Library; McPherson interview, p. 20; Clark interview (1984), pp. 13–15.

55. Oral History Interview of Cyrus Vance, Nov. 3, 1969, pp. 30–31, LBJ Library; "Final Report of Cyrus Vance … Concerning the Detroit Riots, July 23 through August 2, 1967," pp. 7–8, with ibid.; Vance interview (1985), pp. 1–4; Christopher interview, p. 10; Johnson Diary, July 24, 1967.

56. Johnson to Romney, July 24, 1967, Box 232, GR Papers; Detroit Riots Chronology, Box 43, Gaither Files; handwritten notes [July 24, 1967], Box 44, ibid.; Attorney General Calls, July 24 [1967], Box 58, Califano Files.

57. "Vance Report," pp. 8–9; Vance interview (1969), p. 33; Detroit Riots Chronology, Box 43, Gaither Files; Attorney General Calls, July 24 [1967], Box 58, Califano Files; Chronology of Events, July 24, 1200 Hours to July 25, 0900 Hours, Box 15, Christopher Papers; DA/SITREP/1/25 0600, Civil Disturbance File, Task Force Detroit.

58. Fitt interview, p. 25; July 24, 1967, card, Box 345, GR Papers; Transcript of Press Conference, July 31, 1967, Box 319, ibid.; Disturbance Chronology, July 24, 1967, ibid.; "Vance Report," pp. 10, 14; Vance interview (1969), pp. 33–34; Throckmorton, "After Action Report," p. 3, Box 1, RG 78-125; Johnson Memorandum for President, July 29, 1967, Box 72, Appointment File [Diary Backup]; Califano to President, Sept. 12, 1967, and enclosed Clark Statement, Box 11, Califano Files; Christopher interview, p. 12; Clark interview (1969), p. 13; Detroit Riots Chronology, Box 43, Gaither Files; Official Transcript, Aug. 15, 1967, pp. 555–56, Sept. 12, 1967, pp. 883–84, 925–26, Series 1, Box 2, NACCD Records; Department of the Army, Office of the Adjutant General, Operations Report, Lessons Learned Report 5–67, Civil Disorder Task Force Detroit, Sept. 28, 1967, p. 4, microfiche copy in my possession; Wilkins, Man's Life, p. 196. The estimates of the number of Guardsmen in reserve range from 1,900 to 3,000. Cf. "Vance Report," pp. 13–14, and Cassibry Memorandum for the Record, July 24, 1967 (21:30), Box 44, Gaither Files.

59. "Vance Report," pp. 9–10; Transcript of Press Conference, July 31, 1967, Box 319, GR Papers; Throckmorton, "After Action Report," p. 3, Box 1, RG 78-125; Chronology of Events, Box 15, Christopher Papers. Vance maintained that he used the words "insurrection or domestic violence." "Vance Report," p. 10.

60. "Vance Report," pp. 11–12; Throckmorton, "After Action Report," pp. 3, 4, Box 1, RG 78-125; Reconnaissance Survey Field Research Reports, Detroit, Michigan, 2:84, Series 10, Box 46, NACCD Records; Official Transcript, Sept. 12, 1967, p. 949, Series 1, Box 2, ibid.; Sequence of Events, July 24, 1967, Box 345, GR Papers; Transcript of Press Conference, July 31, 1967, Box 319, ibid.; Detroit Riots Chronology, Box 43, Gaither Files; Lessons Learned Report 5-67, p. 7; Sauter and Hines, Nightmare, p. 102; DN, May 18, 1967.

61. "Vance Report," p. 12, app. C; [DPD] Statistical Report, pp. 32, 53; John Nichols to Sidney Fine, Mar. 28, 1986; DFP, July 25, 1967; FBI Confidential Report, July 25, 1967, Box 32, NACCD Records.

62. [Doar] "Lessons Learned," n.d., Box 15, Christopher Papers; Vance interview (1985), p. 31.

63. J. Edgar Hoover to Clyde Tolson et al., July 25, 1967, FBI-FOIA; Detroit Riots Chronology, Box 43, Gaither Files.

64. "Vance Report," pp. 12–13; Vance et al., Press Conference transcript, July 29, 1967, Box 43, Gaither Files; Detroit Riots Chronology, ibid.; Locke, Detroit Riot, pp. 37–38; Disturbance Chronology, July 24, 1967, Box 319, GR Papers; Transcript of Press Conference, July 31, 1967, ibid.; Chronology of Events, Box 15, Christopher Papers; DFP, July 26, 1967; Sauter and Hines, Nightmare, pp. 103, 112–13; Vance to Keith, Aug. 4, 1967, Box 11, Records of the Michigan Civil Rights Commission, RG 74-90, State Archives.

65. "Vance Report," pp. 15–16; Disturbance Chronology, July 24, 1967, Box 319, GR Papers; Transcript of Press Conference, July 31, 1967, ibid.; Detroit Riots Chronology, Box 43, Gaither Files; DN, July 25, Aug. 4, 1967; Cavanagh interview, pp. 48–49.

66. Sauter and Hines, *Nightmare,* pp. 103–4; "Vance Report," p. 16; Trainor tape, July 25 [1967], Box 393, JPC Papers; Transcript of Press Conference, July 31, 1967, Box 319, GR Papers; Romney interview, pp. 20–21; Vance interview (1985), pp. 10–11.

67. "Vance Report," pp. 16–18; Vance interview (1969), pp. 35–37; Throckmorton, "After Action Report," p. 5, Box 1, RG 78-125; *NYT,* July 30, 1967. The number of incidents, according to the Police Incident Summary, rose from 108 between 7:00 and 8:00 P.M. to 147 between 8:00 and 9:00 P.M., 194 between 9:00 and 10:00 P.M., and 231 between 10:00 and 11:00 P.M. "Vance Report," app. C. The White House chronology placed Vance's call recommending deployment at "around 10:20 P.M." Detroit Riots Chronology, Box 43, Gaither Files.

68. Detroit Riots Chronology, Box 43, Gaither Files; Marvin [Watson] Memorandum for President, July 24, 1967, LG/D, LBJ Library; WPR [Reuther] Note, July 31, 1967, Box 369, Walter Reuther Papers, ALHUA; Johnson Memorandum for President, July 25, 1967, Box 71, Appointment File [Diary Backup]; Johnson Diary, July 24, 1967; Johnson, *Vantage Point,* p. 170.

69. Barefoot Sanders Memo for Watson, July 26, 1967, Box 26, HU2/ST22, LBJ Library; Oral History Interview of Clarence Diggs, Jr., Mar. 13, 1969, pp. 8–9, ibid.; *DN,* July 25, 1967.

70. Johnson Memorandum for President, July 25, 1967, Box 71, Appointment File [Diary Backup]; WPR Note, July 31, 1967, Box 369, Reuther Papers; Johnson, *Vantage Point,* p. 170; Hoover to Tolson et al., July 25, 1967, FBI-FOIA.

71. WPR Note, July 31, 1967, Box 369, Reuther Papers; Johnson Memorandum for President, July 25, 1967, Box 71, Appointment File [Diary Backup]; *NYT,* July 30, 1967; "Vance Report," p. 18; Detroit Riots Chronology, Box 43, Gaither Files; Johnson, *Vantage Point,* pp. 170–71.

72. Law and Order in the State of Michigan, July 24, 1967, Box 319, GR Papers; Executive Order, July 24, 1967, ibid.; "Vance Report," p. 18; Throckmorton, "After Action Report," p. 5, Box 1, RG 78-125; Johnson Memorandum for President, July 25, 1967, Box 71, Appointment File [Diary Backup]. The chronology the White House supplied the *NYT* had Vance making his recommendation at 10:30 P.M. and the president signing his proclamation at 10:31 P.M. *NYT,* July 30, 1967. See also Detroit Riots Chronology, Box 43, Gaither Files.

73. Detroit Riots Chronology, Box 43, Gaither Files; *Capability Hearings,* app. 2, pp. 6258, 6264.

74. Detroit Riots Chronology, Box 43, Gaither Files; Johnson Memorandum for President, July 25, 1967, Box 71, Appointment File [Diary Backup]; Johnson Diary, July 24, 1967; Cavanagh interview, p. 50. The text of the Johnson address is in *DN,* July 25, 1967.

75. Harry McPherson, *A Political Education* (Boston: Little, Brown and Co., 1972), p. 359; McPherson Memorandum for the President, July 24, 1967, Box 32, Office Files of Harry McPherson, LBJ Library; McPherson interview, p. 21; *NYT,* July 13, 1968; Senate Committee of the Judiciary, *Nomination of Abe Fortas and Homer Thornberry,* 90th Cong., 2d sess., 1968, pp. 104–5. President Johnson told the Kerner Commission that the speech had been written by "a man who has no political background and a man who thoroughly understands constitutional law." Johnson Memorandum for President, July 29, 1967, Box 72, Appointment File [Diary Backup].

76. Cavanagh interview, pp. 50–51; *DN,* July 25, 1967; *Newsweek* 70 (Aug. 7, 1967): 20; Cavanagh to Johnson, July 25, 1967, Box 232, GR Papers; Sauter and Hines, *Nightmare,* p. 118.

77. McPherson interview, pp. 21–22; McPherson, *Political Education,* p. 360; *DN,* July 26, 1967; *DFP,* July 27, 1967; *NYT,* July 25, 27, 30, 1967; Johnson Memorandum for President, July 29, 1967, Box 72, Appointment File [Diary Backup].

78. McPherson Memorandum for President, July 26, 1967, and LBJ note on same, Box 32, McPherson Files; Douglas Cater for President, July 27, 1967, Box 29, Ramsey Clark Papers, LBJ Library; *DFP,* July 28, 1967.

79. *NYT,* July 30, Aug. 11, 1967; transcript of news conference ..., July 25, 1967, Box 346, GR Papers; Romney's Report to the People, July 30, 1967, Box 319, ibid.; Transcript of Press Conference, July 31, 1967, ibid.; *Capability Hearings,* app. 2, pp. 6272–74.

80. Johnson Diary, July 31, Aug. 1, 1967; Califano for President, Aug. 2, 1967, and enclosed "Response to Romney," Box 26, HU2/ST22; Clark interview (1984), pp. 18–19; Clark Press Conference of Aug. 1, 1967, Box 44, Gaither Files; *DN,* Aug. 2, 1967; *DFP,* Aug. 2, 1967.

81. Release, Aug. 2, 1967, Box 26, HU2/ST22; Cater to Johnson, Aug. 2, 1967, ibid.

82. Hoover Memorandum to Tolson and William Sullivan, Aug. 2, 1967, Cartha D. DeLoach to Tolson, Aug. 3, 1967, FBI-FOIA.

83. *NYT,* Aug. 4, 1967.

84. Panzer Memorandum to President, July 31, 1967, Box 256, White House Name File—Romney; *DFP,* Aug. 8, 1967.

85. Levinson for President, Sept. 5, 1967, Box 256, White House Name File—Romney; Official Transcript, Sept. 12, 1967, pp. 883–85, 922, 925–26, 932–33, 949, Series 1, Box 2, NACCD Records; Califano for President, Sept. 11, 12, 1967, and enclosed Clark Statement, Box 11, Califano Files; *DFP,* Sept. 13, 1967; *NYT,* Sept. 13, 1967; Johnson, *Vantage Point,* pp. 107–8.

86. *DFP,* Aug. 5, 1967; *NYT,* Aug. 23, 1967; Cavanagh interview, p. 50. Cf. *NYT,* Aug. 6, 1967.

2

Benefit of the Redoubt

JEFFREY HORNER

INTRODUCTION

> *We just got tired of running, and we didn't want to have to run again.*
> *—Lillie Mae Wiley, Virginia Park Association*

On the evening of July 23, 1967, the greatest Detroit Tiger ever went two for three in a winning effort in the second game of a home doubleheader, and, after having learned of a major disturbance near his old west side neighborhood, left the stadium while still in uniform in a quixotic attempt to help restore order. William Wattison Horton, just six years earlier, was a baseball phenom at nearby Northwestern High School, and he credits family, friends, and coaches from the Virginia Park neighborhood for his professional career that began right out of Northwestern. Now his old neighborhood was in flames.

The Virginia Park neighborhood, on the near west side of the city, initially developed as a Jewish district in the 1920s. When Detroit's most populous black district, Paradise Valley, was designated as blighted and then razed under urban renewal and the Interstate Highway Act in the late 1950s, many evicted residents moved to the 12th Street commercial district of Virginia Park, where many of them held jobs with Jewish-owned businesses. According to Thomas Sugrue in *The Origins of the Urban Crisis*, pre-WWII black residents were concentrated in only four areas of the city, with about 75 percent living in the Paradise Valley and Black Bottom districts, just east of downtown. With the destruction of that neighborhood, and following a period of significant post-war demographic growth, Virginia Park became a majority-black district by the mid-1960s, in many respects serving as the new home for those displaced from Detroit's lower east side by urban renewal.

On either side of 12th Street were neat, middle class districts. Along 12th Street itself, however, crowded apartment houses created a density of more than 21,000 per square mile, almost double the city average.

The movement of people when the slums of Black Bottom had been cleared for urban renewal had changed 12th Street from an integrated community to an almost totally black one, in which only a number of merchants remained white. Only 18 percent of the residents were homeowners. Twenty-five percent of the housing was considered so substandard as to require clearance. Another 19 percent had major deficiencies.
—Report of the National Advisory Commission on Civil Disorders, 1968

But the path to Virginia Park was a cauldron of day-to-day trials, gross indignities, and threats to one's livelihood, in addition to employment and housing discrimination, much as it had been throughout modern history for African Americans. This essay will examine the quotidian circumstances, the systemic discriminations, and the imbalance of resources leading up to and causing the events in Detroit in July 1967. It will close with a critique of the solutions prescribed by the National Advisory Commission on Civil Disorders in its landmark report, also known as the Kerner Commission Report, released in 1968.

KERNER COMMISSION REPORT FINDINGS

The Kerner Commission, appointed by President Lyndon Johnson just days after order was restored in Detroit, sought to investigate the events, causes, outcomes, and commonalities of twenty-four major incidents in twenty-three cities in the United States throughout the 1960s. In their final report, commissioners found the following ranked causes of endemic civil insurrections in black urban communities throughout the United States:

First Level of Intensity
  1. Police practices
  2. Unemployment and underemployment
  3. Inadequate housing

Second Level of Intensity
  4. Inadequate education
  5. Poor recreation facilities and programs
  6. Ineffectiveness of the political structure and grievance mechanisms

Third Level of Intensity
  7. Disrespectful white attitudes
  8. Discriminatory administration of justice
  9. Inadequacy of federal programs
  10. Inadequacy of municipal services

11. Discriminatory consumer and credit practices
12. Inadequate welfare programs

Several full-length books have already done an excellent job of summarizing the events and causes of Detroit's 1967 Rebellion—including Sidney Fine's *Violence in the Model City* and Hubert Locke's *The Detroit Riot of 1967*. This section of *The Straight Detroit: America's Premier Legacy City* focuses primarily on the fundamental inequities listed in the Kerner Report's first and second levels of causes experienced by blacks in the time leading up to July 1967 in Detroit.

POLICE BRUTALITY AND DISPARATE TREATMENT OF BLACKS

According to the Kerner Report, the most immediate and direct societal inequity was disparate treatment of African Americans by local police forces. Given the city's intransigence toward better integrating its police forces commensurate with its racial populations, and its infamous history of poor race relations between black residents and white police, this finding was hardly surprising.

A thorough and penetrating history of this conflict is offered in Joe Darden and Richard Thomas's *Detroit: Race Riots, Racial Conflicts, and Efforts to Bridge the Racial Divide*. As they point out, its antecedents are directly related to enforcing segregation:

> In some ways, the white police force in the black ghettos functioned as the first line of white defense against the invading "black hordes" that, if not checked, would overwhelm surrounding white neighborhoods. White police brutality, therefore, often functioned, whether deliberately or not, as an effective method of racial social control. During this period, when the black population was rapidly increasing in Detroit and bursting through the seams of the ghettos to which black people were restricted, white police brutality could (and often did) maintain the racial status quo when all other efforts to check black movement failed or were weakening in the face of black protest. (p. 29)

In 1953, *The Michigan Chronicle*, a black-owned newspaper, described police brutality in the most recent ten years as "the symbol of everything that was wrong with Detroit." The same editorial included the commentary that NAACP officials "spent most of their time processing complaints against the police department."

Efforts to eliminate or minimize instances of racially charged police brutality were largely feckless and had been long so before the *Chronicle* editorial. Darden and Thomas write this:

> In late August [of 1939] the Committee to End Police Brutality, still under the leadership of the NAACP Detroit president, Dr. James J. McClendon, staged mass protest meetings on nine playgrounds throughout the city. Speakers discussed the objectives of the meetings and listed incidents of police brutality. People were encouraged to sign

petitions for the removal of the police commissioner from office. The next month the committee submitted a petition to the Detroit Common Council [now City Council] requesting that the Council investigate the policies and practices of the police department, an investigation that, the committee was convinced, would lead to the firing of the police commissioner. (p. 32)

Suffice it to say that the police commissioner kept his job, and reports of police brutality continued apace. Perhaps no statistic better exemplifies the police force's antipathy towards blacks than that

whites in the 1943 riot numbered in the thousands, while blacks numbered in the hundreds, the police killed seventeen blacks (some were shot in the back), but not one white. On Woodward Avenue, a major thoroughfare on the edge of the ghetto, white mobs beat blacks under the very eyes of the police. (p. 33)

The intractability of racial order at the end of a police baton was so ingrained in Detroit that Wayne County sheriff Roman Gribbs, running for mayor two years after the 1967 riot, won on a law-and-order campaign platform. Stepped-up policing practices—and the controversial Stop the Robberies, Enjoy Safe Streets (STRESS) program enacted by police commissioner John Nichols—were politically disastrous, and they contributed in part to Mayor Gribbs opting not to run for reelection in 1973. His successor, Coleman A. Young, pledged to disband STRESS and other racially selective policing practices, and to better integrate the police force. In a city where the population included over 660,000 blacks, he won overwhelmingly.

HISTORIC HOUSING AND EMPLOYMENT DISCRIMINATION IN DETROIT

Finding a suitable residence was an onerous challenge for those displaced by urban renewal, much as it had been throughout the city's history. While blacks had grown to over 40 percent of the city's population, they were still met with hostility in most city neighborhoods. Recent in the minds of many were the deadly 1943 race riots, ignited largely by black residents seeking housing in majority-white neighborhoods on the east side, and increasingly integrating factory floors. Tensions in neighborhoods and factory floors had roiled for years, prompting *Life* magazine to publish a marquee story entitled "Detroit Is Dynamite," ten months before the 1943 riots. Depicted housing conditions were so tenuous and deleterious that *Life*'s publisher limited the story's distribution to North America, presumably to suppress its possible use as anti-American propaganda by Axis powers. When the fuse reached its terminus, Belle Isle, its east side neighborhood, and downtown exploded into all-out war, with numerous outbreaks of hand-to-hand street fighting, murder, arson, vandalism, and property crimes resulting in thirty-four dead (most black), hundreds arrested, and significant property destruction.

Causes of the severe concentration of the vast majority of the city's black residents into a handful of districts included public- and private-sector race discrimination, as well as a severe shortage of new housing. As pointed out by Sugrue, fewer than 10 percent of the city's 545,000 housing units were available to blacks in 1947. In addition, a 1945 housing survey reported an unbelievable 99.2 percent occupancy rate for the city, brought on by a virtual freeze on new residential construction market caused by the war effort.

Even when smatterings of new housing units were being built as the Great Depression wound down, blacks were shut out from being allowed to purchase them. In 1941, a six-foot concrete wall was built adjacent to the historically black Eight Mile Wyoming neighborhood, a Federal Housing Administration–approved "compromise" negotiated between the government and a housing developer to approve loan guarantees to banks writing FHA-insured mortgages to white homeowners on the other side of the wall. Black housing seekers, already profoundly limited in finding safe and secure housing, were literally walled off from accessing new housing in an adjacent neighborhood.

In fact, geographic housing constraints for blacks were so severe that *Collier's* magazine foretold the problems eventually caused by urban renewal in the 1960s:

> Unsolved, the Negro housing dilemma costs Detroit heavily in other ways than jittery nerves. Badly in need of a medical center, express highways, parks and other deferred civic improvements, Detroit must wait indefinitely for them. The land they will occupy now houses hundreds of Negro families who can't be evicted because there's no place for them to go.
>
> —*Collier's*, November 23, 1946

Compounding public and private race discrimination that acutely limited housing choices, an overall housing shortage caused by WWII exacerbated an already dire situation for blacks seeking safe and secure housing.

It is difficult to fully disentangle the sources of racial animus aimed at blacks. But one major dimension arose on crowded factory floors during World War II. Historically, blacks fortunate enough to be hired for automotive factory work were given what Sugrue characterized as the "meanest and dirtiest jobs," although management were nimble at elevating black workers to higher positions when it suited their needs. As described by George Galster, in presentations of his book *Driving Detroit*, the Packard Motor Company, seeking to heighten racial tensions among its mostly white workers in order to sow dissent within the union local, integrated black workers with whites on shop floors, forcing a wildcat walkout by 25,000 white workers. According to Joe Darden, Richard Hill, June Thomas, and Richard Thomas, in their seminal work *Detroit: Race and Uneven Development*, one hate striker commented on the indignity of having to work alongside blacks: "I'd rather see Hitler and Hirohito win than have to work next to a nigger."

Indeed, workplace discrimination was commonplace in many northern states, which hadn't adopted the state-sanctioned discrimination laws allowed by *Plessy v. Ferguson*, known as Jim

Crow. Throughout the south, separate-but-equal was the law of the land, while in the north it was the practice of the land.

As discussed by Reynolds Farley in *Detroit Divided*, in 1940 the Ford Motor Company's 85,000-member local workforce was over 20 percent black, and, remarkably, more than half of all black men employed in the Metro area worked at Ford. While Detroit's role as the arsenal of democracy in WWII changed the employment calculus for blacks in factories, employment discrimination was rife in other sectors.

In nonindustrial employment sectors, blacks faced limited hiring opportunities, and if hired at all, they were given the least desirable jobs. According to Sugrue, blacks fared best in municipal positions, filling a number of positions roughly commensurate to the city population of 36 percent of city jobs in 1946. Many of these positions were as lower-paying janitors, groundskeepers, and sanitation workers. Other industries were less receptive to hiring blacks. Retail sales positions were all but closed to them except for backroom work, as retailers were fearful of their white customers having to interact with black clerks and salespeople.

Apprenticeship programs in trade unions were also all but closed to blacks. This dynamic was especially pernicious, given that most apprentices had a long and higher-paying skilled-trade career after training. The Detroit Urban League reported that as recently as 1966, there were just 41 black apprentices in all skilled-trade unions out of a total of 2,363 apprentices, a rate of 1.7 percent—an actual decline from over 2 percent ten years earlier.

SCHOOLS, RECREATION, AND POLITICS

While Detroit public schools had no official segregation policies, significant evidence suggests that the Detroit school board pursued unofficial policies aimed at promoting racial harmony through segregated schools. In the 1930s, the board transformed Sidney Miller Intermediate School, near the Black Bottom residential district, into a high school, for the intended outcome of deintegrating an adjacent high school. As found by Jeffrey Mirel in *The Rise and Fall of an Urban School System: Detroit, 1907–81*:

> From its inception, Miller fed into Eastern High School. During the depression, when high school enrollments soared, an increasing number of students from Miller went on to Eastern. By September 1933, Eastern, like most Detroit high schools, was severely overcrowded. Unlike the other schools, however, Eastern was also racially integrated. Apparently unwilling to maintain Eastern as an integrated high school, the board transformed Miller into a senior high and announced a liberal policy for students who wished to transfer to other schools. Since the Miller attendance area was almost completely black, the transfer policy allowed the few white students still in the area to leave the school. While the board justifies the creation of the new high school and the transfer policy as legitimate responses to overcrowding, both actions, in effect, created a segregated, black high school in Detroit. The importance of race in these decisions is

underscored by the fact that, despite the severe overcrowding of all the high schools in the city in the 1930s, no other intermediate schools were elevated to senior status and, with the exception of Western High School (which was rebuilt after a fire in 1936), no new schools were constructed during this period. In short, the creation of Miler High School was a clear case of deliberate school segregation. (p. 188)

Private youth and adult recreation options were arguably even more limited than school and employment opportunities, with most such options being limited to inferior experiences if offered at all. In the 1940s, The Bob-Lo Excursion Company, a private, "no colored allowed" transportation service that ferried Detroiters to a Canadian amusement park downriver, was forced by the US Supreme Court (*Bob-Lo Excursion Co. v Michigan*) to integrate their services. Before this decision was handed down, Bob-Lo Excursion ownership interests had relaxed their discriminatory practices to allow blacks and other undesirables to use their services on Mondays only, seemingly because another park with similar offerings open to blacks was doing burgeoning business. Nearby Sugar Island Park shut down for lack of business once Bob-Lo excursions became fully integrated. In the city of Oak Park on Detroit's northern border was the private Crystal Pool, which closed and was sold off to a developer when faced with having to integrate.

Black citizens seeking redress in City Hall were often met with indifference or buck-passing. The fundamental problem was that the nine-member Detroit Common Council was elected on an at-large basis, with each member representing the interests of the entire city. As such, residents of majority-black districts in the city had to compete with the majority-white citywide population for the political affections of Common Council members, whose only black member in 1967 was the Reverend Nicholas Hood Sr. Hood lived only a few blocks from 12th Street and, tellingly, received threats to his personal safety during the riot, causing him and his family to temporarily relocate to another part of the city. One can only speculate whether, if Councilman Hood's political duties were limited to a manageable district that included 12th Street and the Virginia Park neighborhood, he would have received such threats, and whether the riot would have occurred at all.

By and large, the arena of local politics for blacks was defined by private community groups and clergy. With the passage of Open Housing laws in the late 1940s, local community groups fighting neighborhood integration were at the forefront of local politics in the 1950s. Albert Cobo, elected mayor of Detroit in 1949, ran on an explicit platform of opposition to the "Negro invasion" that had been made possible by Open Housing and public housing siting. Not surprisingly, he swept the heavily defended white neighborhood subdivisions on the north side, but surprisingly he won the vote of UAW members, who were more fearful of having to integrate with blacks than they were of what a Republican mayor (and former city treasurer) might try to do to their paychecks. He was reelected in 1953.

During this time, angry black residents of the city began to back increasingly radical players in labor unions and local clergy. Coleman Young's reputation in labor union politics as a street fighter was galvanized in the 1950s, when he all but gave a middle finger to the House Un-American Activities Committee during the Red Scare, going so far as to correct a southern congressman's vernacular pronunciation of the word *negro*. He was elected to the Michigan state senate in 1964, serving there until he was elected mayor of Detroit in 1973.

Albert Cleage was a Presbyterian minister who split with the church in the 1950s in a dispute over how to best minister to the city's disenfranchised black congregants. He then founded the Central Congregational Church to better meet the needs of his followers; after the 1967 rebellion (his term), he renamed the church the Shrine of the Black Madonna.

THE IMPORTANCE OF AN INVESTED COMMUNITY OF STAKEHOLDERS

> Home, boy,
> Home, boy,
> Everybody needs a home.
> —"Home," James Osterberg

And so came an umpteenth indignity in the morning of July 23, 1967, when the police raided and arrested a peaceful gathering of friends and family celebrating the return of two Vietnam soldiers. The action escalated into the Detroit Rebellion of 1967.

A mostly academic discussion has centered on the riot or rebellion question of the conflagration. Sidney Fine cited the incidents as a *riot*, given that chaos, looting, and lawlessness prevailed for days. Hubert Locke described the incidents as a *rebellion*, caused more by police brutality, systemic employment and housing discrimination, and public and private social discrimination, and not by immediate racial antipathies. Ultimately, one's choice of terms is informed by their moral perspective, i.e., rioting is never justified, but rebelling is.

However, given these adverse historical legacies faced by blacks in Detroit, there is another supporting dimension to the *rebellion* descriptor. While arguments for the aptness of the term *race riots* are buttressed by a 95 percent white police force overseeing the residents of a city whose black population was fast approaching 50 percent, a thought experiment presents itself: Would the 12th Street incidents have occurred if the "blind pig" raid and arrests had been carried out by exclusively black police officers? A strong case can be made that even if the raiding police were black, if they had carried out their duties in the same manner as the white police had, a similar incident of international renown would have ensued.

This is because the United Community League for Civic Action, the informal name of the raided establishment, served as a focal point of the community. As such, it served much as bars and speakeasies did in turn-of-the-century urban democratic strongholds—where the bartender was often a ward heeler, if not an elected official, trading information, gossip, favors, and whatever else one frequents social clubs for. While police reports cited the League as an unlicensed, after-hours drinking establishment (in a city more than familiar with the model dating to Prohibition), it nonetheless functioned as an important node of cohesion for a group of people long under siege from severe housing, employment, and police discrimination.

Therefore, it was a particularly gross and exacerbating indignity, after years of open discrimination and prejudice, to have an important social dimension of the community raided and shut down, and its dozens of peaceful congregants handcuffed and taken away for booking. The sanctity of a regularly frequented place of social interaction in the local black community was now destroyed, and neither baseball star Willie Horton, Congressman John Conyers, nor civil rights leader Dr. Arthur Johnson was able to prevent the resulting tragedy.

None of this is meant to suggest that the incidents wouldn't have occurred if the raid on the League had not occurred. As stated by an eyewitness to the events on 12th Street:

> Black folks' discontent, unhappiness, anger, rage—what happened could've happened anywhere. It just so happened to have happened up here on the corner of Clairmount and Twelfth Street. In fact it had almost started a year before, in what was called the Kercheval incident, on the east side.
>
> —Ronald Hewitt, Detroit City Planner

Like the 12th Street uprising, the Kercheval incident occurred on a hot summer night, when rioting broke out after several days of police occupation and stepped-up patrols, in response to allegations of black militants' peace disturbances. Rioting, looting, and civil disorder erupted following a car being pulled over and its occupants arrested. Accounts vary as to how order was restored after only a few hours, with some witnesses suggesting that what effectively quashed the disorder was the active presence of well-known community clergy members, who used their leadership powers to convince cooler heads to prevail.

CONCLUSION—PLANS FORWARD

> As the riot alternately waxed and waned, one area of the ghetto remained insulated. On the northeast side the residents of some 150 square blocks inhabited by 21,000 persons had, in 1966, banded together in the Positive Neighborhood Action Committee (PNAC). With professional help from the Institute of Urban Dynamics, they had organized block clubs and made plans for the improvement of the neighborhood....
>
> When the riot broke out, the residents, through the block clubs, were able to organize quickly. Youngsters, agreeing to stay in the neighborhood, participated in detouring traffic. While many persons reportedly sympathized with the idea of a rebellion against the "system," only two small fires were set—one in an empty building.
>
> Report of the National Advisory Commission on Civil Disorders, 1968

It is striking that despite the Kerner Commission's observation of the effectiveness of the PNAC in quelling violence and vandalism, not one of the commission's dozens of recommendations for action included direct community-building. One is left to wonder whether, if the urban renewal projects of just a few years earlier had included as much community development resources as community destruction resources, the Detroit riot or other civil insurrections would have occurred at all.

Indeed, many Kerner Commission recommendations (which actually called for an expansion of urban renewal programs) advocated for yet more geographically diffuse policies for minority populations. While expansion of Open Housing laws was a laudable objective, given the persistent residential segregation, it did little in terms of strengthening existing majority-black neighborhoods that hadn't burned down, and it may have served to actually weaken them by expanding housing choices for blacks by encouraging the abandonment of established black districts.

Ultimately, preservation of primal human needs for safety, shelter, and sociability is what compelled Willie Horton to travel back in haste to 12th Street after the doubleheader. Would that government had taken heed—both earlier and later—similar to Mr. Horton's of the importance of community fabric and leadership.

3

Conflict Between the Black Community and the White Police

JOE T. DARDEN AND RICHARD THOMAS

COMMUNITY-POLICE RELATIONS DURING THE 1967 RIOT

As riots exploded in cities throughout the nation in the 1960s, former police commissioner Edwards—now a federal judge—could see the connection between the racist practices in police departments and the spreading urban disorders. Two years before the riot in Detroit and in the year of the Watts riot, Judge Edwards once again commented on the volatile nature of the relations between the black community and white police:

> It is clear that in 1965 no one will make excuses for any city's inability to foresee the possibility of racial trouble.... Although local police forces generally regard themselves as public servants with the responsibility of maintaining law and order, they tend to minimize this attitude when they are patrolling areas that are heavily populated with Negro citizens. There they tend to view each person on the streets as a potential criminal and enemy, and all too often that attitude is reciprocated. Indeed, hostility between the Negro communities in our large cities and the police departments is the major problem in law enforcement in this decade. It has been a major cause of all recent race riots. (National Advisory Commission on Civil Disorders, 1968: 85)

In July 1967 a police raid on a "blind pig" in the black ghetto triggered one of the worst riots in U.S. history. When it finally ended, forty-three people were dead, seventeen of whom were shot by police, and the number injured exceeded one thousand; 3,800 were arrested (Fine, 1989: 299). Close to 5,000 people were left homeless—most of them black (National Advisory Commission on Civil Disorders, 1968). The most shocking occurrence of the riots, which would damage black community-police relations for decades, however, was the execution-like slaying by police of three unarmed black men in the Algiers Motel. Police shot these men to death while they were lying or kneeling (Fine, 1989; Widick, 1972).

John Hersey's book *The Algiers Motel* (1968) captured the events that led up to the killings, including the horrendous beating and racist taunting of the victims before they met their deaths at the hands of white officers who could only be described as racist psychopaths. As Hersey wrote, "It is by now, on Monday, July 31, clear that the killings in the Algiers [motel] were not executions of snipers, looters, or arsonists caught red-handed in felonious crimes in the heat of a riot, but rather that they were murders embellished by racist abuse, indiscriminate vengeance, sexual jealousy, voyeurism, wanton blood-letting, and sadistic physical and mental tortures characterized by the tormentors as a game'" (Hersey, 1968: 245–46).

CONFRONTATIONS BETWEEN THE BLACK COMMUNITY AND POLICE:, 1968–1969

Informed social observers and community leaders had little hope that the early postriot period would witness a decrease in tension and confrontation between the predominantly white police department and the black community. Notwithstanding the resistance of some white police officials to increasing the number of blacks in the department, 180 blacks were hired in 1968, making up about 35 percent of the total number hired that year. This was more than the total number of blacks recruited from 1962 to 1967 (Fine, 1989).

The number of blacks hired dropped to 23 percent of the total hires in 1969. Absent any racial discrimination in the department, 239 black police officers in 1968 and 241 in 1969 would have been hired (Fine, 1989). Increased numbers of black police officers would have played a vital role in reducing confrontations between the police and the black community. A predominantly white police department not only lacked racial diversity, but by its very nature nurtured a culture of white racial exclusion. As one black leader explained, "'every confrontation'" between the police and blacks became 'a racial confrontation' because of the largely white complexion of the Police Department" (Fine, 1989: 412).

No wonder that in February 1968 warning signs were beginning to be raised in the still smoldering city. That month, both Mayor Cavanagh and the Michigan Civil Rights Commission were informed that the police and the black community were on a "'direct collision course' and that 'dramatic remedial action' of a kind no city had ever before undertaken was required" (Fine, 1989: 412). In April, Governor Romney received a similar warning from the Michigan State Advisory Committee to the United States Civil Rights Commission informing him that "'the greatest threat to racial peace' in the state was the manner in which law enforcement officers operated in and serviced the black community" (Fine, 1989: 412).

Police Aggression at Cobo Hall I and II and Veterans Memorial, 1968

It appeared that the above warnings went unheeded by Detroit police officials. During 1968, the police department was involved in several incidents directly related to the racial attitudes and actions of white police officers (Georgakas and Surkin, 1998). The first of several incidents occurred on May 3, 1968, several months before the first anniversary of the 1967 riot. The setting was the Poor People's Campaign led by Reverend Ralph Abernathy. According to Georgakas and Surkin, the following events unfolded: "A rally had been scheduled to be held at Cobo Hall, Detroit's Convention Center.... The demonstration, which was being telecast over a local channel, was peaceful and orderly until a car stalled. At that point, the police became extremely agitated and, almost without warning, mounted a cavalry charge upon the demonstrators. Nineteen people were seriously injured in action" (1998: 158).

An official of the U.S. Department of Justice who witnessed the aggressive actions of the police commented, "I saw old ladies being pushed and manhandled, grabbed by the collar and pushed outdoors. I saw young men being beaten with billy clubs ... I saw officers ride horses into a crowd which I judged to be under control. I saw officers strike individual in that crowd for no apparent reason" (Georgakas and Surkin, 1998: 158).

What was most alarming to these U.S. Department of Justice officials was the inability of the police command officers to control their men. "[One official] asked several command officers to pull other officers back. They attempted to but were unsuccessful. In fact, one command officer was knocked down by a patrolman.... All of this over a stalled car well out of traffic. Police were insensitive" (Georgakas and Surkin, 1998: 158–59).

This was still another incident contributing to the tensions between the black community and the Detroit Police Department. Once again blacks and their white allies vented their anger and frustration against this latest in a series of aggressive behavior. In a not-too-veiled threat to the mayor via the black newspaper, the *Michigan Chronicle*, State Senator Coleman Young warned, "if the mayor is afraid to take on the DPOA [Detroit Police Officers Association] then we will do it for him. Otherwise this city is headed for a blood bath" (Georgakas and Surkin, 1998: 159).

Nothing of any substance emerged from the mayor's office sufficient to check future police action, which resulted in still another incident at Cobo Hall on October 29 called Cobo Hall II. Over 1,000 black and white protestors gathered to voice their opposition to George Wallace's presidential candidacy. At some point fistfights broke out, and then, according to some observers, the police revealed their "pro-Wallace sympathies." "They made virtually no attack on Wallace people and seemed to single out white anti-Wallace demonstrators for the roughest treatment. The idea of containing the violence seemed to have no priority at all. The police violence was more fragrant than during Cobo Hall I" (Georgakas and Surkin, 1998: 159).

Few were spared in the melee. "Bystanders, reporters, and photographers were beaten ... even ... a field investigator for Mayor Cavanagh's Community Relations Commission, who was specially assigned to observe the event, was injured by the police" (Georgakas and Surkin, 1998: 159). One incident in particular was pointed out as a glaring example of both police aggression and bias in crowd control. When a busload of "Wallace supporters threw hunks of scrap iron at a group struggling with a Wallace-ite, the people hit by the iron were attacked by the police, while no action was directed toward the bus. Numerous individuals complained of being beaten at the rally and at police headquarters afterwards" (Georgakas and Surkin, 1998: 159). Shelia Murphy, one of the organizers of the protest, would later report that one police officer told her, "We'd kill you if we thought we could get away with it" (Fine, 1989: 416).

Cobo Hall II was not the end of the confrontations between police and the black community in 1968. A far worse racial incident involving white police officers occurred outside Veterans Memorial Hall on the night and early morning of November 1–2, 1968. While the Ebenezer AME Church was sponsoring a high school dance attended by blacks on the sixth floor of the building, the off-duty white police officers were attending a dance organized by the wives of the DPOA. Two black teenagers, the sons of two prominent black families, claimed that as they entered the building they were the targets of racial slurs by white police officers. One youth stated that when the dance on the sixth floor ended and the youth were leaving, he was stopped at gunpoint just outside the building and beaten by six or eight white men, some of whom had been drinking, and none of whom identified themselves as police officers (Fine, 1989).

This youth claimed that he was chased and beaten into unconsciousness by a group of police-men, one of whom fired at least one shot. The youth's mother also stated that a group of whites choked her son in the building's parking lot. When the young men locked themselves in their car for protection, their attackers kicked in the car's fenders and dented the roof (Fine, 1989). One witness, the father of one of the youths, reported that when he arrived at the building at about 2:00 A.M., he saw several policemen in plainclothes "staggering around drunk," one with a gun in his hand (Fine, 1989: 417).

On November 4, in a display of interracial unity against police brutality, an array of black and white community groups rallied to demand an investigation of the incident. More than 400 gathered in the Central Methodist Church and organized the Detroit Task Force for Justice, an interracial organization aimed at controlling police power and one that called for the termination of the DPOA and civilian control of the police department (Fine, 1989). The *Detroit Free Press* added its editorial voice to the movement on the front page and asked, "Who's the Boss of Detroit Police?," adding that the city "faced a growing crisis over the control of its police depart-ment and policemen" (Fine, 1989: 417).

In the end, nine policemen were suspended and on November 16, 1968, a white assistant Wayne County prosecutor issued a public statement in which he stated the police attacks on the black youths were unprovoked. "The policemen, with varying degrees of participation, threat-ened and assaulted the Negro youths without provocation or justification. At no time did any of the police officers identify themselves, make any arrests, or make any report of the incident" (Georgakas and Surkin, 1998: 161).

The New Bethel Incident, 1969

The mounting tension between the black community and white police finally exploded on March 29, 1969, outside of a popular black church in the 1967 riot area. Two white police of-ficers were shot, one killed and the other wounded, while they were (according to some reports) investigating some armed black men attending a meeting of the Republic of New Africa, a black separatist group, at the New Bethel Baptist Church. Police cars from four precincts soon arrived, attempted to enter the church, and claimed that they were fired upon. As police "secured" the church (some observers would say "stormed), four people inside the building were wounded (*Detroit Free Press*, March 31, 1969).

Over a hundred people in the church were arrested and taken to the police headquarters. This mass arrest prompted black state representative James Del Rio to contact Recorders Court judge George Crockett, "claiming suspects' civil rights were violated" (*Detroit Free Press*, March 31, 1969).

When Del Rio and Judge Crockett arrived at police headquarters, Crockett demanded a list of the people arrested. After being told there was no list, Crockett went to the police commissioner's office with a writ demanding that those arrested but not charged be released. Several hours later Judge Crockett held court on the first floor of the police headquarters and released thirty-nine prisoners. That afternoon, the judge kept two men in jail and released the remaining prisoners (*Detroit Free Press*, March 31, 1969). As a result of the release, a firestorm of white criticism encircled the African American judge and fueled more racial polarization.

Blacks and whites differed widely over the actual facts of the shooting incident and Judge George Crockett's handling of the incident as reported in the mass media (Warren, 1972). In the April issue of *Tuebor*, "The official organ of the Detroit Police Officers Association," the large-print headline read: "FULL STORY OF ASSASSINATION OF PATROLMAN M. CZAPSKI." According to the paper, the following took place:

> Patrolman Michael Czapski, age 22, and patrolman Richard Worobec, 28, cruising near Linwood and Euclid observed ten to twelve men dressed in green military fatigue uniforms with leopard skin epaulet armed with rifles and carbines in front of the New Bethel Baptist Church. They immediately stopped the scout car got out to investigate. *Neither drew his gun. Upon seeing the Officers, the would-be-killers, in guerrilla fashion, turned and fired Patrolman Czapski, fatally wounded, felt Patrolman Worobec, although critically wounded managed to crawl to the scout car and call for assistance.* Patrolman Czapski, brutally shot seven times, was dead upon arrival at Ford hospital. The scout car was riddled with bullets. Patrolman Worobec escaped with his life.
>
> The assassins ran into the New Bethel Baptist Church. Patrolman Worobec's cries for help were heard over the police radio. Within seconds, supporting scout cars arrived on the scene. Black as well as White Officers responded. Fellow officers removed Czapski and Worobec while under fire from the church. *A ranking officer at the scene pounded repeatedly on the locked door of the church and demanded entry. The only answer received was gun fire.* The Officers then broke into the darkened barricaded building. Immediately they were fired upon from the center of the alter by a rifleman. The man dove for cover behind an overturned table near the pulpit. Shots were being

fired from all over. Other officers came in and turned on the lights. Everyone was ordered to stand with their hands up. Slowly they began to rise as directed. One hundred forty-two (142) adults including five (injured persons, as well as five (5) juveniles were in the building.

The majority, both men and women, were wearing paramilitary fatigues with leopard skin epaulets, and combat boots, the uniform of the Republic of New Africa. Requests for information brought only silence. Nor one person offered assistance or cooperation. Nine weapons, including rifles, handguns, gas ejecting spray and a quantity of ammunition was recovered from inside the church building.... The ranking officers at the scene ordered all those present arrested. (*Tuebor*, April 1969)

Blacks had a different interpretation of the incident. Reverend C. L. Franklin, the pastor of the church, claimed that while the incident did "'regrettably and unfortunately' involve the death of a police officer and the wounding of five other people charged that police over-reacted to the shooting" *(Michigan Chronicle*, April 12, 1969). The police overreaction involved, the pastor explained, "the wounding of four Black attendants of the affair" (public meeting sponsored by the Republic of New Africa) and "flagrant shooting into a crowd which included … men, women and very small children who obviously could not all have been guilty" *(Michigan Chronicle*, April 12, 1969).

Black state representative Neil Saunders, who interviewed some of the blacks arrested that fateful night, accused the police of "unnecessary rough tactics in effecting arrests of people who offered no resistance." "Women told us how their dresses were pulled up over their heads and how they were patted down—an illegal act by police officers—the women also told us how the police kicked them and their children and how they hit men who were innocent of any wrong. Men and women told how they were dragged from the floor and how they were hit over their heads and about their bodies with guns" *(Michigan Chronicle*, April 12, 1969). Both Representative Saunders and Reverend Franklin claimed that the police did not give any "warning to the people inside the church about the shooting outside" *(Michigan Chronicle*, April 12, 1969). According to what some of the victims told Saunders, the people in the church were not told to "come out with their hands up or they would be arrested" *(Michigan Chronicle*, April 12, 1969).

Black nationalist leader Milton R. Henry, vice president of the Republic of New Africa, called the police storming of the church "uncivilized and unjustified … a bloody, storm trooper attack" *(Detroit Free Press*, April 1, 1969). Henry claimed the two police officers provoked the situation, citing two unidentified witnesses who said that "the two police officers got out of their car with guns drawn, provoked their assailants in some way and that the assailants fired at the officers in self-defense" *(Detroit Free Press*, April 1, 1969).

Several days after the shooting, close to 100 off-duty policemen and their wives picketed the Tenth Precinct—the home station of the two officers—to protest the handling of the prisoners taken at the church. Some carried picket signs saying "Crockett Justice? Release killers. Prosecute prosecutors. Give license to kill policemen" (*Detroit Free Press*, April 1, 1969). As the public outcry—mainly white—grew, more policemen and their wives picketed the Recorder's Court, completely ringing the building. Some police wives went to the office of the U.S. Attorney Robert Grace, where they demanded "a federal investigation of Crockett and of Detroit's city administration." Angry telephone calls into Recorders Court were coming in "at a rate of one a minute." The majority of the calls either demanded Judge Crockett's resignation or were seeking information about how he could be removed from office (*Detroit News,* April I, 1969).

Three days after the shooting and Judge Crockett's controversial release of the black arrestees at the church, Governor Milliken and Mayor Cavanagh added their views to the controversy concerning Crockett's decision. During his weekly news conference, the governor said that he was "extremely concerned about the allegations made with regard to Judge Crockett's handling of the matter ... and [wanted] to strongly encourage the tenure commission to investigate the case thoroughly. This is the logical and proper approach" (*Detroit Free Press*, April 3, 1969). Milliken explained that he was not trying to prejudge Crockett but had "deep concern" over the police contentions that Crockett's release of suspects "could hamper their investigation" (*Detroit Free Press*, April 3, 1969).

Mayor Cavanagh described Crockett's decision as "highly unusual (and) to some degree questionable" and that he supported a state Judicial Tenure Commission probe of Judge Crockett. "The investigative procedures the police were following were made extremely difficult by the highly unusual, to some degree questionable, but nonetheless unusual incidents that took place, including that of Judge Crockett's participation in the case," the mayor argued. "I think Judge Crockett acted with haste in exercising what obviously are his judicial prerogatives" (*Detroit Free Press*, April 3, 1969).

The controversy over Judge Crockett's actions soon erupted in the state senate, where black and white legislators engaged in a bitter debate. After the debate, the senate adopted a resolution that asked the Judicial Tenure Commission to conduct the investigation of Crockett's actions. One white member of the house of representatives introduced a resolution to remove Crockett from the bench, accusing the judge of "unlawful and unjudicial interference" with the office of the Wayne County prosecutor. He asked the legislature to "direct Gov. Milliken to fire the Judge." State Senator Coleman Young, black Democrat of Detroit and soon to be the city's first black mayor, called the proceedings a "Senate lynching session" (*Detroit Free Press,* April 2, 1969).

Michigan's thirteen black legislators were not about to stand idly by and allow that to happen. In the midst of the Crockett controversy they did not allow the white public to forget the police storming of New Bethel Baptist Church and the resulting damage done to the $600,000 structure. After viewing the damage done to the church by police bullets, the three black senators and ten black representatives initiated a fund to repair the damage *(Michigan Chronicle,* April 12, 1969).

One black representative, Jackie Vaughn III, proposed that New Bethel Baptist Church be designated as a "shrine and place of pilgrimage for all people dedicated to freedom and civil liberty" *(Michigan Chronicle,* April 19, 1969). He suggested in a telegram to C. L. Franklin, the pastor of the church, "that March 30, the day of the shooting, be declared a 'day of infamy' in commemoration of the police attack' on the church" and that the church "be preserved as it was after the police had fired shots into doors, walls, furniture, the pulpit and pews" *(Michigan Chronicle,* April 19, 1969).

On the same day Milliken and Cavanagh made their public statements about Crockett, William T. Patrick (who had been Detroit's first black city council person and was now serving as president of New Detroit), along with a coalition of black groups, organized to protest what they described as a police invasion of the church. In a private letter to Judge Crockett a day after he released the prisoners, Patrick described him as "an authentic hero of these trying times" and his action as "a beacon of light" that probably prevented widespread racial confrontation throughout the city *(Detroit Free Press,* April 3, 1969). This was an obvious reference to the 1967 riot.

Patrick praised Crockett for his actions. "I view your historic actions of [Sunday] ... as being another peak of achievement for you. Your insistence on the full utilization of the law as a servant of this community in a time of great stress was most remarkable." In another reference to the 1967 riot, Patrick wrote, "I think you may have spared our community most disastrous consequences as the result of your forthright stand" *(Detroit Free Press*, April 3, 1969).

While Patrick viewed Crockett's action as preventative of another possible race riot, Mayor Cavanagh justified the police raid on the black church and the mass arrests of blacks as the police's "only appropriate way." According to the mayor, "had any other tactics been used other than to quickly assemble a group and enter the building and try to effect the arrest of 150 people, then the chances of having maybe a full-scale riot or something equally serious were great" *(Detroit Free Press,* April 2, 1969).

The local chapter of the NAACP, with its long history of protesting police brutality in Detroit, also supported Crockett's decision to release the prisoners of the mass arrest. In a letter published in the April 12 issue of the *Michigan Chronicle,* the organization commended the judge for his "courageous action in helping to secure the release of many members of the black community who were arrested in connection with the New Bethel incident. Too often in the past, the voice of justice has been silent in order to permit certain highly questionable police procedures. That these procedures have been in derogation of the basic fundamental constitutional rights guaranteed to every citizen," the letter continued, "has meant little or nothing if the person detained was poor, black or ignorant. It is indeed comforting to know that such is not nor ever will be the case while you are Judge of the Recorders Court" *(Michigan Chronicle,* April 12, 1969).

The letter mentioned attacks on Judge Crockett by the white news media. "We at the NAACP are well aware of the gross distortions reported by the news media and particularly the *Detroit News*, with reference to your handling of what was a potentially explosive situation. Absent your intervention, Detroit could well have been on its way to a repeat of 1967. That the news media chose to delete this from the consideration of the public is deplorable. but alas consistent with their efforts to discredit you in their hate campaign" *(Michigan Chronicle,* April 12, 1969).

The NAACP informed the judge that, by his actions, he had "helped to insure that there will be equal justice under the law for all people. We are proud that you have exhibited a fierce dedication to the principles upon which this great nation was founded in the face of the unwarranted attack by many who should support you. We are proud that you have shown us that the independence of the judiciary is essential to the concept of an orderly society. And lastly, but far from least, we are proud that you are Black" (*Michigan Chronicle,* April 12, 1969).

As hundreds of white policemen and their wives and supporters protested Judge Crockett's actions, a new black organization formed to protest the police action at the church and to support Judge Crockett. This new coalition group called itself the Black United Front (BUF) and was led by Dan Aldridge, who worked for the Detroit Commission on Children and Youth. Other members of the BUF included Black Panthers, the Wayne State University Association of Black Students, the Guardians (a black police officers group), the Eastside Voice of independent Detroit, two black churches, and "representatives of Democratic Congress man Charles Diggs and John Conyers and State Rep. James Del Rio, D-Detroit" (*Michigan Chronicle,* April 12, 1969). The group was formed, Aldridge said, because "we are concerned with the inexcusable conduct of a police force [that] indiscriminately fired into a church and upon defenseless women and children" (*Michigan Chronicle,* April 12, 1969).

Letters to the editor of the two white daily newspapers revealed just how deeply these events had racially polarized the community. One reader wrote:

> It was with shock, anger and disgust I read of Judge Crockett's infamous behavior concerning die persons brought in for questioning in the case of two Detroit policemen.... When one in so high a place ... uses his authority to exercise his personal bias, the people of Detroit should not sit idly by. This man has made a mockery of our judicial system.

Another reader had still another view of the events:

> It is small wonder that most black people in Detroit have little respect or love for the Detroit police. The latest police action in their private war against the black man was the invasion of a black church and indiscriminately shooting it up.... Is nothing sacred to the police? Does the fact that people are black give the police the license to kill or fire into a gathering of men, women and children under the pretext of law enforcement? There was no armed attack on the white church which sheltered a draft dodger. I wonder why. (*Detroit Free Press*, April 1, 1969)

The *Detroit News*, the more conservative of the two daily newspapers, questioned wherever Judge Crockett had abused his power. In an editorial, "An Abuse of Power?" the paper asked: "Have law enforcement and justice taken another beating from Recorder's Court Judge Crockett, Jr.? Certainly the judge owes the community an explanation of his disturbing conduct of last weekend.... It appears possible that in his haste to release the prisoners the judge may have stretched his own authority beyond its legal boundary" (April 1, 1969). After questioning the manner in which Crockett processed and finally released the majority of those arrested, the newspaper argued that the questions it raised, while not "all the questions by any means," were "sufficient ... to justify an investigation into Judge Crockett's conduct by the state judicial tenure commission recently established to probe abuses of judicial power" *(Detroit News,* May 1, 1969).

In a *Detroit Free Press* editorial on Wednesday, April 2 (three days after the shooting), entitled "Let's See Each Other Instead of Stereotypes," the paper attempted to shed some light on the events. "The clamor growing out of last weekend's Linwood Avenue incident shows just how difficult it is for human beings to communicate across racial lines. It is so easy, at such a moment, to think strictly in racial stereotypes. The white man is tempted to see only a judge turning loose suspects after a policeman has been shot in cold blood. The black man is tempted to see only the invasion of a black church and the mass arrest of suspects and innocents alike" *(Detroit Free Press,* April 2, 1969). The editors then spoke to those of reason among black and white Detroiters:

> The reasonable man—and Detroit can thank a kindly fate that there are still many reasonable men around—knows that the truth is more complicated. He knows that a man has been killed and five others wounded in a tragic incident. He knows that the black nationalists are peddling an empty doctrine and trying to stir up those who do not share their political views. He knows that most black citizens know this. He knows that it must have been scary beyond belief to be either inside or outside New Bethel Baptist Church. He knows and regrets deeply—that a church did get shot up and this is not the sort of thing we want to be happening.
>
> The reasonable man knows that the police undoubtedly did swoop up some innocents ... that the writ of habeas corpus was not intended to interfere with normal and routine investigation procedures, The reasonable man knows all these things, and he will keep the Linwood Avenue tragedy in perspective. The only further danger to Detroit from such an episode is that the reasonable men will let the stereotype-builders run away with things and drive us apart. Heaven knows we have had enough trouble understanding each other in the past.
>
> Somewhere in human experience there must be the tools to bridge the chasm across which we so often glare at each other in righteous indignation. Somewhere there must be the wellspring of compassion that could make us weep ungrudgingly over a dead white policeman and over the injured, of whatever race.
>
> Il we are not wary, though, this event—which should simply be an isolated human tragedy—will become larger then life. A white man's special truth will butt head on into a black man's special truth, and peace will be lost somewhere in the no-man's land between. No one has the right to feel sell-righteous in this. Wrongs have been done, now and in the past. But we can—we must overcome them, do a little forgiving

and try to make our city work. To paraphrase the words that are so much in the minds of Christians this week: Father forgive us, for we know not what we do to each other. *(Detroit Free Press,* April 2, 1969)

The clamor over the actions of Judge Crockett would continue in the media for some time, but meanwhile some parties were trying to educate the public as to the legality of his actions. On May 2, 1969, the New Detroit Board of Trustees adopted a report entitled, "The New Bethel Report: 'The Law on Trial,'" which emerged from a request from its Law Committee "to determine whether the administration of justice had functioned effectively in the aftermath of the tragedy" *(New Bethel Report,* 1969: 3). The report concluded, "Based upon our examination of the facts and law involved in this case, we are convinced that Judge Crockett's actions were taken in good faith with ample legal basic. We hope that this will end the matter" *(New Bethel Report,* 1969: 31). Unfortunately, it would not end the Detroit police Officers Associations (DPOA) relentlessness *(Detroit News,* May 1, 1969; *Tuebor,* June and July 1969).

Changes in the attitudes of some of the news media played a role in ending the matter. As Warren points out, "The media coverage of events relating to the New Bethel shooting incident took on a somewhat different character following the initial controversy. The months of May and June brought several occurrences which had a potential for altering the original perceptions of the affair" (1972: 125). He referred to the *Detroit Free Press* admitting to "inaccuracies in its reporting of the incident: 'In the confusion that swirled around the courtroom proceeding that day [March 30] the facts of what took place were reported inaccurately by many media including this paper. We have since corrected these errors and we think they are human factors which explain, but the original inaccuracy cannot be excused. In part the error was ours and we regret it'" (Warren, 1972: 125).

On June 16, 1970, a jury of ten blacks and two whites voted for acquittal of the two men accused of shooting the two officers outside of New Bethel church *(Detroit Free Press,* June 17 and 18, 1970; *Detroit News,* June 16, 1970; *Michigan Chronicle,* June 27, 1970).

STOP THE ROBBERIES, ENJOY SAFE STREETS (STRESS)

A year later, the police and the black community were on another collision course.

The harsh realities of urban life in Detroit during the 1970s fostered continued racial tensions and conflicts between the growing black community and the predominantly white police department. Violence was on the rise, and as Georgakas and Surkin explain: "By 1970 the situation was clearly out of hand. There were more than 23,000 reported robberies, which meant that at least one out of every 65 Detroiters had been a victim. An army of drug addicts lived in the remains of 15,000 inner-city houses abandoned for an urban renewal program which never materialized" (1998: 167).

The worst part of this scenario was the alarming rise of gun ownership. "More than 1 million guns were in the hands of the population, and union officials estimated that half the workers came to the plants armed with one weapon or another." Add to this mix the related fact that, according to Georgakas and Surkin, by early 1971 "the atmosphere of permissiveness regarding police misconduct and the growing chaos in the streets had prepared the way for a new police unity called STRESS (Stop the Robberies, Enjoy Safe Streets). This unit was a secret, elite section of Detroit's undercover assault squads" (1998: 167).

The preferred policing method used by STRESS was the "decoy" operation, "in which one police officer acted as a potential victim in some area where a crime was likely to occur. As the decoy was attacked, other STRESS officers moved in for the arrest" (Georgakas and Surkin, 1998: 167). Most of the high-crime areas in which STRESS operated were predominantly black, which increased confrontations between the black community and the police. The decoy method, therefore, soon turned into a form of illegal entrapment, which resulted in a record number of police killing of blacks. For example, during its first year of operation the Detroit Police Department had the "highest number of civilian killings per capita of any American police department. The Detroit police killed civilians a the rate of 7.17 per 1,000 officers in 1971.... More than one-third of the killings in Detroit were done by STRESS, which represented, at most 2 percent of the department" (Georgakas and Surkin, 1998: 168).

The unit was also accused of conducting 500 raids without the use of search warrants and killing twenty people within thirty months. In their own defense, STRESS officers countered that the disproportionate number of killings by their unit was because they were engaged in dangerous work Fighting street crime "on the only terms that criminals understood." In fact, they Felt that they deserved to be "commended For bravery rather than criticized" (Georgakas and Surkin, 1998: 168).

In its first year of existence STRESS had a checkered reputation. At the beginning the victims of crime welcomed the anticrime unit, but between January 13, 1971, and June 10, 1971, when their operation made its first report, fifteen people had been killed, of whom thirteen were black (*Michigan Chronicle*, June 10, 1972).

The worst case was the September 17 shooting death of two unarmed black teenagers, aged fifteen and sixteen, by STRESS officer Richard Worobec, who had been wounded during the New Bethel incident in 1969. Worobec claimed that he was attacked by the youths while he was acting as a drunk. He said he shot them as they fled after he identified himself as a police officer (*Benton Harbor News Palladium*, December 14, 1971; *Detroit Free Press,* December 14, 1971; *Detroit News,* December 14, 1971).

Some questioned whether Worobec volunteered for the unit because it would provide him the greatest opportunity to avenge the 1969 killing of his partner, Tom Turner, the black president of the Metropolitan Detroit AFL-CIO Council, raised the question in a letter to Mayor Gribbs concerning the STRESS program: "I do not want to prejudge Patrolman Worobec, but 1 do suggest that it may be a serious error of judgment to involve policemen who some believe may have old scores to settle" (*Michigan Chronicle,* June 10, 1971).

It did not take long for community groups to respond to STRESS'S activities. On September 23, 1971, the State of Emergency Committee was formed to protest the killings of the two black youths. Thousands of people marched to demand the abolition of STRESS. On October 2, a memorandum by a city agency, the Detroit Commission on Community Relations, called for suspension of STRESS operations and asked that STRESS resources be transferred to other programs for citizen cooperation (*Michigan Chronicle*, June 10, 1971).

On December 13, 1971, the Michigan Civil Rights Commission held a press conference and issued the following statement:

> As a result of the expression of public concern following the September 17 slaying of two Detroit youths by a Detroit Police officer, the Michigan Civil Rights Commission directed that an investigation be conducted into the activities and procedures of … STRESS…. As of this date, eleven (11) citizens have been killed by STRESS officers. Ten of these fatalities occurred in instances where the decoy method was being employed. Ten of the eleven victims were black …, Our review disclosed that one officer and several of his partners participated in a total of seven of the eleven STRESS fatalities. This same officer had been involved in a relatively larger number of citizen-officer injury incidents prior to joining STRESS. Another officer was assigned to STRESS while awaiting a Trial Board Hearing on charges of mistreating a black prisoner, although he was subsequently exonerated. Police Department statistics indicate that crimes of robbery have decreased where STRESS has been assigned, but there is no indication that the decrease is attributable to the employment of the decoy techniques. (Michigan Civil Rights Commission, 1971)

As a result of its preliminary review, the Michigan Civil Rights Commission directed eight recommendations to the Detroit Police Department. The first one, "that the decoy method be immediately discontinued as a STRESS technique," and the sixth, "that the Michigan Civil Rights Commission staff will participate in human relations training programs, particularly for STRESS officers," were both rejected by John Nichols, the police commissioner *(Detroit News,* December 14, 1971).

Nichols wasted little time holding his own press conference to defend STRESS and the use of the decoy method. He said that the decoy method would be "retained because it was legal, properly managed and definitely effective." He claimed that the black community approved of STRESS "in its entirety" but said "some are falling prey to vociferous members of the community pretending to represent all black citizens" (*Detroit News,* December 14, 1971).

Not surprisingly, given the increase in crime in many black neighborhoods, some blacks agreed with Nichols's support of STRESS, but were concerned about its abuses. In his letter to the mayor. Turner pointed out that many black leaders had approved of the "innovative program," but notwithstanding their support, "he was uneasy about some aspects of STRESS." He accepted the fact that the decoy method was a "legitimate form of police protection," but he was "especially uneasy about a White police decoy in a Black neighborhood because it invites suspicion and provocation" *(Michigan Chronicle,* June 10, 1971).

Some blacks, however, did not fault STRESS, and criticized blacks who were protesting the abuses of STRESS instead of focusing on crime. In November 1971, a black columnist for the *Michigan Chronicle* described these protestors as "short on foresight." "The biggest issue in Detroit for the past four years has been crime in the streets," he wrote. "In recent months more aggressive enforcement, plus participation by citizens, has lessened the problem somewhat. The big controversy recently, of course, has been over the STRESS unit ... the average citizen condones the STRESS operation when it isn't approached with a racist attitude" (*Michigan Chronicle,* October 16, 1971).

He reminded his readers that "there are Black officers in the STRESS unit, and according to this column's information, Blacks were there the night two youths were slain." For the writer, "law and order" was the real issue, and he "bore in mind that without law there is no order. And no matter how much havoc, hell and protest are stirred up, the police will prevail/ ... To advocate that we abolish STRESS shows a lack of foresight on the part of many Blacks, even though they are justified in being concerned" *(Michigan Chronicle*, October 16, 1971). For this writer, "the real concern and the protest march should have been directed toward combating crime a couple of years ago. Perhaps then the young brothers would have been spared the need for STRESS decoys" *(Michigan Chronicle*, October 16, 1971). In short, the reporter's position was that the black youth were fully responsible for their slaying by a white police officer!

There is no doubt that crime in the black community was a major problem in the postriot period, but the writer seemed determined to pile all the blame upon the black community and excuse police abuse:

> The civil disturbances of 1967 should remind Black people not to attempt to destroy something they can't replace. There is no merit in biting the hand that feeds you. Neither is there merit in destroying the forces that protect the community, especially when the majority of Blacks are afraid to join forces to protect themselves.... If you say "let the police do it," then cut out the complaining and shut up. *(Michigan Chronicle*, October 16, 1971)

In early March 1972, another confrontation between STRESS and the black community erupted, but with a complicated racial twist. In an incident called the "Rochester Street Massacre," three black STRESS officers claimed they saw a man with a gun enter an apartment building. He was later identified as a Wayne County sheriff's deputy. The STRESS unit called other police and together they entered the apartment, firing their weapons. All four were Wayne County sheriff's deputies. One man in the apartment was killed and three were seriously wounded. One deputy was shot six times as he stood with his back to the wall, and his hands in the air, holding his ID badge in his hand (Georgakas and Surkin, 1998). The deputies and the three STRESS police officers were in plain clothes. All were black *(Detroit Free Press,* March 10, 1972). In the end, three officers were indicted and acquitted (Georgakas and Surkin, 1998).

Although there were a few black police officers in STRESS, the Guardians of Michigan, an African American police officers association, demanded that STRESS be abolished. The Guardians joined thousands of blacks in an anti-STRESS march in the wake of the Rochester Street incident. Tom Moss, the president of the Guardians, argued that putting STRESS officers dressed as decoys on the street "is just like laying a $5 bill in the middle of the floor." Other members of the Guardians agreed. A former president claimed that "STRESS, by its mere existence, makes more criminal types out of members of the Black community. It uses Black people to put fear in the minds of so-called criminals" *(Michigan Chronicle,* March 18, 1972).

Notwithstanding the Guardians' position on STRESS, some black STRESS officers saw themselves as playing a vital role in fighting crime in the black community. While they did not mention the decoy method, they did see their role in STRESS as defending the black community from criminals. "'We're out here to serve the people," one black STRESS officer explained. "We all grew up in the ghetto. We know what its like to have some junkie come in and clean out your house.... The other day a junkie caught a lady with a baby in her arms coming out of a bank. He put a gun up to the baby's head and told the women to give him her money. Now, if he's desperate enough to do that to a baby you know what he'd do [to you]." Another STRESS officer said:

> That's why we lean on dope houses. Little six and seven year old kids tell us "that's the dope house." If you go through all the steps of the procedure to bust the cat ... usually the worst thing that happens to him is a reduced charge of attempted possession and sale. We can't let guys like (hat feed off out people. So we go by and let him know were on to him. We get a lot of "gas" from the department and we understand their point, but we're not going to let that guy operate if we can help it.... It's dangerous operating that way, but we get the job done. *(Michigan Chronicle,* May 20, 1972)

While some segments of the black community and liberal and radical groups were clamoring for the abolishment of STRESS, other segments—also concerned about the program's abuses—were worried about the rising crime rate in the city. A few weeks after the Rochester Street incident, the Interdenominational Ministerial Alliance of Detroit and Vicinity, which had a combined membership of 300,000, issued a statement: "The 1971 crime rate in the city of Detroit has brought to our realization the need for better protection of people and property in the city. Six hundred and ninety murders were committed in the city of Detroit last year. Of these, approximately 570 were committed by Blacks on Blacks" *(Michigan Chronicle,* April 8, 1972).

The ministers' group described the impact of the rising crime rate on their communities and families. "Our communities have been victimized to the extreme with muggings, breaking and entering, rapes, purse snatching, kidnappings and arsons," the ministers stated. They were particularly worried about the most vulnerable members of their communities and the decreasing sense of security. "Senior citizens, men, women and school children have been open prey for the criminal elements of our city. So much so, that many are afraid to go out day or night. Churches, schools, homes and places of business have all felt this menace—crime. Drug traffic is rampant in the schools, on the streets, and in the community in general" *(Michigan Chronicle,* April 8, 1972).

One of the ministers shared a story of how three black youth robbed him outside his church. "Three of them met me right outside the church doors early one evening. One had a deer rifle, and the other a handgun. They took my money, my watch and my Masonic ring. I didn't see three kids—I saw that great big deer rifle barrel" *(Michigan Chronicle,* April 8, 1972).

One would have thought that the ministers' group would have embraced STRESS unconditionally. Instead, they explained that their statement was not a "blanket endorsement of STRESS." One member of the group said, "We don't believe an honest investigation of the Rochester St. incident was conducted. We think an outside agency should investigate. We intend to ask for a grand jury investigation." Another member felt that "there should be a court case against STRESS. Let them prove themselves. We want nothing swept under the covers. There is something wrong there—all the pieces of the puzzle don't fit" *(Michigan Chronicle,* April 8, 1972).

Before the end of the year, another incident between STRESS officers and members of the black community grabbed the attention of the public. On December 4, 1972, four STRESS officers had a shootout with three young black men who, according to one source, "had been waging a private war against big-time heroin dealers in their neighborhoods" (Georgakas and Surkin, 1998: 206). While staking out a dope house that "three vigilantes" had attacked, STRESS went after the armed men instead of the dope pushers. During the resulting shootout four STRESS officers were wounded and the four armed black men escaped. Several weeks later, during a second shootout with the same black men, a STRESS officer was killed and another wounded. The armed black men escaped again (Georgakas and Surkin, 1998).

During the following weeks, "STRESS put the black neighborhoods under martial law in the most massive and ruthless police manhunt in Detroit history. Hundreds of black families had their doors literally broken down and their lives threatened by groups of white men in plain clothes who had no search warrants and often did not bother to identify themselves as police" (Georgakas and Surkin, 1998: 171).

This police action resulted in "56 fully documented cases of illegal procedure [being] brought against the department." Unfortunately, one black victim of this massive and illegal manhunt was a fifty-seven-year-old unemployed man who was killed by STRESS officers when he shot at them, believing they were a gang of robbers invading his home. On January 12, 1973, one of the black vigilantes, Hayward Brown, was finally captured. The other two were killed in a shootout with police in Atlanta (Georgakas and Surkin, 1998: 171).

The trial that followed featured the famous radical black lawyer Ken Cockrel, who, in defending his client, put STRESS on trial. In the process of defending Browns participation in the one killing and several woundings, "Cockrel invoked the Algiers Motel, Cobo Hall I, Cobo Hall II, Veterans Memorial, New Bethel, the Rochester Street Massacre, and the whole record of STRESS and the Detroit Police Department" (Georgakas and Surkin, 1998: 171).

Brown was acquitted in 1972, He later became sort of a folk hero, speaking on radio and television. Some saw him and his companions as heroes who had "taken on a job that the STRESS squad, for all its bloody fingers, had not been able to handle" (Georgakas and Surkin, 1998).

The controversy over STRESS would not end until the election of Coleman Young, the first black mayor of Detroit, in 1973. During his mayoral campaign against John Nichols, Young focused on STRESS. "We want professionals, not Keystone Cops," he said (Rich, 1989: 104). Not surprisingly, blacks' votes for Young reflected their anger at STRESS, and three months into his first term as the first black mayor of Detroit, Young announced the disbanding of STRESS. This ended one of the bloodiest periods in black community-police relations in Detroit, but other confrontations were destined to arise as the city and the police department became more racially polarized.

THE BEATING DEATH OF MALICE GREEN, 1992–1997

Close to twenty years after Mayor Coleman Young closed down the STRESS operation, another highly racialized incident occurred. On November 5, 1992, two white police officers, Walter Budzyn and Larry Nevers, attempted to arrest a thirty-five-year-old black male named Malice Green outside a West Warren Avenue crack cocaine house. According to one newspaper report taken from police officials and witnesses, the two white plainclothes officers, in an unmarked car, stopped Green's car. They asked him for his driver's license. When he opened his door and glove box to get it, one of the officers, apparently suspicious of what was in Green's hand, asked him what he was holding and to let it go. One of the officers jumped into Green's car and started beating his hands with his flashlight while the other officer leaped into the car on the other side. By then Green, hanging halfway out of his car, dropped what was his hand: a piece of paper. He was struck in the chest and, according to witnesses, appeared dazed (*Detroit News* and *Free Press,* November 7, 1992).

Soon other police arrived, including Sgt. Freddie Douglas, a black officer. According to some witnesses, "One of the arrivals, a white male officer, pulls Green off his seat and beats him with his fist in the face, chest and stomach. Another officer stands on Green's neck as handcuffs are put on. At least two other uniformed officers reportedly hit Green, who drops some keys" (*Detroit Nexus* and *Free Press,* November 7, 1992).

The police then flagged down two EFMS units. Once on the scene, one of the technicians sent a message to his supervisor, asking, "What should I do if I witness police brutality/murder?"

The incident caused Green to go into a seizure. He was rushed to Detroit Receiving Hospital, where he was dead on arrival. The Medical Examiner's Office reported that the cause of death was homicide from "blunt force trauma to the head" and that Green had sustained seventeen blows to his head, hands, and body (*Detroit News* and *Free Press,* November 7, 1992).

Budzyn and Nevers were charged with second-degree murder for their participation in Green's murder. Another white officer, Robert Lessnau, "was charged with assault to commit great bodily harm," and Freddie Douglas, the black officer, was "charged with manslaughter for allegedly failing to stop the officers" (*Detroit Free Press,* August 24, 1993).

Nevers and Budzyn were partners and were known on the streets by the nicknames Starsky and Hutch, the two characters of the popular cop TV show. Each of them had more than twenty-five citizen complaints filed against them during his career.

At the time of the fatal beating of Green, Budzyn, forty-seven, had been a policeman for nineteen years. In 1988 he was sued for an assault that cost the City of Detroit $10,000. A year earlier he had been named precinct patrol officer of the year.

Larry Nevers, fifty-two, had been on the police force for twenty-four years and had been sued "at least twice for alleged brutality." The city settled both suits. During the early 1970s he was a member of the controversial STRESS unit. According to Nevers's colleagues, however, he was a hardworking, aggressive cop. "He goes out and digs and looks for what's going on.... Everyone in the precinct, black and white, they want to work with Larry." Several hours after Green's death, Nevers told a *Free Press* reporter, "I must've done something wrong—a guy died" (*Detroit Free Press,* November 17, 1992).

This unfortunate incident took place in the wake of the Los Angles riots of 1992 brought about by the acquittal of white police officers who were videotaped beating black motorist Rodney King. In a city already burdened with a long and tragic history of racial conflict and racial polarization, it did not take long for the brutal murder of Malice Green by a white police officer to unleash anger and indignation within the black community. The well-known black minister Charles G. Adams wrote in his *Michigan Chronicle* column, "The high cost of racism is clearly evident in the brutal beating of Rodney King in Los Angeles and the heinous murder of Malice Green in Detroit. Look at the astronomical costs to those cities in terms of legal fees and claims! How many millions will Detroit have to pay because a few cops vented racial rage against a citizen they should have been protecting." Some white officers of the Detroit Police Department "have never accepted the fact that for almost 20 years they have had to work under the authority of African American leadership in the DPD and the city," Adams wrote. "When they saw Malice Green, they saw Coleman Young and tried their best to beat his brains out, costing the city millions of dollars in legal fees and claims" (*Michigan Chronicle,* November 18–24, 1992).

A day after the police killing of Green, mourners and protesters erected a makeshift shrine composed of posters, signs, flowers, and a soapbox where Green's death supposedly occurred. A few weeks later the shrine "began to overflow with offerings. Art work, handbills and mementos adorn[ed] the rundown building hovering over the site. Some spoke to specific business, political and other interests now hooked into the Green tragedy" (*Michigan Chronicle*, December 2–8, 1992).

As expected, Green's killing reverberated throughout the media. One writer from pre domi-nantly white Dearborn Heights wrote, "Why do the media portray the beating of Malice Green as racially motivated? Why are people in these stories described as black or white? It seems you are trying to turn this incident into something it is not." Another writer accused the media of having "done a great disservice to police officers" and shifted the blame for Green's death to Green himself. "If Green had to reach into his glove department to retrieve requested documents, he should have informed the officers of his intent. Once Green allegedly tried to hide his possession of an illegal substance from officers, and circumvent their seizure of the substance through physical resistance, any consequence resulting from his struggle lay at Greens feet alone." Reflecting an opposite view, another writer wrote, "I am appalled that two white officers beat one black motorist. This incident proves that white motorists are treated differently from black motorists by police officers." Another writer wrote, "Too often, as a European American, I forget the discrimination, unfairness and hate that many Americans put up with daily. I doubt a European American would have been treated the same way" *(Detroit Free Press,* November 17, 1992).

Soon after charges were filed against the four officers, two related issues emerged: a change of venue for the trial and the fact that few police officers in Detroit had ever been convicted of first- or second-degree murder. There was the possibility that a fight over a change of venue could happen, but according to legal officials at the time, "not since the infamous Algiers Motel incident during the 1967 riots has a major local criminal trial been removed from Detroit." They also could not recall a case "where an on-duty officer was convicted of any offense higher than manslaughter in the death of a civilian" (*Detroit Free Press*, November 17, 1992).

Blacks in Detroit had not forgotten how three young black men were shotgunned to death at close range in the motel by white police officers who also threw racial and sexual slurs at them. Nor could blacks forget how the initial police report falsely accused the victims of being snipers killed during a gun battle with police (Heresy, 1968). As if this was not enough to bear, in 1969 the black community had to endure the movement of the trial of one of the police officers charged with the murders to Mason, Michigan, a short distance from Lansing, where an all-white jury acquitted him (Fine, 1989). The lawyer for the police officer fully understood how to take advantage of the still seething postriot racial tension and conflicts at the time and admitted that he had no difficulty getting the trial moved to Mason. "It was a hot potato. The Recorder's Court was happy to get rid of it," he said. Once the trial was moved to Mason, the lawyer had no trouble getting an all-white jury. On the other hand, however, "'From the victims' perspective, and the prosecutors,' it was an uncomfortable atmosphere,'" he added (*Detroit Free Press*, November 18, 1992). Clearly this lawyer knew how to play the racial card to benefit his white client.

By 1992 the black community/police relationship had undergone radical changes. Detroit was a black majority city with blacks comprising 76 percent of its population. Community activists who had labored for decades against white police brutality could no longer claim that the DPD functioned as an occupying army. Notwithstanding these changes, there was yet some lingering doubt that the officers would be convicted of murder in the beating death of Green.

Serious questions surfaced during the preliminary examination of the four officers: "Was Green experiencing an 'adrenaline cocaine phenomenon' or were Detroit police officers overly aggressive? Did police officials wipe blood from Green's car?" (*Michigan Chronicle*, December 2–8, 1992). Green's longtime friend Ralph Fletcher, one of the last people to see him alive, testified that he saw Budzyn and Nevers "wiping blood off Greens car" and that "the car was pushed closer to the intersection" (*Michigan Chronicle*, December 16–22, 1992).

Defense attorneys wasted little time questioning "the credibility and characters of Green and ... prosecution witnesses in the case." During cross examination by Michael B. Batchelor, a black lawyer representing Budzyn, Fletcher admitted that he permitted crack users to smoke crack in his home in exchange for cash. He also admitted that he did not witness Nevers hitting Green, but he did see Nevers swing his flashlight. It probably did not help the prosecution's case that an autopsy revealed cocaine and alcohol in Green's system. Yet when questioned by the defense attorneys, the medical examiner insisted that repeated blows to Green's head resulted in his death (*Michigan Chronicle*, December 2–8, 1992).

In late December the charge of involuntary manslaughter against Sgt. Freddie Douglas, the only black officer and supervisor present during the beating death of Green, was thrown out. The judge rejected the prosecutor's argument that Douglas could have saved Green's life had he intervened in the beating. Instead, the judge countered that the blows resulting in Green's death could have been delivered before Douglas arrived on the scene. On hearing the judges decision, an emotional Douglas "shuddered, rubbed his teary eyes and raised his folded hands in thankful prayer." Later he said, "I never gave up hope." The decision greatly upset Green's sister, who complained "why did they let him off. He should have stopped it. All he did was stand there and look." Douglas still faced a misdemeanor charge of neglect, however (*Detroit Free Press*, December 24, 1992).

According to Douglas's lawyer, the only reason his client was charged was because prosecutors were influenced by the beating of Rodney King and the riot that occurred in the wake of the officers' acquittal. He did not think the beating death of Green was racist, but believed that the charge against his client was racist because "the mayor and the prosecuting attorney for Wayne County decided to defuse a situation that could have been volatile and charge a black" (*Detroit Free Press*, December 24, 1992). People in the neighborhood where Green grew up and was so brutally murdered were divided over the charges against Douglas being dropped. Some argued that Douglas should have stopped the beating, while others argued that he did not hit Green and he did tell them—Budyzn and Nevers—to stop the beating (*Detroit Free Press*, December 24, 1992).

On December 23, 1992, in an attempt to settle a $61 million lawsuit over Green's death, the City of Detroit countered with a proposal of $5.1 million payment to fourteen members of his family. Less than a month later, U.S. District Court Judge Gerald Rosen blocked the settlement and on April 13, 1993, called the Green family lawyers greedy and refused to allow the city to pay the $5.1 million settlement. Legal fights over the money would continue for four more years.

For the next nine months Detroit became the center of the most intense racial drama in decades. On January 21, Judge George Crockett III, the son of the judge known for his intervention in the New Bethel incident, was selected to preside over the Recorder's Court trials. On two occasions, one in May and the other in June, Crockett denied defense lawyers' motions to move the trial out of Detroit. February brought more suspicion and drama when someone shot and killed Robert Knox, one of the witnesses to Green's beating. According to the police chief the shooting was drug-related (*Detroit Free Press*, August 26, 1993).

The trials began on June 2, 1993, with the selection of juries for Nevers and Budzyn. (Lessnau, the other white officer involved, accepted a nonjury trial to be decided by Crockett.) Eight days later, Nevers's jury selection was completed. A change of venue was requested again, and once again Crockett refused to move the trial out of Detroit. On June 16, Officer Budzyn's jury was ready to hear his case (*Detroit Free Press,* August 26, 1993).

As expected, much of the controversy surrounding the trial related to the coroner's report and the exact cause of Malice Greens death. Defense lawyers challenged Wayne Country assistant medical examiner Dr. Kalil Jirakis testimony that Green died from fourteen blows from large flashlights. The medical experts for the defense countered that Green's death was caused by his cocaine use or, they conceded, by a combination of cocaine and the beating. One defense expert, Oakland County Chief Medical Examiner Ljubisa Dragovic, disagreed with Jiraki's autopsy. He argued that Green's brain was "wired up" from cocaine use and the police beating "triggered the massive seizure" that killed Green. After much prodding by a "relentless prosecutor," Dragovic reluctantly concluded that Green's death was a homicide (*Detroit Free Press*, July 27, 1993). Philadelphia medical examiner Haresh Mirchandani attributed Green's death to an irregular heartbeat "brought on by cocaine intoxication, blunt injuries to the head and physical and mental exertion" (*Detroit Free Press,* July 28, 1993).

On July 19 the prosecution rested its case against Budzyn, Nevers, and Lessnau. The following day, Budzyn testified, "I never hit anybody." When Nevers took the stand on August 3, he testified that he hit Green because he tried to grab Nevers's holstered gun, a claim that no doubt resonated with his supporters, who knew that Nevers had once almost been killed by a suspect who grabbed his gun (*Detroit Free Press*, August 26, 1993).

On August 9, the defense lawyers for Budzyn and Nevers saw an opportunity for mistrials because the films provided as entertainment for the jurors included *Malcolm X,* which showed scenes of the police beating of Rodney King in Los Angles. Their motions for mistrials were denied. On August 13, just four days later, the jury began its deliberation on a case that had already begun to divide the metropolitan community along racial lines. On August 23, the jury arrived at a verdict: Budzyn and Nevers were guilty of second-degree murder, Lessnau not guilty. A photo on the front page of the *Detroit Free Press* under the large headline, "IT WAS MURDER, JURIES RULE," graphically displayed the impact of the guilty verdict on the two officers: "After hearing they were found guilty, a sobbing Larry Nevers leans against the chair of a stoic Walter Budzyn in Detroit Recorder's Court on Monday" *(Detroit Free Press*, August 26, 1993).

Responses to the Verdicts

Susan Watson, an African American columnist for the *Detroit Free Press,* was moved by Nevers's display of emotion, but reserved most of her sentiment for Malice Green:

It was hard to look at pictures of Larry Nevers and not feel a twinge of emotion. The veteran cop dropped his head into his hands and sobbed when jurors convicted him and his partner of murder in the death of Malice Green. Nevers' chest heaved, and he seemed to struggle for breath. The weight of the verdict physically overwhelmed him. It was sad, but sadder still is the fact that Malice Green is dead. I remembered that as I watched Nevers. Alter the verdicts were read, Nevers rose from his seat and left the courtroom.... As bleak as his life may seem right now, he still has tomorrow ... he still has a chance to find some new meaning in life ... And that's something that was denied Green when he had his encounter with a street version of the criminal justice system last November. (August 26, 1993)

Family Responses

Although Green's relatives were pleased with the verdict, they still felt a heavy sense of loss of a son, brother, father, and husband. His sister said they would not be satisfied until the officers were sentenced. Green's mother, while also pleased with the verdict, commented that it would not bring back her son. "I will never be able to see my son again. The officers' families will be able to visit them." One of Green's daughters added that the case had been "hard on all of us. They took our father away." One of the sisters reported that the most difficult part for the family was "just sitting listening to the testimony.... We were just praying before they read the verdict." Listening to Budyzn's testimony troubled her. "He didn't hear nothing, he didn't see nothing, and he didn't do nothing ... I guess my brother got them 14 blow upside the head from the goddamn instrument in the car" (*Detroit Free Press*, August 26, 1993).

The relatives and friends of the convicted officers were also overwhelmed with emotion as they closed ranks around them. Budzyn's family vented their anger at the verdict. His daughter described how her father would do anything for anyone, and recalled how he used his own money to pay for hotel rooms to shelter battered women running from their attackers. Budzyn's father blamed his conviction on the jury of eleven blacks and one white. Budzyn's ex-wife rallied to his defense, saying that she thought it was "a sad day when five crack addicts can convict in-nocent police officers of second-degree murder." She felt that the jurors were intimidated by the possibility of a riot of the masses. "I feel that this jury found him guilty of second-degree murder to placate the masses. I don't understand what evidence they had. There was no blood on the flashlight. There was no blood on him" (*Detroit Free Press*, August 26, 1993).

After hearing the verdict Nevers went home and stayed inside, "sheltered behind blinds drawn tightly shut." He was visited by somber friends and relatives. His sister-in-law, who viewed the coverage of the verdict on television, said that they were devastated. When Nevers returned home from the court, she hugged him. "I don't think we even talked," she said (*Detroit Free Press*, August 26, 1993).

Police Response

It was expected that the verdict would have a powerful impact on police officers in Detroit and the suburbs. Given the history of racial tensions in Detroit and the dramatic change in the racial makeup of the police department during the Young administration, it was no wonder that the police reactions to the verdict reflected the social and racial fissures in the larger metropolitan society. Some officers speculated that Green's use of cocaine may have been a contributing factor to his death, echoing what medical experts for the defense had argued. Tom Schneider, a white policeman and head of the Detroit Police Officers Association (DPOA), issued a statement calling the guilty verdicts "a victory for the drug addicts, dope dealers, pimps and prostitutes," and claimed that the officers were not able to get a fair and impartial trial because of public statements by Mayor Young, Chief Stanley Knox, and the news media (*Detroit Free Press,* August 26, 1993).

Some police officers had different views on how much their colleagues' responses to the verdicts were racially based. One officer stated that "the black investigators feel the verdict was justified; the white ones feel the officers were just doing their jobs." Still another officer explained, "It definitely wasn't a black or white thing. It was a situation that got out of control, and they lost it. Every day there are blacks killing blacks in the streets of Detroit and that's the greatest injustice" (*Detroit Free Press*, August 24, 1993).

Notwithstanding the range of reactions to the verdicts among Detroit police, reflecting some racial sentiments, two newspaper writers reported that "the fatal beating of Malice Green and convictions of fired white officers Larry Nevers and Walter Budzyn have not worsened race relations in the department. In fact, some said the slaying brought officers closer together, sort of in an 'us-versus-criminal mentality'" (*Detroit Free Press,* August 28, 1993).

Predictably, the guilty verdict of the two white police officers generated much heat among letters to the newspapers. The letters revealed the vast difference—mainly racial—between those who supported the officers and those who did not. One letter writer wrote: "It is not by coincidence that the officers feel they did no wrong. They were nurtured in a society that told them they are superior to the African-American male, and their badges simply gave them a stamp of approval." Another writer felt the "trials were comparable to a black being tried before the Ku Klux Klan. The case should have been tried in Macomb or Oakland County." These were and still are mostly white areas. According to still another writer, "Malice Green was a victim of a society in which police officers are supposed to make us feel safe. The police who were supposed to protect Malice Green beat him to death. How safe does that make us feel?" Another writer blamed Green and his drug use for causing the officers to overreact and implied that the guilty verdict was motivated by the fear that a nonguilty verdict would have triggered a riot similar to the recent disorders in Los Angeles. "The officers may have used excessive force in gaining control of Malice Green, but shouldn't Green have been accountable for his actions? Without cocaine in his system would these officers have been on trial for murder? Were the verdicts rendered to prevent a riot in Detroit? Nevers and Budzyn were sacrificial lambs" *(Detroit Free Press,* August 28, 1993).

The *Detroit Free Press* can be credited with publishing a balanced editorial in the wake of yet another racial incident in the already racially polarized Detroit metropolitan community. "Justice appears to have been served by the murder convictions of two former Detroit police officers for the fatal beating of Malice Green," the editors wrote. "Although no one can properly take pleasure in the guilty verdicts, or in the horrifying events that led to them, the community can derive a measure of quiet satisfaction from the fact that its criminal justice system seems to have worked as it is supposed to work: openly and fairly." They praised the two officers for their years of service to the city and expressed sympathy for Nevers' sobbing response to the verdict. "Nevers and Budzyn were veteran officers who often distinguished themselves in tough jobs patrolling the city's mean streets. The image of Mr. Nevers burying his face in his hands and sobbing as his conviction was announced likely will prove indelible for many people who saw it." But, in balance, the editors added, "such matters in no way mitigate the officers' deadly, irreversible misconduct in the Green case. To suggest otherwise would do a disservice to all other police officers with equally dangerous and thankless jobs who do not illegally resort to fatal force to maintain public order" *(Detroit Free Press*, August 28, 1993).

The editorial did not stop there. "The Green trial suggests—again-that brutality remains a systemic, not individual, problem in the Detroit Police Department, despite marked overall improvements in police-community relations in the past 20 years. Monday's convictions will not erase that problem, and Detroit's next mayor will have to address it in a way that incumbent Coleman Young has not." The Detroit Recorder's Court juries were praised for their "diligence and patience throughout the long weeks of testimony and deliberations," and the prosecuting and defense attorneys were described as "sincere and passionate advocates for their positions." Judge George Crockett III "worked hard and generally well to manage his courtroom during the tense trials, although we disagreed with some of his harsh and peremptory orders to the news media. Other decisions by the judge arc likely to be cited on appeal." Predictions of postverdict violence were overplayed, particularly given the fact that the juries were predominantly black and the judge was African American. "The verdicts in the Green case make counterproductive any extra-legal responses by Detroit—although predictions of such disturbances struck us as exaggerated. The trials were heard by an African-American judge and by juries whose composition reflected the community in which Mr. Green lived and died, bolstering the legitimacy of whatever verdicts were reached" *(Detroit Free Press,* August 24, 1993).

The editors ended with both a note of sadness and hope. "A dignified sadness would seem the most appropriate reaction to this personal and community tragedy. There is room for relief that the trails ended in a way that should inspire renewed confidence in Detroit's institutions of justice. But for the city, its police department—and especially for Malice Green and his family—the price of that renewal was unacceptably high" *(Detroit Free Press*, August 24, 1993).

The television coverage of the trial and the verdict was well balanced and avoided the temptation to exploit the situation, particularly the emotionally charged moment when the verdicts were announced. "As verdicts were rendered in the Malice Green trials, images from the courtroom were filled with a haunting, almost unbearable tension, especially when Larry Nevers was pronounced guilty of second-degree murder and emotionally unraveled before viewer's eyes." While it "was an incredibly dramatic TV slice of real life ... to their credit, Detroit's local TV stations for the most part refused to exploit the drama." Carol Rueppel, news director of WVID-TV (Channel 4) said that they "wanted to be on top of the story, but not alarmist." Another news director, Mort Meisner of WJBK-TV (Channel 2), said, "You stay away from a lot of speculation." Even Bill Bonds, the white, "often flamboyant" anchor at WXYZ (Channel 7), reined himself in when he asked a reporter on the scene before the verdicts, "I'm not trying to hype this thing ... but what's going on down there?" *(Detroit Free Press,* August 26, 1993).

In the wake of the verdicts expressions of joy combined with caution could be heard on Detroit's two major news radio stations, WQBH-AM (1400) and WCHB (1200), which served predominantly black audiences. After a review of the verdicts Martha Jean (the Queen) Steinberg, the very popular black WQBH radio personality, played a gospel song, "A Good Day." During her regular program of gospel music and commercials, however, she interspersed postverdict advice to her radio audience, cautioning them to "maintain calm." "I'm asking you to be real cool," she said *(Detroit Free Press,* August 26, 1993).

Talk radio WCBH provided blacks the opportunity to discuss the verdicts from their unique perspective. Most callers supported the guilty verdicts. Some accused the white media outlets of "conducting an inflammatory riot watch." For example, on the talk show the Reverend Wendell Anthony, president of the Detroit chapter of the NAACP, implied that "some in the media have done more inciting than informing" (*Detroit Free Press,* August 26, 1993). But, according to one reporter, "Local TV already had set the tone for restraint" (*Detroit Free Press,* August 26, 1993).

Protestors and Riot Prevention

In the tense moments after the verdicts were announced, several black community leaders stepped up to the plate to avert riots. As a crowd of 200 to 300 gathered around the spot where Green was beaten to death by the two convicted police officers, Rev. Darnell Taylor noticed that the crowd was growing and becoming unruly and out of control. He and others decided to take the crowd on a march. Soon Taylor was leading 150 people down West Warren toward a location where a teenager was killed by a policeman a month earlier "after allegedly pointing a gun at the officer." As Taylor led the crowd on the march, "they sang, laughed and called to spectators to join them. When they got to the site, they joined hands, formed a circle and prayed and sang. Then they dispersed—peacefully." Other community leaders as well as responsible members of the crowd also joined in to help keep the peace. As one reporter explained, "It was no accident; it was the preaching, cajoling at times, physical intervention of community leaders that kept the outpouring of emotions largely peaceful after the verdicts were announced. It was not always community activists who provided the leadership," he added, "Several times, provocateurs were restrained or shouted down by people in the crowd" (*Detroit Free Press,* August 28, 1993).

After the announcement of the verdicts, police strategy appeared to be to allow the protestors to vent their emotions. Warren Street, the site of Green's murder, was closed to traffic. Little wonder, therefore, that police chief Stanley Knox expressed his gratitude to community leaders like Taylor, "who constantly exhort[ed] the crowd to remain peaceful over a makeshift sound system rally organizers had set up. He simply drowned out rabble-rousers" (*Detroit Free Press,* August 28, 1993).

Posttrial Complications

At a news conference after the guilty verdicts were announced another drama began to unfold, adding yet another complication to the already racially tense postconviction mood of the city. The lone white member of the Walter Budzyn's jury complained that "duress" compelled him to vote to convict Budzyn of second-degree murder. "It was a very hard and difficult decision for me to make.… I didn't think it was proven, as far as intent," he said. While he always believed that Budzyn was guilty, he was not convinced that it was second-degree murder. It appeared that he blamed much of his duress on the pressure put on him by black jurors, claiming that after they screamed at him, he just gave in. According to this juror, there was intense discussion in the Budzyn's jury room during the last few days as the black jurors tried to convince him to side with them. "It was felt by some people, that because I was white and having an opposing view to theirs, they felt it was racial. But it definitely was not racially motivated in any way, shape or form" (*Detroit Free Press*, August 26, 1993).

The white juror claimed that racial tensions in the jury room increased after he remarked to the black jurors, "It seems like you people want to turn this into a Rodney King situation." Angry at the name-calling, he banged his hand into a door, causing bruises that were clearly visible during the news conference. Disappointed and angry because he did not hold out, he conceded that "in the end, the verdict sheet was in front of me and I just signed it, and said 'Boom, here it is.'" Although he had one last opportunity to change his mind when Judge Crocket III polled the jurors, he decided not to do so (*Detroit Free Press*, August 24 1993).

The white juror also called a WXYT-AM radio talk show to apologize for the verdict to Budzyn's lawyer, who was on the show. Later, the lawyer said, "The fact that he felt he owed an apology was an indication to me that maybe an injustice had been done." When the lawyer asked the juror if Budzyn had gotten a fair trial, the juror replied, "No." On hearing this, chief Recorder's Court judge Dalton Roberson responded, "I think he's … having some emotional problems with the verdict, and he needs to avail himself of our psychological counseling services." The juror turned down the offer, saying, "I don't think I am deranged or otherwise have lost my mental faculties … I definitely have some problems with the verdict that I came to" (*Detroit Free Press,* August 28, 1993).

The black jurors "were stunned" by the white juror's depiction of what happened in the jury room. One black juror said she and the white juror were "close, very close. We talked a lot … I never would have thought he would have done some of the things he is doing today." They had sat near each other and discussed evidence together. "We didn't try to persuade him. What we did was put all the evidence before him" (*Detroit Free Press*, August 26, 1993).

Another black juror argued that race was not a factor. Instead, she claimed that the white juror tended to side with the police because of his years of military experience. She felt that he "initially put a lot of his feelings and beliefs into the decision. We kept telling him that he couldn't go by his beliefs, that you have to go by the facts and the decisions" *(Detroit Free Press,* August 24, 1993). One of the black jurors mentioned that the white juror told her that "because of the decision he made he was going to have to go home and face his people." She told him, "we all do" (*Detroit Free Press,* October 13, 1993).

The Sentencing of Budzyn and Nevers

On October 12, 1993, Detroit braced for the sentencing of Budzyn and Nevers. Before hearing his sentence, Nevers approached the bench and in an emotional voice told Judge George Crockett, "I never had the opportunity to express to the Green family my sincere apologies for the loss of their son, husband and father ... Your honor, I did not kill Malice Green. I never intended to hurt him, to do anything to him other than to arrest him for a felony." Malice Green's stepdaughter was not moved by Nevers's apology. "He wasn't apologizing to me. He was trying to protect himself," she said.

Before he imposed the sentence on Nevers, Crockett told him, "Mr. Nevers, you were the senior officer that evening, the most experienced, the elder. Yours were the blows that resulted in the death of Malice Green.... What you did was excessive in the extreme" (*Detroit Free Press*, October 13, 1993).

Next it was Budzyn's turn to approach the bench before sentencing. Unlike his stoic reaction to his conviction months earlier, this time he "brushed away uncharacteristic tears and spoke quickly, almost inaudibly." He told the judge that he was sorry for what happened, that there was nothing that he could ever do to change it. "I was just doing my job and I was arresting him for narcotics. I never struck Mr. Green." When Crockett asked, "What do you mean, never?" Budzyn said, "I did not strike that man." Judge Crockett asked if he had hit Green on the knuckles and knees as he had testified at his trial. Budzyn replied that he had not, which contradicted his testimony. When asked if he had struck Green at all, he said, "No, sir." It took only a brief moment for Crockett to respond to this obvious contradiction. "Mr. Budzyn, I believe from the evidence I heard that you did in fact strike Mr. Green." In addition to striking Green and then contradicting his own testimony, Crockett held Budzyn responsible for Green's death by his inaction and failure to stop Nevers from beating Green *(Detroit Free Press,* October 13, 1993).

Seated in the front row of the courtroom, the Green family waited for the sentences to be announced. Malice Green's widow, Rose Mary Green, told Crockett, "It is time for the world to see through the excuses and face the truth—being black, unemployed and having used drugs did not kill Malice. Mr. Budzyn and Mr. Nevers killed my husband" (*Detroit Free Press*, October 13, 1993).

Judge Crockett sentenced Nevers to twelve to twenty-five years in prison, where he would have to spend no less than nine years and eight months in a maximum security prison before seeking parole. Budzyn received eight to eighteen years in prison with at least six years and five months in prison *(Detroit Free Press,* October 13, 1993).

The sentences aroused deep feelings among the families, friends, and supporters on both sides. Malice Greens father found little satisfaction in the sentence because he had lost a son forever. "No. I'm not satisfied, but what can I do? Nothing," he said. Budzyn's ex-wife had expected a lighter sentence and expressed disgust at the way in which he was portrayed. "I don't want to hear any more of this garbage. Walter Budzyn doesn't deserve this. Walter Budzyn is not going to do any eight years in jail. He's going to have people fighting for him," she exclaimed. Green's younger sister shared her family's anguish over how they had been treated since the verdicts. "We have been hurt and insulted by many who support these ex-officers and act as if my brother, who they never knew, did not have a right to live" *(Detroit Free Press,* October 13, 1993).

As expected, politicians shared their views on the sentences. A spokesman for the Macomb Coalition for Republicans—a largely white suburban organization—said, "We all watched the politicians and special interest groups in the form of Mayor Young and the NAACP railroad two people through the criminal justice system ... this will go down as one of the saddest days in the city's history" *(Detroit Free Press,* October 13, 1993).

Judge Crockett acknowledged the conflicting and painful divisions as the result of his sentences, but voiced pride in both the city and the legal system. Before be rose to leave the bench, he addressed the courtroom:

> No one in this community will be completely satisfied with what has transpired this day. Mr. Green's family will never, ever set him again. The defendants' families will not see them. The circumstances that gave rise to the loss of life of Mr. Green touched all of us. I have abiding faith in the cool heads that live in this community, in its sense of fair justice and fair play. This trial has demonstrated this city is without peer in this nation. This is Detroit, Michigan, *(Detroit Free Press,* October 13, 1993)

Few people were surprised at the reactions to the sentences that predictably followed time-worn racial city/suburban pathways. Following the former white police officers' convictions, old racial antagonisms constantly resurfaced in the letters in newspapers and talk shows, revealing racial division between blacks and whites and city and suburban communities. Not that there had not been racial divisions before. There were still historic wounds that had barely healed from past racial conflicts going back to the 1967 riots and the days of STRESS. On October 13, the *Detroit Free Press* ran a huge headline, "Ex-cops get prison." Underneath this one ran another slightly smaller caption, "Episode tore open city's racial wounds." The writer reported that letters to newspapers showed "a deep division between black and white people, city and suburban community ... church leaders say it's time for healing. It's time, they say, for making sure the fatal beating of Green doesn't leave a lasting rift between Detroit area black and white people" *(Detroit Free Press,* October 13, 1993).

In the midst of the storm of racial anger and frustration that followed in the wake of the sentences, there were steady voices calling for racial calm and reconciliation. These healing voices had always emerged during periods of racial conflicts. A resident of Wyandotte remarked that city and suburban residents should "stop being angry with one another and stop living in the past." Referring to the trials, verdicts, and sentences, she added, "The whole thing seems to have been made into a black and White issue rather than what it really is—people being punished for something they did…. People have to get past color and begin trusting each other again." The Reverend Edgar Vann, pastor of Detroit's Ebenezer Church, confessed that healing the recent rift in the community would not be easy, but believed that "if there's any entity that can heal, it's the church…. The church can bring stability to this community." The pastor planned to discuss the sentences in his next Sunday sermon and expected that other ministers would do the same. In his sermon he planned to make appeals for community restraint and offer prayers for the families of Green, Budzyn, and the city. Based on his firm faith in the role of the church to heal Detroit's racial wounds—particularly in the wake of the sentences—the pastor believed that churches had "a great role to play in terms of keeping people calm, of healing and of helping to disseminate the proper information" *(Detroit Free Press,* October 13, 1993).

Not everyone was convinced that Detroit's long-standing racial wounds could be healed anytime soon. Professor Lyn Lewis, chairperson of the sociology department at the University of Detroit-Mercy, said, "Before Malice Green, there was racial division, there was discrimination and there was prejudice in all sphere of life. And that stuff will remain. All we're seeing now is what has existed all along and now people have a Malice Green case around which to voice their opinions." Lewis was not convinced that the Green case would be "a forum in which people will heal the rift because people don't see themselves as being wounded. There are no politicians, no social scientist or community leader who can effectively bridge this gap" *(Detroit Free Press,* October 13, 1993).

Unfortunately, the professor was partially correct. Due to years of appeals and further legal actions, the Green case was prevented from becoming an effective forum for the healing of the racial wounds of the Detroit metro community. Instead, the opposing sides hardened their positions as the legal fight over the conviction of the two white ex-officers continued.

Retrials of Budzyn and Nevers

Both Budzyn and Nevers appealed their convictions, "alleging jury tainting, jury bias, erroneous jury instruction, insufficient evidence and improper denial of a change of venue to lessen pre-trial media impact" *(Detroit News*, November 11, 1996). On July 31, 1997, the Michigan Stare Supreme Court agreed that the jury had been tainted, mainly by the showing of the *Malcolm X* film, and granted Budzyn a new trial. Their decision, however, only affected Budzyn's conviction because the evidence against him was less compelling than the evidence against Nevers *(Detroit*

News, August 17, 1997). On March 19, 1998, he was retried and again found guilty, this time for the lesser crime of involuntary manslaughter. Unlike the predominantly black jury in the first trial drawn from predominantly black Detroit, accused by some Whites of racial bias, the jury for the retrial was more racially diverse, made up of eight whites, one Asian, and three blacks. This jury resulted from the merging of the Detroit and suburban Wayne County court systems ("White Ex-Officer Guilty in Black Motorist's Death," 1998). In January 1999, the Michigan Court of Appeals reinstated the earlier sentence of four to fifteen years. Since Budzyn had already served the minimum under the first conviction, he was released *(Detroit Free Press,* January 13, 1999, April 19, 2000).

Nevers lost his 1997 appeal to the Michigan Supreme Court. However, he won his appeal in federal court, which overturned the verdict two years later. As in Budzyn's case, the court of appeals based it decision on the showing of *Malcolm X* in addition to the jury hearing about preparation for riots in case the white ex-officers were acquitted. The appeals court decision was then appealed to the U.S. Supreme Court, which allowed the decision to stand. In May 2000, Nevers was convicted of involuntary manslaughter and sentenced to seven to fifteen years in prison. Three years later, in March 2003, the state appeals court overturned this conviction. In September 2003, the conviction was upheld by the State Supreme Court. This long legal process finally ended for Nevers in 2001 *(Detroit Free Press*, September 23, 2003).

The protracted legal process weighted heavily on the families involved. During the retrial of Larry Nevers in March 2000, Malice Green's mother, Patricia Green, mentioned that the trials were causing her heart to fail and said that her doctor told her that she might not be able to sit through the trial. As a grieving mother, however, she felt very strongly that her son was murdered and that Nevers should return to prison. "This new trial just opens up new wounds," she said. "I can't get no rest and I know he's not resting" *(Detroit Free Press*, April 19, 2000).

CONCLUSION

Long before the 1967 riot, the racial practices of the Detroit Police Department towards the black community represented the single most important source of racial conflict in Detroit. In many ways it was a form of social control and intimidation that forced the Detroit branch of the NAACP to expend enormous energy processing complaints from black citizens about white police abuse.

In both the 1943 and the 1967 riots, many white police officers abused their power by brutalizing and killing black people. Police action sparked the 1967 riot. Racial conflict over police practices, for example, STRESS, played a key role in the election of Coleman Young, the first black mayor of Detroit. Yet Young's election and long tenure as mayor and his creation of a racially integrated police department did not prevent the brutal murder of a black motorist, Malice Green, by two white police officers.

4

Emergence of Black Political Power After 1967

JOE T. DARDEN AND RICHARD THOMAS

B
lack political power was one of the most historically significant developments after the civil disorders in 1967. White flight to the suburbs paved the way for a black majority in Detroit. Radical and some moderate black leaders wanted nothing less than black political control of the city. And the time was ripe! The political zeitgeist sweeping Detroit—primarily expressed through the election of a black mayor of the city—would change race relations in metropolitan Detroit for decades.

In 1968 the Reverend Albert Cleage Jr., a leader of several black nationalist groups in Detroit during the 1960s, stressed the importance of black political power in areas where blacks were in the majority: "We can vote Black and we can control political structures in any area in which we are a majority. This is a reality, and it's exactly the same thing that Whites would do if they were Black." Blacks would soon be a majority in Detroit, Cleage stated, affirming that "by voting Black we can elect a Black mayor, a Black council and a Black school board." A black candidate's only necessary qualification, according to Cleage, was that he be "devoted to the Black nation, putting his dedication to Black people first" (1968: 18).

Cleage and other black nationalist leaders rejected the traditional biracial liberal coalition politics that had dominated black political history for decades. According to his political calculations after the 1967 "rebellion," blacks would soon control the city and whites could have the suburbs. "We would appreciate it ... if people in the suburbs [whites] would stay in the suburbs, if they would stop trying to live in the suburbs and run our Black community, if they would stop living in the suburbs while holding ... political offices in the cities" (Cleage, 1968: 18). Cleage's view of black political independence saw whites as playing little or no role in the future of black politics in Detroit.

With regard to the whites who still lived in a black-majority city, black nationalists such as Cleage believed they would have to accept, reluctantly or otherwise, black majority rule in the city. This political scenario did not materialize in quite the way that some black nationalists desired, however. Many black moderate activists, no less "nationalist" than Cleage and other radicals, pursued the same political goals but without the rhetoric and fanfare.

The late Robert Millender was one such moderate political activist. A brilliant political strategist, Millender contributed more to black political development in Detroit during the 1967–73 period than all the black radicals and other moderate political activists combined. He was the "kingmaker" of the period. In 1968 he engineered Robert Tindal's election to the city council. A year later he worked on behalf of the unsuccessful Richard Austin campaign for mayor in the closest race in the history of Detroit. Three years later Millender added an impressive black political victory to his record by masterminding the election of Erma Henderson to the city council to replace Tindal, who had died in office. Millender's biggest political success came in 1973, when he managed Coleman Young's campaign to become Detroit's first African American mayor. By then he had overcome his bitterness against Cole-man Young for allegedly failing to marshal votes for Austin (Tyson, 1980).

In the early postriot period, as more whites were leaving Detroit for the suburbs and many of those remaining engaged in last-ditch efforts to maintain political power, the political future of Detroit became one of the major topics of discussion. In the summer of 1968, *Detroit Scope* magazine broached the racially sensitive subject, "Will Detroit's Next Mayor Be a Negro?" Interestingly enough, it linked the election of a black man as mayor to both race and gender. "Whether 1969 will be the year Detroit elects its first Negro mayor—or whether the political inevitable will be delayed until 1973—boils down to a more specific and very intriguing question: Will White women vote for a Negro?" (Mollison, 1968: 5).

The writer reasoned that if Detroit's black population "does not reach 50 percent by next year [1969], or 50 percent of voter registration, a black candidate would need White votes," and since "Detroit has 47,500 more women than men registered to vote … and women outnumber men in 23 of the 24 election districts, it is apparent that this dominance is bi-racial." Furthermore, "since Black women could be counted upon to vote for the Black candidate under almost any circumstance, it is the White women who could hold the balance of power" (Mollison, 1968: 5).

According to this analysis, any black who was preparing to run for mayor in 1969 would have to consider the fact that, because "Negro registration tends to lag behind White registration, and because the expanding Black population has stretched the Negro get-out-the-vote organization to the breaking point, a Negro mayor in 1969 would need White support" (Mollison, 1968: 6). White support for a black candidate, therefore, would be the challenge in 1969 and the litmus test for racial healing in the immediate postriot era.

In the spring of 1969, the *Michigan Chronicle* published an editorial entitled "A Black Mayor May be Detroit's Answer":

> A great city teeters on the brink of ruin, its life blood being sapped by a number of
> ills. Detroiters, in this election year, must come up with the Great Physician who can

diagnose, treat and eventually cure the chronic maladies plaguing the city. We sincerely believe that a capable qualified Black man in the mayor's seat is the wherewithal for starting Detroit on the road to recovery. The time is appropriate, the need is imperative. Across the nation, Whites continue to abandon the cities to Blacks, leaving behind a legacy of woes—soaring crime rates, deteriorating race relations, substandard and insufficient housing, poor school systems, and empty tax coffers. Left behind are the apathetic and disenchanted, with no investment in the future of the city and any trust or respect for existing governments. (*Michigan Chronicle*, April 26, 1969)

The editorial writers realized that "a Black mayor is no panacea," as "Cleveland's Mayor Carl Stokes has warned." They correctly pointed out that "no one is naïve enough to believe that miracles will be wrought overnight just because a man of darker hue occupies the mayor's seat. But we believe that such a man could provide the injection to restore the interest, dedication and vitality needed to get the city moving again" (*Michigan Chronicle*, April 26, 1969). Realizing that Detroit was becoming increasingly polarized by "fear and race tension," the writers claimed that "in view of recent events its growing Black population is going to hold suspect any White administration. And along the same line, Whites who harbor fear that a Black mayor will automatically show partially to Blacks are needlessly worrying" (*Michigan Chronicle*, April 26, 1969).

RICHARD AUSTIN: THE FIRST BLACK MAYORAL CANDIDATE

In 1969, Richard Austin was the ideal black candidate for mayor. Austin was the first black in Detroit to win a mayoral primary, although he lost the final election to Roman S. Gribbs. Austin was a black moderate who not only believed in the liberal coalition but also understood the pragmatism of biracial politics as one means to achieve black political ends after 1967. Like other blacks of his generation, Austin had achieved several black "firsts." He was the first black in Michigan to become a certified public accountant (CPA); the first to achieve membership in the American Institute of CPAs; the first to serve on the board of directors of the Certified Public Accountant Association; and the first to be elected Wayne County auditor (*Michigan Chronicle*, September 6, 1969).

By any objective standard of merit Austin had the professional experience and achievements to become the first black mayor of Detroit. That he did not win election was testimony both to the irrational racism of whites, who two years after the 1967 riot were still trapped in phobias of blacks taking over the city, and to the yet underdeveloped political consciousness of certain segments of the black community.

Some blacks believed that 1969 was not the year to elect a black mayor. Earlier in the year, however, Congressman John Conyers triggered interest among Detroit blacks in the possibility of a black mayor by pushing hard for a black mayoral candidate. Initially, the choice of his old political rival, Richard Austin, for this historic achievement did not excite Conyers. In 1964, they had competed in a close congressional race in which Conyers beat Austin (Tyson, 1980). However, in the mayoral contest Conyers rallied behind his former opponent. Austin came in first in the primary election with 45,856 votes, and Wayne County sheriff Gribbs came in second with 34,650. The white vote was largely split between Gribbs and Mary Beck, a white conservative, who placed third and received 26,480 of the total votes (*Detroit Free Press*, September 10, 1969).

The primary clearly demonstrated the influence of race on local politics. Austin received most of his votes from the black community. He had hoped to get 15 percent of the white vote, but received less than 10 percent. Gribbs and Beck received tremendous support from the white community for their emphasis on "law and order" (which had become a code word among many white suburbanites for controlling black unrest in the city). Gribbs, a white moderate who believed in integration, had antagonized many black leaders when, as assistant Wayne County prosecutor in 1963, he aggressively prosecuted black protesters who participated in the sit-in at the first Federal and Loan Association. As Wayne County sheriff, Gribbs also alienated many people, particularly blacks, when he attempted to get approval for his officers to use Mace, a controversial form of pepper spray. He decided to be a candidate for mayor twenty-four hours before the filing deadline to save the city from a field of what he considered less than acceptable candidates (*Detroit Free Press*, September 10, 1969; *Michigan Chronicle*, September 6, 1969).

Given the state of racial polarization two years after the riot, there can be little doubt that many whites saw Gribbs as their last "white hope" to hold on to their beloved city hopelessly but inevitably falling into the hands of the growing black population. This explains the almost instant response from the powerful white financial community who rallied to support him. Gribbs received financial backing from executives at major banking, business, and legal establishments in the city, including General Motors. Ninety percent of Gribbs's support during the primary came from managers, executives, and lawyers. Most of his financial support was centered in the suburbs. Austin's support, meanwhile, came mainly from Detroiters, most of whom were doctors, dentists, and small business owners (*Detroit Free Press*, September 28, 1969).

This election would set the stage for understanding the political implications of the racial divide between the white suburban and black city populations, which was rapidly widening in the early postriot era. Although whites were fleeing to the suburbs in increasing numbers, claiming it as their new base of white economic and political power in the region, many still wanted to maintain control of an increasingly black city. As Reverend Cleage had commented more than a year earlier, white suburbanites should "stop trying to live in the suburbs while ... holding political offices in the cities" (Cleage, 1968).

As the two top vote-getters in the primary prepared for the November mayoral election, everyone knew that race would be the determining factor in the outcome. For some it was the elephant in the room. The *Free Press* was not alone in recognizing the racial challenge facing

Austin in his bid to become Detroit's first black mayor in a city where many whites were determined to hold on to city hall as long as possible. In September the paper commented, "Although he finished first in the primary, Austin must woo many white voters to win in November ... on the surface it looks like a tough assignment, given the racial polarization shown by Tuesday's overall voting patterns" (*Detroit Free Press*, September 10, 1969).

Austin refused to believe that whites would not vote for a black as mayor of Detroit, but he had no illusions that race was not a key issue. Attacking Gribbs, who had denied that race was a factor, Austin told a group of students in northwest Detroit, "I wish to God he was right. Race is relevant to too many people in this election" (*Michigan Chronicle*, September 20 and November 1, 1969).

How could race not be relevant to many people in 1969 in the wake of the New Bethel incident and the controversy over the role of Judge Crockett in the events of March 1969? Race had to be a major factor to both blacks and whites, as many on both sides of the racial divide rallied for and against the judge for releasing blacks mass-arrested at the church after the killing of one white officer and the wounding of another white officer (see chapter 2). The year had been the most racially polarizing year since the 1967 riot. As much as Austin refused to believe that whites would not vote for a black and Gribbs denied that race was a factor, race loomed large and ominous over the upcoming election.

Interestingly, race seemed far more important to whites than to blacks in the city. For example, blacks pursued a voting pattern similar to the 1965 city council elections when they voted for both black and white candidates, in contrast to white voters who tended to vote only for white candidates (Lewis, 1969). Likewise, in the 1969 election many blacks once again demonstrated their belief in biracial politics by voting for both white and black candidates, while most white voters repeated their 1965 pattern. A citizen research group, the Citizen's Committee for Equal Opportunity, discovered that in the primary election "White voters in appalling numbers simply did not vote for black candidates at all, or in instances where they [considered doing so], gave them such low consideration as to virtually exclude them from serious consideration" (*Michigan Chronicle*, November 1, 1969). The committee reported that, unlike many black voters, white voters were not demonstrating a belief "in the bi-racial future of the city and in the bi-racial representation in city government" (*Michigan Chronicle*, November 1, 1969). In short, many white voters barely acknowledged black political candidates as worthy of holding certain political offices.

The 1969 elections peeled the onion of white racism by examining layer after layer of thinly veiled white racial phobias. That year, a *Detroit Free Press* survey of voters revealed that white voters were mainly concerned about welfare, crime, and "the colored taking over" (*Detroit Free Press*, September 11, 1969). One could only guess as to why so many whites were afraid of blacks having the political power that whites had enjoyed for so long.

The 1969 primary elections also revealed levels of white acceptance or tolerance for degrees of black political power. While some white voters supported blacks for seats on the Detroit

Common Council, they held back on supporting a black for the top office of the mayor. One white west-side residential area made the point clearly when it gave black councilman Nicholas Hood 35 percent of its votes, but gave Austin only 10 percent. No wonder a group of white leaders supporting Austin put full-page advertisements in local newspapers asking white voters, "Can you vote for a black mayor?" (*Detroit Free Press*, November 2, 1969).

Many whites had no problem responding in the negative. Reflecting the views of many white homeowners on the northeast side of Detroit, a newspaper informed its readers that if Austin were elected as Detroit's first black mayor, it would mean the beginning of the end "for the white, tax-paying homeowner." Another paper in the same area warned its readers, "Unless the white conservative voting element in this election exhibits a sudden wave of political intelligence, the election of Negro candidate Richard Austin as Detroit's first black mayor is a foregone conclusion" (*Detroit Free Press*, October 21, 1969).

The most tragic aspect of the 1969 mayoral election was that far too many whites viewed it as a last-ditch effort to maintain white political control in Detroit instead of an opportunity to build a biracial future. As surveys repeatedly demonstrated, the vast majority of whites rejected Austin, this gentle black moderate, solely on the basis of race (*Detroit Free Press*, September 11 and 19, 1969). This grim racial reality was difficult to bear for Austin, who sincerely wanted to bridge the growing post-1967 racial gap. Because he needed white votes to win, Austin campaigned in white communities as he had done in the primary. However, the odds were running against him.

Austin's black supporters who had marshaled the black votes that won him first place in the primary were becoming increasingly frustrated by white voters' blatant refusal to vote for a qualified black candidate because of race, instead of considering merit. Such white racial attitudes reinforced the black nationalist tendencies among some of Austin's followers and eroded the black moderates' faith in the future of racial integration. In his column in the local black newspaper, black nationalist Reverend Albert B. Cleage Jr. shared his frustration: "I support Dick Austin and I feel that he should receive the total Black vote, but inasmuch as his election is dependent upon a large White vote, I see no possibility of his election" (*Michigan Chronicle*, August 23, 1969). After criticizing the black community for not registering enough blacks, Cleage warned, "The White racist syndrome will wipe out White support for Black candidates by election day" (*Michigan Chronicle*, August 23, 1969).

Cleage may have been justified in expressing what seemed like a form of black political fatalism. If blacks failed to register to vote, how could they overcome "the white racist syndrome"? In short, white racism and black political apathy could sabotage the future of black political development in Detroit. The future of the black-white political coalition was also at stake. A writer for the *Michigan Chronicle* (September 23, 1969) explained it best when he put white liberals on notice that if blacks did not come out of the November election "with a healthy victory," there would not be any more black/white coalitions. The writer argued that, in past elections, black/white coalitions had mainly benefited white politicians, and warned that "the Black community is not going to accept the short end or the blind, lame or dead horse in the trade this time."

The black leadership supporting Austin knew all too well that white liberals were not working hard enough to get white votes for black candidates. At a meeting of the black and white liberal politicians and labor leaders, black leaders informed their white allies that "the records will show we in the Black community can deliver votes better than the White community. We are sick and tired of delivering votes for White folks and listening to their excuses later. We are going to stop delivering if you don't deliver for Dick Austin and other Black candidates we have selected" (*Michigan Chronicle*, September 23, 1969).

Black/white coalition politics had reached the first in several critical junctures in the early postdisorder era. Black political activists and strategists had long realized they could call the shots in local coalition politics. Increasingly becoming a minority faction in the coalition, liberal whites had to face the fact that as blacks became a numerical majority in Detroit, they would be less responsive to the dictates of the previously white-dominated liberal coalition. That time was certainly not in November 1969, however. Dick Austin badly needed the coalition in order to win, but the coalition could not deliver sufficient white votes to give Austin the victory and the office of the mayor. Sadly, Austin lost the election, but left his indelible mark on the political history of black and white Detroit (*Detroit Free Press*, September 19, 1969).

This was a major political defeat for the black community, but their growing numbers dictated that eventually they would prevail against the protracted political rearguard action of those whites who were determined to hold on to political power in an increasingly black city. As one very perceptive white reporter observed, "After years of fitful and sometimes explosive growth, a new politics has emerged in Detroit. It belongs not to the left or the right, but to the steadily growing black community.... Within a very few years, most of the burdens and benefits of local political power will rest with blacks" (*Detroit Free Press*, October 21, 1969).

Most whites—even those who feared and resisted it—realized that it would only be a matter of time before the black community had enough votes to elect a black mayor and a predominantly black common council without heavy reliance on white votes. Black political activists and strategists had always known that black population growth and white flight would eventually win the day. Veteran politician Coleman Young, sitting in the state senate, bided his time, knowing that he was destined to play a major role in the "new politics" of Detroit.

COLEMAN YOUNG: THE FIRST BLACK MAYOR OF DETROIT

State Senator Coleman Young and Richard Austin could not have been more different in their personal history and political style. Austin had a quiet and accommodating political demeanor and style that had served him well in becoming the first black in various professional and political positions. Young, in contrast, had a more rough-and-tumble, combative political demeanor and style developed in the labor and black radical movements of the late 1930s and ensuing years. Young's father had been forced to flee Tuscaloosa, Alabama, where Young was born, because he was considered to be an "uppity nigger." As Young explained in his autobiography, "my father and his brothers were ambitious, more learned than most blacks in that part of the county.... My father got [whites'] attention after he moved his family to Tuscaloosa ... because he sold and circulated black newspapers like the *Pittsburgh Courier* and the *Chicago Defender*." These northern newspapers were threatening to whites "because [they] encouraged black people to read ... and put all sorts of Northern ideas in their heads, such as voting and integrated schools and labor unions." His father was forced to take the family to Detroit (Young and Wheeler, 1994: 13).

As a young man working at Ford Motor Company, Young hit a racist foreman in the head with a steel bar and as a result lost his job. His early involvement in the labor movement and his military experiences as a second lieutenant in the famous Tuskegee Airmen—in a Jim Crow army—had a profound influence on his later political views and positions on combating racial discrimination. During World War II he was arrested along with 100 other black officers for attempting to integrate an all-white officers club at Freeman Field, Indiana (Young and Wheeler, 1994). Three years after the war ended, in 1948, Young became the Michigan chair of Henry Wallace's Progressive Party presidential campaign (Tyson, 1980).

His uncompromising radicalism continued in the 1950s when he helped organize the National Negro Labor Council (NNLC), the most radical black labor organization of that period, and became its executive director. When the House Committee on Un-American Activities (HUAC) began investigating the Detroit chapter of the NNLC, Young found himself in the national limelight. In February 1952 Young stood his ground and defiantly told the members of the committee: "I am part of the Negro people. I am now in process of fighting against what I consider to be attacks and discrimination against my people. I am fighting against un-American activities such as lynching and denial of the vote. I am dedicated to that fight and I don't think I have to apologize or explain it to anybody" (Foner, 1981; Young and Wheeler, 1994: 128).

Young was one of the first radicals, black or white, to stand up to HUAC, making it clear that he would not be a "stool pigeon." When one of the committee's southern members mispronounced "Negro" as "Niggra," Young corrected him: "As a Negro, I resent the slurring of the name of my race" (Young and Wheeler, 1994: 121). Such bold defiance of the dreaded HUAC was captured on phonograph records that soon began circulating throughout the black community, elevating Young to the status of a local folk hero (Young and Wheeler, 1994).

Predictably Young's radicalism soon caught the attention of the head of the Detroit FBI. In 1954, he wrote to J. Edgar Hoover describing Young as a "dangerous individual" who "should be one of the first to be picked up in an emergency and one of the first to be considered for future prosecution" (Thompson, 2001: 195).

In 1961 Young was elected to participate in the rewriting of the Michigan state constitution. In 1964 he was elected to the state senate and moved to the position of Democratic leader (Rich, 1989: 84–85). Four years later, he became the new Democratic leader committeeman from Michigan, becoming the first black in the nation to be elected to that position. His election to this position proved to Young that racial attitudes were changing and whites were beginning to vote for candidates based on their qualifications instead of their color. At this juncture of his political career, the future mayor still believed in the efficacy of the liberal coalition for black political development, but with qualifications: "I am a Negro first and a Democrat second," he said (*Detroit Free Press*, January 4, 1976; *Lansing State Journal*, July 7, 1968). During the black nationalist period, when black separatists talked about carving out their own country in the southern United States, Young said they were "just smoking marijuana." To Young, a coalition with liberal whites was "the only way" (*Detroit Free Press*, September 22, 1968).

Senator Coleman Young seriously considered becoming a candidate for mayor of Detroit in 1969 but was prevented from doing so by a Michigan Supreme Court ruling that barred a state legislator from running for another office before the expiration of his or her current term. Young, then a three-term senator, had wanted to run because he believed that Austin had not caught on and had failed to give "the people anything to sink their teeth into as far as what he could do as mayor." According to Young, Austin's biggest shortcoming was his failure to commit himself publicly to such issues as civilian control of the police department (*Detroit Free Press*, September 10, 1969).

Some people believed that Young was not willing to support Austin. In a 1986 interview, however, Young claimed that he was not asked to participate in the Austin mayoral campaign. "I went down to the Austin headquarters and asked to help. I didn't know they had a small room in the back where they decided strategy. I was told to get out the vote in my district. I felt it was insulting. I asked, what can you do for my district? There was no consultation. Austin lost because the numbers were not right. He also took the black vote for granted" (Rich, 1989: 96).

In 1973, four years after the disappointing defeat of Richard Austin, the black community began to rally behind Young. He was ready not only to run for mayor but, most importantly, to make control of the police department a central part of his campaign. In a speech kicking off his primary campaign, Young put the police department and Police Commissioner John Nichols on notice that STRESS was a major problem in a city divided by race. "One of the problems is that the police run the city ... STRESS is responsible for the explosive polarization that now exists; STRESS is an execution squad rather than an enforcement squad. As mayor, I will get rid of STRESS" (*Detroit Free Press*, May 11, 1973). He added, "The whole attitude of the whole Police Department, historically, has been one of intimidation and that citizens can be kept in line with clubs and guns rather than respect. The present department under Nichols is following the old blackjack rule by terror. If elected, I would fire Nichols" (*Detroit Free Press*, May 11, 1973). The police responded by endorsing Nichols, who was also running for mayor (Ashton, 1981).

In the primary Nichols and Young came in first and second respectively in a field of five, with Nichols getting 33.8 percent of the vote and Young getting 21.1 percent. The voting patterns revealed that each candidate would have to appeal to both black and white voters in order to have a chance of winning in November (Ashton, 1981).

Young had more than a growing black political base on his side. His broad political experience in local, state, and national politics gave him an important edge over the single-issue Nichols. Notwithstanding this edge, Nichols had the advantage of exploiting white fear of black crime in the street. Young knew better than to ignore crime, but his appeal to white voters emphasized economic development for the city. He promised to lead a "business resurgence" that would produce thousands of jobs and would include "new park facilities, a stadium, rapid transit, recreational facilities and housing." Young also advised the business elite of Detroit to invest in the city instead of the suburbs. In contrast, Nichols focused on crime in the street, which he argued was the most important issue in the city (Ashton, 1981).

Although Young stressed economic programs in his campaign, he never lost sight of the need to control the predominately white police department. He explained, "With the field narrowed to Nichols and me, the election was reduced to a showdown over law enforcement policies. I regretted that insufficient attention was being paid to the matter of Detroit's reconstruction, but was pleased to have the battle waged over an issue I felt so strongly about" (Young and Wheeler, 1994). According to Young, the debate over the role of the police department was crucial to Detroit's future. Nichols had to be defeated because he represented a national trend of increased police power in postriot cities.

As Young put it, "I genuinely believed that a victory by Nichols would deliver a troubling, oppressive message to the rest of the country and goose it along toward a coast-to-coast police state. Somebody had to stop the cops." Young saw himself as that person. "At street level," Young explained, "the campaign boiled down essentially to one question: Should white officers be allowed to continue to kill black people in the name of law enforcement?" (Young and Wheeler, 1994: 58).

To their credit, both Young and Nichols tried to avoid race, but any dialogue about the police became by extension a dialogue about race. Young admitted,

> The race was about race. Everybody in the city was aware of that, despite the fact that Nichols and I tried to hold our tongues whenever the issue turned to color. For me, it was only prudent to assume a conciliatory tone, because the white voters seemed to harbor a preconception that I would run them off with guns or spears or something and turn the city into a black empire. To assuage those fears, I assured them that my hiring practices would reflect a fifty-fifty racial balance. (Young and Wheeler, 1994)

During one of the "Great Debates" between the mayoral candidates, Nichols was asked why blacks should vote for him. He said, "I would hope that if there's one white man out there who's going to vote for me simply because I am white, that he would stay home on Election Day. I don't think that the criteria should be how much we can appeal to each other's ethnic group, but rather how much we can appeal to the broad base of citizens" (Rich, 1989: 104). Referring to his opponent in the race, Nichol added, "I would hope that the senator shares this belief in that we should be selected for what we stand for and not for who we are or what our accident of birth have made us in terms of skin pigmentation" (Rich, 1989: 104).

Young responded that he didn't have any problem "with that general approach. I have said before that I'm running on a program. I espouse no position which is good for blacks which I don't consider to be good for whites and vice versa. I hope to be judged and I expect to be judged based on my program. I am not naïve," Young stated. "I know that there is polarization in this city. I'm seeking to close that polarization and to unite the differences between the races. And I believe that based upon my experience, again in the legislature, the labor movement, and across the spectrum of my public life, I have been able to appeal to all groups" (Rich, 1989: 104).

The November poll revealed that whites could only equalize the ballot by turning out at a rate 6 percent higher than blacks, "but the Nichols campaign was not generating that kind of interest among white voters" (Rich, 1989: 105). Possibly most of the 58,000 new registrants that fall were black, clearly a good sign for Young. In the end, Young won the election by "a city-wide total of only 16,741 votes" (Rich, 1989: 105), becoming Detroit's first black mayor. Two decades later, reflecting back on that historic day, Young wrote:

> On Election Day, I became the goddamn mayor of Detroit. There wasn't a single precinct in the city that was close—Nichols took the white ones and I took the black ones.... Afterwards, I was hard-put to place the day in perspective. On one hand—the hand in which I gripped memories of the Boblo guide who turned me away from the park, the Catholic school priest who had torn up my application, Tuskegee, Freeman Field, Walter Reuther ... the Un-American Activities Committee, the attorney general, and all the jobs I had lost over the years—it was a preposterous, impossible dream come true, an only-in-America kind of thing. On the other hand, I knew that this had only happened because, for once in my life, I was in the right place at the right time, and that my fortune was a direct result of my city's misfortune—of the same fear and loathing that had caused all of my problems and Detroit's problems in the first place. I was taking over the administration of Detroit because the white people didn't want the damn thing anymore. They were getting the hell out, more than happy to turn over their troubles to some black sucker like me. (Young and Wheeler, 1994: 200)

At that moment in 1973 Young had won a much-coveted prize for the black community, which was still in the throes of the aftermath of the 1967 riot. The results of this historic election demonstrated the valuable lessons black politicians had learned since the disappointing Austin defeat in 1969: "They now knew how to target their appeals, and they had their man campaign in white districts, even though there was an equal risk in those areas of losing votes as there was in gaining them." This was not merely a "symbolic gesture" to get white votes, but instead "it helped to show a commitment to both white and black voters that the candidate intended to conduct a fair administration. During and after the campaign, the newly elected mayor reiterated his commitment to a 50/50 administration" (Rich, 1989: 105).

The victory did not blind Mayor Young to the need to bring the races together in a city that was half black and half white. Soon after his victory he proclaimed to his supporters, "I didn't win; we won. All of Detroit won" (*Detroit Free Press*, November 8, 1973). Although he emphasized racial unity in his inaugural address, saying, "What is good for the black people in this city is good for the white people in this city," Young and his black and white supporters could not conceal their unabashed enthusiasm for the newly emerging political order. This was a black political victory, plain and simple.

A writer for the *Detroit Free Press*, one of the two white daily newspapers, understood the significance of the moment:

> The factors that led to state Sen. Coleman A. Young's election Tuesday as Detroit's first black mayor represents a major turning point in the city's racial and political history. After half a decade of falling just short, Detroit's blacks finally have wrested the balance of power from the city's whites. Blacks now have the deciding vote in major elections, especially in ones as clearly drawn as the race between Young and the white former police commissioner, John Nichols. (*Detroit Free Press*, November 8, 1973)

A few days after the historic election, a *Detroit Free Press* editorial, "Watershed Election Offers Opportunity, Hope for City" (1973), explained another benefit of the historical election: the campaign itself. The quality of the campaign between the two men, while contentious, at times was "open beyond belief. It was not racist. It was issue-oriented. John Nichols can move on to other endeavors secure in the knowledge that he, even in losing, has made a strong contribution to the stability and health of the city that he loves." Young, on the other hand,

> brings to his new office a wealth of experience in dealing with people of varied backgrounds and philosophies.... In his campaign he enjoyed the support of a number of institutions and organizations with multiracial leadership, and while these did not translate into massive white support, they do at least provide him a base for building the confidence of the city's white population. (*Detroit Free Press*, November 8, 1973)

Coming out of such a close election in a racially polarized city, the *Detroit Free Press* editorial writers understood all too well the burden of race that the new black mayor would have to shoulder. "In any close election, the victor comes to office needing to overcome the doubts and fears of those who did not support him," the writers argued, "He must govern everybody. That is particularly true now, when Mayor Young will have to overcome the fears left over from this city's past difficulty in keeping race from being a problem" (*Detroit Free Press*, November 8, 1973).

Sadly, most of the "doubts and fears" were among those whites who had voted against Austin and supported Nichols strictly on the basis on race, and who now saw "their city" being taken over by blacks. Some white northeast residents interviewed late Tuesday, the day of the election, talked about blacks "taking over the city" and planned on moving out (*Detroit Free Press*, November 8, 1973). Notwithstanding this all too pervasive white racial attitude, the editorial sounded a much-needed hopeful note:

> We believed Detroit is mature enough and sophisticated enough to be able to accommodate this change, to become more stable rather than less, to provide justice and

security for whites and blacks alike. It is, as the mayor-elect said Tuesday, time for Detroit to become a great city again. Detroit has had enough of division and distrust. Let us build a city that will make us proud. Let us build it together. (*Detroit Free Press*, November 8, 1973)

Two days after the election, George Romney, former governor and former secretary of U.S. Department of Housing and Urban Development, commented that Young did not have a chance of coping effectively with Detroit's critical problems. He believed that no politician could solve these problems because of the nature of the American political system. "We expect too much from the political process," Romney concluded, reflecting his belief that the American political system was incapable of solving the real ills of the nation (*Detroit Free Press*, January 3, 1973).

The *Detroit Free Press* editorial writers took issue with Romney, however. Commenting that mayor-elect Young was "setting the right tone for his administration," they wrote that Young "has an opportunity that is unique in the city's history … to show this city, which has suffered through two of the worst race-related riots in American history, that we can put all that behind us—that we can work together to make Detroit a less fearsome place and a more hopeful city." Referring to Romney's doomsday scenario of the future of Detroit, the writers explained that Young's mission "is perhaps as important as any that ever confronted a mayor of the city of Detroit. It is a mission that, as former Gov. George Romney glumly observed, the system will tend to frustrate. But the new mayor-elect simply cannot accept Mr. Romney's verdict that his mission is foredoomed to failure. Detroit and Michigan cannot accept it either" (*Detroit Free Press*, November 13, 1973).

The Police Reaction

Predictably, many white officers were upset over the election of Young. At police headquarters the morning after the election, "there was an undertone of disappointment, irritation—maybe even betrayal—over the fact that Detroit had elected a black mayor. Nichols had been their man. He had put 30 years in the force and worked his way up the hard way from patrolman to commissioner." Young, on the other hand, "was a constant critic of the police force. He talked of abolishing the STRESS unit and bringing more blacks into the department" (*Detroit Free Press*, November 8, 1973).

One STRESS officer with twenty-two years in the department described the postelection atmosphere: "Things were kind of gloomy around here this morning. The guys are usually clowning around, but this morning they were kind of quiet. But finally I told them, there've been mayors before and they're all politicians. What's so different about this one?" (*Detroit Free Press*, November 8, 1973). To his credit, Nichols, in his defeat, asked the city to support the new mayor, which undoubtedly influenced the attitudes of some white police officers. During his concession speech, Nichols was asked if the police department "will survive." He resounded with a laugh and said, "The police department will always survive. The police department has resilience and it has strength and it will survive" (*Detroit Free Press*, November 8, 1973).

While some white police officers lamented the future under a black mayor, others took the change in stride. As one white plainclothes officers told his gloomy partner, "Look at it this way, there's always going to be crooks in Detroit and somebody has to catch them and put them in jail. Young's not going to change that, is he?" Other white officers speculated that maybe a black mayor might help them do their job better. "Maybe now," one white officer commented, "these black kids will have somebody to look up to" (*Detroit Free Press*, November 8, 1973).

One white inspector reported that he was "completely calm and confident that either one of the candidates would have made a successful mayor." In fact, he and many other white officers were more worried about the new city charter that was approved, with its provision for an ombudsman who would investigate complaints against the police, than the election of Coleman as the first black mayor. According to the above inspector, "the charter—that's the real Pandora's Box. That part about the ombudsman is fantastic. Whoever gets that is going [to be] a real dictator" (*Detroit Free Press*, November 8, 1973). No doubt he was referring to the ten-year term and wide powers that would be given to the ombudsman by the city council to "investigate city agencies for incompetence or corruption, and to help citizens with complaints about the bureaucracy" (*Detroit Free Press*, November 7, 1973).

The police department had reason to be concerned. The city charter, which passed by 44,000 votes, eliminated the office of police commissioner and established a five-person civilian board of commissioners appointed by the mayor. The mayor, in turn, would "appoint a police chief for administrative purposes, and complaints against the department will be handled by a civilian board, an idea that is repugnant to most policemen." Furthermore, the charter provided for an ombudsman to be appointed by the city council "to handle citizen's complaints in city departments" (*Detroit Free Press*, November 8, 1973).

Some writers for the *Michigan Chronicle*, the largest black weekly newspaper in the state, tempered their enthusiasm for the historic moment with advice for the future. In an open letter to the community entitled "Young Can't Do It By Himself," one writer wrote:

> For the first time in the history of Detroit, the nation's fifth largest city, a Black man has been elected as its chief executive and jubilance abounds throughout the Black community because of that victory. The election of Coleman A. Young to the mayor's seat is a dream come true for many of us who have worked long and hard to muster enough political clout to make that dream a reality ... [However,] amid the celebration and joy over the fact that, as Mayor-Elect Young said, "We have won our place in the sun," we are sobered by the Herculean task that faces our new mayor.... It is on this sobering note that we convey this open letter to urge one and all to rise to the occasion and put our collective shoulders to the wheel as we have never done before. We have a right to be joyful, but at the same time we must keep the realistic fact of life before

us that the hard work and diligent efforts have just begun. So there is no time to relax in victory. (*Michigan Chronicle*, November 12, 1973)

Inauguration Day, 1974

On the morning before the inaugural luncheon in January 1974, some of Young's followers held a prayer meeting, during which the Reverend Charles Butler of the New Calvary Baptist Church, referring to Young, cited the biblical phrase "Behold this man." As one newspaper observed, although members of Detroit's power elite were present, "for the first time in Detroit the street people who knew 'Coleman' when he was down and struggling were in on things, watching from the edges of the crowd, smiling as if they had been graced by greatness" (*Detroit Free Press*, January 3, 1974).

Like other joyful but wary black leaders and observers, federal judge Damon J. Keith knew the mayor would soon be facing formidable challenges. During the prayer breakfast he presented some sage advice to the new mayor:

> Always let it be known that your administration will treat all citizens with dignity and promote self-respect. I invite your attention to the fact that all those who have reached the level of excellence are characterized by their fairness, their humility and the manner in which they deal with those who are subordinate to them. Few persons have ever attained high position and remained in those high positions very long by demeaning others ... personal integrity is an absolute and necessary quality in our public officials, especially during these troubled times. (*Michigan Chronicle*, January 5, 1974)

Judge Keith next addressed what everyone knew would be one of the greatest challenges facing the new Young administration: crime, especially black-on-black crime, and the police:

> We must devise a means of riding this city, root and branch, of the criminals who are committing murders, rapes and assaults on the people of this city. I am aware of all the sociological reasons as to why crimes are committed and understand most of them, but I say to you that while we work to eliminate poverty, substandard housing, inadequate education and all the evils that are the byproduct of a racist society, we must also, without delay or equivocation, strive to make this city of ours a safe place in which to live, in which to raise our children, in which to enjoy the fruits of our labors and our God-given rights. (*Michigan Chronicle*, January 5, 1974)

Keith then addressed the sensitive issue of black-on-black crime. "Let us look, not with shame but with cold logic at the record. The crime problem, which has won for our city an unprecedented degree of adverse publicity, is essentially a wave sparked by Black criminals preying upon Black victims. Tragically," the judge explained, "this crime wave is aided and abetted by

Black people, by an 'it's no business of mine' attitude. When police come, nobody is there who remembers seeing anything" (*Michigan Chronicle*, January 5, 1974).

Keith then turned the topic to the challenges facing the Detroit Police Department in an unjust society. "Our police today are assigned an almost impossible task. They are asked by the larger society to maintain order in an unjust society, a society which has systematically and illegally frustrated Blacks in their efforts to survive. But the police alone cannot keep order unless and until the major institutions in the larger society demand justice" (*Michigan Chronicle*, January 5, 1974).

He then turned his attention to the new mayor, saying, "It is you who can awaken every citizen, Black and White, to the truism that policemen alone cannot do the job that is the obligation of every citizen and a part of citizenship to cooperate with the police." The judge told Mayor Young, "Your call, loudly given, and responded to, can reverse the crime trend in this city and prove more than any other one thing that a Black man can run a city in an outstanding manner and bring it new honors. Thus, Mr. Mayor, you must lead a revolt of the people of this community for justice and against crime" (*Michigan Chronicle*, January 5, 1974).

Keith ended his talk by returning to the solemn purpose of the spiritual breakfast:

> Let it be said as we go forth this morning, from this monumental and historic prayer breakfast, that this is one of Detroit's finest hours. In the years to come, let it be said that Coleman A. Young contributed mightily to freedom, prosperity and dignity for all people during his administration, and that this quality of freedom which we hold so precious and which is indeed so unique, will be his legacy to our city, our children and to our country. (*Michigan Chronicle*, January 5, 1974)

That afternoon, Detroit Corporate and labor leaders gathered at the Cobo inaugural luncheon to honor the new mayor. Among them were such notables as Henry Ford II, chairman of the Ford Motor Company, and Leonard Woodcock, UAW president. Ford explained the significance of the new day. "We, here in this room, represent the beginning of a new coalition of business and labor, brought together by our mutual desire to pledge our support to the newly inaugurated mayor" (*Detroit Free Press*, January 3, 1974). Ford's support would be crucial in the coming years because black political power in Detroit, personified by the new black mayor, would still need powerful and willing white allies to rebuild the city. While some of Young's black followers might have been too drunk with the wine of victory to see or want it, of necessity the "new politics" would include the biracial liberal coalition.

This was, indeed, a new and glorious day for blacks in Detroit as they and their white allies engaged in a three-day inaugural celebration and the new mayor told the criminals to hit the road (Rich, 1989). Notwithstanding the well-deserved jubilation, the harsh realities of running a troubled city were waiting in the wings for the curtain to rise on this new era of black political control:

As the band played, singer Diana Ross performed, Judge Damon Keith spoke, and the crowd cheered for Young's success, the city was reacting to the recession of 1974. The first black mayor of Detroit had inherited a politically rich city but an economically poor one. In his first four years of office, he would have a fiscal crisis in 1975, a near riot, a police confrontation over layoffs and residency rules, and the threat to close Chrysler's Jefferson Avenue plant. (Rich, 1989: 105–6)

Continued Tensions in Detroit

One of the first racial crises of the Young's administration occurred in 1975, when a black teenager named Obie Wynn was shot in the back and killed by a white bar owner. The situation had the potential of becoming another 1967 riot. Angry black protestors looted the bar and burned its carpet before they were chased away. As soon as he was informed of the crisis, Mayor Young ordered his white police chief, Philip Tannian, to send every black officer in the department to the scene, "the idea being to merge them with white officers and make a show of racial unity on the street." When the police chief informed the mayor "that he had no way of knowing which of his officers were black," the mayor, in his well-known manner, responded: "Bullshit, I said. In about an hour, they were all there" (Young and Wheeler, 1994: 207).

When Mayor Young and a group of community leaders were unable to calm the situation, Young decided to "fight attitude with attitude." He climbed up on a car and, as he recalled years later, "spoke to the people as angrily and sternly as I dared without turning them against me, figuring that the only way to check their mood was with a passionate petition of reason." He told them that "Detroit was their city and they should not tear it apart; also, that there was a difference between justice and vigilante violence and that I, like them, was interested in the former" (Young and Wheeler, 1994: 207).

The recent memory of John Conyers being stoned when he tried to calm a mob from the top of a car during the 1967 riot was not lost on Young. "When other black leaders had stood on cars during the 1967 uprising, the community had shouted them down," he recalled. "But this time was different, because the crowd knew that my words were more than rhetoric: I was the goddamn mayor. I guess they figured they owed me one more chance to prove myself. It probably didn't hurt my case when somebody threw a rock at me, which earned me some sympathy points." Young passed this first test. He had prevented more violence and a repeat of the 1967 riot, but people were still angry, and he was criticized from both sides (Young and Wheeler, 1994: 207).

The situation worsened when a Polish baker returning home soon after Wynn's killing was pulled from his car and stoned to death. Young marshaled black and white community leaders, including the parish bishop and Polish community leaders, to ease the situation. He visited the widow and mother of the victim, assuring them that justice would be served. Reflecting back on this crisis, Young wrote: "We were probably on the verge of another major riot at that moment. But it never materialized, and I firmly believe that it was our community presence which ultimately saved the day—the cooperative effort of neighborhood leaders and black and white police officers" (Young and Wheeler, 1994: 208).

Young was clearly thankful for how things turned out and attributed the outcome to the newly instituted police reforms: "Black and white police officers—including some of the newly hired women on the force—were performing in a very professional manner despite extreme provocation in the form of bricks and the like." Given the death toll of the 1967 riot, he was quick to acknowledge that this racially integrated police presence, including women, was able to restore order without firing a single shot. "If we had gone about cracking heads in the Detroit tradition, there would have been hell to pay. It was a trial by fire for our police reforms, and thank God they worked." It would not have worked, however, if the mayor had not ordered his police chief to send all black police officers in the department to the scene. This was a race-relations stroke of genius rooted in Young's understanding of how white police departments too often have mishandled racial crises. "That may have been the first time in Detroit history that black police officers had been called upon for emergency work" (Young and Wheeler, 1994: 208).

Changes to the Police Department

The greatest evidence of rising black political power in Detroit during Mayor Young's first term in office was the radical change in the racial makeup of the police department—not an easy task, considering the resistance of many white police officers and their unions. After several years of power struggles and countless bouts of negotiations, Young made some progress in changing a predominantly white police department into one that was at least in the process of becoming more racially integrated. By the end of 1976 Detroit boasted its first black police chief and a top command structure that was half black and half white. One hundred black officers had been hired since Young's election, increasing black representation from 17 percent to 22 percent (Ashton, 1981).

The "old boy's network," which had perpetuated and maintained white male privilege in promotions for decades, was forced to give way to Young's aggressive affirmative action program. As a result of this program, blacks went from 5 percent of all officers holding the rank of sergeant to 15 percent (Ashton, 1981). As Young explained in his autobiography, the police unions fought change at every turn: "As the issues played out, the battle was joined over two policies we instituted in order to bring parity to the racial balance of the department and make it more community-oriented. First, we began to enforce the city's residency rule, under which it was mandatory for police officers and other city employees to live within the city limits of Detroit." This rule, Young points out, "had been on the books since 1914 but was largely winked at by administrations prior to mine." Therefore, he argued, "Given the prevailing 'us versus them' law-enforcement climate in Detroit, the residency rule was vital to our efforts to increase the community element in the neighbor-hood. Consequently, we stuck with it in spite of vehement objections from the veteran cops" (Young and Wheeler, 1994: 209).

The other policy was "the existing police promotion procedures," which was based on testing which Mayor Young believed "was culturally biased and effectively discriminated against black officers." This proved to be a major challenge to the Young administration. "Without ripping apart the system," Young claimed, "we profoundly modified it by establishing two lists of test scores—one for white officers and for black. After a qualifying mark was established as a cut-off for eligibility, promotions were made alternately by selecting the officers with the highest score from the white list, then the officer with the highest score from the black list" (Young and Wheeler, 1994: 210).

Young argued that this approach did not favor black officers because they were not promoted unless "they had passed the test." In fact, Young continued, "records show that in the oral-board portion of the test, black officers on the average have scored higher than whites." This policy was not limited to blacks and whites, but also "ensure[ed] that women, who constituted only 1 percent of the department in 1974, were hired in far greater numbers" (Young and Wheeler, 1994: 210).

As expected, white police officers did not like Young's two-list policy and filed suit against him and the city of Detroit, arguing that the policy constituted reverse discrimination. Young's attitude was, "You're damn right—the only way to arrest discrimination is to reverse it." It was a long struggle, but as Young tells the story, "The final round, resolved ten years later after it was filed, was heard by the United States Supreme Court, which upheld the appellate court's decision that our policies constituted 'a valid and permissible remedy' for past discrimination."

Another police suit "contesting the promotion of officers to sergeant" through three appeals also went the way of the city, but it took twenty years. The final ruling on the case from the Sixth Circuit Court of Appeals in Cincinnati was delivered in late March 1993. When Mayor Young heard of the decision, he told the media, "After twenty years of pursuing a persistent program of affirmative action, fighting with one hand in the courts all the way, for the first time we can say we have reached our goal. The department is truly fifty-fifty, both across the board and in command ranks, including sergeant" (Young and Wheeler, 1994: 210–11).

Young and the Carter Administration

Mayor Young ended his first term in office by helping to put Jimmy Carter in the White House. As a major black figure in national Democratic politics and in labor and business circles, Young had both the power and credibility to deliver powerful black voting blocs to Carter. Young possessed such influence that when Carter slipped during the 1976 presidential campaign, saying that he saw nothing wrong with "ethnic purity"—a statement many interpreted as advocating racial purity—Young defended the Democratic candidate, explaining that he had been misunderstood. Carter was still apologizing when he met Young at the Detroit airport. As soon as Young boarded Carter's plane, he told Carter, "Get up off your knees and keep on walking" (Tyson, 1980: 38; Young and Wheeler, 1994: 223).

In 1976 during a speech in Providence, Rhode Island, Young was asked why he supported Carter: "In my view his record as the Governor of Georgia was an outstanding one. It certainly demonstrates concern for poor people, for minorities, and support for civil rights. Coming from Georgia, I think that's an outstanding thing" (Young, 1976). When asked how he felt about Carter's reservations about bussing and whether it bothered him, Young did not hesitate to express a view at odds with many black leaders. "No, no, it doesn't bother me at all; I share his reservations. I think 'bussing' is a kind of catch-all; it's not an automatic cure-all. Putting a little White kid and a little Black kid in those schools is no chemical or magical guarantee for a quality education," he argued. "I don't give a damn how you mix up Black and White within the city of Detroit; it's still only something dividing the children. No amount of integration is going to do it: improve education" (Young, 1976). In response to another question about Carter's stance on bussing and racial code words, Young continued to defend Carter.

"He fought to have Blacks admitted to the Baptist Church in Plains, Georgia, where he's a member. Now if there's anything that is more personal than school, it's church. And he does live in an integrated community" (Young, 1976).

When Carter became president, Mayor Young's political power multiplied by virtue of the leverage he now had in the White House. Carter's urban policies reflected Young's. Young's appointees ended up in the Carter administration, channeling federal money to Detroit. During the Carter administration, Mayor Young could be seen operating in the country's highest councils (Tyson, 1980).

Campaigning for Carter's reelection in Chicago on October 19, 1980, Young recounted how Detroit had suffered under President Ford and the Republicans. "We were having great difficulty in Washington with President Ford. We had two Bills passed in '76 that would have brought some money to our city, and Mr. Ford vetoed both of them," Young said. "The Republican Party had literally turned its back on the cities," he continued. "They started talking about the silent majority and middle America. And in doing so, literally wrote off the cities, blue collar workers, poor folks, and, and minorities. They said they didn't need us.... Reagan's coming from the same place" (Young, 1980: 1). Young reminded his audience that President Carter had fought for programs to support the survival of cities whereas the Republicans had adopted an approach that in part placed people "in a so-called silent majority—that means white suburbs—and then literally turn them against the white people that live in the cities and divide the nation along those lines." On the other hand, Carter's support had helped Detroit to reduce crime in the last three years. "That can be attributed very directly to what ... I unabashedly call—Jimmy Carter dollars" (Young, 1980: 3). When Carter lost his reelection bid, Mayor Young and the city lost its most important supporter.

Reflections on Young's First Term: Interview with the Michigan Chronicle

After three years in office and on the eve of his own reelection bid, Young spoke about his successes and failures in various areas of race relations. In an interview with the *Michigan Chronicle* he was asked if his affirmative action policies were working out to his satisfaction. He replied: "No. There have been peaks and valleys. We won some and lost some. But it's mandated in the city charter and we intend to continue working for it. We've made some progress in the Police Department; we haven't done as well in the Fire Department. But we plan to continue our fight there" (*Michigan Chronicle*, January 22, 1977).

The interviewer then mentioned that Mayor Young's "chances for reelection and indeed the wellbeing and future of the city depend on the quality of race relations," and posed the question, "How do you feel about the current state of race relations in the city and what do you believe your administration has contributed in that area?" Young replied that "there is much less tension between Blacks and Whites than there was three years ago. As far as my administration is concerned, I have tried to demonstrate in my appointments which have been 50/50, that it is possible to have a fair distribution of jobs and all the other possible things among peoples of different races and creeds." Notwithstanding the ongoing challenges to his affirmative action policies, Young informed the interviewer that the policies in "the Police Department and other areas of city government … have resulted in good relations. One of the best examples is the Police Department. Under Chief Hart, who is Black, that department is united, more so than it was under a White chief. Chief Hart is doing a good job and is respected" (*Michigan Chronicle*, January 22, 1977).

Young went on to mention a morning prayer breakfast he had just attended as another example of good race relations. "I was at a prayer breakfast attended by clerical and lay representatives of all denominations and persuasions, Black, White and Latino. I saw it as a possible educational experience. Everyone knows that 11 A.M. on Sunday is the most segregated hour in the week," Young said, "but I think we do a bit better here than in most places. It may seem a small thing but it's important" (*Michigan Chronicle*, January 22, 1977).

Asked about the high and low points of his term to date, Young responded, "Sometimes you can have a high point when you avoid disaster." He was obviously referring to the near riot he faced after the shooting of the black teenager. Young explained that the high point in that case occurred "when we found a police department, which had been guilty of excesses in the past, being professional and, even under provocation, not firing a single shot. We also found leaders, Black and White, who had the courage to get out there in front of angry citizens and helped keep the peace." Mayor Young then expanded on that high point in race relations, which involved avoiding another 1967-type riot. "When we emerged from what could have been even worse than 1967 without a single person being killed as a result of police action, or actions of citizens against police, that to me was significant. Because it involved people of all races and religions, it told me that Detroit has picked itself up." When asked about his biggest disappointment, he pointed to the fact that Detroit has been in a "depression for the two and a half years that [he has] been in office. That has meant that I've had my back against the wall. Most of my time has been spent putting out fires instead of going ahead with our plans for the city" (*Michigan Chronicle*, January 22, 1977).

One of the biggest questions related to race relations was "the fear of crime which has so many people in Detroit scared to death." Young reported that he had recalled all the police officers who had been laid off and planned to add more. "But," he added, "there also has to be an educational approach. We have to teach people to look out for one another, to get away from that ... city attitude that everyone has to mind his own business. When a man's house is broken into, it isn't just that man's business. I think a change in the attitude can reduce the fear of crime." Asked about what legacy he would like to leave behind, Young answered, "A rebuilt and unified city ... a city in which the dry rot and deterioration have been stopped ... a city with an educational system in which our young people can get a decent education ... a city which doesn't have the disgraceful situation of a 40 percent unemployment rate for its young people" (*Michigan Chronicle*, January 22, 1977).

In August 1977, Young's reelection campaign included addresses to both the Police Academy's and the firefighters' graduation classes. They were designed to focus attention on Young's efforts in changing the racial and gender makeup of both departments. On August 20, 1977, Young told the Police Academy graduation class, "I volunteered to do something about discrimination against Blacks. Now we are hiring, as you know, new police officers. The percentage of Blacks in the Department today ... is now ranging about 32%." This statement was greeted by applause. Continuing, Mayor Young told the class, "This City will employ about 750 new police officers. We're over halfway there, and when we get there it will be because I have given preference and importance to Black police officers as a correcting affirmative action, in the same way folks directed me to give preference to women officers by corrective Affirmative Action." Young predicted that the police department "should be, within the next month or two months, approximately 40% Black. That's a long way from where it was four years ago" (Young, Speech, 1977a).

Young understood many of the problems this new class had faced and would face in the future as the system slowly changed. He explained that it takes "a hell of a long time to turn a bureaucracy around that's ingrained and filled with bigotry, and we're still dealing with too much of that in the Police Department." But, he assured his audience that "we will deal with it. The next four years will be a hell of a lot better than the last four" (Young, 1977a).

Mayor Young made it clear to the police graduates, however, that he would not tolerate police brutality. "I'll back you to the hilt as you enforce the law fairly and I'll hang you high if you mess over a citizen. We've had too much of that. Responding to the criticism of the police graduation class of 1977, Young told the class, "We hear of 'lack of preparation,' we hear criticism, and I know what is wrong with the class of '77: It's too damn Black and too many women. It's just that simple" (Young, 1977a).

He then addressed the women police graduates. "I did not hesitate when the Court ordered me to take corrective action," he told them; "but, I must admit that I, like almost every male, had a few misgivings on how effective they would be. And I'm sure that many of the male Police Officers felt the same." He confessed that after three years of observation and experience, "women police officers are every bit as effective as men on the street and off the street, and in many cases, more effective" (Young, 1977a). This last statement brought applause. Turning his remarks to the male police officers, he told them: "Let's face it brothers, this is the way of the future. When we say equal opportunity, it goes across the board, it doesn't stop with blacks. Our women Police Officers are playing an important role—they are protecting us. They are part of the reason that our Police Department is protecting the people" (Young, 1977a).

Since this was an election year, Mayor Young could not resist bragging about his accomplishments in expanding the police force and radically changing its racial and gender makeup. "We will have, in the next six to eight weeks at the longest, between 5700 and 5800 Police Officers on the Detroit Police force. That's the highest number in the history of this City. We will have the most integrated police force in the United States," he said, again to applause (Young, 1977a).

A week later, Mayor Young presented essentially the same message to the firefighters' graduating class. "I want our Fire Department to reflect the population of this City. For a long time, there was discrimination against people because of their color," he told them. "We are seeking now to eliminate that as quickly as we can, and you are a reflection of that effort" (Young, 1977b). Young mentioned a police case in which a federal judge had found the city guilty of discriminating against women and ordered them "to go down the list of women who tried to become police officers and to hire one woman for every man until we have exhausted every woman on that list." He said, "We have done that. The Police Department is no worse for having hired women" (Young, 1977b.)

Young then explained to the graduating class how the fire department would be undergoing similar changes. "Everyone in this class—and you might as well face it, you will be integrated with women before this next three months is over, (applause) and I don't think that's going to injure your ability to perform as a fireperson—and I say 'fireperson.'" He added, "Any person who can pass the examination and who possesses all of the needed requirements, including the physical agility—any person, regardless of race, religion, or sex, as far as I am concerned, is entitled to a job with the City of Detroit." As he had with the police graduating class, Young left the firefighters with an inspiring message about their mission. "You are, indeed, a new kind of Fire Department because you are of the people. You reflect all the people in this City" (Young, 1977b).

Mayor Young ran for reelection against black councilman Ernest Browne in 1977. He was supported by Ford Motor Company chairman Henry Ford II, UAW president Douglas Fraser, and President Jimmy Carter. This was the first general election in a mayor city in which both mayoral candidates were black. Black voters rejected Browne both in the primary and in the general election. Browne's strategy of a winning coalition of a majority of white voters and a minority of black voters failed. The campaign turned ugly when Young accused Browne of selling out blacks for political gain and Browne accused Young of using racist tactics (*Detroit Free Press*, November 7, 1977).

Young's Second Term in Office

Mayor Young had won a second term in office and fulfilled some key campaign promises during his first term by using affirmative action initiatives to steadily transform the racial makeup of various city departments, particularly the police department. In the summer of 1978, when the NAACP came to Detroit to discuss affirmative action, Mayor Young welcomed the visitors with the following statement: "Welcome to Detroit, the Affirmative Action City ... I can't think of any recent issue that is more important to the future of minorities and women and the whole American people than the issue of affirmative action" (Young, 1978). Young started out his talk by pointing to what most of those in the NAACP gathering understood only too well, that affirmative action was often seen as reverse discrimination, "some penalty on White America." He talked about the "unfinished business of the Civil War," of blacks being denied their "forty acres and a mule," of the mistake of "burying Reconstruction in blood and reaction." He warned that "unless we recognize that [history], today, we could be on the verge of a similar attempt, and I do say attempt, cause Black folks ain't going so mildly this time" (Young, 1978).

Warming to his topic, Young expanded his talk to the global implications of racial change in the United States:

> In the interest of America, we live today in a new world in which non-White people are also important. It's no longer a White man's world. There is an ascending Africa, Asia, and South America. Non-Whites, colored people—Black, brown, yellow—are very important to the world scene. To the degree that we remain a world power, indeed, to the degree that we deserve to claimed leadership in this new world, then we must deal with the problems of minorities within our own ranks. (Young, 1978)

Young linked the problems of minorities to the achievement of unity within the United States. "Unity cannot be achieved on the basis of a continual repression and suppression of any segment of our society. We should have learned [that] in '66 and '67. I hope we are learning now." So, in fighting for affirmative action, he told the audience, "we are fighting in the best interests of all Americans—all Americans. It is just as essential to the sorriest White bigot that we have equal opportunity and unity in this country, as it is essential to the lowliest Black" (Young, 1978).

He then turned to the topic of the role of government leaders at this crucial time in the history of affirmative action following the *Bakke* decision. "The perception of defeat that exists in wide sectors of the Black community, as the result of Bakke, calls upon the leadership of America to speak out in re-affirmation of the course that we have undertaken in regard to affirmative action." That means, Young advised the gathering, that during this election year blacks "ought to measure every candidate for office, whether governor, or Congress, or state legislature, or community college candidate, on 'Where do you stand on Bakke?' That's the scale; that's the measure" (Young, 1978).

Acknowledging that there have been demands that President Carter speak out on affirmative action, Young produced a memorandum that he had just received from Washington that was to be released to the press. The memorandum was addressed to "Heads of Executive Departments and Agencies":

Since my administration began, I have been strongly committed to a policy of affirmative action. It is through such programs that we can expect to remove the effects of discrimination and ensure equal opportunities for all Americans.

With your help, this administration has been able to develop and implement meaningful affirmative action programs throughout the federal government, and as a result, minority employment has increased to its highest level in history. The recent decision by the Supreme Court in Bakke enables us to continue those efforts without interruption. That historic decision indicates that properly tailored affirmative action programs, which provide minorities with increased access to federal programs and jobs, and which are fair to all Americans, are consistent with the Civil Rights Act of 1964 and with the Constitution. I want to make certain that in the aftermath of Bakke you continue to develop, implement, and enforce vigorously affirmative action programs. I also want to make certain that the administration's strong commitment to equal opportunity and affirmative action is recognized and understood by all Americans. (Young, 1978)

The president's letter of support for affirmative action outlined a post-*Bakke* strategy in his administration. Others, however, had a vital role to play as well, as Young explained to the gathering: "Ladies and gentlemen, I believe that this is the proper basis upon which to begin these discussions. It is up to us now to police this mandate at every federal, state, and local level, to see to it that it is pursued at every level of the private sector" (Young, 1978).

Mayor Young faced even tougher issues during his second term, the worst of which was a budget crisis in 1981 that forced Detroit voters to approve an income tax hike and city officials to sell $125 million in emergency bonds (*Detroit Free Press*, January 5, 1981). Young not only had to persuade city voters to go along with his plan to save the city from bankruptcy, but he also had to convince the state legislature and twist the arms of municipal workers to accept a two-year wage freeze. Black unemployment in the city remained at 25 percent as Young prepared to run for his third term. Not even the impressive Renaissance Center complex could lift the gloom of a declining city. Times were tough in the Motor City and getting tougher, especially for many blacks who still saw Mayor Young as the "big daddy," a symbol of their power and success (*Detroit Free Press*, January 1, 1984; *Lansing State Journal*, 1981).

When Carter lost his bid for reelection it hurt Detroit and severed the ties that once provided so much financial support for the struggling city. True to his street style of politics, the change in Washington did not prevent Young from calling President Reagan "prune face" and accusing him of "lacking any compassion for urban residents and the poor." In his third inaugural address, Mayor Young told Detroiters to "circle the wagons" and to "close ranks and send a message to the President … [This country] can't go forward if its cities are sinkholes of poverty and starvation" (*Detroit Free Press*, January 1, 1984).

Assessing his first decade as mayor of Detroit, Young focused on black unemployment and its relationship to crime. "The primary problem that we face now is unemployment," he mentioned, "the fact that in the Black community one out of four are out of a job, and among young people we have 65 to 70 % unemployment. That's a devastating figure. There's a direct relationship between that and crime" (*Michigan Chronicle*, January 14, 1984).

Being mayor of a predominantly black city surrounded by predominantly white suburbs meant that Young could never escape the covert and overt forces of racism. Many white suburbanites could not understand Young's periodic antagonism toward the suburbs, and why, according to them, he was always talking about racism. On August 22, 1984, in a talk to the Booker T. Washington Business Association, he spoke to the topic. "Now, I can't remember any recent period in this Country, and in this State, because I think it is worse in this State than it is in most of the Country, when racism has been more open and more overt. As you know," he explained, "many people get angry, particularly white people, when I talk about racism. They get angry with anybody who talks about racism. Just because they get angry does not mean that racism does not exist (Applause)" (Young, 1984).

Young argued that racism in the city and state was at "an all-time high." He accused the suburbs of wanting to control "our water and our City." Furthermore, Young continued, "We also know that there has been a reach for our transportation system. There has been a reach for the Detroit Art Institute." This "reaching," Young claimed, was a source both of conflict between suburbs and city conflict and of racism. "As long as Detroit and its suburbs keep fighting each other, as long as this feeling among those in the suburbs is that they aren't going to stand for Black folks to run a damn thing, they are going to destroy it or control it. As long as that feeling exists, let me tell you, we will all be destroyed" (Young, 1984).

Another example of racism Young discussed related to the white press's accusation that he was not reaching out to the suburbs, that he should show some leadership. In his typical brash style, Young told his audience, "Hell, I go across Eight Mile Road every other month. Do you ever hear of those sons-of-bitches coming here? (laughter). You know me; you can reach two ways, right?" He said that he has been reaching out and that he would continue to do so. "But I want somebody, sometime, to reach in. Those damn expressways run two ways. If I can get out to Ten Mile Road, those sons-of-bitches can get down here" (Laughter) (Young, 1984).

Young understood the need for suburban-city cooperation as essential for regional growth. The city could not exist without the suburbs and the suburbs could not exist without the city. In the same way, he said, downtown could not exist without the neighborhoods and the neighborhoods could not exist without downtown. But again, he argued, suburban racism was the major barrier. "None of us can exist with the blind racism that characterizes this area, which many, many people in the suburbs would just as soon see the damn thing go down before they would help Detroit," he remarked (Young, 1984).

A year later, in his annual "State of the City" report to the Economic Club of Detroit, Mayor Young devoted more than a third of his report to crime and the need for more prison space, and mentioned that economic, social, and educational deprivation is the underlying cause of crime. Rising crime had to be addressed, and Young made it clear that he did "not approve of vigilantism, but [did] approve of citizen involvement" (*Michigan Chronicle*, February 16, 1985). He did not limit himself to the problems of Detroit, however. He noted and praised "the resiliency of the people of Detroit," whom he compared to a cat with nine lives—"always capable of rebounding in [the] face of economic setbacks." Young used this opportunity to discuss the link between the economic turnaround of the city and the surrounding metropolitan region, and called for increased cooperation between the city and its suburbs in attracting more jobs into the area. He added that he was working with the county executives in this effort (*Michigan Chronicle*, February 16, 1985).

Young's Accomplishments

As Young prepared for his fourth term as mayor of Detroit, he addressed his critics by listing many of the projects he claimed had been successful during his administration. Among these projects were the Riverfront, Millender, and Trolley Plaza apartments with close to 1,800 units. He emphasized that these apartments were "50 percent Black and 50 percent White, half come from within Detroit and half from outside." To Young, this project represented economic and racial integration. He also mentioned that in other downtown areas 7,000 to 8,000 units were "subsidized and moderate income." Some critics in the black community, however, saw this "integration" as Young's attempt to stop white flight at the expense of inner-city blacks. Young denied that he had "caved in to gentrification" like other cities. "Those cities are gentrifying Black folks out of the ghettoes," Young explained. "Whites come in, take over the area, invest a lot of money in it and it becomes a lily White area. It becomes just the reverse of what it was. That's one of the things we have avoided and one of the things I am most proud of" (*Michigan Chronicle*, November 2, 1985).

While it was undeniable that Detroit had suffered a loss of 800,000 people, Young attributed the 40 percent drop in population primarily to the deterioration of neighborhoods. As whites deserted the city in the wake of the 1967 riot, blacks moved into better housing and abandoned neighborhoods in the Linwood, Mack, and Kercheval areas. The problems were compounded by exploitive slumlords who purchased property, "drained it and then left it vacant." According to Young, this resulted in the urban sprawl that left about 40 percent of Detroit's land unused. Being the optimist he had to be, running a city in decline, Young did not waste time worrying about the problems, but instead came up with ways to correct some of the imbalances between land and people. For those critics who said that the city had deteriorated since he became mayor, Young countered, "The deterioration was well advanced before I became mayor." Linwood, Mack, and Kercheval were already decaying in 1967, the year of the riot. "All of them were damn near burned down in '67," he reminded his critics. "You asked what are we going to do about Linwood, Mack and Kercheval. What were they before? 12th Street was worse than Linwood before we rebuilt it. So was Black Bottom, [which] we rebuilt. So was Hastings, and we rebuilt it." While he admitted that he had not been able to turn all the problems around, Young said he had "turned [a] significant portion of it around" (*Michigan Chronicle*, November 2, 1985).

The 12th Street area, the epicenter of the 1967 riot, was rebuilt during Young's term in office, a project that he did not hesitate to claim as his own. "I'm the one who built 12th street back up," he said. "When I took office seven years after the riots, 12th street was still lined with cinders and burned out homes and stores. Today it's a far cry from that." He went on to list the devastated areas that had been redeveloped since he became mayor. New homes in Black Bottom had quadrupled, and the area boasted a new shopping center and community center; brand-new housing was built on both sides of the Chrysler Freeway (the old Hasting Street) extending from downtown to Farnsworth; the Warren and Chrysler centers had been built, as well as the Seven Mile–Livernois shopping center, the Seven Mile–Gratiot commercial strip, and the Kern Gardens housing project; Belle Isle underwent renovations; and there were "ongoing city lighting improvements" (*Michigan Chronicle*, November 2, 1985).

Young also included the controversial GM plant built on the foundation of Poletown as an accomplishment. Young saw this project as especially significant because it was "the only one in the nation built in a central city and it will provide as many as 6,000 badly needed jobs. It is one of the best things I have been able to do since I became mayor ... for every thousand jobs ... there will be 6,000 more jobs created in supplier plants" (*Michigan Chronicle*, November 2, 1985).

While Young could point to various accomplishments during this election year, critics could point to lingering problems, such as the increase in violent crime. Most alarming during this election year was the dramatic increase in black teenage violence. As one reporter described it, "Teenage violence has escalated at such a rate that as authorities arrest one teen gunman, another is committing a similar crime in another part of town. More than 200 Detroit Public School children have been shot in 1985 resulting in 24 teenaged deaths" (*Michigan Chronicle*, November 2, 1985). This had to be a heavy burden for the first black mayor of Detroit, who more than anything wanted to be a role model for black youth.

The Impact of the Beating Death of Malice Green

Mayor Young's last term in office was marred by the police beating death of Malice Green on November 5, 1992 (see chapter 2). A writer for the *Detroit News and Free Press* expressed the effect of this event on Young's mayoralty: "The foundation upon which Mayor Coleman Young built his career and his administration was rocked Thursday by the beating death of a Detroit man at the hands of Detroit police officers" (November 7, 1992). As he would later write, "nothing knocked me cold like the beating death of an unemployed father of five named Malice Green ... I would have sworn—in fact, I probably had sworn—that it could never happen in Detroit." It was his "worst nightmare coming true." It was especially disturbing that one of the white officers involved had been a member of the STRESS unit Young had abolished during his first months in office (Young and Wheeler, 1994: 322).

This tragedy cut to the very heart of Young's two-decade-long struggle to improve relations between the black community and the police. "For nearly twenty years," he said, "I had emphasized a firm but respectful style of law enforcement. I had campaigned on that issue and fought over it with veteran cops." Changing the attitudes of the Detroit Police Department had been the first priority of his first term as mayor, and as he put it, "I was damn proud of the progress we had made since then in our relationship with the people, much of which could be attributed to the affirmative action measures we so diligently pursued for two trying decades" (Young and Wheeler, 1994: 321).

Young issued a statement after the shooting in which he said he was "shocked and sickened" at what he had learned about the role of several police officers in the death of a "citizen of the city." He "ordered an immediate, complete investigation to determine exactly what happened," and warned that

> Every officer found to be guilty of any misconduct in connection with this tragic incident will be dealt with in the harshest manner possible. I have worked too long and too hard to build a community-based police department to have something like this happen. So long as I am mayor, we will not tolerate any mistreatment of the citizens of this city by the police department. (Young and Wheeler, 1994: 322)

Malice Green's beating death by two white police came on the heels of the L.A. riots following the not-guilty verdict in the trail of white police officers accusing of beating Rodney King (who fortunately did not die). Mayor Young knew all too well how volatile the situation could become. Some of Young's critics in the media attacked him for referring to the Green incident as "murder" on *NBC Nightly News*. Young retorted, "Didn't [they] understand that I had an angry city to con- sider? Whatever I had to say about the Malice Green incident, I had to say with the city in mind" (Young and Wheeler, 1994: 323).

Young knew that Detroit was not out of the woods when it came to riots triggered by careless and brutal police action compounded by insensitive public officials:

> The people of Los Angles had just staged the most devastating riot in American history because they thought—and with damn good reason—that the authorities showed no remorse over what happened to Rodney King, were not appropriately appalled, and did not object profoundly enough to renounce it or to take even symbolic action against the perpetrators. I could not let that happen in Detroit. I was in no hurry to win back the riot championship. (Young and Wheeler, 1994: 323)

Young's mention of "riot championship" was an obvious reference to the Detroit riot of 1967, often referred to as the worst riot in U.S. history. The memory of the 1967 riot and its possible recurrence haunted black and white Detroiters for decades. Every serious racial incident had the potential—in the collective memory of Detroiters—of blowing up into another riot. Now that the L.A. riot had taken center stage in the recent history of urban riots, city officials like Young could either ignore or learn from its lessons. "My charge … was to convince the people of Detroit that I was on their side, Young stated, "and that I was just as outraged about what had happened as they were. My job was to learn from Los Angles; to alienate myself from any official attitude against which the people of my city might revolt" (Young and Wheeler, 1994: 323).

After twenty years as the first black mayor of Detroit, Young decided not to run again. His health was failing and, as he would later put it, "I didn't want to sleep through my last term the way Ronald Reagan did" (Young and Wheeler, 1994: 328). As he prepared to leave office, he could look back on several major accomplishments. Chief among them were "affirmative action in the police department, economic development downtown and elsewhere, and the successful management of two fiscal crises" (Rich, 1989: 265).

Undoubtedly, integrating the police department was one of Young's greatest accomplishments in the broad area of race relations. In fact, one could argue that since most of the riots of the 1960s had been provoked by practices of predominantly white police departments, Young's affirmative action policy in the police department was one of the most important contributions to racial equality and interracial cooperation in the post-1967 period. Had the police department remained predominantly white in a predominantly black city, constant conflict between the two would have been inevitable and extremely costly in lives and property.

Increases in minority hiring ranks as an equally impressive accomplishment. When Young was elected mayor in 1973, the city had granted minority contractors less than $20,000. In contrast, Young claimed, "Since 1988 we had averaged more than $125 million, the most awarded by any city" (Young and Wheeler, 1994: 329). Notwithstanding his efforts to improve minority hiring, he never abandoned his commitment to racial balance in hiring. Even though the white population was declining when Young became mayor, he promised to share political power with whites on a fifty-fifty basis. This policy on race reflected his belief that blacks and whites could live harmoniously in cities with black mayors (Rich, 1989).

Young practiced this belief throughout his years as mayor.

> I've done my damnedest, in the office of mayor, to carry forward the pursuit of unity on both the intramural and extramural levels. Inevitably, my most immediate, conspicuous opportunities have occurred through the vehicle of city hiring, and I have used, as my instruments in the campaign, racial balance and affirmative action, among other means. (Young and Wheeler, 1994: 330)

He was so committed to racial balance in city hiring that whenever he could, he made sure to go "out in public with two security officers, one black, one white." Unfortunately, this display of interracial unity did not satisfy many of his critics. "Despite my record of fifty-fifty hiring," Young protested, "I have been boorishly charged over the years with 'racial politics' and 'playing the race card.' I prefer to think of it as 'equal opportunity politics' and 'playing the equality card'" (Young and Wheeler, 1994: 330). Not able to resist a jab at the suburbs, he said, "I only wish that my fellow public servants in the suburbs were held to the same standards. To the contrary, I submit that many of them would severely endanger their reelection potential if they dared to hire on a fifty-fifty basis" (Young and Wheeler, 1994: 330).

As Mayor Young was leaving office, he noted sarcastically that "the usual dignitaries paid their respect, many of them spewing forth in uncharacteristically benevolent tones—mindful of course, that I have finally loosened my grip upon the city's top office and no longer pose an institutional threat to their agendas." True to his Black Bottom roots, however, the mayor really appreciated the "flattering remark" from JoAnn Watson, then executive director of the Detroit Chapter of the NAACP, who said, "He's the only mayor I've known in my lifetime about whom the brothers stand out on the corner and slap hands and say, 'my man'" (Young and Wheeler, 1994: 330–31)

Young reflected, "That comment was especially meaningful to me in view of the fact that it was the brothers on the corner of Black Bottom, I among them, for whom I embarked on my life's work more than fifty years ago. And it was ... with their modern counterparts in mind that, as mayor of Detroit, I bargained with presidents and collaborated with captains of industry." In the end, Young still held this street corner brothers firm in his heart. He knew that as he ended his long tenure as the first black mayor, there was another generation of black males still struggling to survive. "If, as I suspect, those brothers slapping hands are younger men out of luck, searching for human respect and a living wage—and Detroit is full of that kind, believe me—then hell yes, I'm honored to have been their man for the last two decades, and eager to continue in that capacity, however it might shake down in the years ahead" (Young and Wheeler, 1994: 331).

DENNIS WAYNE ARCHER, MAYOR OF DETROIT, 1993–2001: CITY-SUBURBAN BRIDGE BUILDER

The next black mayor of Detroit was a glaring contrast to Mayor Young. Dennis Wayne Archer became mayor at a far less racially polarized and volatile period. Those whites still in the city had grown used to living in a black-majority city. If they feared that "the colored were taking over," they either moved or adjusted. One of the greatest sources of racial tension, the predominantly white police force, had been transformed into one of the most racially integrated police forces in the nation. While many whites in the surrounding suburbs disliked and demonized Young, they were forced to recognize his powerful and defiant regional presence. They knew that he did not care what they thought of him. In fact, it took a "streetwise" tough-taking black personality like Young for many whites to appreciate Archer.

While he was a successful lawyer and a justice of the Michigan Supreme Court, Dennis Archer was by no means a product of the black upper class. In fact, his early life and struggles in rural Cassopolis, Michigan, were far more difficult than Young's somewhat middle-class upbringing in Black Bottom. Archer was born on January 1, 1942, on Detroit's east side. Before his birth his father lost his left arm in an automobile accident that left him partially disabled and limited his job opportunities. The Archer family moved to Cassopolis when Dennis was five, where his father, "in spite of his disability, managed to support his family as a caretaker of a summer home."

He "mowed the lawn, washed the car and cared for the summer home, all for a paycheck of $75 every two weeks—and only $37 every two weeks during the winter months" ("Dennis Archer," n.d.-a).

At age eight, Dennis Archer began to contribute to the family well-being by working at jobs as a golf caddy, pin-setter at a bowling alley, and a bakery which required him to rise "in the dark at 3 A.M … walking a mile, mopping the floor, then walking back home for another hour or two of sleep before he got up for school" ("Dennis Archer," n.d.-a).

After high school, Archer moved to Detroit to find work to finance his college education. Here again, he worked a variety of jobs to achieve his goals, including painting houses, working as a stock boy in a drug store, and becoming "the first African American worker in the Henry Ford Hospital medical records department." In college, Archer continued working menial jobs to make ends meet, such as dishwashing in Western Michigan University dormitory kitchens prior to graduating with a degree in teaching in 1965 (Johnson and Henderson, n.d.).

At that stage in his life, Archer's dream was to become a schoolteacher. He moved to Detroit and worked with emotionally disabled youngsters in the public school system. While teaching, he met his wife, Trudy DunCombe, also a teacher. They were married in 1967. She encouraged him to attend law school. Later he would return the favor by encouraging Trudy to attend law school as well. Archer began his legal education by taking night courses at the Detroit College of Law, where he earned his degree in 1970. After passing the bar, he moved from teaching to the law firm of Gragg & Gardner. A year later he switched to Hall, Stone, Archer & Glen, where he was made a partner (Johnson and Henderson, n.d.).

Archer had an outstanding career as a lawyer before he ran for the office of mayor of Detroit. He was active in the Wolverine Bar Association, a predominantly black lawyer organization, which elected him president in 1979. Four years later, in 1983, the National Bar Association, the nationwide organization of black lawyers, elected Archer as its president. In 1984, the same year that *Ebony* magazine named him one of the "100 Most Influential Black Americans," he was elected president of the State Bar of Michigan. The next year, 1985, the *National Law Journal* included Archer in its list of "100 Most Powerful Attorneys in the United States" and voted him as one of the "100 Most Influential Lawyers" ("Dennis Archer," n.d.-a).

The crowning accomplishment of 1985 was Governor James Blanchard's appointment of Archer to a vacancy on the Michigan Supreme Court, a position that Archer had earned after fifteen years as a trial lawyer. In 1986, Archer was "elected to an eight-year term on the Supreme Court by the people of the State of Michigan. He was the first Black to sit on that Court in nearly 20 years and only the second in Michigan's history" ("Dennis Archer," n.d.-a).

The State Supreme Court appointment could have easily lured Archer into a sense of a glorious final personal accomplishment. Not only did the appointment "seem to signal an end to Archer's political career," but as one observer put it, "It was a prestigious posting that could be expected to continue indefinitely. He was only two years away from a guaranteed annual pension of $50,000, when he decided in 1990, to step down from the bench, return to private practice of law, and seek the mayoralty of Detroit" (Johnson and Henderson, n.d.).

Archer was not a novice in politics when he entered the Detroit mayoral race in 1993. As far back as 1969, Archer was busy "stuffing envelopes, putting together advance teams and other odd jobs for Richard Austin's unsuccessful campaign for mayor of Detroit" ("Dennis Archer," n.d.-a). Politics "fascinated" Archer to the extent that he later worked as campaign manager for both George Crockett Jr.'s successful race for Congress in 1982 and Mayor Coleman Young's successful 1977 mayoral campaign. In addition, Archer "subsequently served in high positions in the campaigns of Secretary of State Richard Austin, Governor James Blanchard, and the United States Senator Carl Levin, as well as working for the election of his friend, William Jefferson Clinton, to be president of the United States" ("Dennis Archer," n.d.-a).

When Archer decided to run for mayor in 1990, he had a private meeting with Mayor Young and told him that he would like to "emulate" what the mayor had done. Young, who was very ill and in his seventies, refused to commit himself to his onetime reelection campaign manager, no doubt because he was contemplating running for a sixth term. Regardless, according to one writer, "As the months passed, Archer made it plain that he planned to run for mayor of Detroit even if it meant facing Coleman Young in a race. It was an audacious decision. Despite his failing health, Young remained wildly popular in Detroit" (Johnson and Henderson, n.d.). Those who had always supported him saw him as a "fiercely independent politician who would guard the city against the 'hostile' forces in the predominantly white suburbs" (Johnson and Henderson, n.d.)

Archer's conciliatory approach to the suburbs as a "campaign tactic" in his formal announcement in November 1992 no doubt alarmed many blacks, who had countless reasons to distrust white suburbanites. Having decided to challenge the ailing but still formidable Mayor Young, Archer decided to pull out all the stops and "fearlessly blasted Young for his style of government." He told the *Detroit Free Press*, "The days when a handful of politicians can sit in a back room and carve up this city are over. It is time for opening the window and letting fresh air into City Hall" (Johnson and Henderson, n.d.).

As could be expected, Young was offended by Archer's comment, and after deciding not to run himself for a sixth term, endorsed Sharon McPhail, a rival candidate. Young's endorsement of McPhail

> gave McPhail an instant organization and within days, at least $250,000 through a $5,000-a-head fund raiser attended by many city officials or businesspeople who were investing in their jobs or city contracts. But it also played into Archer's hands ... [by] linking McPhail to a tired city government that was short on services and battered by a reputation for cronyism and corruption. Young's endorsement [of McPhail] helped Archer crystallize the race as a contest between new and old, change and more of the same. (Johnson and Henderson, n.d.)

Comments from a 1992 focus group revealed a range of opinions about Archer, such as: "Heard he's always with White people. Doesn't care anything about Black people," or "[The elitist charge] is just a label. He's intelligent, articulate, educated." Several members of the focus group saw Archer as providing a "fresh attitude" and bringing "a broader base of support to the table" and a "new spirit to Detroit" ("Focus Group, Election Campaign," 1992).

While the focus group comments shed some light on how people viewed Archer, the 1993 campaign would reveal just how much the race and class card could be played in a majority-black city. As one observer explained, "From the outset of his campaign, Dennis Archer had been troubled by what he called 'the drumbeat.' It began as a whisper. Archer was upper-crust, elitist, distant by choice from the middle and lower-class blacks who made up the bulk of Detroit." To many blacks, that was bad enough, but "after he had lunch with Oakland County Executive L. Brooks Patterson, the embodiment of mean-spirited suburban racism to many black Detroiters, Archer was labeled a lackey of some vague, white power brokers who wanted to reclaim the city. Archer, in sum, wasn't black enough to be a mayor of a city that was about 80 percent African American." What had started out as a whisper from McPhail's camp "turned ... to a roar, playing the race card early and often" (Johnson and Henderson, n.d.).

A month before the November 1993 election, at a McPhail fund-raiser the anti-Archer race-baiting got out of hand. Reverend Charles Adams, one of Detroit's most respected and well-known black ministers and community leaders, told the gathering, "They want a nice mayor. They want a mayor to shuffle when he's not going anywhere, scratch when he's not itching and grin when he's not tickled" (Johnson and Henderson, n.d.). This was an obvious reference to the repeated claims that Archer was only interested in courting powerful white interests in the suburbs.

This attack deeply hurt Archer, coming as it did from such a respectable leader in the black community. He could not allow it to go unchallenged; as he told the *Detroit Free Press*, "I wasn't born wearing the kind of clothes I'm wearing. I wasn't born driving the kind of car I'm driving. I wasn't born making the money I'm making.... What kind of message does that [campaign tactic] send our children? Does that mean you have to turn your hat around backward and call somebody names in order to be considered worthy of being part of the community?" Archer concluded by pointing out that he wanted to work with those who were interested in improving Detroit, black, white, Arabic, Jewish, suburban, or city dweller (Johnson and Henderson, n.d.).

To his credit, Revered Adams realized his mistake, and before a week had passed apologized by phone to Archer. Several weeks later, on the eve of the election, Adams invited Archer to address his congregation. Taking the pulpit, Archer clarified his views about Detroit and many blacks' fear of a white suburban takeover of Detroit.

> It has been said throughout this campaign that "they" want to take the city back and "they" have a candidate. I hope to let you know who they are and who I represent. I rep-resent the people who can't get their garbage picked up on time ... their streetlights to

stay on all night ... their phone calls answered at city hall. I stand before you representing children who are more concerned about surviving the school day ... the homeless, the disenfranchised and the working poor who want affordable housing, and a clean and decent place in which to live. (Johnson and Henderson, n.d.)

When he ended his speech, Reverend Adams hugged him (Johnson and Henderson, n.d.).

With just a few weeks remaining in the campaign, Gail Parrish, an African American and the executive director of the Race Relations Council of Metropolitan Detroit (RRCMD), in an article in the *Detroit Free Press* entitled "Stereotyping Allows Suburbs to Set Agenda for Detroit," presented some sage advice concerning racial labeling in the campaign and black fears and anxiety about white suburban influence on the election.

There has been a great deal of concern about racial labeling in this election. One of the most troubling aspects of this labeling and stereotyping is the degree to which it is framed as a response to suburbia. This may sound naïve, but does it really matter what suburban intentions are for Detroit? (*Detroit Free Press*, October 21, 1993)

She warned her readers not to focus "too much attention on the concerns and intentions of the suburbs" because by doing so, "we Detroiters risk falling into a trap that would keep us in a powerless reactionary stance, charting a course that is anything but independent. We risk losing the opportunity to frame effectively our own vision for the future." While she acknowledged that there were some suburban interests who were racist and "ill-intentioned," some were not. Therefore, she argued, "We are handing power that is rightfully ours to others by letting suburbanites, who have no vote in this election, frame the agenda for our city" (*Detroit Free Press*, October 21, 1993).

The city-suburban issue had been a regional issue for years, so it was no surprise that it would raise its troubling head during the campaign. Several months earlier, the RRCMD had sponsored a forum to allow the mayoral candidates to answer questions related to the racial and ethnic relations of Detroit. Dennis Archer and Sharon McPhail were among the six candidates attending the forum. Unfortunately, as reported by an observer, "It was clear by the forum's end, that the big question in the minds of those attending was still unanswered: 'Who is the best person to lead Detroit into a multiculturally harmonious future?'" (Race Relations Alert, 1993).

In September, the RRCMD sponsored its first major race and ethnic relations conference, which had the uplifting title "Tear Down the Walls: A Call for City-Suburban Reconciliation." The major focus was on "bridging the mostly white suburbs and the mostly black city," and the "possibility that a new Detroit mayor could bring new cooperation between the city and the suburbs" (*Detroit Free Press*, October 21, 1993). The keynote speaker, Clarence Page, an African American columnist for the *Chicago Tribune*, reminded the participants that the upcoming mayoral contest between Dennis Archer and Sharon McPhail would revolve around two questions: "Who is going to work the hardest for urban-suburban cooperation? And is that a bad thing or a good thing?" He added that the recent pattern of blacks moving to the suburbs may have contributed to improved relations between Detroit and its suburbs (*Detroit Free Press*, October 21, 1993).

During the campaign various news and citizens' organizations sent questionnaires to Archer to obtain his views and future policies—if he were elected—related to race and ethnic relations. The Latino News Publication was concerned about the growing Hispanic population in Detroit, and asked: "Hispanics comprise a significant portion in Detroit's population. How are you going to interact with Hispanics to bring out their voice in your administration?" Archer responded: "I began meeting with Hispanic community leaders two years ago and my advisory council, Amigos de Archer, has been an integral part of my campaign seeking the office of Mayor of the City of Detroit." Furthermore, he assured the *Latino News*, "I am committed to improving the quality of life in the areas of education, jobs, safety and security ... and to substantially increase the number of Hispanics in all areas of city government." He promised to have more Hispanic police officers and firefighters, to "give more concentrated attention to the gangs in the community," have "members of the Hispanic community as his appointees," and to "continue to work on a regular basis with the Hispanic community" ("Dennis Archer," n.d.-b).

The *Detroit News* candidate questionnaire wanted to know what Archer "would do to bring about improved relations between Detroit and its suburban neighbors?" Predictably, Archer promised to be "personally involved in building bridges between city and suburbs and ... actively participate in the Big Four meetings ... and to accept speaking engagements in the suburbs." Most importantly, he said he would "look for ways to promote the many things we have in common and work to resolve the differences and misunderstandings" ("*Detroit News* Candidate Questionnaire," n.d.).

When asked in another *Detroit News* questionnaire, "What is the state of race relations in Metro Detroit today? What would you do to ease racial tension in the region," Archer admitted that race relations were not good, but said they could be improved. His administration, he promised, "will be one of inclusion, not of exclusion. My administration will reflect the ethnic diversity of our community and will work with block clubs, neighborhood and community groups to listen to and address issues of importance and concern to our residents." Furthermore, he promised to be "personally involved in reducing racial tension rather than relying solely on the efforts of the NAACP, New Detroit, ACCESS, The NCCJ and others" ("*Detroit News* Candidate Questionnaire," n.d.).

Archer won the November 1993 election with a margin of victory over McPhail of 57 percent to 43 percent. The exit polls revealed some of the underlying racial dynamics of the election. Archer "received 90 percent of the votes by white Detroiters but only 47 percent of the black vote—to McPhail's 52 percent" (Johnson and Henderson, n.d.). During his inauguration and swearing-in ceremony, Mayor Archer threw out a challenge to Detroiters to contribute their part to improving the city. "Sweep the sidewalk in front of your house ... clean the rubbish from the storm sewers on the street. Pick up the broken glass in your alley. Go with your neighbor to cut the weeds in the lot down the way on your street." As he had promised throughout his campaign, he called for the healing of the divide between Detroit and its suburbs. "Tell our friends in Birmingham, Dearborn, Mt. Clemens and Windsor," Archer said, "we're in this together and we're in it for the long haul" (*Michigan Chronicle*, January 5–11, 1994).

Former mayor Coleman Young was prevented from participating in the program because of illness, but the new mayor and Detroit City Council President Maryann Mahaffey paid tribute to Young's five terms as mayor of Detroit. "Today as we launch a new chapter, we cannot forget the contribution of a truly monumental figure in Detroit's history—Coleman Young." Mahaffey said that the city council would present Young "with an official testimony and medallion recognizing his public service" (*Michigan Chronicle*, January 5–11, 1994).

As Archer took office, it became abundantly clear that he was serious about reaching out to the surrounding suburbs. In July 1994, at the Greater Detroit Chamber of Commerce's Fourteenth Annual Mackinac Conference, he was a major presence and participant in the discussions about new regional partnerships, seen as a beacon of hope for the region. In a photo in the *Detroiter* magazine, Archer was even seen smiling alongside a smiling Oakland County executive L. Brooks Patterson, long considered by African Americans in Detroit as a sworn enemy of the city. As a writer for the *Detroiter* pointed out, however, "The new mayoral leadership in the city of Detroit was seen at Mackinac as the catalyst for a new partnering in Southeast Michigan." Obviously referring to the racial tensions between Detroit under Young and the present Archer administration, the writer said, "The olive branch finally has been extended across Eight Mile Road and the dust shaken out of the welcome mat between such diverse entities as Detroit and its suburbs, Southeast Michigan and state government, Metro Detroit and Western Michigan, Democrats and Republicans, and most of all, the business community and the city of Detroit" (*Detroiter*, July 1994).

There can be no doubt that Mayor Archer introduced a fresh, new approach to running a predominantly black city surrounded by predominantly white and largely hostile suburbs. Young had been on a war-footing with many elements in the suburbs for decades, and his legacy was still smoldering in the hearts of many blacks who had more than enough reasons to distrust white suburbia—and to distrust Archer for reaching out to them. Archer was not Young, however. He came with a different vision. One urban scholar explains, "At the root of his vision for Detroit was adherence to a view that to stabilize and revitalize the city required bridge-building, negotiation and compromise with the suburbs and the white business elites. It is a vision that sees cultural separatism as an economic dead end for African Americans" (Neill, 2003: 140). While "cultural separatism" had its downside, Archer's vision for Detroit had potential risks for his credibility among Detroit blacks. "The vision has been the assertion of the possibility of a multicultural city in a regional context where persistent racism makes this an uphill task, risking the charge of being 'a silk-stocking' elitist, a synonym for 'the white man's candidate'" (Neill, 2003: 140).

Black urban planners under Archer articulated this vision, which departed from the "separatist" tendency of Young's planners. "The tone of the two Planning and Development Department directors appointed under Archer was far removed from the outlook of the separatist Ron

Hewitt," writes one scholar. Gloria Robinson, the first planner appointed under Archer, "pointed to how Archer had not played the 'victim card' in the manner of Young but also mentioned the 'difficulty of sending an inclusive cultural message to the suburbs when the mayor knows the reality of the racism out there driving sprawl.'" Another black planner who replaced Robinson restated this vision for Detroit as "a city where diversity is celebrated and different people can live side by side" (Neill, 2003: 140).

It could be argued that one of Archer's greatest contributions to both the economic development of Detroit as a "black city" and the limited improvement of city-suburban race relations was his success in attracting new businesses to Detroit, such as Compuware, the computer giant (Johnson and Henderson, n.d.). Prestigious white businesses coming to Detroit had the tendency to "soften" white suburbanites' view of the "black city."

During his tenure as mayor, Archer launched negotiations for the Detroit Tigers' new baseball stadium, named Comerica Park, which opened in 2000. The renaming of the stadium after the bank is interesting as a commentary on race and the city. As one writer put it, "The new stadium is called Comerica Park—ironically named after a bank in the early 1990s that changed its name from Detroit Bank and Trust in order to disassociate itself from the negative image of Detroit" (Neill, 2004: 144). Archer also paved the way for the return of the Detroit Lions from Pontiac to Detroit with a new stadium in the fall of 2002 (Johnson and Henderson, n.d.).

Perhaps Mayor Archer's "most defining moment [was] the day when voters okayed three casinos in the city limits" (Johnson and Henderson, n.d.), a project that the late Coleman Young had supported as a means to "create jobs and bring a measure of fiscal independence to Detroit in the form of local betting taxes" (Neill, 2003: 144). Things soon turned sour, however, when none of the three casino licenses issued went to an African American, "despite the fact that a prominent African American Detroiter had experience in this area." Robinson, one of Archer's Planning and Development directors, defended her boss's decision. "The city was not interested in cronyism," she said, "but in the best bids. The economic interests of the city were put ahead of race" (Neill, 2003: 148).

Mayor Archer's casino decision was one of the major reasons behind a recall petition organized by the Black Slate, the political arm of the Shrine of the Black Madonna and the New Marcus Garvey Movement. Ron Hewitt, one of the planning directors under Young who at the time was the regional chair of the Black Slate, was driving the effort (Neill, 2003). Some of the recall leaders expressed the same time-worn racial views heard during the 1993 mayoral campaign that Archer was "not black enough" to be mayor of Detroit. For example, Hewitt said that Archer is "somebody who doesn't take into account the needs and aspirations of black people against the background of our experiences in America." Another supporter of the recall effort labeled Archer an elitist who didn't listen to the concerns of "everyday black Detroiters." "You shouldn't have to have a college degree for the mayor to stop and pay attention to people. A real black person wouldn't ignore black people" (Detroit Free Press, June 9, 1999).

Detroit Free Press writer Heath Meriwether described this recall attempt among certain black critics of Archer, saying, "The not-black-enough disease strikes again." She argued that the "recall attempt flies in the face of Archer's approval rating among Detroit residents, his national prominence as a co-chair of Vice President Al Gore's presidential election campaign, and his proven ability to sell Detroit as a place where you want to do business." While Archer's critics "cite a variety of issues for wanting to oust him from his job—including the enduring one of poor city services to neighborhood, the recall boils down to this: Archer somehow is not black enough to lead Detroit" (*Detroit Free Press*, June 9, 1999).

One prominent black lawyer who disagreed with the black recall attempt argued that several of Archer's projects, such as the stadium, the casinos, and Campus Martius, provided work for a range of black companies and created well-paying jobs that enabled Detroiters to invest in homes and provide college education for their children. Furthermore, the critics had to face the fact that crime and unemployment were down and "large scale development is underway" (*Detroit Free Press*, May 23, 1999). In May 1999, a *Detroit Free Press* poll, 65 percent of 350 registered voters in Detroit "said they wanted to keep Archer in office" (June 9, 1999).

In the end, the recall attempt failed. Concerned about the divisiveness the recall attempt had caused in the black community, the Rev. Wendell Anthony, head of the Detroit chapter of the NAACP, tried to build bridges between Archer and the groups leagued against him (*Detroit Free Press*, June 9, 1999).

One of Mayor Archer's last projects, designed to carry out his vision of a multicultural metropolitan community, occurred in 2001 and was itself a sad commentary on suburban commitment to the vision. As urban planner scholar William J. V. Neill describes it:

> The Detroit 300 tricentennial celebrations in 2001 showcased efforts under Archer to project an image of a multicultural city alongside a Detroit civic identity which offered an inclusive invitation to join to the rest of the metropolitan area. Celebrations reached a high point in July with a free waterfront concert by Motown recording artist Stevie Wonder, a Tall Ships Visit and a musical concert. The publicity matter for the latter, part-sponsored by the *Detroit Free Press*, included the powerful logo: "D" for diversity. Banners extensively festooned from city lamp-posts proclaimed the direct message "Proud People." Suburban identification with this civic sentiment that could also be read as a cultural statement was modest as evidenced by a shameful reluctance to contribute financially to tricentennial events as put by one local politician from the suburb of Novi: "For us to say no subjects us to criticism about a white enclave turning its back on a black community, and I'm sensitive to the charge. (Neill, 2003: 148)

After two terms in office, Archer surprised his many supporters when he decided not to seek a third term as mayor (*New York Times*, April 18, 2001). As the clouds of future economic and fiscal woes began forming over the Motor City, one scholar wrote, "it is likely that Greater Detroit under Archer missed its last chance to embrace the concept of progressive multicultural regionalism" (Neill, 2003: 156). The reasons for this missed opportunity are complex, but as urban scholar June M. Thomas argues, "If Young were indeed the main cause of estrangement [between the city and its surrounding suburbs], Archer's election should have resolved all such problems.... In contrast, Archer was a natural diplomat.... White citizens and institutions would have been hard pressed to find a capable Black mayor more open to negotiation and cooperation." Unfortunately, Thomas continues, "Once elected, Archer soon found that his willingness to cooperate did not automatically eliminate suburban noncooperation. During his first year in office, battles with regional leaders—particularly over a proposed merger of city and regional transit systems—were bruising affairs" (Thomas, 1997: 205).

KWAME KILPATRICK: THE HIP-HOP MAYOR OF DETROIT, 2001–2008

Kwame Kilpatrick was born in Detroit in 1970 and raised on Detroit's west side. According to one source, Kilpatrick "knew by the fifth grade that he wanted to be mayor," which he considered his dream job. Such youthful aspirations were not unusual, given his family's political background. His mother, Congresswoman Carolyn Cheeks Kilpatrick, had been serving as state representative from Detroit's Ninth District for two years, an office she would hold for eighteen years. His father, Bernard Kilpatrick, worked in the Wayne County Executive Office (Rochelle, n.d.).

After graduating from the prestigious and selective Cass Technical High School, Kilpatrick attended Florida A&M University, a historically black college, and graduated with a BSc degree in political science in 1992 (Stevens, 2008). Before returning home to Detroit, Kilpatrick spent a short time teaching at Richards High School in Florida. Back in Detroit Kilpatrick continued his teaching career at the Marcus Garvey Academy. During his four years at the academy, Kilpatrick was more than a teacher: "He took on the role of basketball coach and the more important role of mentor" (Rochelle, n.d.). He enrolled in the Detroit College of Law and earned his juris doctorate (Stevens, 2008).

Unlike his two predecessors, Kilpatrick was primed for office by his powerful political family. When his mother was elected to the U.S. House of Representatives, her seat was available for her son. Kilpatrick succeeded her in the Michigan House of Representatives at age twenty-six. His mother went on to serve in the U.S. Congress and to become chairwomen of the Congressional Black Caucus; meanwhile, Kwame Kilpatrick was leading the Democrats in the state legislature as minority leader, the first African American to do so. During his time in the legislature Kilpatrick "brokered the Clean Michigan Initiative, which promoted urban renewal through new funding and also secured a deal to preserve healthcare funding for those on low income" (Stevens, 2008). Sixty percent of this $675 million in funds went to Detroit. Kilpatrick also played a major role in securing millions of dollars to fight lead poisoning in the city. At the time, more child-related lead-poisoning cases were reported in Detroit than in the rest of the state combined (Rochelle, n.d.).

Kilpatrick entered the national spotlight at the 2000 Democratic Convention in Los Angles when he addressed the gathering. Four years later, he spoke again at the Boston convention. At this early age, Kilpatrick was well on his way to becoming one of the most impressive black rising stars in the state and the nation. His considerable political talents and experiences were catching the eye of the national Democratic leadership: "In 2000, the Democratic Leadership Council, the modernizing faction that came to prominence under Clinton and Gore, tipped Kilpatrick as 'one to watch'" (Stevens, 2008). Just as Kilpatrick was maturing in the role as minority leader in the state house, Mayor Archer announced in April 2001 that he was not going to run for reelection, and Kilpatrick saw his opportunity to achieve his longtime dream.

As in the three previous mayoral elections, race played its part. In contrast to Archer's attempt to build bridges between the city and its suburbs, a preelection survey revealed that "suburban healing had ranked low as a quality the next mayor should have" (Neill, 2003: 155). The pendulum was swinging back to the harsh realities of city-suburban racial and innercity intraracial politics. In the final battle between the two main candidates, both Kilpatrick and his competitor, seventy-year-old Gill Hill, president of the Detroit City Council and former mayor Young's chief homicide detective, "underplayed bridge-building and rapprochement with the suburbs characteristic of Archer's election campaign eight years earlier." Kilpatrick "presented himself as 'a son of the city' ... to whom Coleman Young was a 'hero'" (Neill, 2003: 155). In the end, Kilpatrick defeated Hill with 54 percent of the vote to become, at thirty-one, the youngest mayor in the history of Detroit (Neill, 2003).

This would not be the last time that Kilpatrick would be forced to engage in racial politics. In 2005, when he found himself behind in the polls during the reelection fight with Freeman Hendrix, his campaign tried to focus attention on Hendrix's suburban support. In the August primary race Hendrix had beaten Kilpatrick 44 percent to 34 percent, creating a historical first by "making Kilpatrick the first incumbent mayor to finish second in a primary in at least 60 years" (Osinio, 2005). The polls showed that black voters had split their votes between the two black candidates, and a majority of white Detroit voters and other minorities, which made up 20 percent of the voting population, supported Hendrix. In desperation, Kilpatrick fell back on the old tactic of suburban-baiting. In the first of three debates with Hendrix, Kilpatrick said, "In Birmingham and Bloomfield Hills and all these places, they do more meth, they do more Ecstasy and they do more acid than all the schools in the city of Detroit" (Osinio, 2005).

As could be expected, county and school district officials were outraged at Kilpatrick's comments. Oakland County executive L. Brooks Patterson was quick to respond: "These comments insulted the residents of Birmingham and Bloomfield Hills, insulted the students and impugned the reputation of two of our finest, exemplary school districts" (Osinio, 2005). Patterson compared Kilpatrick to the former Mayor Young, saying (somewhat incorrectly) that Young had refused to cooperate with the surrounding communities. Patterson had been around long enough to understand racial politics and had contributed his share to the playbook. He admitted, however, that he and Kilpatrick had worked together. "Kwame has largely been a very affable person to work with, but once in a while he makes comments like these that really hurt relations. I'll continue to work with him because he's the leader of Michigan's largest city, but he's not going to be on my Christmas card list" (Osinio, 2005).

Recognizing he had made a tactical political error by engaging in suburban-baiting, and before the county executive had demanded an apology, Kilpatrick made a somewhat feeble attempt at damage control by issuing a statement that read: "Character issues such as drug abuse are not exclusive to Detroit Public Schools. My reference to substance abuse, not intended to focus on any particular school district, was simply used to illustrate this position" (Osinio, 2005). Patterson appeared confused about why Kilpatrick would use such "inflammatory" statements about two of Oakland County's "most prosperous communities," unless, Patterson concluded, he was doing it to win votes (Osinio, 2005). One pollster was not surprised by Kilpatrick's desperate attempt at suburban-baiting and its impact on future city-suburban relations, saying, "Mayor Kilpatrick doesn't care about suburban relations right now ... he just cares about the election. The problem with comments like this is that they're only made for the moment" (Osinio, 2005). Falling back on the playbook used by the McPhail campaign against Archer, Kilpatrick's strategy was to create an "us versus them" mind-set by labeling Hendrix as the candidate favored by the suburbs in hopes of winning more of the black vote (Osinio, 2005).

It did not help Kilpatrick that 2005 was also the year that *Time* magazine named him as one of America's worst mayors. In an interview with *Time*, Kilpatrick acknowledged that some of his "boneheaded behavior" during his first term could be attributed to his youth and early inexperience in running a major city (Gray, 2007). Wearing an earring, hosting a hip-hop summit, and other aspects of his image that earned him the title of the nation's "first hip-hop" mayor by "cultural icon" Russell Simmons (Gray, 2007) alienated many of Detroit's black professionals. His lifestyle and attempts to "cast himself as a racial martyr sent the message," as explained Mildred Gaddis, fifty-three, one of Detroit's popular talk-show hosts, "This is our city now, and the thug life is OK ... This hip-hop thing ... turned off a lot of people who initially supported him," Gaddis said, herself among them (Gray, 2007).

In the November 2005 election Mayor Kilpatrick managed to survive his historic primary loss to Hendrix, and beat his opponent 53 percent to 47 percent, thus holding onto the office of the mayor. Unfortunately, more serious challenges were waiting in the wings.

Two years later, the young mayor of Detroit was fighting for his job and his political life when he was caught up in a sex scandal involving his chief of staff, Christine Beatty. Dating back to a 2003 whistle-blower trial in which Kilpatrick's police ex-bodyguard, Harold Nelthrope, and former deputy police chief Gary Brown, claimed they were fired because of an internal investigation into the mayor's personal life. They filed a civil lawsuit against the mayor. Both Kilpatrick and Beatty denied that they had been involved in an extramarital affair. When the trial ended on September 11, 2007, with a verdict awarding the plaintiffs $6.5 million in damages, Kilpatrick once again played the race/suburban card by blaming the "wrong verdict" on white suburban jurors (Rochelle, n.d.).

Unwilling to take the blame for his obvious wrongdoing and pledging to appeal the verdict, Kilpatrick went on radio attacking the verdict, declaring that he did not receive a fair trial and unabashedly declaring that he would not be prevented from leading the city because "I believe with all my heart and my soul that God anointed me to do this. And I believe something bad would happen to me if I walked away from this blessing" (*Detroit Free Press*, September 13, 2007). Once again playing the race card, he strongly implied that the verdict against him should be seen as an attack on all black men in Detroit. "All of a sudden, you just get corrupt, ignorant, stupid, lazy and promiscuous.... I just think this is a reality check—not just on Kwame Kilpatrick because, you know, I'm God's guy; I'm going to be all right—I think this is for all black men right now in the city of Detroit" (*Detroit Free Press*, September 13, 2007).

Kilpatrick's race-baiting arguments were rapidly unraveling even among black men whom he had supported for high public office, such as Amos Williams. In 2006, Kilpatrick had supported Williams as the Democratic candidate for Michigan attorney general, but the former disagreed with Kilpatrick's rather transparent and contradictory arguments. "It wasn't like the jury went out and drummed up some charges. This was litigation brought by two black men who thought the mayor had misused his power to damage their careers" (*Detroit Free Press*, September 13, 2007).

The beginning of the end of Mayor Kilpatrick's political career occurred in late January 2008 when two *Detroit Free Press* investigative reporters revealed that Kilpatrick and Beatty had lied under oath about their affair in the police whistleblower lawsuit. The mayor then made a secret deal in which he agreed to settle the lawsuit for over $9 million in exchange for keeping the private text messages between himself and Beatty about their affair secret. Kilpatrick would spend months in court battles trying to keep the text messages and secret settlement documents from being released to the public, to no avail (*Detroit Free Press*, September 5, 2008).

When the text messages were finally released and made public, they revealed that Kilpatrick and Beatty had lied about not having an affair—both were married to other people—and about not intending to fire Brown. As the two investigative reporters explained, "The Kilpatrick-Beatty relationship and Brown's dismissal were central to the whistle-blower suit filed by Brown and Harold Nelthrope ... the two cops accused Kilpatrick of retaliating against them because of their role in an internal investigation of the mayor's security team—a probe that could have potentially exposed the affair" (Schaefer and Elrick, 2008)

In January 2008, during his seventh "State of the City" address to Detroit, Kilpatrick focused on several positive changes occurring throughout the city; then, before completing the speech, he launched into the controversy swirling around him. Once again casting himself in the role of a racial martyr, he said:

In the past 30 days I've been called a nigger more than any time in my entire life. In the past three days I've received more death threats than I have in my entire administration. I've heard these words before but I've never heard them say them about my wife and children. I have to say this because it's very personal to me. I don't believe that a Nielsen rating is worth the life of my children or your children. This unethical, illegal lynch mob mentality has to stop. And it's seriously time. We've never been here before. And I don't care if they cut the TV. off. We've never been in a situation like this before. Where you can say anything, do anything, have no facts, no research, no nothing and you launch a hate-driven bigoted assault on a family. I humbly ask members of the council, I humbly ask the religious community, I humbly ask the brothers and sisters of the city of Detroit—I humbly asked that we say "no more" together. I love this city with every part of my being. I will continue to stay focused on building the next Detroit. God Bless you, Detroit, I love you. (Rochelle, n.d.)

The address backfired badly in some quarters. Some observers felt Kilpatrick's speech amounted to race-baiting to save his political career. Even his former political advisor, Sam Riddle, described the address as a race-baiting speech, "an act of desperation," an attempt to regain his base by playing the race card. "He's gone to that well one too many times" (Rochelle, n.d.). Carmen Harlan, an African American news anchor at a local Detroit affiliate, countered Kilpatrick's characterization of the media coverage of his scandals as a baseless "hate-driven bigoted assault on a family":

Mr. Mayor, I'd like to address you directly. You were absolutely right tonight when you said that death-threats and racial slurs are wrong. I'll even go further, they're inexcusable and inappropriate, but to say that we, the media, are to blame for the mess isn't fair either. Using emotionally driven words, like the N-word, phrases like "hate-driven" and "bigoted assault," even "lynch mob mentality," stirs the very core of even my emotions. You see, I love the city too, as much as you do. Like you, we [the media] have a job to do too. I've asked you to sit down with me; explain what we don't understand and how we may have gotten it wrong. I'm still waiting for that phone call. And I quote you, "No more, I humbly ask! The Kwame Kilpatrick roller coaster has to stop." (Rochelle, n.d.)

Notwithstanding his fading light brought on by recent criminal charges associated with the text message scandal, Kilpatrick refused to resign and fully accept blame for the millions of dollars his actions had cost the city. In February 2008, during a morning radio show he was asked if he would be willing to repay taxpayers the $8.4 million for the (secret) settlement that the city paid to the two officers. Uncontrite as ever, Kilpatrick responded: "I pay it back every day. When I go out and do an economic stimulus package for hundreds of millions of dollars. When I go find a way to do a deal on the tunnel for $75 million dollars. When I go and bust my butt every day from six in the morning to ten–eleven o'clock at night.… I work every day to make sure the city gets what it's owned" (WWJ AM, Detroit, February 28, 2008).

Despite the heavy burden of shame and money Kilpatrick had cost the city, he still had many supporters who refused to abandon him, or for that matter press him to resign. They became his blind enablers, willing to forgive and forget their young "hip-hop" mayor's moral failings. Kilpatrick knew this and played upon it. In March 2008, the mayor's supporters packed a church where they rallied to the chants of "I can make it through the storm" augmented by the rousing choruses of a gospel choir. Kilpatrick assured the crowd that he would not resign. When Kilpatrick, standing behind the pulpit, told them, "I will humbly serve you till the day I die," the crowd exploded in deafening applause (*Detroit Free Press*, March 28, 2008). Seeking to minimize the seriousness of his misdeeds, the mayor claimed that the text message scandal involved more than that since other people had done worse things and did not lose their freedom. He then changed the subject to one sure to elicit even more sympathy from his supporters. The real issue, he said, was really about Detroit's future and resources. "We're at a time when the most precocious resource in the world is not oil, it's water," he said. He was referring to the fact that since Detroit owns and operated the water system that supplies water to most of southeast Michigan, the suburbs that had been fighting for years to have some control in its operation (*Detroit Free Press*, March 28, 2008).

As if he did not have enough controversy, Kilpatrick's use of the N-word compounded his trouble and further eroded his credibility among some former supporters. A year earlier he had joined with the NAACP at its Ninety-eighth Annual Convention to effectively bury the N-word in an event "billed as the funeral for the racial slur that has been used against blacks for more than a century" (Sieh, 2008). Yet even this controversy was the least of his troubles. As a result of the text messages that revealed that Kilpatrick and Beatty had been involved in a love affair and had in fact committed perjury, both were charged with "obstruction of justice, conspiracy, misconduct in office and perjury" (Rochelle, n.d.).

For some strange reason, Mayor Kilpatrick refused to accept the terms of the bond in his perjury case requiring that he inform the court before leaving the city. Perhaps the heady arrogance of power and status was too much for Kilpatrick when in July he decided to violate his bond and travel to Canada on a business trip. His actions forced the hand of the county prosecutor's office to request that he be punished. Kilpatrick apologized to the court, saying, "I've been living in an incredible state of pressure and scrutiny." His apology was not sufficient. On August 6, 2008, District Court Judge Ronald Giles informed Mayor Kilpatrick that he would receive the same treatment as any other defendant and sent him to jail for the night ("Detroit Mayor Ordered Jailed," 2008). The next morning, he made history by "becoming the first sitting mayor in Detroit's 307-year history to spend a night behind bars" (Elrick and Swickard, 2008).

As his legal battles mounted, a chorus of voices began calling for his resignation. In early August *Detroit Free Press* readers shared their frustration, anger, and sadness over the troubles the mayor had brought both upon himself and the city he so often claimed he loved (*Detroit Free Press*, August 10, 2008). One reader wrote, "I am sad for our city that has lost a bright young mayor to his ego. It happens. He should resign for his own good and that of the city he loves."

Another reader reminded fellow Detroiters, "Remember, my fellow citizens, that we, not any politician, are the city, and this all will pass. I hope the churches that have supported him will speak out and encourage him to resign." According to one reader, "The legacy of Coleman Young and Dennis Archer, two principled mayors who did their best for the City of Detroit, has been trashed one more time by the Hip-Hop Mayor. Somehow, Mayor Kilpatrick doesn't think the rules apply to him" (*Detroit Free Press*, August 10, 2008).

One reader blamed Kilpatrick for setting back race relations in the city and embarrassing the black community, especially black men:

> As a black man, I view Mayor Kwame Kilpatrick as the new black man's burden. Shame on the city of Detroit for putting up with this sham.... I can't think of any case that is more embarrassing or detrimental to African Americans everywhere than the Kilpatrick situation. It fans the glowing embers of racism and leads many non-blacks to ask: "What in the hell is wrong with you people? How can you allow this?" How indeed? (*Detroit Free Press*, August 10, 2008)

By this time, some city leaders and some of Kilpatrick's main supporters were beginning to realize that they had to cut bait in order to salvage what was left of the city's reputation. The court battles and legal challenges were bogging the city down in an ongoing legal morass. In August 2008, the influential Council of Baptist Pastors of Detroit and Vicinity abandoned its earlier reluctance to call for the mayor's resignation and issued a statement through its president saying, "We humbly urge the mayor to consider resignation from his office." The president added that "resignation would be an act of good faith that the mayor has the best interest of the city at heart ... there is an uncertain time line for resolution of charges against the mayor ... The legal process threatens to mire the city in a mess for an indefinite period." As a result Kilpatrick's ability to lead had been "rendered ineffective" (*Detroit Free Press*, August 10, 2008).

On September 4, 2008, after the city had endured months of regional, national, and international embarrassment, shame amid the public spectacle of legal wrangling, Mayor Kwame Kilpatrick pled guilty to two felonies and no contest to a charge of assaulting a police officer in July who was in the process of serving papers on one of the mayor's best friends. As part of the settlement Kilpatrick agreed to resign as mayor of Detroit, repay $1 million in restitution to the city, give up his law license, hold no public office for five years, spend 120 days in jail, and serve five years probation (Saulny and Bunkly, 2008; *Detroit Free Press*, September 5, 2008).

The news soon spread around the nation and the world. As quoted in the *Detroit Free Press* (September 5, 2008), the British Broadcasting Company reported the sad end of Mayor Kilpatrick: "A prominent African-African who was elected mayor at the age of 31, Mr. Kilpatrick had been considered one of the rising stars of the Democratic Party." The *Wall Street Journal* pointed to the racial tensions between the city and the suburbs produced by Kilpatrick's troubles. "The mayor's troubles exposed the long-standing resentments between the largely African-American city and its white suburban population. Many of the city's residents support the mayor and consider his legal troubles an attack on him from his political enemies. Suburban residents, many of whom left the city after the 1967 riot, called for his resignation" (*Detroit Free Press*, September 5, 2008). The *New York Times* argued that Kilpatrick's "refusal to resign delighted a certain segment of the city's mostly poor, mostly black population, who felt pride in Mr. Kilpatrick's rise from the Detroit Public Schools to the mayor's office. But others here found Mr. Kilpatrick arrogant and stubborn" (*Detroit Free Press*, September 5, 2008). *Time* magazine, quoted in the *Detroit Free Press*, assessed the costs of Kilpatrick's problems on the city. "The cost to Detroit taxpayers for Kilpatrick's abuse of power has been high—over $10 million so far, including legal fees and an $8.4 million confidential settlement paid to whistle-blowers ... the same sum could put several hundred new police officers on the streets of the country's most violent city. Or knock down more than a thousand of the abandoned buildings that dot Detroit's streets and breed crime" (*Detroit Free Press*, September 5, 2008).

It would be difficult to imagine that all this attention was lost on the mayor. If he felt any remorse over the enormous burden he had laid on the city, he did not express it at the news conference after he pled guilty. Instead the ex-mayor could not resist yet another gesture of empty bravado, pledging to overcome his conviction and heaping blame on the media and Governor Jennifer Granholm "for damaging his marriage and career." Worse still, he issued yet another sad and tragic pledge to the gathering, "Y'all done set me up for a comeback." A month later, at his sentencing, the ex-mayor showed little remorse, "shaking his head as the judge chastised him for his crime, smiling at family and friends, at time clowning with the prosecutors who helped put him behind bars." He maintained his defiance even in the face of Wayne County Circuit Judge David Groner, who scolded him for his arrogance and sentenced him to 120 days in jail. Upset over Kilpatrick's comments at the news conference, the judge told him, "The community expected to hear a message of humility, remorse and apology. Instead, we heard an arrogant and defiant man who accused the governor, among others for his downfall. Your statements were incredible given the fact that you had just pled guilty" (*Detroit Free Press*, October 28, 2008). Then as he was led away, Kilpatrick waved at his family and friends and said, "Y'all take it easy" (*Detroit Free Press*, October 28, 2008).

Kilpatrick had the potential to become a major leader and model for a new generation of youth, especially black youth in Detroit, who sorely needed a model beyond reproach. This "hip-hop" generation looked up to him, and for good reason: he was smart and charismatic and had accumulated an impressive list of accomplishments at a young age. Notwithstanding the scandal that brought him down while in office, Kilpatrick did accomplish some goals worthy of mentioning: he relocated some businesses downtown, including Home Depot, Borders, and Quicken Loans, revised "the development agreement with Detroit's three casinos so that permanent casinos/hotels would actually be built ... [and] successfully closed the deal for the $180 million renovation of the historic Book-Cadillac Hotel" (Sternberg, n.d.). To his credit, he made efforts to revitalize neighborhoods by establishing "the Detroit Riverfront conservatory to redevelop Detroit's riverfront ... [and] he also established Next Detroit, a 5-year project aimed at enhancing

6 neighborhoods through improved maintenance and new investment" (Sternberg, n.d.). The opening of career centers "to provide job retraining in high-demand areas" was certainly a key accomplishment. Other accomplishments could be added to the list as well, such as building "upon the success of 2005/2006 sporting events to attract other events, such as the National Association for the Advancement of Colored People (NAACP)'s 98th annual National convention and 2009 NCAA Men's Basketball Final Four" (Sternberg, n.d.). As one writer said, "Mayor Kilpatrick has style, presence, confidence and enthusiasm, qualities that help investors believe in his vision for Detroit" (Sternberg n.d.). He also had the political experience to resume bridging bridges across the city-suburban divide.

In spite of all this potential for greatness, he squandered it for show and sex. Among the tragic consequences of his transgressions—besides destroying the trust of the black community—was the grist he provided for the anti-Detroit mill. Black Detroiters did not need more negative press about its leaders or its city. Furthermore, the image of Detroit as a black majority-run city was damaged beyond measure by Kilpatrick's conduct while in office. No other black leader in Detroit's history has brought such shame and humiliation on a community in a constant struggle to do its best in the midst of poverty, crime, and violence.

History would not only credit him with being the youngest mayor elected as mayor in Detroit but unfortunately the only mayor in the history of Detroit to be charged with a felony while in office (Rochelle, n.d.).

CONCLUSION

The growth of black political power was the most significant development in the black community after 1967. White flight to the suburbs in the wake of the disorders made possible the growth of a black-majority city determined to take control of city hall. The election of Coleman Young as the first black mayor of Detroit signaled the end of white political control of the office of the mayor, and the beginning of the era of black mayors as the symbol of black political power. This development also contributed to the racial divide between the white suburbs and the black city. Mayor Young was the pioneer of this era of black mayors. While

he was often a well-deserved thorn in the side of white suburbia with its unabashed history of racism, there can be no doubt that he made his greatest contribution to race relations by disbanding STRESS and radically changing a predominantly white police department into a racially integrated one. Mayor Archer was the brilliant lawyer and bridge builder between the white suburbs and the black city, after the suburban/city racial tension of the Young era. Sadly, Mayor Kilpatrick, the youngest of the three black mayors to be elected, brought great shame on the city of Detroit.

SECTION IV

READINGS

PLANNING AND REGIONAL RELATIONS

INTRODUCTION

This section, on planning and regional growth, opens with **Sidney Fine's** description of Detroit's status as a National Model City leading up to the 1967 Rebellion. Next, **Nathaniel Jones**, who argued the *Milliken v. Bradley* case before the US Supreme Court, reflects on the backstory to one of the greatest conflicts between Detroit and its suburbs: desegregation through busing. Mid-twentieth-century urban politics and efforts toward metropolitan-wide governance are described by **Joe T. Darden, Richard Child Hill, June Thomas, and Richard Thomas**, followed by a brief history of federal urban renewal and its effects on Detroit, by **Emily Smith**. The section closes with a comprehensive piece, by **Marissa Mewitz**, on the history and future of public transit in Detroit.

1

The Model City

SIDNEY FINE

Whatever its racial problems, Detroit acquired a national reputation while Cavanagh was mayor as a model city in terms of its ability to cope with the problems that all big cities faced in the 1960s, especially racial problems. "Detroit," the *New York Times* editorialized when it became evident on July 23, 1967, that the city did not have a patent on racial peace, "probably had more going for it than any other major city in the North." Those who saw Detroit as a model city noted that it had a large and prosperous black middle class and that its blue collar workers had jobs in the auto industry that paid the unskilled wages that were 20 percent above the average for unskilled workers in the nation. Detroit as of 1967 drew attention as the only city to have two black congressmen—they made up half of the black representation in Congress. There was only one black on the Common Council, but there were three black judges in Detroit in 1965; two blacks served on the Board of Education in 1966; two of the five members of the Housing Commission in 1966 were black; and twelve Detroit blacks were members of the Michigan legislature in 1967. Detroit was lauded for its ability to secure federal funds, having one of the best per capita records in the nation in this respect. Most of the money Detroit received from Washington was directed to the inner city. "If the white middle-class knew how disproportionate our expenditures on the inner city were," a high-ranking city official declared during the 1967 riot, "we'd probably have a white revolt on our hands."[1]

Detroit's black housing left a great deal to be desired, but visitors from other cities thought that this housing was superior to what was available to blacks in their cities. Although "intolerable" in a few areas, housing was "not a terribly serious problem," an aide advised President Johnson in May 1967 after a visit to Detroit. The quality of black housing was, indeed, slightly above that of New York, Chicago, Cleveland, and Philadelphia. Although a racially segregated city, Detroit as of 1960 was somewhat less segregated than the mean for large cities in the nation. Detroit's school system before the riot was regarded by some as "noticeably better" than that of any other large midwestern city, and the *Washington Post* praised Detroit's inner-city schools as "one of the

Sidney Fine, "The Model City," *Violence in the Model City: The Cavanagh Administration, Race Relations, and the Detroit Riot of 1967*, pp. 32-37, 477-479. Copyright © 2007 by Michigan State University Press. Reprinted with permission.

country's leading examples of forceful reform in education." Detroit's poverty program, the *Post* also noted, was "regularly cited as the most effective in the United States." Even more important, the Department of Justice's Office of Law Enforcement Assistance designated Detroit as the nation's "model for police-community relations."[2]

What especially attracted favorable attention to Detroit in the years immediately preceding the 1967 riot was the reputed state of its race relations. "Of all the accomplishments in the recent history of the city," a writer in *Fortune* asserted in 1965, "the most significant is the progress Detroit has made in race relations." Detroit, the head of the National Urban League stated the next year, was on the way to becoming a "demonstration city" in the area of race relations. Not only had the leading citizens of the community come together in the CCEO and in church organizations to improve race relations, but blacks reputedly had access to City Hall and saw themselves for the first time as "part of the city." Cavanagh estimated early in 1967 that he was spending three quarters of his long working day dealing with the problems of the inner city.[3]

Detroit, Judge Horace W. Gilmore, the head of the CCEO's Police-Community Relations Subcommittee, declared in 1965, was "the most sophisticated city in the country on the matter of intergroup relations." The black deputy director of the CRC did not delude himself that Detroit had solved or was even near solving its racial problems, but he nevertheless stated at the beginning of 1966 that Detroit's "good image" was "justly reflective of a degree of communication and cooperation between white and Negro" that was "unmatched anywhere else in the United States," with the possible exception of Atlanta. The same point was made even more strongly in May 1967 by Detroit's only black councilman. "With all of its problems," Nicholas Hood declared, "Detroit is far ahead of any major city in America because we have a city administration that will not only listen to the concerns brought to it but will set out to work on these concerns."[4]

Proud of Detroit's race-relations image, Cavanagh stated a few weeks before the July 1967 riot that, in Detroit, you did not "need to throw a brick to communicate with City Hall." It was, indeed, the fact that blacks were not throwing bricks at City Hall at a time when racially related riots were spreading across the land that made Detroit appear to be a national symbol of hope. Detroit, as we shall see, experienced a minidisturbance in the summer of 1966, but the city quelled it so easily and bloodlessly that what had occurred actually enhanced Detroit's model city image. The Cavanagh administration, understandably, was willing "to promote" that image and, to a degree, to believe in its validity. "It is no accident," Cavanagh declared a month before the July riot, "that Detroit has escaped any great amount of civic unrest." It was due rather, he said, to the city's responsiveness to the "needs in the streets."[5]

Social scientists visited Detroit in the Cavanagh years to learn how a city could deal successfully with its racial problems. Detroit and its mayor became the subjects of praise in the nation's magazines and news papers, admiring articles appearing in such places as *Fortune, Newsweek, Harper's, U.S. News & World Report, Look,* the *Wall Street Journal,* the *Christian Science Monitor,* the *Los Angeles Times,* and the *Cleveland Plain Dealer.* The view of the city in the periodical press was echoed by the Department of Justice's Summer Project, which pointed to Detroit as "a racial model." In 1965 the American Institute of Architects gave Detroit and one other city its first awards for urban redevelopment plans that "successfully realized the objective of creating vital environments for the core of American cities." In March 1967 the National Municipal League and *Look* magazine designated Detroit an "All-America City" because of the development of its $250 million cultural center, thus reversing thirty years of "under-emphasis on culture," its urban renewal and redevelopment plans, and the manner in which it had reacted to its small 1966 disturbance.[6]

Jerry Cavanagh, an aide remarked, "not only got a great deal of press, he got brilliant press." The "best known" and most "glamorous" city mayor of the time, he was portrayed nationally as "The Dynamo in Detroit" who had pulled "a once dead industrial city out of its physical, economic and cultural doldrums" and as having gone further than other mayors in responding to slum problems. *Life* selected "the hot young mayor" as one of the one hundred members of the "Take Over Generation," and the United States Junior Chamber of Commerce named him one of the ten "outstanding young men" of the nation. Although Cavanagh had his enemies in Detroit, he was reported at the end of 1963 to be "the object of nearly constant worship" by the city's press and its civic, business, and labor leaders. Two years later a writer in *Fortune* described Cavanagh as the "image" of the city's new consensus, "the symbol of the city's aspirations." When someone said to the president of Michigan Bell that the unemployment rate among Detroit's black youth was disturbingly high, he replied, "One of these days Jerry Cavanagh will get a few people together and come up with a program."

When Cavanagh ran for reelection in 1965, he received a crushing 69 percent of the vote. The next year he became the first mayor simultaneously to head both the United States Conference of Mayors and the National League of Cities. His advice was sought by the White House, he came to be seen as a presidential possibility himself, and he relished the idea. "On a clear day," an aide said of Cavanagh, he could "see the White House." The mayor's favorite song was said to be "Impossible Dream," and he appeared for a time to be living it.[7]

Things began to turn sour for Cavanagh in 1966. Believing himself "politically hot," he decided to challenge former Michigan Governor G. Mennen Williams for the Democratic nomination for the United States Senate. The electoral problem for Cavanagh in what was certainly a political blunder was that Williams appealed to the same labor, liberal, and black constituency as the mayor, and Williams had endeared himself to those groups as governor before Cavanagh had appeared on the political scene. Williams defeated Cavanagh in the primary, swamping the mayor in Detroit's black precincts. Cavanagh's candidacy not only "alienated" some of his Detroit supporters, but it also dealt a blow to assumptions about his political invincibility and raised the ire of Democrats, who blamed the divisive primary for Williams's defeat in the final election. By that time, moreover, Cavanagh had come out against America's involvement in the war in Vietnam and had criticized federal spending for space exploration, positions that did not endear the mayor to President Johnson. Cavanagh soon "detected ... somewhat of a chill around the White House" where he was concerned.[8]

Misfortune seemed to plague Cavanagh from 1966 onward. The Detroit TV and radio personality Lou Gordon, once an ardent supporter of the mayor, turned on Cavanagh, questioning his character and integrity and claiming that his senatorial candidacy had been a betrayal of a promise to serve out his second term as mayor. Councilwoman Mary Beck, seizing on the emotional crime issue, mounted a recall campaign against the mayor in the spring of 1967. A grand jury investigation of the Police Department spawned a crop of nasty rumors that involved the mayor. There were rumors also that the Catholic mayor was having marital difficulties, rumors that were confirmed when the mayor's wife and the mother of their eight children filed for separate maintenance on July 18, 1967. Fed information and misinformation by the mayor's Detroit foes, the nationally syndicated columnist Drew Pearson wrote a particularly venomous piece about Cavanagh in May 1967. On July 21, 1967, two days before the Detroit riot, a Cavanagh aide remarked, "You know, the only thing the poor guy has not had is a riot."[9]

It would be a mistake to assume that Cavanagh, despite a sea of troubles, saw his career at an end on the eve of the July 1967 riot or that his national image had dimmed to any significant degree. Whatever the view of him in Detroit—and an independent survey in June 1967 revealed that he was still solidly backed by the Detroit electorate—he remained an admired national personage. *Newsweek* in March 1967 not only hailed Cavanagh as "urban America's most articulate spokesman" but placed him and New York's John Lindsay at the top of any list of mayors who might have national political futures. Echoing *Newsweek*, the *Detroit News* reported just a few days before the Detroit riot began that the city and the nation were still looking closely at Jerry Cavanagh because of the reputation that he enjoyed across the land. As the national reaction to the Detroit riot made abundantly clear, the mayor's troubles, in any event, had not rubbed off on his city, which continued up to July 23, 1967, to enjoy a reputation as a model city.[10]

Did Detroit deserve its reputation as a model city, particularly in its race relations? That the city's reputation was grossly inflated in an absolute sense goes almost without saying. Detroit blacks during the Cavanagh years before the 1967 riot complained with good reason about unemployment, job discrimination, and the quality of the housing and the public education available to them; and their relationship with the Police Department was one of mutual antagonism and constant strain. Detroit had its CCR, its CCEO, and its Archbishop's Committee on Human Relations; but it also had its white homeowners who adamantly opposed open housing, and almost 70 percent of the white respondents in a postriot survey indicated that they thought blacks had been "pushing too fast" for what they wanted.[11]

As a successful black businessman in the city stated just after the riot, Detroit offered considerable opportunity to "the enterprising Negro," but its numerous programs did not appear to be reaching the very poor and the hard-core unemployed. Putting the matter somewhat differently, a Cavanagh aide, in assessing the performance of the Cavanagh administration as of September 1966, concluded, "I would say that up to now we have played with heady ideas ... [but] we still have to produce the major part of what we set out to do."[12]

For all of the publicity that it received about its open lines of communication to the black community, the Cavanagh administration was not really in close touch with the ghetto poor and the unemployed youngsters on the street corners. Cavanagh conceded the point after the riot. Hard as his administration had tried, he stated, it had failed to "get down to the streets" and did not really know what was going on there. There was actually a good deal of unrest in Detroit, but it was not apparent on the surface. Councilman Mel Ravitz compared Detroit in February 1966 to an iceberg, a city with "a bright, attractive, well-publicized face but [with] submerged dangers" that could not "readily be seen."[13]

Inadequate as were its efforts to deal with its problems in any absolute sense, Detroit, in a comparative sense, may nevertheless have deserved its preriot model city reputation. This was, indeed, the view of Detroit's first black councilman, William T. Patrick, Jr., who said just after the riot that although Detroit, "in a pure sense," had "many problems," relations between the races were good "in a relative sense compared with the rest of the nation." "Detroit," he remarked, "is damn good compared with other cities." When a *Detroit News* reporter compared Detroit with four other large midwestern cities in May 1967, he concluded that Detroit, although not "the ideal city" or "the perfect model," was responding more successfully to the urban problems of the day than the other cities were. However little progress it had made in the areas to which its programs were addressed, Detroit, Cavanagh correctly said during the riot, had done "more of the textbook things than any other city."[14]

The evidence is conflicting as to whether Detroit blacks thought that they were better off than blacks in other cities. A compilation of mean dissatisfaction scores for city services based on a survey of blacks aged 16 to 69 in fifteen major cities in early 1968, after the riot, revealed that Detroit blacks stood at about the midpoint in terms of their level of dissatisfaction with four city services: schools, parks, police, and garbage collection. Detroit blacks also did not differ appreciably from blacks in the other cities in their estimation of whether their mayor was trying as hard as he could or fairly hard to solve city problems. On the other hand, when the Detroit Urban League and the *Detroit Free Press* in a postriot random sample survey asked blacks in the principal Detroit riot areas to compare their lot with that of blacks in other northern cities, 45.5 percent responded that Detroit blacks had "better than average income," as compared to 8 percent who thought the opposite; 39 percent thought that they had better jobs, as compared to 8 percent who thought they had worse jobs; and 24.5 percent thought that they had received a "better than average education," as compared to 10 percent who thought the reverse.[15]

In the final analysis, how Detroit blacks compared their condition with that of blacks elsewhere may be of less significance in ascertaining the degree of their dissatisfaction than the comparison they made between themselves and Detroit's whites. "Black Detroiters," a black official at the time of the riot later stated, "didn't compare their lot in life to Black Wattsites, Black Harlemites or Black anywhere else. Black Detroiters compared their lot in life to white Detroiters." As we have seen, whites had more income, better homes, and better jobs, and suffered less unemployment than the city's blacks. Whites were also more satisfied than blacks with the quality of their schools and parks and the police protection they received, and Detroit blacks, no doubt, thought that there was good reason for this.[16]

That Detroit could be compared so favorably with other Northern cities in terms of its ability to cope with racial problems should be taken as less an indication of Detroit's success than of the even greater inadequacy of what was being done elsewhere. Cavanagh, indeed, conceded after the riot that the Detroit effort had been "like putting a bandaid on a severe wound."[17] It is easy enough to disparage the Detroit effort, but the problems of the black ghetto and poverty that Detroit and other big cities faced in the 1960s were not all that tractable, as the record of the years that have followed makes painfully evident.

The two faces presented by Detroit just before the riot, the city so proud of its accomplishments, so often under attack from inside for its shortcomings, was nicely illustrated when Detroit received its All-America City award in March 1967. Since the award was, in part, based on the city's urban rehabilitation and housing efforts in the WCO area of Detroit, the city government invited the WCO to attend the award ceremony. The organization's president responded that the award was nothing but "a big joke" and that the WCO did not want to be included in "such a hypocritical ceremony."[18]

NOTES

1. *NYT,* July 25, 1967; Northrup, *Automobile Industry,* p. 35; *Wall Street Journal,* Aug. 12, 1964; MC, Jan. 8, 1966; *Los Angeles Times,* Feb. 2, 1966, DRSB No. 1; Van Gordon Sauter and Burleigh Hines, *Nightmare in Detroit: A Rebellion and Its Victims* (Chicago: Henry Regnery Co., 1968), p. 220; Lukas, "Whitey"; *Washington Post,* July 25, 1967; Brown, "Detroit," p. 144; *DN,* Mar. 1, 1966; Cavanagh, "Civil Rights: The Next Frontier," July 8, 1966, Box 301, JPC Papers.

2. *Wall Street Journal,* Aug. 12, 1964; Sauter and Hines, *Nightmare,* p. 220; Gaither for President, May 9, 1967, Box 29, WE9, WHCF; Lukas, "Whitey"; Karl E. and Alma F. Taeuber, *Negroes in Cities: Residential Segregation and Neighborhood Change* (Chicago: Aldine Publishing Co., 1966), pp. 32, 37; *DN,* Apr. 30, May 28, 1967; *Washington Post,* July 25, 1967; Ross Speech, enclosed with Ross to Locke, Nov. 18, 1965, Box 37, ORA Papers; Locke, *Detroit Riot,* p. 65.

3. *Wall Street Journal,* Aug. 12, 1964; Brown, "Detroit," p. 144; MC, Apr. 23, 1966; *Los Angeles Times,* Feb. 6, 1966, DRSB No. 1; *Look,* Sept. 21, 1965, copy in Box 212, JPC Papers; *Newsweek* 69 (Mar. 13, 1967): 43.

4. Gilmore to Editor, *DN,* July 15, 1965; Box 1, Gilmore Papers; MC, Jan. 8, 1966; *DN,* May 13, 1967.

5. *DFP,* May 18, June 27, 1967; Locke to Fine, Jan. 4, 1984. See chap. 6.

6. Locke, *Detroit Riot,* p. 65; Locke to Fine, Jan. 4, 1984; Brown, "Detroit," pp. 142–45ff; *Newsweek* 69 (Mar. 13, 1967): 42–43; *U.S. News and World Report,* May 23, 1966, p. 37; CCEO, "Race Relations in Detroit—Summer 1965," n.d., Box 18, ORA Papers; *Los Angeles Times,* Feb. 6, 1966, DRSB No. 1; Nicholson, "Surprising Mayor," pp. 76–82; *Look,* Sept. 21, 1965, copy in Box 212, JPC Papers; *Cleveland Plain Dealer,* Jan. 3, 1965, in ibid.; *Wall Street Journal,* Aug. 12, 1964; *NYT,* Apr. 4, 1965; Lukas, "Whitey"; *DFP,* Mar. 24, 1967; Reconnaissance Survey Field Research Reports, Detroit, Michigan, 1:3, Box 46, NACCD Records.

7. Serrin, "One Big City"; Nicholson, "Surprising Mayor," p. 76; Brown, "Detroit," pp. 144, 256, 262; *Cleveland Plain Dealer*, Jan. 3, 1965, in Box 212, JPC Papers; *Look*, Sept. 21, 1965, copy in ibid.

8. *DFP*, Aug. 3, 4, 1966, Sept. 3, 1967; Nicholas interview with Bernard Klein [1982], copy of tape in my possession; Johnson interview, p. 49; Serrin, "One Big City"; Gordon, "Racial Gap," p. 25; Cavanagh Oral History Interview, Mar. 22, 1971, pp. 18, 36–38, LBJ Library; Marvin Watson to Bill Moyers, Box 9, Watson Office Files, LBJ Library; Widick, *Detroit*, pp. 163–64; *DN*, Aug. 18, 1968.

9. Cavanagh interview, p. 40; *DFP*, June 13, July 19, 20, Sept. 3, 1967; Locke, *Detroit Riot*, pp. 66–67; transcripts of Gordon broadcasts, Box 353, JPC Papers; Pearson column, May 14 [1967], typed copy in Box 339, ibid.; Cavanagh to Benjamin Bradlee, May 12, 1967, Cavanagh to Celestin J. Steiner, July 18, 1967, ibid.; Serrin, "One Big City"; Gordon, "Racial Gap," p. 25; *NYT*, July 25, 1967; Nicholas interview with Patricia Knox [1982], copy of tape in my possession; *DN*, May 14, July 20, 1967, Aug. 18, 1968. After six weeks of effort, Beck was able to gather only 42,000 of the 114,118 signatures required for an election to recall the mayor. *DFP*, June 13, 1967.

10. *DN*, May 14, June 11, 19, 1967; *Newsweek* 69 (Mar. 13, 1967): 38; *Washington Post*, July 25, 1967; *NYT*, July 25, 1967.

11. See *DN*, Feb. 3, 1965, and White File, No. 262, Inter-University Consortium for Political and Social Research, Detroit data for Angus Campbell and Howard Schuman, "Racial Attitudes in Fifteen American Cities," in *Supplemental Studies for the National Advisory Commission on Civil Disorders* (Washington: GPO, 1968).

12. Raschard Memorandum to Wilson (interview with Michael Ward), n.d., Series 4, Box 22, NACCD Records; Tom Popp Memorandum to Wilson, Oct. 26, 1967, ibid.; John Ursu Memorandum to Wilson (interview with John Feikens), n.d., ibid.; Black to Cavanagh, Sept. 8, 1966, Box 271, JPC Papers; National Commission on Urban Problems, *Hearings,* 5:3; Potts Speech, June 8, 1967, Box 24, ORA Papers; *Los Angeles Times*, July 30, 1967, DRSB No. 1.

13. Remarks by Cavanagh … , Sept. 26, 1967, Box 386, JPC Papers; Girardin to Jeanelle L. Baker, Aug. 11, 1967, Box 3, Girardin Papers; *MC*, Mar. 19, Apr. 23, 1966; *DN*, Oct. 10, 1967; *NACCD Report*, p. 149.

14. Bernard Dobranski Memorandum to Wilson (interview with Patrick), Oct. 13, 1967, Series 59, Box 2, NACCD Records; *DN*, May 28, July 31, 1967; Gaither for President, May 9, 1967, Box 29, WE9, WHCF; Serrin, "One Big City."

15. Howard Schuman and Barry Gruenberg, "Dissatisfaction with City Services … ," in Harlan Hahn, ed., *People and Politics in Urban Society* (Beverly Hills: Sage Publications, 1972), p. 374; Campbell and Schuman, "Racial Attitudes," pp. 22, 41; Black File, Nos. 183–87, 193, Detroit data for ibid.; *The People Beyond 12th Street: A Survey of Attitudes of Detroit Negroes after 1967* (Detroit: Detroit Urban League, 1967).

16. *MC*, July 24, 1982; Joel D. Aberbach and Jack L. Walker, *Race in the City* (Boston: Little, Brown and Co., 1973), p. 35.

17. *DN*, July 31, 1967.

18. Archie Perry to Cavanagh, May 10, 1967, Box 368, JPC Papers.

2

Milliken v. Bradley; A Judicial Betrayal of Brown

While I was serving as counsel to the Kerner Commission in 1968, and shortly after I became the general counsel of the NAACP in 1969, the extent of the spread of Northern school segregation was becoming increasingly apparent. In particular, the officers of the Detroit branch of the NAACP were concerned by these patterns. I met with these officers, at their request, during the 1970 NAACP annual national convention to discuss developments in that city.

They informed me about recently signed legislation in Michigan (Act 48[1]), signed into law by Governor William Milliken, which virtually enjoined the Detroit school board from implementing a very modest desegregation plan that would have affected 10,000 white students out of a school system of about 300,000. This desegregation plan created a political firestorm. Additionally, the inferior quality of education that was being provided to black children was a cause of deep concern to the local NAACP officers. For example, Michigan law required that children be exposed to six hours of education a day, but in overcrowded schools black children were limited to just half that time. Rather than reassign the students in the overcrowded black schools into the adjacent white schools that had excess capacity, the state policy shortened the educational day for black children.

When I returned from the convention to my office in New York, I called a meeting of my legal team and the Detroit school board lawyers, who were interested in having the NAACP intervene. At the meeting, I concluded that the legislation was a clear case of interposition and nullification by the state because when the state passed Act 48, it halted the actions of the Detroit school board to comply with the command of *Brown*. That was tantamount to Governor George Wallace of Alabama standing in the schoolhouse door, and to Governor Orval Faubus of Arkansas interfering with the order of the district court to integrate Little Rock High School.

I made it clear to the Detroit school board lawyers that our strategy would have to include joining the Detroit school board as a defendant. That infuriated them and their lawyer. In fact, when

Nathaniel R. Jones, "Milliken v. Bradley: A Judicial Betrayal of Brown," *The Pursuit of Racial and Ethnic Equality in American Public Schools: Mendez, Brown, and Beyond*, ed. Kristi L. Bowman, pp. 171-175. Copyright © 2015 by Michigan State University Press. Reprinted with permission.

the lawyer for the Detroit school board, George Bushnell Jr., who had been an ally of the NAACP, realized that his client would be a nominal defendant, he said: "I'll whip your asses in court." I responded, "You'll have to do that, because we have no choice but to join you as a party."

There were, however, two Sixth Circuit precedents that stood in our way. We decided that we would have to develop a strategy that would allow us to distinguish *Craggett v. Cleveland Board of Education*[2] and *Deal v. Cincinnati Board of Education*.[3] In those cases, the Sixth Circuit, in the 1960s, had held that the racial imbalance in schools that was being complained of by black plaintiffs did not result from state action, and without state action the federal courts had no jurisdiction.

We drafted our lawsuit to indicate that we could prove that the racial imbalance in Detroit's schools was a result of official action by the state of Michigan as well as by the Detroit school board. The initial reaction by the trial judge, Stephen Roth, was skeptical, if not hostile. He made it clear to us that he was a long-time resident of Michigan, had been the Attorney General of Michigan, knew the "good people" of Michigan, and that the allegations we made in that complaint with regard to the conduct of the officials in Detroit and in Michigan just could not be sustained. Therefore, he was not going to grant us any temporary relief. On appeal, the Sixth Circuit later did grant temporary relief, and took a different view of our complaint.

Eventually, Judge Roth became a convert. He made it very clear, as we proceeded on the merits, that he thought we could make our case. We had to show that discriminatory housing policies and school policies combined to form a nexus. For instance, we offered proof of restrictive housing covenants and their effect in maintaining segregated owner-occupied neighborhoods in Detroit. Additionally, we offered proof of public housing policies that ensured when public housing was constructed in Detroit, it was constructed on a segregated basis, and that the school board accommodated the practice by committing to build schools where the housing authorities were planning to put the segregated housing. Without such a commitment from the school board, the public housing would not have been built. Furthermore, the policies of the real estate industry, the banking industry, and the FHA had all worked together to create and maintain residential segregation.

We also developed a huge map of Detroit as an exhibit in the case, which Judge Roth allowed us to post on a wall in the courtroom. It had overlays of every five years, which showed racial population shifts, student assignment changes, and transfer policies of the Detroit school board. As the black citizens of Detroit were being moved around the city through discriminatory housing policies, the school boundary lines also shifted. It was irrefutable that the student assignment policies had a racial motive.

Judge Roth made specific findings on the interaction that occurred between school officials, housing officials, and banking officials to create the racial isolation that existed in schools. The Sixth Circuit's decisions in the *Deal* and *Craggett* cases in the 1960s had held that the policies of housing were separate and apart from school policies—that school officials had no control over what the housing industry did. We proved that there was a connection. Our evidence tied them together, showing the interrelationship between the housing industry and the policies of the school board. That was sufficient for Judge Roth, and for the Sixth Circuit. But, unfortunately, the Sixth Circuit did not include that as a factor in its affirmance of the district court holding that there were enough other segregative acts by the state and Detroit officials to establish their culpability.[4]

After Judge Roth made his findings with regard to the intentional acts that provided jurisdiction to the federal courts, we then proceeded to have hearings on the remedy. After taking considerable testimony, Judge Roth concluded that a remedy limited to the political boundaries of Detroit would not last very long because of the massive nature of the constitutional violations he identified. The evidence showed that the state of Michigan, through the application of its policies or the failure to enforce its proclaimed non-discrimination policies, was a participant in creating segregation and isolation in Detroit. Therefore, as a joint tortfeasor, the state could be required by the Court to participate in the remedy. When Judge Roth made his finding, he directed the state of Michigan to join with the Detroit school district in formulating a desegregation plan. He didn't say what the plan should be, but he indicated that the plan should not be hemmed in by the political boundaries between Detroit and the various suburban communities. That was where things stood at the time an appeal was taken to the United States Supreme Court.

The issue placed before the Supreme Court was: Could the suburban districts be required to participate in a remedy, of a two-way nature, that would have students in suburban schools being assigned to some schools in Detroit and some children in Detroit being assigned to some schools in the suburbs? As Professor Joyce Baugh's book *The Detroit School Busing Case:* Milliken v. Bradley *and the Controversy over Desegregation* suggests, neither Justice Potter Stewart nor Chief Justice Burger could bring themselves to affirm a plan that was going to disturb suburban white children.[5] Thus, what the Supreme Court did was ignore the fact that the state of Michigan was the parent of education. Local school districts were sub-units of the state, created by the state. In fact, we offered evidence that in one fell swoop, the state had dissolved some 300 school districts without the consent of the affected citizens—an action that was consistent with the state's power. So, we argued, the state had the power to participate in a remedy that would realign student attendance policies so as to enhance desegregation. Ultimately, this argument was unsuccessful.

The significance of the case to me has only grown since the time it was litigated. I knew then that we had the ability to break the back of urban segregation. We had devised a means by which, if the precedents established in the South were followed in the Northern cases, we could achieve a significant reformation of Northern and urban conditions. In the 1973 decision of the Sixth Circuit that was appealed to the Supreme Court, the Honorable George Edwards, then the Chief Judge of the Sixth Circuit, wrote an opinion that stated: "The instant case calls up haunting memories of the now long overruled and discredited separate but equal doctrine of *Plessy v. Ferguson*. If we hold that school district boundaries are absolute barriers to a Detroit school desegregation plan, we would be opening a way to nullify *Brown v. Board of Education*, which overruled *Plessy*."[6] But when the Supreme Court issued its first decision in *Milliken* in 1974, the Court rejected and abandoned the precedents it had established in the Southern cases.[7] It retreated from *Brown*.

If we look at the condition of education today in urban America, we see that Judge Edwards was absolutely right. If one more justice had followed the Court's clearly established precedents, the educational landscape of this country would be dramatically different, all to the good of America and its children.

NOTES

1. Act approved July 7, 1970, 1970 Michigan Public Acts 136 (repealed by Act of January 13, 1977, 1976 Michigan Public Acts 1541).
2. Craggett v. Cleveland Board of Education, 338 F.2d 941 (6th Cir. 1964).
3. Deal v. Cincinnati Board of Education, 369 F.2d 55 (6th Cir. 1966), certiorari denied 389 U.S. 847 (1967), appeal after 1966 decision remanded to the district court, 419 F.2d 1387 (6th Cir. 1969), certiorari denied 402 U.S. 962 (1971).
4. Bradley v. Milliken, 338 F. Supp. 582 (E.D. Mich. 1971); Bradley v. Milliken, 345 F. Supp. 914 (E.D. Mich. 1972). Both district court opinions were affirmed by *Bradley v. Milliken* 484 F.2d 215 (6th Cir. 1973), which was reversed and remanded by *Milliken v. Bradley* 418 U.S. 717 (1974).
5. JOYCE A. BAUGH, THE DETROIT SCHOOL BUSING CASE: *MILLIKEN V. BRADLEY* AND THE CONTROVERSY OVER DESEGREGATION (University Press of Kansas 2011).
6. Bradley v. Milliken, 484 F.2d 215, 249 (6th Cir. 1973).
7. Milliken v. Bradley, 418 U.S. 717 (1974).

3

Politics and Policy in Metropolitan Detroit

JOE T. DARDEN, RICHARD CHILD HILL,
JUNE THOMAS, AND RICHARD THOMAS

All of the issues discussed thus far—the economy of the region, patterns of race and class, race relations, redevelopment strategies—relate in some sense to politics. Although the political environment has not always determined the course of events in the Detroit metropolis, it has certainly helped shape them. The political fragmentation of the region is the single variable that best explains why certain areas of the region suffer the most from the effects of the massive extremes in regional economic development.

If, as had happened in metropolitan regions in the southern United States, the city of Detroit had been able merely to annex the developing region instead of watch helplessly as outlying areas incorporated, it would have mattered little to the tax base of the city whether development decentralized. The political fragmentation that did occur exacerbated race and class conflicts that had already begun to take place within the central city. Soon it became fairly easy for whites to escape diversity, merely by moving to one of many suburbs surrounding the city. Redevelopment policies constantly intertwined with politics within the city, especially as mayors used redevelopment to try to gain political favor with voters. They failed to address problems of race and income discrimination or inequity because of the political environment on national and local levels.

This chapter examines three aspects of politics and policy in Detroit. Rather than recite a litany of mayors and councils within the city throughout the years, it is more instructive to look specifically at politics in the region, as related to race and regional conflict and cooperation.

The first part of the chapter offers a history of the ascendency of black political power within the central city and the region. Beginning in the era when even one black political candidacy was a victory, it explains how blacks eventually succeeded in electing many blacks to political office, including the present mayor. Throughout this era the natural tension between the black moderate coalition builders and the black radicals, or nationalists, influenced the contours of black political power.

The second section examines a policy case study that illustrates the conflicts over school desegregation. The issue of whether schools should be substantially integrated by race offers a microcosm of the conflicts between cities and suburbs that spilled over into the judicial as well as the political arena.

The last section picks up on an earlier chapter's discussion of racial and income inequality between municipalities within the region. It also reviews the efforts that have been made to reduce inequities and to institutionalize regional governance and cooperation.

As a whole, the chapter suggests that the rise of black political power has been a victory for those concerned with creating a democratic society. But the current inequities between the municipalities of the region have given black political ascendency a hollow ring. Proposals for increased metropolitan cooperation have failed, because so many people within the region gain from political fragmentation. Because of the importance of black political power in Detroit, little interest exists even in Detroit, one of the most disadvantaged municipalities—in instituting meaningful metropolitan reorganization.

BLACK POLITICAL POWER IN DETROIT

One of the most remarkable stories in the constellation of potential narratives about politics in the Detroit region is the story of the growth and development of black political power.

This story actually begins with the black migration during and after World War I that paved the way for black political power in Detroit. By the mid-1930s blacks had begun to shift from the Republican party, the party of Abraham Lincoln and Henry Ford (bestowers of freedom and jobs, respectively), to the Democratic party. Charles C. Diggs, Sr., the first black Democrat to be elected to a state office, represented a political coalition of blacks and of labor-based, ethnic, and liberal white Democrats.[1] He was reelected several times after his first victory in 1938, but he fell from power when he was convicted of accepting bribes in 1944. He was jailed from 1948 to 1950, Because of that conviction, the state senate refused to seat him after his reelection in 1950. Between 1946 and 1962 eight blacks, including several black women, won election to the Michigan legislature. One of these was Charles C. Diggs, Jr., who in 1951 won election to the seat that had been refused his father.[2] The steady stream of black lawmakers from Detroit reflected the expanding black population in districts where blacks were rapidly becoming the majority.

Throughout the 1950s a coalition of black, labor, and liberal organizations worked to elect blacks to state and city political and judicial positions. One crucial election was that of William T. Patrick, Jr., a former assistant prosecuting attorney, who became the first black in the city's history to win a seat on the Detroit Common Council.[3]

The liberal coalition that had elected other blacks exercised caution in choosing Patrick. Patrick's education, moderate speech, and action—in short, his overall cultivation as an acceptable member of the black upper class—rendered him sufficiently suitable for upper-class whites' political taste. Patrick's election reflected the period in the history of black political development in Detroit when black, upper-class professionals were becoming increasingly interested in liberal politics. Patrick believed in the politics of the liberal coalition and demonstrated this belief by campaigning with Councilman Ed Carey, a UAW official and minority leader in the Michigan House of Representatives, and with another candidate of Polish descent, taking both of them into black precincts. They, in turn, took Patrick into their precincts. Because he was the candidate of the liberal coalition. Patrick stayed away from racial appeals to black voters. However, he still ran four-to-one ahead of the nearer whites in black areas and four-to-one behind Polish candidates in Polish areas.[4] Regardless of the liberal coalition's nonracial political posture, race still dominated politics in Detroit elections.

As important as the liberal coalition had been and would still be to the election of blacks to political office in Detroit, the growth, expansion, and increasing politicalization of the black population were rapidly becoming the dominant factors in the black community's political development. Liberal coalition politics of necessity placed ideological constraints on independent black political development. Not unlike other ethnic and nationality groups in Detroit and other cities, blacks in Detroit and elsewhere were straining at the political leash for their turn to lead big city politics. It would only be a matter of time before liberal coalition politics would collide with the movement for increased black political independence, But in the late 1950s liberal coalition politics continued to benefit black political development in Detroit.

Of all the blacks elected to public office in Detroit in the 1950s, Congressman Charles C. Diggs, Jr., best symbolized black political progress during the decade. Diggs lost a race for the Detroit Common Council in 1953, but the close results strongly suggested the possibility of victory in the 13th U.S. Congressional District, which corresponded to the 3d Senatorial District, which Diggs represented in the state senate. He challenged and defeated the white 14-year incumbent. Democratic congress man George D. O'Brien, in the 1954 Democratic primary. He then went against three opponents—including Republican Landon Knight, son of John S. Knight, the newspaper publisher—and won. It was a great victory! Diggs had not only polled more than two-thirds of all the votes cast, but had accomplished this political feat in an area 55 percent white, made up of Greek, Jewish, Mexican. Chinese, Lebanese, Maltese, Irish, and Italian ethnic minorities. Diggs became Michigan's first black congressman. When he traveled to Washington for the swearing in ceremonies. 400 blacks went along with him on a special train. The gallery was so crowded that the late Sam Rayburn had to conduct two swearing in ceremonies so all the visitors could witness this historic occasion.[5]

Once in Washington. Diggs wasted no time in making his political views known and refused to be restrained by his party's politics. Though not as independent and outspoken as New York's black congressman Adam Clayton Powell, he was much more so than Chicago's black congressman William L. Dawson. During his first month as a congressman. Diggs introduced 11 civil rights bills and attacked the Veterans Administration for racial discrimination. He considered himself a "fighter against injustice" and put his own party on notice that he would not be their "tool" where black interests were involved. He challenged his party's views on civil rights and in 1956 threatened to bolt the party if it did not "stop pussyfooting on civil rights views."[6]

When Diggs won reelection in the fall of 1958 for a third term, he had become one of the major black political figures in the nation and the symbol of the decade of black political development in the Motor City.[7]

Black Consciousness and the Road to Black Political Independence

Black political consciousness and power in Detroit quickened in the tumultuous 1960s. Early in the decade blacks rallied against the excessive police power of Mayor Louis C. Miriani and succeeded in throwing him out of office. Black radicals, unimpressed with the incremental political progress of the past, rejected the idols of black and white liberalism as "false gods" used to maintain and perpetuate black political subservience to "the white establishment" Black rebellion punctuated the decade, placing in question the efficacy of an entire tradition of liberal coalition politics in Detroit. Just before the end of the decade. Detroit came close to electing its first black mayor.

In 1961 blacks comprised about one-third of the total population in Detroit. This percentage would expand as whites left for the suburbs. Black political awareness was moving apace with the expanding black population, as white politicians nervously eyed their districts' rapidly changing complexions. The most pressing issue to politically aware blacks in 1960 was to get rid of Mayor Miriani, who had instituted a police crackdown that translated into wholesale arrests of black citizens. Not everyone was dissatisfied with Miriani. The white power structure in Detroit, including members of the liberal coalition such as the UAW, gave Miriani strong support. This was perhaps the first sign of divergence of blacks and key white segments of the liberal coalition. Blacks rallied behind Jerome P. Cavanaugh, who was challenging Miriani for the office. The Trade Union Leadership Council (TULC), a black labor organization with a history of conflicts with the white leadership of the UAW, mobilized the black community behind Cavanaugh, giving him the votes necessary to win the election.[8] By demonstrating their political power in this mayoral campaign, called "the biggest political upset in Michigan politics in 32 years," blacks also demonstrated that they would no longer let the liberal coalition determine their political direction.[9] Consequently, this election widened the gap between liberal whites and blacks in the coalition.[10]

In response to the groundswell of black activism, some blacks in Detroit abandoned liberal coalition politics for a more nationalistic approach to black political development. In 1962 blacks of this political persuasion started a campaign to elect blacks to replace white congressmen in predominantly black districts. While this effort received some black support, the entrenched black political leadership, still tied to the liberal coalition, rejected such appeals to race.[11]

By the early 1960s the Freedom-Now party was sufficiently organized in Detroit to put forward a slate of candidates for local public offices as well as for Congress. The Freedom-Now party's attempts failed, but the mood of black political independence remained strong and persistent.[12] When William Patrick resigned from the Common Council in 1964, some black leaders mobilized to fill his seat and two other seats with three blacks in the 1965 council elections. "Crime-in-the-streets" for whites and "black support for black candidates" soon became the only issues of the campaign.[13]

Just before the primary, pandemonium ensued when the *Detroit News* published an article questioning the credentials of Jackie Vaughn, one of the black candidates. The Wayne County AFL-CIO (American Federation of Labor and Congress of Industrial Organizations) sided with the *Detroit News* and endorsed ex-mayor Miriam. Black groups, led by the TULC, accused the white political elite of trying to impose white candidates on the black community. Some community support for Vaughn took on the appearance of a crusade.[14]

As if this were not enough excitement for one election campaign, the *Detroit News* triggered another round of conflict when it published statistics revealing that whites supported only white candidates. In contrast, blacks supported both black and white candidates. In response, a group of black ministers, the Interdenominational Ministries Alliance (IMA), threatened to call a boycott of all white candidates if whites did not show more respect for black candidates. A similar campaign, organized by black nationalist the Reverend Albert B. Cleage, Jr., urged blacks to support only the four black candidates. This group's rallying cry was "four and no more."[15]

The IMA threat attracted much white media attention but in the process turned off moderate black organizations like the TULC, which opposed the boycott. The threat did stimulate some liberal white religious and labor organizations to action. Concerned that white liberal candidates could not defeat white conservative candidates without black votes, they began a modest push for white support of black candidates. Moderate black politicians rejected the radical approach of the IMA, but benefited from such approaches. For example, the IMA boycott threat opened doors in white areas to such moderate candidates as Nicholas Hood, who normally would not have been acceptable to many whites.[16] Whites perceived the Nicholas Hoods of the black community as "safe" alternatives to the more radical political activists. Obviously bowing to the black political moderates, IMA decided to withdraw its boycott threat. Other black organizations, however, continued supporting only black candidates. These organizations included the Inner-City Voters' League, the League of Negro Women Voters, and the National Organization on Negro Education. Out of the four black candidates, only Nicholas Hood, who came in eighth, won a seat on the Detroit Common Council.[17]

In the 1960s the threat of radical black politics—or at least black politics to the left of black moderates in the liberal coalition—posed problems for the established black politicians, but the threat never materialized into any substantial challenge. The Freedom-Now party vaporized before it even registered in the consciousness of the average black voter. Political indifference among many blacks in Detroit was due to preoccupation with the countless problems associated with surviving in a harsh urban environment. In Wayne County in 1964 only 175,000 of 300,000 potential black voters were registered. Since only about one-third of those registered actually voted, black political activists faced a problem of black political apathy.[18]

Black radicals did help redefine black political independence in Detroit. This meant more than just a redistribution of political power within a coalition under the perpetual control of the white political and business elite. In 1968 the Reverend Albert Cleage, Jr., a major leader of the Group on Advanced Leadership (GOAL), one of several black nationalist groups in Detroit, stressed the importance of black political power in areas where blacks were in the majority: "We can vote black and we can control political structures in any area in which we are a majority. This is a reality, and it's exactly the same thing that whites would do if they were black." Blacks would soon be a majority in Detroit, the Reverend Mr. Cleage stated, and "by voting black we can elect a black mayor, a black council and a black school board." A black candidate's only necessary qualification, according to Cleage. was that he be "devoted to the black nation, putting his dedication to black people first."[19] Clearly, this political philosophy had no room or patience for traditional liberal coalition politics.

What role would whites play in the black political community as envisioned by Cleage? "We would appreciate it ... if people in the suburbs [whites] would stay in the suburbs, if they would stop trying to live in the suburbs and run our black community, if they would stop living in the suburbs while holding ... political offices in the cities."[20] According to Cleage's views of black political independence, therefore, white suburbanites. even those within the liberal coalition, had little or no role to play in the future of black politics in Detroit. With regard to whites who still lived in a black-majority city, one could only speculate that black nationalists such as Cleage would see them accepting, reluctant or otherwise, black majority rule in the city.

This black political scenario, however, did not materialize in quite the way that some black nationalists desired. Several black moderate activists, no less "nationalistic" than Cleage and other black radicals, pursued the same political goals but without the rhetoric and fanfare.

The "King Maker"

The late Robert Millender was one such moderate political activist. A brilliant political strategist, Millender contributed more to black political development in Detroit between 1964 and 1973 than all the black radicals and moderate political activists combined. He first became involved in politics in the late 1940s while studying law at the Detroit College of Law. There he met fellow student Zolton Ferency, the future chairman of the Michigan Democratic party, who introduced him to politics. Ferency started what the law students called a Democratic Study Club, in which Millender participated. Millender's first big opportunity to become involved in a political campaign came in 1948 when he worked for the election of "Soapy" Williams for governor. He joined the TULC soon after it was organized in 1957, as one of the two nonlabor members. John Conyers, the current congressman, was the other nonlabor member. Millender also played an active role in the 1957 campaign to elect William T. Patrick, Jr., to the Detroit Common Council.[21]

The remarkable skills in political strategy that Millender would use to foster black political development in Detroit were honed in 1960 when he became co-manager of Zolton Ferency's campaign to defeat Prosecuting Attorney Samuel Olsen. Unfortunately, Ferency lost the election, but in the process Millender earned the respect of political observers for his skills in managing the campaign. Here was a man, according to predictions, destined to become "one of the most outstanding political strategists in the city and the state."[22]

Beginning in 1964 Millender began using the considerable political skills that would earn him the title of "King Maker." Soon after Michigan realigned its congressional districts, Millender devised a plan that not only protected Diggs's district as a black district but also made it possible for another black person to be elected from the first district in Detroit. Incidentally, his plan also helped out-state Republican incumbents to hold on to their districts and pitted five incumbent Democrats against one another. Millender came up with the master stroke to get his plan adopted. He convinced black Democratic legislators to vote with their political rivals, the Republicans, to reapportion the state.[23] After reapportionment Millender successfully managed the congressional campaign of John Conyers, Jr., in a close and bitter race with Richard Austin, also black. Conyers's victory made him the second black congressman from Michigan and made Detroit "the first city to be represented by two black congressmen."[24]

This black political advance came at great cost to the larger black community: It split the black leadership. When the first district was newly reapportioned, a group of concerned citizens sent Millender to ask TULC labor leader Horace Sheffield to run for congressman from the district. He refused, telling Millender that if a black could win, which he doubted, his candidate would be Richard Austin. Millender informed Sheffield that he was their first choice, and if he did not accept, the group would support Conyers. Millender and his group went on to campaign for Conyers. Sheffield and other major black labor leaders, along with the Democratic party's white leadership, rallied behind Austin. The wounds of this campaign between two prominent blacks took years to heal.[25]

Millender's efforts to get George Crockett elected to the Detroit Common Council in 1965 failed, but a year later Crockett won election to the Detroit Recorder's Court. In 1968 Millender scored again by quarter-backing Robert Tindal's election to the council. Overcoming the rift caused by the Conyers and Austin campaigns, in 1969 Millender worked on behalf of Richard Austin for mayor in the closest race in the history of Detroit. Roman Gribbs edged Austin by a margin of only 6.194 votes. Three years later Millender added another impressive black political victory to his record by masterminding the election of Erma Henderson to the council to replace Tindal, who had died in office. Millender's biggest political success came in 1973 when he managed Young's campaign to become the city's first black mayor. By then he had overcome his bitterness against Coleman Young for allegedly failing to marshal votes for Austin.[26]

Richard Austin: First Black Bid for Mayor of Detroit

Richard Austin's bid for mayor in 1969 was a momentous occasion for the city. Although eclipsed by Young after the 1973 election, Austin became the first black in Detroit to win a mayoral primary. He lost the final election in what went down in Detroit's annals as the closest political contest in the city's history, but his campaign lingered in the hearts and minds of both black and white Detroiters for many years.

Richard Austin was a black moderate who not only believed in the liberal coalition but also understood the pragmatism of biracial politics as one means to achieve black political ends. Like other blacks of his generation, he had achieved several black "firsts." He was the first black in

Michigan to become a certified public accountant (CPA), the first black to achieve membership in the American Institute of CPAs, the first black to serve on the board of directors of the Certified Public Accountant Association, the first black financial advisor to the U.S. Commission of Internal Revenue, and the first black to be elected Wayne County auditor.[27] By any objective standard of merit, Austin had the experience and background to become the first black mayor of Detroit. That he did not was testimony both to the irrational racism of whites, who two years after the black rebellion were still trapped in their self-imposed phobias and fantasies of blacks taking over the city, and to the yet underdeveloped political consciousness of significant segments of the black community.

Some blacks believed that 1969 was not the year to elect a black mayor. But Congressman John Conyers ignited a spark in the black community earlier in the year by pushing hard for a black mayoral candidate. While the choice of his old political rival, Austin, for this historic achievement did not initially excite Conyers, he rallied behind him. Austin came in first in the primary election with 45,856 of the votes, and Wayne County's Sheriff Roman S. Gribbs came in second with 34,650. The white vote was largely split between Gribbs and Mary Beck, a white conservative, who placed third and received 26,480 of the total votes.[28]

The primary clearly demonstrated the influence of race on local politics. Austin received most of his votes from the black community. He hoped to get 15 percent of the white vote but received less than 10 percent. Gribbs and Beck received tremendous support from the white community for their emphasis on "law and order." Gribbs, a moderate who believed in integration, had antagonized many black leaders when, as assistant Wayne County prosecutor in 1963, he aggressively prosecuted black protesters who participated in the sit-in at the First Federal Savings and Loan Association. As Wayne County sheriff, Gribbs also alienated many people, particularly blacks, when he attempted to get approval for his officers to use Mace, a controversial form of gas. He decided to be a candidate for mayor 24 hours before the filing deadline to save the city from a field of what he considered less than acceptable candidates.[29]

Almost overnight Gribbs received financial backing from executives at major banking, business, and legal establishments in the city, including General Motors. Ninety percent of Gribbs's support during the primary came from managers, executives, and lawyers; and most of his financial support was centered in the suburbs. Austin's support came mainly from Detroiters, most of whom were doctors, dentists, and small business owners.[30]

As the two top runners prepared for the November election, everyone knew that race would be the determining factor in the outcome. As the *Detroit Free Press* stated in September, "Although he finished first in the primary, Austin must woo many white voters to win in November.... On the surface it looks like a tough assignment, given the racial polarization shown by Tuesday's overall voting patterns."[31] Austin refused to believe that whites would not vote for a black to be mayor of Detroit, but he had no illusion that race was not a key issue. Attacking Gribbs, who had denied that race was a factor, Austin told a group of students in northwest Detroit, "I wish to God he was right. Race is relevant to too many people in this election."[32]

Race seemed far more important to whites in the city than to blacks. For example, following a racial voting pattern much like that of the 1965 city election, black voters voted for both black and white candidates, while white voters tended to vote only for white candidates. A citizen research group, the Citizen's Committee for Equal Opportunity, discovered that in the primary election "white voters in appalling numbers simply did not vote for black candidates at all, or in instances where they did so, gave them such low consideration as to virtually exclude them from serious consideration." The committee reported that, unlike many black voters, white voters were not demonstrating a belief "in the bi-racial future of the city and in bi-racial representation in city government."[33]

A white reader's letter to the editor of the *Detroit Free Press* asked the question, "Will whites help elect the best council candidates?" Pointing out that the November election would be a crucial test in race relations, the writer lamented the fact that the "best qualified candidate for mayor might not be elected because he is black," considering the fact that "two-thirds of the white voters have acknowledged his superiority in a poll—but only half of that group indicated that they would support him."[34]

A *Detroit Free Press* survey of voter attitudes during the year revealed that white voters were mainly concerned about welfare, crime, and "the colored taking over."[35] Yet the primary election also revealed that while whites supported blacks for seats on the Detroit Common Council, they held back on supporting a black for the top office of mayor. A case in point was that one white west-side residential area gave black Councilman Nicholas Hood 35 percent of the vote but gave Austin only 10 percent of the vote. No wonder a group of white leaders supporting Austin put full-page advertisements in local newspapers asking white voters, "Can you vote for a black mayor?"[36] For many whites the answer was a resounding no. A northeast Detroit paper, reflecting the views of many white homeowners in that section of Detroit, informed its readers that if Austin was elected as Detroit's first black mayor, it would mean the beginning of the end "for the white, tax-paying homeowner." Another paper in the same area, considered the official voice of the Northeast Council of Homeowners Association, warned its readers, "Unless the white conservative voting element of this city exhibits a sudden wave of political intelligence, the election of Negro candidate Richard Austin as Detroit's first black mayor is a foregone conclusion."[37]

Surveys repeatedly indicated that the vast majority of white voters in Detroit rejected Austin solely on the basis of race.[18] This fact greatly disturbed the quiet black moderate who sincerely wanted to bridge the racial gap in Detroit. Realizing that he needed white votes, Austin campaigned in white communities as he had done before. But many of his black supporters—those who had marshalled the black vote that won him first place in the primary—were becoming increasingly frustrated by white voters' reluctance to vote on merit instead of race. The Reverend Albert B. Cleage, Jr., of past black nationalist fame, wrote in his column published in the local black newspaper: "I support Dick Austin and I feel that he should receive the total black vote, but inasmuch as his election is dependent upon a large white vote, I see no possibility of his election.... [We] could elect Dick Austin mayor and ... could elect a majority of the city council

[but] we probably won't do either because we won't try hard enough." After criticizing the fact that blacks had not registered enough blacks, Cleage said, "The white racist syndrome will wipe out white support for black candidates by election day."[39]

Another writer for the same newspaper put white liberals on notice that if blacks did not come out of the November election "with a healthy victory," there would not be any more black/white coalitions. Complaining that in past elections black/white coalitions had mainly benefited white politicians, the writer warned, "The black community is not going to accept the short end or the blind, lame or dead horse in the trade this time."[40]

Black leaders supporting Austin knew all too well that white liberals were not working hard enough to get white votes for black candidates. At a meeting of the black and white liberal politicians and labor leaders, the black leaders informed their white allies: "The records will show we in the black community can deliver votes better than the white community. We are sick and tired of delivering votes for white folks and listening to their excuses later. We are going to stop delivering if you don't deliver for Dick Austin and other black candidates we have selected."[41]

Black political activists and strategists had reached the point where they realized that they could call the shots in coalition politics. Liberal whites in the coalition, now reduced to a minority faction, had to face up to the fact that, as blacks became a numerical majority in Detroit, they would be less responsive to the dictates of the liberal coalition. But that time was surely not in 1969. Dick Austin badly needed the coalition in order to win. The coalition, however, could not deliver sufficient white votes to give Austin the lead. Austin lost the election but left his indelible mark on the political history of black and white Detroit.[42] Subsequently, Austin was elected to the office of secretary of state of Michigan and became an even more visible presence for state residents than he would have as mayor of Detroit.

Coleman Young: Detroit's First Black Mayor

Blacks lost a major political battle in the 1969 mayoral election, but they were winning the protracted political war in the city. As one very perceptive white reporter observed after Austin's defeat. "After years of fitful and sometimes explosive growth, a new politics has emerged in Detroit. It belongs not to the left or the right, but to the steadily growing black community.... Within a very few years, most of the burdens and benefits of local political power will rest with blacks."[43] Most whites knew that it would only be a matter of time before blacks would have enough votes to elect a black mayor and a predominately black common council without heavy reliance on white votes. Black political activists and strategists also knew this. Coleman Young, sitting in the state senate, bided his time, foreseeing that he was destined to play a major role in the "new politics" of Detroit.

Senator Coleman Young was a striking contrast to Richard Austin. Unlike Austin, with his quiet and accommodating political demeanor and style, developed through the process of being the "first black" in countless white-only situations. Young evolved a more combative political demeanor and style so evident in the black radical tradition of the late 1930s and early 1940s.

Young's father had been forced to flee Tuscaloosa, Alabama, where Young was born, because he was considered an "uppity nigger." As a young man working at Ford. Young hit a racist white foreman in the head with a steel bar and as a result lost his job. He became involved in the UAW-CIO (United Auto Workers and Congress of Industrial Organizations) union drives in Detroit and later won election as the Wayne County CIO's first black organizational secretary. But he was ousted, along with other radicals, after Walter Reuther became UAW president. Always disturbed by racial discrimination. Young, as a second lieutenant in the famous Tuskegee Airmen, found himself constantly at odds with the U.S. Army's Jim-Crow regulations. He was arrested along with 100 other black officers for attempting to integrate an officers' club at Freeman Field, Indiana. In 1948 Young assumed the Michigan chair of Henry Wallace's Progressive party presidential campaign.[44]

In 1951 Young contributed to the formation of the National Negro Labor Council (NNLC), the most radical black labor organization of that period, and became its executive director. The redbaiting witch hunts of the early 1950s, led by Senator Joseph McCarthy, soon began focusing on the NNLC. The House Committee on Un-American Activities investigated the Detroit chapter of the NNLC, in which Young was involved. In February 1952 Young stood his ground and defiantly told the members of the committee: "I am part of the Negro people. I am now in process of fighting against what I consider to be attacks and discrimination against my people. I am fighting against un-American activities such as lynchings and denial of the vote. I am dedicated to that fight, and I don't think I have to apologize or explain it to anybody."[45]

Young was one of the first radicals, black or white, to stand up to the committee. Informing them that he would not be a "stool pigeon," Young proceeded to lecture the southern congressional representatives and staff members on the correct pronunciation of "Negro." Such brash and bold behavior elevated Young to the status of a local hero in the black community. Soon phonograph records of his testimony were circulating throughout the black community.[46]

Coleman Young began his political career in 1960 as an elected delegate to the state constitutional convention. He drafted the first version of the Civil Rights Commission Act. In 1964 he was elected to the state senate and moved to the position of Democratic leader in the senate. And in 1968 he was elected the new Democratic national committeeman from Michigan amidst the upheavals of the Chicago Democratic Convention. Young became the first black in the nation to be elected to that position. To Young, his election proved that racial attitudes were changing and that whites were beginning to vote regardless of the candidate's color. At this point in his political career. Young still believed in the efficacy of the liberal coalition for black political development but with qualifications: "I am a Negro first and a Democrat second."[47] At the height of the black nationalist period in the nation and Detroit when separatists talked about carving out their own country in the South, Young said they were "just smoking marijuana." To Young, coalition with liberal whites was "the only way."[48]

Senator Coleman Young seriously considered becoming a candidate for mayor of Detroit in 1969 but was prevented from doing so by a Michigan Supreme Court ruling that barred a state legislator from running for another office before the expiration of his current term. Young, then a three-term senator, had wanted to run because Austin, according to Young, had not caught on and had failed to give "the people anything to sink their teeth into as far as what he would do as mayor." Austin's biggest shortcoming, Young felt, centered on his failure to commit himself publicly to such issues as civilian control of the police department.[49]

In 1973, four years later. Young was ready not only to run for mayor but also to make control of the police a central part of his campaign. He filed early enough to provide himself ample time to appeal a Wayne County Circuit Court ruling against his running. When the Michigan Supreme Court ruled in his favor and Austin, then secretary of state, announced that he was not in the running. Young became a serious mayoral candidate.[50] In a speech kicking off his primary campaign. Young put the police department and Police Commissioner John Nichols on notice:

> Detroit today is a racially polarized city, and now is the time we need to have a black mayor. One of the problems is that the police run the city.... STRESS [a controversial undercover police operation] is responsible for the explosive polarization that now exists; STRESS is an execution squad rather than a law enforcement squad. As mayor, I will get rid of STRESS.... The whole attitude of the whole Detroit Police Department, historically, has been one of intimidation and that citizens can be kept in line with clubs and guns rather than respect. The present department under Nichols is following the old blackjack rule by terror. If elected, I would fire Nichols.[51]

The white police responded by endorsing Nichols.[52]

In the primary Nichols and Young came in first and second, respectively, with Nichols getting 33.8 percent of the vote and Young getting 21.1 per cent. The remaining votes went to the other three candidates. The voting patterns revealed that each candidate would have to appeal to both black and white voters in order to have a chance of winning in November.[53]

Young's broad political experience in local, state, and national politics gave him an edge over the single-issue Nichols. Yet Nichols did have the advantage that exploiting white fears of black crime in the street gave him. Young knew better than to ignore crime, but his appeal to white voters emphasized economic development for the city. Young promised to lead a "business resurgence" that would produce thousands of jobs and would include "new park facilities, a stadium, rapid transit, recreational facilities, and housing." Speaking at the Economic Club of Detroit, Young advised the assembled cream of the Detroit business class to invest in the city instead of the suburbs. Nichols could do little better than accuse Young of being a professional politician compared with himself, a practical man heading one of the city's largest departments. Predictably, Nichols fell back on crime in the street, which he argued was the most important issue in the city.[54] In the end. Young—with the support of many business groups, the support of the Urban Alliance (a nonprofit, interfaith, nonpartisan voter information organization), and significant financial support—won the election and became Detroit's first black mayor.

The victory did not blind Mayor Young to the need to bring the races together in a city half black and half white. Soon after his victory he proclaimed to his supporters, "I didn't win; we won. All of Detroit won."[55] Although he emphasized racial unity in his inaugural address, saying, "What is good for the black people in this city is good for the white people in this city," Young and his black and white supporters surely knew that the "new politics" was emerging in full bloom. This was a black political victory, plain and simple. On the morning before the inaugural luncheon, some of Young's followers held a prayer meeting, and the Reverend Charles Butler of the New Calvary Baptist Church, referring to Young, cited the biblical phrase "Behold this man." Although the power elite were present, "for the first time in Detroit the street people who knew 'Coleman' when he was down and struggling were in on things, watching from the edges of the crowd, smiling as if they had been graced by greatness"[56]

At the Cobo Hall inaugural luncheon, world corporate leaders such as Henry Ford 11 (chairman of the Ford Motor Company) and labor leaders such as Leonard Woodcock (UAW president) gathered around a smiling, former radical, now the mayor of one of the world's largest industrial cities. Henry Ford got up and explained what the new day really meant: "We, here in this room, represent the beginning of a new coalition of business and labor, brought together by our mutual desire to pledge our support to the newly inaugurated mayor."[57] Black political power in Detroit personified by Mayor Young would still need powerful and willing white allies to rebuild the city. While some of Young's black followers might have been too drunk with the wine of victory to see or want it. of necessity the "new politics" would include the liberal coalition.

The greatest evidence of black political power in Detroit during Young's first term of office was the radical change in the racial makeup of the police department. This was not an easy task because of the resistance of white police officers and their union. After several years of power struggles and countless bouts of negotiations, Young made some progress in changing a predominantly white police department into one that was at least in the process of becoming more racially integrated. By the end of 1976 Detroit boasted its first black police chief and a top command structure that was half black and half white. One hundred black officers had been hired since Young's election, increasing black representation from 17 percent to 22 percent.[58] The "old boys network," which had perpetuated and maintained white, male privilege in promotions for decades, had to give way to Young's aggressive affirmative action program. As this program began to take hold, blacks went from 5 percent of all officers holding the rank of sergeant to 15 percent.[59] Young would continue to have problems with the police department. but never again would it be the symbol of white, official oppression.

Mayor Young ended his first term in office by helping to put Jimmy Carter into the White House. As a major black figure in national Democratic politics and in labor and business circles. Young had both the power and credibility to deliver powerful black voting blocks to Carter. Young possessed such influence that when Carter slipped during the 1976 presidential campaign, saying that he saw nothing wrong with "ethnic purity," a statement many interpreted as advocating racial purity. Young defended the Democratic candidate, explaining that he had been misunderstood. Carter was still apologizing when he met Mayor Young at the Detroit airport. As soon as Young boarded Carter's plane, he told Carter, "Get up off your knees and keep on walking."[60]

When Carter became president Mayor Young's political power multiplied by virtue of the leverage he now had in the White House. Carter's urban policies reflected the influence of the mayor of Detroit. Young's appointees ended up in the Carter administration, channeling federal money to Detroit. All during the Carter administration. Young could be seen operating in the country's highest councils.[61]

Mayor Young ran for reelection against black councilman Ernest Browne in 1977. Young was supported by Henry Ford II (chairman of the Ford Motor Company), Douglas Fraser (president of the UAW), and President Carter. This was the first general election in a major city in which both mayoral candidates were black. Black voters rejected Browne both in the primary and in the general election, so Browne hoped for a winning coalition of a majority of white voters and a minority of black voters. It did not work. Young won handily. The campaign turned bitter when Young accused Browne of selling out blacks for political gain and Browne retorted that Young used racist tactics.[62]

The mayor faced even tougher times during his second term, the worst of which was a budget crisis in 1981 that forced Detroit voters to approve an income tax hike and city officials to sell $125 million in emergency bonds.[63] Young not only had to persuade city voters to go along with his plan to save the city from bankruptcy but he also had to convince the state legislature and twist the arms of municipal workers to accept a two-year wage freeze. Black unemployment in the city remained a problem and stood at 25 percent as Young prepared to run for his third term. Even the impressive Renaissance Center complex could not lift the gloom. Times were tough in the Motor City and getting tougher, especially for many blacks who still saw Young as the "big daddy." a symbol of their power and success.[64]

The loss of Carter as president hurt Detroit and cut the ties that had once provided so much financial lifeblood to the struggling city. But that did not prevent Mayor Young from calling President Reagan "pruneface" and accusing him of "lacking any compassion for urban residents and the poor." In his third inaugural address, he told Detroiters to "circle the wagon" and to "close ranks and send a message to the President.... [This country] can't go forward if its cities are sinkholes of poverty and starvation."[65]

Now that Detroit has had a black mayor for more than a decade and boasts a predominantly black city council, has Detroit become a hollow prize? If political observers have learned nothing else about the long history of black political development in Detroit and other cities, they have learned this: Black political development alone cannot solve the basic economic problems affecting the black urban masses in the major cities of the nations.

William Lucas: A New Breed

For close to a decade Mayor Young was the premier black politician in the metropolitan community. But even as his political star continued to rise, dimmed only slightly by the ignominious fall of Jimmy Carter in 1980 and the spectacular victory of Ronald Reagan, another local political star also rose. Democrat William Lucas's political career represents a sharp break in the historical patterns of black political development.

Lucas first became involved in Wayne County politics in 1968 when he was appointed under-sheriff by then Wayne County sheriff, Roman Gribbs. Gribbs had convinced Lucas to leave the FBI to take the job. After Gribbs became mayor of Detroit in 1969, Lucas was appointed Wayne County sheriff. He won reelection to the office three times. After 14 years as Wayne County sheriff. Lucas won election to the newly created office of Wayne County executive, with strong support from the Black Slate, the most powerful black political organization in the metropolitan area and in the state. This organization had played a key role in Coleman Young's first victory and since then had been successful in electing other black candidates to office. Mayor Young, however, did not endorse Lucas for the office of county executive.[66]

Soon after Lucas took office, he not only hired a prominent, white Republican as an advisor but also sharply reduced the county budget, which included curtailing services essential to the poor, most of whom were blacks living in Detroit, These decisions enraged the Black Slate: "[Lucas's] political decisions and associations are fraught with evidence of a lack of sensitivity and a lack of concern for the effects of the political process on the lives of black and poor people." The organization attempted to recall Lucas but failed. While Mayor Young shared the concerns of the Black Slate, he did not support its recall movement, even though some of his strongest supporters were behind it. Instead, Young expressed the view, "To the degree that Lucas is not living up to his promise ... we ought to speak out loudly and make it be known.... We ought to let Lucas know that those of us who elected him are disappointed with what he is doing and we will see him at the next election," Young's decision not to support the recall movement disappointed the Black Slate. Lucas, however, commented that Young's decision not to join the recall movement was what he had expected: "He's a straight-forward individual."[67]

In less than three years as Wayne County executive, Lucas transformed many aspects of county government, ruffling many feathers on the way, including those of his own party. Often called "Cool Hand Luke," he took on established labor leaders, abolished the powerful Wayne County Road Commission, greatly reduced the county's work force, and set up a blue-ribbon commission to push for additional prison space in the county. Observers in Washington, D.C., first noticed Lucas when he initiated a trade mission to Japan. To some political observers, Lucas had "given Wayne County a badly needed dose of respect."[68]

After years of fighting with members of the Democratic party, in May 1985 Lucas switched to the Republican party and invited other blacks to join him. Meeting with President Reagan at the White House soon after his switch, Lucas said, "I am not here to say they [blacks] all have to rush and join in, but just think. Just think about the value of your vote. Just think about attaching some degree of importance to the political process and not just following blindly everyone's lead."[69]

Leading Democrats were not surprised by Lucas's switch. Lieutenant Governor Martha Griffiths, among others, had already accused Lucas of openly flirting with Republicans, who, Griffiths claimed, were "trying to lure him out of the Democratic Party to cut up the black vote."[70] A month before Lucas switched to the Republicans, Mayor Young called the anticipated move "desperate" and commented, "There's a hell of a lot wrong with the Democratic Party. I've often said I'm a Democrat, not because they are perfect. They have a lot of bastards in the Democratic Party, but I think there are more in the Republican party, and that explains my party preference."[71]

By mid-1985 the Republicans in Michigan were busy showboating their newest black convert, who they hoped to run for governor against the Democratic party's Governor Blanchard. Leading white Republicans, such as former governor George Romney and Richard DeVos (president of Amway Corporation and one of the major financial contributors to the Republican party) seemed eager to dump longtime party regulars who were in line to run on the Republican ticket for governor of Michigan to support Lucas instead. Many white Michigan Republicans felt Lucas would not offend white voters. "He [Lucas] is not a [Jesse] Jackson or a Coleman Young," explained Romney. "Jackson tends to turn a lot of white people off. Coleman has clearly conducted a racist administration in the city of Detroit."[72] Lucas ran and lost the race for governor.

It certainly was one of the most intriguing dramas in the political history of the state. A black politician had gained the top political office in the county, governing an area much larger than the majority-black city, yet had thereafter distanced himself from the Democratic party and, some claimed, from his black constituency. Nevertheless, the possibility existed that he would be catapulted to state office.

All of this offered amazing possibilities, considering that two decades before, the likelihood of having even a black city mayor had seemed remote. Blacks had come far in the political realm, not only because of population shifts in the city and region but also because of the special talents and efforts of politicians and political organizers. In the process they had moved from fragile coalition predicated on the acceptability of black candidates to white sensibilities, to black political power supportive of the most outspoken ethnic politicians. The steady ascendency of black political prowess, however, had not bridged racial chasms in the region.

METROPOLITAN SCHOOL DESEGREGATION: A POLICY ISSUE

Although school desegregation policy is not always thought of as a political issue, school district boundaries have become as important as (or more important than) political jurisdictional boundaries in many regions of the country. In the previous section of this chapter it became obvious that over the years blacks gained great political power and influence in the city of Detroit and, to a more limited extent, in the region. This portion of the chapter suggests that one reaction of white citizens to increasing black visibility and political power was first to retreat to whiter areas of the city of Detroit and then to retreat even farther to whiter school districts.

Schools and housing have been the most contested areas in the racial struggle that has taken place in Detroit. Schools, like houses, represented racial territory and social status. More important, schools have always been among the most central institutions in any community. Like the neighborhood church, the neighborhood school often embodies the collective values of the surrounding community. One reason why Detroit whites resisted blacks' moving into their neighborhoods was that they knew residential integration would lead to school integration. This would further challenge their claim to what they perceived as their exclusive right to their racial space.

By 1953 black students attended two-thirds of the schools in the city of Detroit. However, many white teachers and principals and a few white administrators seemed completely oblivious and insensitive to the racial changes occurring in their midst. Some schools responded to these racial changes by lowering curriculum standards to accommodate prevalent white stereotypes of blacks as a class of people unable to learn as fast as whites. Black teachers were still largely confined to predominantly black schools and were becoming frustrated over being forced to teach in schools considered inferior. White teachers in these mostly black schools shared their frustration.[73]

Racial conflicts in the school system punctuated the decade of the 1960s setting the stage for the protracted bussing controversy that tested the racial tolerance of blacks and whites in metropolitan Detroit. Many school-related racial conflicts seemed inevitable, originating as they did from un predictable and largely uncontrollable changes in the racial demography of Detroit. But some school-related racial conflicts could have been foreseen and perhaps controlled, if not prevented. These conflicts erupted as a direct result of urban renewal policies of the 1940s and 1950s that forced the relocation of thousands of blacks from one overcrowded ghetto to another equally overcrowded ghetto, overloading already seriously handicapped schools.

Racial Segregation in the Schools

In 1960, as ghetto schools strained to accommodate more students, the Detroit Board of Education opted to bus black students from the overcrowded center-district schools to the closest schools with sufficient student capacity. Predominantly white schools located on the extreme northwest side of Detroit and in surrounding neighborhoods were extremely hostile to this bussing plan be-cause they perceived it to be an invasion of their community by vastly inferior black students. As soon as the bussing plan was made public, whites on the far northwest side of Detroit organized a meeting of some 500 people. They circulated petitions to recall the members of the Detroit Board of Education and encouraged parents to boycott classes for three days. When school opened, 30 percent of the children boycotted classes at one school and 67 percent at another. Some parents who participated in the boycott did so only because they feared violence.[74]

Anticipating the possibility of racial conflict, the Detroit Commission on Community Relations set up meetings with the press, police officials, the Catholic Archdiocese of Detroit, representa-tives of the Council of Churches, and the religious leaders in the neighborhood to discuss the racial problems associated with the bussing plan. They condemned the actions of the people who organized the boycott and circulated the petitions.[75] But the fear of bussing ran deep, and even liberal whites who chose to live in integrated neighborhoods began to worry about the declining quality of their schools as black students were bussed in from overcrowded ghetto schools. A common statement at the time was "I'll stay until the school declines." As more black students arrived, white teachers began asking for transfers.

Meanwhile black parents were up in arms over inadequate and segregated schools in black neighborhoods. Their protests were justified, based as they were on charges of racial discrimination in the school system, and confirmed in 1962 by the Citizens Advisory Committee on Equal Educational Opportunities. The Detroit Board of Education had directed this committee to identify "the factors which affect equality of educational opportunities in the Detroit Public Schools and to recommend to the Board of Education ways which would increase equality of opportunities for all pupils."[76] The committee boldly acknowledged the presence of racism in the Detroit school system and recommended bussing as one solution for ending segregation. The committee also censured the historical practice of segregated teacher placement: "While the Detroit Public School system has employed a large number of Negro teachers in recent years, the committee found a clear-cut pattern of racial discrimination in the assignment of teachers and principals to schools throughout the city."[77] This practice, the committee stated, "of assigning teachers, principals, and other school employees on the basis of race is educationally, legally, and morally unsound and weakens the democratic opportunities of children in the Detroit Public Schools. We urge that immediate action be taken to remedy this situation."[78]

The main responsibility for implementing the committee's recommendations was correctly placed upon the Detroit Board of Education, but support from the community at large was needed for the successful implementation of the recommendations. The school system could not be expected to carry the entire burden of uprooting racism and ending discrimination.

Black parents began to organize. They were encouraged by leaders such as radical black minister the Reverend Mr. Cleage, who said, "It is deplorable that years of protests by a generation of parents has not sufficiently impressed the board with the fact that the administrators were busy as beavers establishing Jim Crow districts, Jim Crow curricula, and Jim Crow schools. Now that the facts are known, now that the board sees the patterns of segregation and second rate facilities foisted on Negro children, the course of necessary action is obvious."[79] The committee report came on the heels of a groundswell of black community protest against segregated schools, sparked in part by a race discrimination suit filed in federal court against the school board by a group of black parents from Sherill School. The Sherill School Parents Committee was soon joined by other interested organizations.

Two months before the school committee report came out, these protest organizations formed a citywide group called Parents Committee for School Integration. They agreed to concentrate their efforts on combating racial discrimination in the school system, leaving nonracial school problems to the Parent-Teacher Association (PTA).[80] The parent group proved so effective that a local black newspaper commented: "The school report would already be as dead as a dinosaur if it were not for the Sherill School Parents' bias suit."[81] Essentially a grass-roots movement of concerned black parents, the Sherill School Parents Committee put the local NAACP in the embarrassing position of trying to catch up with a school desegregation struggle in Detroit that had been initiated without its support or guidance. As one writer put it, "The NAACP ... must understand that any action it may wish to take at this time must be taken in cooperation with the Sherill School Parents Committee."[82]

The committee report paved the way for as much racial cooperation as racial conflict. Its recommendations exposed previously contested aspects of racism in the school system and provided official sanctions for the continuation of bussing, which angered many whites. The report also increased the expectations of black parents for a speedy and significant change.

In 1964, two years after the report was issued, Detroit's liberal groups received a long-awaited opportunity to effect further change in Detroit's school system. When three school board members decided not to run for reelection, the liberal groups saw their chance to install a liberal majority on the school board. They formed a coalition, rounded up candidates, organized a campaign, and won the victory, a high point in the history of interracial political cooperation in Detroit. In the following years the liberal-dominated school board altered school boundaries to promote racial integration, increased the number of black teachers and administrators, and pressured publishers to produce textbooks that provided a more accurate picture of the races. "Every decision, every appointment, every statement," one observer commented, "reflected the board's overriding commitment to the goal of racial integration."[83]

For all their good intentions, guided by the visions of an integrated school system, the liberals on the board were soon swept into the unpredictable crosscurrents of racial change. The 1967 rebellion polarized blacks and whites all over the country and especially in Detroit. The death of Martin Luther King in 1968 mortally wounded the spirit of interracial cooperation, which had so inspired the liberal school board members after their election victory and subsequent successes. "Black power" was becoming increasingly more popular within the black community. In March of 1968 the *Michigan Chronicle* newspaper reported, "The crisis in Detroit's inner-city schools is fast approaching the dimensions of a forest fire."[84] The "forest fire" was the outbreak of racial conflicts that swept through Detroit schools. Black students became enraged at their fellow white students at Pershing High School when they refused to accept the elected black student government. On Detroit's east side black parents at the Marcy and Stephen schools were organizing efforts to eliminate white administrators. Black community control organizations and black parent groups were springing up all over the city, demanding black community control over their schools. A month earlier white parents at Finney High School had threatened to keep their kids at home if any more black students were transferred to the school.[85] The school board was caught between the proverbial rock and a hard place. And although it was for different reasons, a significant number of blacks and whites opposed racial integration in the schools.

In 1969 the Michigan legislature passed a law that required the decentralization of Detroit's public school system. In the Detroit school board's view, decentralization, or "increased community involvement," would help bridge the gap between them and the black community, but integration remained the board's primary goal. Decentralization was only a means to that goal. The goal, however, seemed to be rapidly slipping away. As A. L. Zwerdling, president of the school board, sadly informed a group of school administrators in Washington, D.C., in 1969, "No one who came to our public meetings on decentralization was interested in integration. Everyone wanted segregation so they would be assured a little piece of control; you cannot have both integration and community control."[86] Zwerdling made it clear that if he had to choose between the two, he would choose integration. He had not become the president of the Detroit Board of Education, he later informed the League of Women Voters, "to preside over the liquidation of integrated school systems."[87]

The School Board Recall and the Roth Decision

Events in 1970 and 1971 illustrated the extent to which school desegregation had become a political issue. In 1970 a plan for desegregation of the Detroit school system spurred a bitter school board recall election. This in turn led to a series of events that culminated in a court-ordered plan for the desegregation of the school systems of the entire metropolitan area.

The recall came about because of a modest proposal to desegregate city high schools. On April 7, 1970, the Detroit Board of Education voluntarily adopted a plan to effect a more balanced distribution of black and white students in 12 of 21 Detroit high schools. The so-called April 7 Plan was to take effect over a three-year period, applying initially to those students entering the 10th grade in September 1970. For the 11th grade, the plan was to be instituted at the opening of the 1971–1972 school year and for the 12th grade, at the beginning of the 1972–1973 school year. The plan was designed to reduce segregation in a school system that then was 63.6 percent black.

On July 7, 1970, however, the governor of Michigan signed into law Act 48, Public Acts of 1970. Section 12 of that act had the effect of delaying and ultimately blocking the implementation of Detroit's April 7 high school desegregation plan.

In the meantime predominantly white groups from the northwest and northeast neighborhoods in Detroit spearheaded a recall drive that succeeded in removing four members of the board who supported the April 7 Plan. According to the *Free Press* education writer, the recall election "was the only successful recall election in the history of the school system ... and ... left the city's liberals and its civil rights groups reeling from the shock."[88]

After the recall, the governor of Michigan appointed four new board members. These four members, together with the incumbents who had originally opposed the April 7 action, rescinded the plan. This decision generated a complaint, filed by the parents of individual black and white school children and the Detroit branch of the NAACP, against the board of education of the city of Detroit and its members, the superintendent of schools, the governor, the attorney general, and the superintendent of public instruction of the state of Michigan.

The complaint alleged that the Detroit public school system was segregated on the basis of race, as the result of actions and policies of the Detroit Board of Education and the state of Michigan. The complaint specifically challenged the constitutionality of Act 48 of the Public Acts of 1970 of the state of Michigan.

In an opinion announced October 13, 1970, the U.S. Court of Appeals for the Sixth Circuit held that Section 12 of Michigan's Public Act 48, and hence the blocking of the April 7 desegregation plan, was unconstitutional.[89] In addition, the court of appeals ordered the district court to hear the case involving school segregation in Detroit on its merits. The trial of the case began April 6, 1971, and continued until July 22, 1971.

After extensive hearings U.S. District Court Judge Stephen J. Roth ruled that *de jure* segregation existed in the Detroit public schools. Roth indicated that the principal causes were population movement and housing patterns, but state and local governmental actions, including school board actions, played a substantial role in promoting segregation. Roth also blamed federal, state, and local governmental officers and agencies, lending institutions, and real estate firms for establishing and maintaining the segregated residential patterns that led to school segregation.

According to Judge Roth, school districts were accountable for the natural, probable, and foreseeable consequences of their policies and practices, and where racially identifiable schools were the result of these policies, the school authorities bore the burden of showing that the policies were based on educationally required, nonracial considerations.

The court case uncovered a number of discriminatory policies practiced by the Detroit school board. For example, beginning in 1950 the board created and maintained optional attendance zones within neighborhoods undergoing racial transition and between high school areas of opposite predominant racial compositions. In 1959 there were eight basic optional attendance areas affecting 21 schools. Optional attendance areas provided pupils living within certain elementary school neighborhoods a choice of attendance at 1 of 2 high schools. At least one optional area existed in 1960 between 2 junior high schools of opposite predominant racial components.[90] All of the optional high school areas except 2 were in neighborhoods undergoing racial transition, from white to black, during the 1950s. The effect of these optional zone policies was to allow white youngsters to escape identifiably black schools.[91] The school board also had a policy, supposedly to relieve overcrowding, that included the bussing of black students past or away from closer white schools with available space to more distant black schools. This practice continued until the late 1960s. In addition, the board had created and altered attendance zones, maintained and altered grade structures, and altered feeder school patterns in a manner that had the effect of continuing black and white students in racially segregated schools. Until 1970 the board separated school attendance zones of opposite racial compositions by north-south boundary lines despite the board's awareness (since at least 1962) that drawing boundary lines in an east-west direction would result in significant racial integration. The effect of the board's actions or its failure to act was to perpetuate school segregation. Finally, the board constructed schools on sites that guaranteed racially identifiable schools. Of the 14 schools that opened in 1970–1971, 11 opened with 90 percent black students, and 1 opened with over 90 percent white students.[92]

In summary, most of the evidence suggested that the state and its agencies, such as the school board, acted directly to control and maintain the pattern of racial segregation in the Detroit schools. Until 1970 the state refused to provide authorization of funds for the transportation of pupils within Detroit, regardless of their poverty or distance from the school to which they were assigned. On the other hand, the state willingly provided funds for transportation to adjacent, mostly white suburban districts. This action, along with other differences imposed on Detroit *vis-à-vis* the suburbs, created and perpetuated systematic educational inequalities.

After his findings of *de jure* segregation. Judge Roth grappled with the problem of fashioning a remedy in accordance with *Swan v. Board of Education, Monroe v. Board of Commissioners. Green v. County School Board*, and *Brown v. Board of Education*[91] Initially, he contemplated a "Detroit only" solution. Judge Roth required the school board defendants, Detroit and state, to develop and submit plans of desegregation "designed to achieve the greatest possible degree of actual desegregation, taking into account the practicalities of the situation."[94] Three "Detroit only" desegregation plans were submitted by the plaintiffs and by the Detroit Board of Education.

Judge Roth found that none of the plans would result in the desegregation of the public schools of the Detroit school district and that desegregation could not be accomplished within the corporate geographical limits of the city.[95] Judge Roth concluded that he had the duty to look beyond the limits of the Detroit School District for a solution to the illegal segregation in the Detroit public schools. Any desegregation plan involving only the city of Detroit would lead directly to a single segregated school district overwhelmingly black in all of its schools, surrounded by a ring of suburbs and suburban school districts overwhelmingly white. This seemed uncalled for in a state in which the racial composition was 87 percent white and 13 percent black.[96] Accordingly, the court ruled that it had to consider a metropolitan remedy for segregation. Judge Roth proceeded to request that each party submit plans for metropolitan desegregation. The parties submitted a number of plans, including one by the Michigan Board of Education, but Roth rejected all of them. The proposals submitted by the plaintiffs were all good-faith efforts to accomplish desegregation in the Detroit metropolitan area. All would have incorporated geographically most, if not all, of the three county areas of Wayne, Oakland, and Macomb. However, none of the proposals represented a complete plan for the effective and equitable desegregation of the metropolitan area.

Judge Roth appointed a nine-member panel to prepare and submit an effective metropolitan desegregation plan. The court identified the 54 metropolitan-area school districts that the plan was to include. It also directed that transportation and pupil assignment were to be a two-way process, with both black and white pupils sharing the responsibility for transportation requirements at all grade levels. In all, there were 780,000 students in the affected area, about a third of all public school students in the state. At the time of the ruling, the Detroit public school system was 65 percent black, and the suburban schools were less than 10 percent black.

City/Suburban Reaction to the Roth Decision

Suburban reaction indicated deep-seated and widespread opposition to the cross-district desegregation decision. A sampling of the opinions of suburban Detroit officials, teachers, parents, and students showed nearly unanimous disapproval. Many said they had no objection to blacks' being bussed into the suburbs, but they opposed suburban children's being bussed to Detroit schools.[97] Suburban school officials almost overwhelmingly opposed the metropolitan desegregation decision.

Opposition also came from some suburban mayors and municipal officials. The city commissioners of Royal Oak, for example, proposed an ordinance to make cross-district desegregation difficult and expensive. Some of the provisions of the ordinance were that all busses have speed governors to keep them traveling at less than 25 miles per hour and have seat belts and that all drivers have three years of college and three months of driver training.[98]

Opposition to metropolitan desegregation in Detroit impacted every level of the political arena. One day after the court decision. President Nixon phoned Michigan's Governor Milliken to stress that the decision clearly demonstrated the need for a moratorium against bussing until 1973. Instead of a moratorium, the U.S. House and Senate passed a bill that sought to prohibit the carrying out of any court-ordered bussing until all appeals of a case had been heard by the U.S. Supreme Court. This bill was supported by the five Democratic members of the Michigan congressional delegation. The five—John Dingell, William Ford. Martha Griffiths, James O'Hara, and Lucien Nedzi—voted for the bill with the hope that it would prevent bussing in Detroit.[99]

Among many suburban residents, Judge Roth became known as the "bussing judge." His name appeared on bumper stickers throughout metropolitan Detroit with such comments as "Roth is a four letter word" and "Roth is a child molester." Hatred for Judge Roth descended to such depths that in July of 1974, when he lay dying in his hospital bed, many suburban Detroit residents called to express their joy that he was near death.[100]

Although a minority, some civic and religious groups spoke out in support of the metropolitan school desegregation decision. The League of Women Voters of Metropolitan Detroit urged peaceful and thoughtful compliance with the desegregation order. The league asked the citizens of metropolitan Detroit to devote their best energies to making the desegregation process peaceful and constructive for the education of all the children in the area.[101]

Also, nine Detroit-area religious leaders urged the community to unite behind the federal court order. The joint statement, stressing the urgency of the goals behind the court order, said, "We must put aside differences.... We have an opportunity to make the classrooms of the metropolitan area a living lesson in American pluralism, and this great lesson can go beyond the classroom and renew the spirit of our country.[102] The statement released by the Metropolitan Detroit Council of Churches was signed by representatives of several denominations and faiths. Despite the support by some civic and religious groups, the widespread suburban opposition to metropolitan desegregation speeded up the appeal of the decision.

Before the panel appointed by Judge Roth could make a report on the specifics of metropolitan school desegregation in Detroit, the Court of Appeals for the Sixth Circuit remanded the case to the district court for the taking of additional evidence, because several of the suburban school districts had not been heard or had had no opportunity to be heard. In other words, as a prerequisite to the implementation of a desegregation plan affecting any school district, "the affected district must be made a party to the litigation and afforded an opportunity to be heard."[103]

The U.S. Supreme Court reversed the decision of the court of appeals, holding that no remedy involving any school district other than Detroit would be within the equitable power of the district court without evidence that the suburban district or districts had committed acts of *de jure* segregation.[104]

There were no findings that the differing racial composition between schools in the city and in the outlying suburbs was caused by official activity or collusion between the central city and suburban school districts. Thus, the decision to include in the desegregation plan pupils from school districts outside Detroit was not predicated upon any constitutional violation involving those school districts. According to *Swan v. Charlotte Mecklenburg Board of Education,* the nature of the violation determines the scope of the remedy.[105] Therefore, the court of appeals approval of a remedy that would reach beyond the limits of the city of Detroit to correct a constitutional violation found to have occurred solely within that city went beyond the governing equitable principles established by the U.S. Supreme Court.[106] Despite Judge Roth's conclusion that school desegregation could not be accomplished within the corporate geographical limits of the city, future school desegregation plans were based on Detroit only. Detroit was to remain a very racially segregated school system.

Suburban School Desegregation

The Roth cross-district plan was not the only generator of controversy over bussing. For example, Pontiac. Michigan—an industrial suburb 25 miles northwest of Detroit—was outside the scope of Roth's cross-district plan yet had its own court case. Appalachian whites and southern blacks in Pontiac shared a history of racial conflict. As one observer put it, "Racial clashes are endless here." At one time black and white neighborhoods fought over the location of a new $15 million high school, "turning one school board meeting into a chair-throwing melee." [107] The bussing controversy emerged in Pontiac in 1969. as a result of the local NAACP's charge that the Pontiac school board was perpetuating segregationist practices. District Judge Damon J. Keith, a black man from Detroit, ruled that the school board had maintained a segregated school system by planned site selection and teacher placement. In fact, the district had changed its boundaries six different times since 1948 to maintain segregated schools.

Judge Keith ordered the school district to come up with a desegregation plan. The plan that eventually evolved required only that 37 percent of the student population be bussed to 36 predominantly white schools, which worked out to a black mix of 20 to 36 percent. The plan was relatively modest, but it was still too much for the school board. The board appealed Judge Keith's decision and lost. Immediately, a group of irate white mothers set about organizing an antibussing group called the National Action Group (NAG) to frustrate compliance with the court order. Irene McCabe, the housewife who led the group, claimed NAG's opposition to bussing was not racially motivated. Yet the organization's first public act was sponsorship of a stadium rally attended by 5,000 people and featuring George Wallace, famed opponent of Alabama school desegregation and champion of white rights.

A week before school opened, ten Pontiac school busses were blown up, at a loss of $50,000. NAG leaders repudiated the bombing but carried on a campaign that created more racial conflict and violence. On the first day of school five women chained themselves to the bus yard gates to prevent the busses from moving, and other women sat down in front of the gates. As the first black children arrived, the NAG pickets joined the white bystanders in yelling "nigger, nigger" at the black children filing into school.[108]

Massive demonstrations continued for three days. Police responsible for providing security "idled on the sidewalk," which was understandable given that the Pontiac Police Officer Association had contributed $300 to NAG. Neither local union leadership nor General Motors intervened to resolve the racial conflict. In the end the Parent-Teacher Association and many students labored to bring forth some semblance of racial peace. When school opened again in the fall of 1972, a racial trouble-shooter commented that it was "the quietest school opening since '63; it's even hard for us to understand."[109] Twelve years later in 1984, Pontiac's school superintendent. Odell Nails made an even more positive evaluation of the racial climate in the school system: "Pontiac has worked itself out of the confusion. Not everybody likes it. But the great majority have accepted it and are cooperating"[110]

Desegregation gradually took place in other suburbs but with much less racial conflict and fanfare. The Department of Health. Education and Welfare (HEW) withheld funds from Ferndale in 1969 for illegally segregating black elementary students in a single school. The school district also maintained racially segregated school faculties and student populations within easy walking distance of each other. Segregation persisted and in 1972 funds were cut off. In 1980 the Court of Appeals for the Sixth Circuit ordered Ferndale to come up with a plan to end racial segregation in its elementary schools. In 1981 the city came up with a voluntary desegregation plan.[111]

When the Ecorse school board voted for a voluntary desegregation plan in 1976, board members who voted for it were recalled. Five years later the new school board finally got rid of the plan. And the NAACP responded with a lawsuit, charging both the school system and the state board of education with *de jure* segregation. The suit claimed that Ecorse built an elementary school in 1939 to deliberately segregate black and white students. When the black student population increased, the suit maintained, white officials expanded the school rather than allow black students to attend white schools. The school system was found guilty and ordered by a federal judge to take all the necessary steps to desegregate the system. In 1981 a desegregation plan went into effect.[112]

In rare cases blacks and whites were able to achieve desegregation without court orders. Southfield is one of the best examples in Michigan, and probably the nation, of a suburb whose school system was integrated without a court order, thanks in part to a history of integrated housing. Such a positive interracial history obviously influenced race relations at Southfield High. According to one writer, "Racial integration is not merely an anomaly ... but a deeply held matter of faith." Between 1977 and 1984 black enrollment in the school increased from 7 percent to 43 percent without any major racial conflicts.

The most impressive feature of this racial transformation is the existence of interracial friendship outside the school. Southfield High does have its special problems, such as not enough black staff and a fear among both blacks and whites that the school might become segregated, but for now it is a positive model of racial cooperation.[113]

In general, however, the reactions of suburban whites to bussing raised grave questions about the possibilities for metropolitan political cooperation. Their reactions to bussing were not unlike the responses of the white South during the Civil Rights Movement in the 1960s. During the 1970s white, northern suburbanites suddenly discovered that they had a serious racial problem, which many had denied existed. Many were surprised by their responses, which, however benign they appeared, were no less racist than those of their southern counterparts. Surely southern whites must have savored the moments when they, long maligned by northern whites for their rude and vicious form of race relations, could witness white, northern racist antics on the six o'clock news.

Antibussing sentiments became so intense in the Detroit metro area during the 1970s that advocates organized seven major antibussing groups; Roseville Action Group, Citizens Against Busing, National Action Group (NAG), Save Our Children, Concerned Citizens for Quality Education (CCQE). Tri-county Citizens for Intervention in Federal School Actions (TCIFSA), and Kids Attend Their Schools (KATS).[114]

While these groups shared basically the same aims, they varied in size and strategies of resistance. NAG, described in the infamous Pontiac case, had about 20 operating chapters in 20 Detroit suburbs. TCIFSA had a membership of close to 48,000 people, each of whom contributed one dollar to finance the fight against the Roth decision. KATS had supporters mainly in Warren and in Berkley and the rest of Oakland County. They wanted freedom of choice and preferred private to integrated schools. CCQE boasted 1,800 members in Grosse Pointe and had members who threatened to go to jail rather than send their children to schools in Detroit.

White suburbanites' reaction to cross-district bussing revealed a wide range of racist feelings toward blacks in Detroit, feelings similar to the mass racial hysteria that had driven many of them out of Detroit. Many white suburbanites perceived bussing as an assault upon the last bastion of white society and culture. As one observer pointed out, "Bussing threaten[s] the whole way of life for hundreds of thousands of white people whose culture, whose options, whose ambitions all point away from the city."[115] In order to protect his way of life, one white suburbanite threatened to "go out and get a gun." "I've never done anything like that before," he said, "but this is one thing I'd go to war for." Another said, "I'd throw myself in front of a bus before I'd let them take my children to Detroit.... My kids will never go to Detroit; I will move to the Upper Peninsula."[116]

White suburbanites who could see no way out of the bussing situation contemplated relocating to their former home states. West Virginia, Virginia, Georgia, and elsewhere. In 1971 a group of whites in Warren, seeking a way to evade racial integration by establishing a private school system, was given permission by the city's consolidated school board to use its public building after regular school hours. Warren's residents also signed pledges protesting bussing:

> We _____, residents of the City of Warren, do hereby pledge that we shall not allow our children to attend school if bussing is ordered by the courts, whether it is our child or our neighbors' child that is chosen to be bussed.[117]

While some white suburbanites accepted one-way bussing of black students to suburban schools as opposed to having their children bussed into Detroit, many whites wanted to avoid all contact with blacks, particularly those whites who had moved to the suburbs to get away from blacks in Detroit.

A small yet significant minority of suburban whites accepted school desegregation. They believed that black and white children should get to know one another and that white parents were doing a disservice to their children by not letting them know any black children: "Children should learn to appreciate differences," asserted proponents of this view. "Too many children [are] growing up in unrealistic settings. If youngsters are going to live and work successfully in a world that's getting smaller all the time, they're going to have to be in contact with people who are not just like themselves." The most progressive of these whites believed in racial integration even if it meant cross-district bussing: "I believe in integration and I don't know how else we're going to achieve it, because no one will sell their house to a black person here in Wyandotte. In order to change things that aren't right, you're going to have to make sacrifices." From this perspective, antibussing whites seemed pathetic: "They are so afraid and the sad thing is they really don't know what they are afraid of."[118]

White suburban attitudes toward school desegregation were just a pale reflection of their negative attitudes toward the city of Detroit and its citizens. And black parental attitudes, while far milder, suggested that the level of estrangement was deep, for many of those blacks had moved to a philosophy of community self-control. Education had become a battlefield.

Toward Metropolitan Cooperation

Neither the regional experience concerning racial politics in the city nor the record of school desegregation battles bode well for regional governmental cooperation in the Detroit area. Nevertheless, over the years some individuals and groups have made efforts to increase metropolitan cooperation within the region. These have ranged from nonprofit corporations devoted to good government and greater efficiency to politicians sincerely concerned about the increasing isolation of municipalities in the region.

The following portion of the chapter reviews some of the major efforts made to promote regionalism. It starts with a description of the great political fragmentation that exists within the region, and then it describes the movement toward voluntary metropolitan cooperation supported in the mid-1960s, efforts initiated by the state of Michigan to equalize school financing, subsequent proposals for a strong metropolitan authority supported by state representative William Ryan, and recent changes in the functions and powers of Wayne County (the county that includes the city of Detroit and other municipalities). The overall assessment of the chapter is that, in spite of numerous efforts to decrease political isolationism and increase cooperation, the region remains severely fragmented and that this fragmentation has a number of deleterious effects on the poorest of the municipalities, including Detroit. Yet little evidence suggests that this situation will change, in part because Detroit politicians now jealously guard their black political base and in part because the largely white suburban municipalities feel perfectly content with their political isolation.

Separation and Cooperation

As Maps 2.1 to 2.5 illustrate, the number and size of suburban municipalities greatly increased during the years from 1940 to 1980. Much of this expansion took place by the 1960s. By 1980 the region was very much fragmented, isolated, and in some sense antagonistic. A report issued by the Metropolitan Fund, Inc. in 1965 documented the extent to which such fragmentation had taken place by the mid-1960s.[119]

In 1965 the southeast area of the state—including Wayne, Oakland, Macomb, Monroe, St. Clair, and Washtenaw counties—contained a total of 404 units of government, including the 6 counties, 67 cities, 39 villages, 109 townships, 165 school districts, and other districts and authorities dealing with services such as sanitation, water, hospitals, and incinerators. Wayne County alone contained 94 of these units of government, Oakland County had 98, and Macomb had 54. By 1982 the number of units of government in Wayne County had dropped only slightly to 91, and the number in Oakland to 93. In Macomb County the number remained at 54. Between 1945 and 1964, 41 new municipalities (cities and villages) had incorporated in the 6 counties, although during that time period only 3 municipalities in the area had annexed land exceeding a quarter of a square mile. No such annexation occurred in the 3 central counties of the region: Wayne. Oakland, and Macomb.[120] As in many other northern states, communities have defensively incorporated to prevent absorption by larger municipalities, and state laws have made such incorporation much easier and quicker than annexation.

Nevertheless, examples of regional cooperation do exist, mainly in the form of authorities, special districts, and cooperative agreements. For example. the Huron-Clinton Metropolitan Authority has existed since 1940. and it developed and maintained parks and recreational areas for the residents of five counties. Although not without conflict—central-city mayors constantly complained that the authority provided more services for suburbanites than for their constituencies—it did offer an example of longstanding, albeit single-purpose, cooperation.

Other authorities and special districts have included single-purpose agencies that sometimes served a portion of a county, such as the People's Community Hospital Authority in western Wayne County, the Southeast Oakland County Water Authority, and the South Macomb Sanitary District. Cooperative agreements between municipalities proliferated in the region, including service contracts under which one unit of government would pay another to supervise its tax assessing activities or to provide police, fire protection, utility, park, public health, or planning services. The premier example of such agreements was the city of Detroit's provision of water for dozens of local units of government in southeast Michigan. Municipalities have also entered into joint service agreements to provide mutual assistance for library facilities, refuse disposal, fire fighting in times of need, and other services.[121]

Some forms of regionwide planning and program development also existed in early years in the southeast Michigan region. The Detroit Metropolitan Area Regional Planning Commission, established in 1947, included Wayne, Oakland, and Macomb counties as consistent members, with Monroe and Washtenaw counties as members for part of its history. Financed by county contributions, this agency undertook comprehensive planning research throughout the 1950s and 1960s. Another regional organization was the Supervisors' Inter-county Committee (SICC), formed by the members of the boards of supervisors of first five and then six southeast Michigan counties—the same counties involved in the regional planning commission, plus St. Clair County. This voluntary cooperative council, granted legal status in 1957, provided a forum for discussions of mutual concerns and for setting up and managing cooperative agreements. SICC also established a research arm that eventually became the Metropolitan Fund, Inc., a leader in promoting regional thought and fact gathering.

However, all of these agreements, authorities, and organizations did not add up to meaningful political cooperation. The SICC, for example, only included county levels of government, and the Metropolitan Area Regional Planning Commission did not link planning and governance. In the mid-1960s discussion began about the possibility of increasing the level of regional cooperation in the southeast Michigan area.

In 1964 the Metropolitan Fund asked the Citizens Research Council of Michigan to write several papers assessing the status of regional cooperation and suggesting improved structures. The council's report encouraged the Metropolitan Fund to establish a small policy committee in 1965. The policy committee concluded that two primary options existed: A metropolitan government with areawide authority and jurisdiction could be established, (an option that the policy committee said was not feasible politically) or the existing framework of local government and interlocal cooperation could be strengthened in several ways, including by the establishment of a voluntary Council of Governments (COG). The policy committee favored the second option and suggested that SICC and the Metropolitan Area Regional Planning Commission merge into a new council of governments. The chairman of the Metropolitan Fund appointed a new multimember body, the Committee of 100, to develop a specific proposal for a COG to include governments in six counties—a proposal that dele gates to a prospective council approved in substance in 1967. The new council, the Southeast Michigan Council of Governments (SEMCOG), was formally created on January 1, 1968.[122]

The state of the region today would have been vastly different if the Metropolitan Fund's policy committee had chosen to press for a stronger metropolitan governance system. About the same time that these deliberations were taking place, in the mid-1960s, citizens in other regions of the country—such as Nashville, Tennessee; Jacksonville, Florida; and Indianapolis, Indiana—were approving new governmental structures that combined cities with their surrounding counties. In those cases, of course, only one county was involved, but the new structures did provide broader territory and thus broader taxing powers for the cities.[123] And it was about the same time that Minnesota's Twin Cities, Minneapolis and St. Paul, were developing a structure of regionalism that eventually led to a pioneering tax base-sharing agreement for that region.[124]

Southeast Michigan, however, was apparently ready for nothing stronger than a voluntary council, SEMCOG. While this council in its early years made great strides in promoting regional cooperation, it has always operated within strong limitations. With its establishment the membership abolished SICC, and the Metropolitan Area Regional Planning Commission was absorbed into SEMCOG as its planning unit, thus reducing the possibility of duplication. But at first only slightly more than 100 of the 400 eligible units of government joined. As a COG the organization functioned well, undertaking comprehensive land use planning as well as eventually supervising comprehensive planning of regional criminal justice, waste treatment, public health, and other services.[125] The COG structure, however, is by definition weak. SEMCOG, for example, could not force membership, which remains voluntary, or undertake activities as ambitious as tax base sharing. Though many metropolitan-area political leaders opposed any greater degree of regional cooperation in governance, the financial situations of the central city of Detroit and several other urban municipalities in the region were becoming so acute that it was obvious that some larger unit of government would have to help.

In the early 1970s that unit appeared to be the state government. Although metropolitan governance in the Detroit region did not succeed greatly, the state stepped in to assist redistribution of financial resources in some small fashion. This is apparent in several program areas, but we would like to focus on the issue of equitable financing for school districts, an issue of importance beyond the Detroit region but one pushed to the fore because of the crisis of the Detroit public school system.

Fiscal Crisis in the Detroit Public School System

The fiscal crisis of the public schools of Detroit offered an example of the effects of fiscal inequity in the region. In November 1972 the nation's fourth largest school system, responsible for instructing one in seven students in the state, was bankrupt.

The basis of the problem was escalating school costs in the face of declining revenues. The rising costs were due to inflation, rising expenditures for the special service needs of poor children, and increasing labor costs.[126] At the same time property taxes, which accounted for 85 percent of Detroit's locally raised school revenues, became insufficient as property values declined and voters refused millage increases.[127] Detroit's total property value actually declined by $865 million between the 1960–1961 and 1967–1968 school years. By 1971–1972 the city of Detroit was finally worth on the market what it had been in 1960–1961. But by then the Detroit school system had lost over $91 million in taxes.[128]

Detroit faced a contradiction. The city could try to tax itself at a higher rate to provide the services needed by an ever poorer population. To follow that path was to risk driving more firms and well-off families out of the city to the suburbs and to bring on tougher tax resistance among those who stayed in town.[129] Or the city could keep taxes steady and cut services, thus decreasing the quality of life not just in the city but in the whole region.

Central cities must provide services that more affluent communities can avoid, such as redevelopment projects and welfare. Central cities also provide services that suburbanites use but do not pay for, such as libraries, museums, and water and sewage systems. This kind of central-city overburden explains why Detroit's school millage rate fell well below that of most of its suburbs in the early 1970s, while its municipal tax rate ranged from two to five times that of its neighbors.[130] Detroit could not focus its financial energy on its school system the way many suburbs could, yet the city was subsidizing the suburbs to the tune of tens of millions of dollars each year.[131]

Because the distribution of the tax base among local governments bore no relationship to the educational requirements of the metropolitan population, fiscal revenues were divorced from social needs, and this perpetuated race and class inequality in the Detroit region. In 1970–1971, the average property value per pupil among the wealthiest tenth of Detroit-area school districts ($47,035) was over five times that of the average property value of the poorest tenth ($9,339). (See Table 3.1.) So poorer school districts had to impose higher tax rates than their wealthier

Table 3.1 Relationship of school district to tax rates, local revenue per pupil, and total expenditures per pupil for the 86 school districts in the Detroit metropolitan area, 1970–1971 school year

School districts (in deciles)	Average state equalized valuation per pupil	Average equalized millage rates	Local revenue per pupil	Total operation expenditure per pupil[a]
Poorest tenth (n = 9)	$ 9,339	35.2	$ 311	$ 756
Next tenth (n = 9)	11,803	32.1	337	772
Next tenth (n = 9)	13,152	34.3	398	766
Next tenth (n = 8)	14,730	34.4	446	797
Next tenth (n = 8)	16,034	34.4	517	803
Next tenth (n = 8)	18,063	32.4	545	865
Next tenth (n = 8)	20,581	32.1	605	869
Next tenth (n = 9)	23,994	30.8	652	917
Next tenth (n = 9)	29,433	32.4	865	1013
Richest tenth (n = 9)	47,035	24.5	1055	1085
Detroit	18,325	22.9	441	895

Source: Calculated from raw data provided in (1) Michigan Education Association, Research Division, *Michigan Public School District Data 1970–71*, East Lansing, Mich. and (2) Michigan Department of Education, *Local School District Results, the Fourth Report of the 1971–72 Michigan Educational Assessment Program*, Lansing, Mich. September 1972.

[a]Total expenditure by local, state, and federal governments.

Table 3.2 Distribution of taxable property and pupil enrollment among the 86 school districts in the Detroit metropolitan area, 1970–1971 school year

School districts (in deciles)	(A) Percentage of total taxable property in metropolitan area	(B) Percentage of total public school pupils in metropolitan area	A/B
Poorest tenth (*n* = 9)	3.0	6.2	.48
Next tenth (*n* = 9)	4.5	7.5	.60
Next tenth (*n* = 9)	4.9	7.1	.69
Next tenth (*n* = 8)	3.7	4.8	.77
Next tenth (*n* = 8)	4.4	5.2	.85
Next tenth (*n* = 8)	34.2	39.9	.86
Next tenth (*n* = 8)	10.5	10.2	1.03
Next tenth (*n* = 9)	7.5	5.9	1.27
Next tenth (*n* = 9)	13.9	9.0	1.54
Richest tenth (*n* = 9)	13.1	4.2	3.12
Total (*n* = 86)	99.7	100.0	
Detroit	27.5	29.2	.94

Source: Calculated from raw data provided in (1) Michigan Education Association, Research Division, *Michigan Public School District Data 1970–71*, East Lansing, Mich. and (2) Michigan Department of Education, *Local School District Results, the Fourth Report of the 1971–72 Michigan Educational Assessment Program*, Lansing, Mich., September 1972.

neighbors if they wanted to raise equivalent resources for their students. For example, the tax base in Dearborn, the home of Ford Motor Company, was $45,339 per pupil. Next door was Dearborn Heights with a tax base of $9,206 per pupil. At that time Dearborn Heights would have had to levy a 5 percent property tax to come up with the same school revenues that Dearborn could raise with a 1 percent tax. Obviously, Detroit was not the only school district suffering from fiscal inequity.

As Table 3.1 illustrates, while the property tax rates among the wealthiest tenth of school districts in the Detroit metropolitan area averaged only 70 percent that of the poorest tenth, per-pupil expenditures among the wealthiest tenth exceeded those of the poorest tenth by an average of 44 percent. And while the poorest tenth of school districts instructed 6.2 percent of the area's students with 3 percent of the metropolitan area's property wealth, the wealthiest tenth of school districts instructed only 4.2 percent of the area's student population with 13.1 percent of the area's taxable wealth (see Table 3.2).[132]

The primary emergency of the early 1970s, however, was the status of the Detroit school system. How difficult it would be to find genuine solutions to the fiscal crisis of education in the city of Detroit was clearly revealed in the events of 1972–1973. After lengthy debate, the Michigan legislature responded to the school district's financial collapse by authorizing special loans to pay off the debt. The legislature then passed a law requiring the Detroit school board to impose a 1 percent income tax to remain in effect until Detroit voters passed a millage renewal. The education income tax would automatically come into force whenever the school millage fell below the state mandated operating level.[133] Detroit residents were left with a choice: They could pass a millage renewal or they could continue to pay the state-imposed income tax. On September 11, 1973, Detroit voters passed a seven-mill tax increase by a two-to-one margin, and the income tax was rescinded.[134]

The Michigan legislature's decision to disenfranchise Detroit residents and impose a solution was an emergency measure. A more durable policy was clearly called for. The fiscal crisis was easily solved in theory. All that was necessary was to shift fiscal responsibility to a higher level of government—to a regional government, the state, or Washington, D.C. The higher government could collect taxes and distribute the money to local school districts according to a formula based on the number of students and educational need. Most national planning bodies, including the President's Commission on School Finance Reform, were then recommending state or federal financing of schools.[135] State or federal financing, supporters argued, would remove local incentives for fiscal zoning, curb regressive features of the local tax system, tie growth in local tax revenues to growth in the national economy, and help increase educational productivity by circumventing the duplication that comes from the fragmented system of local school districts.

William Milliken, Michigan's Republican governor in the early 1970s, was a national leader in the movement for state financing of public education. Milliken was one of the first U.S. governors to attack inequities in school finance. In his alternative plan, he argued that every school system in Michigan should get the same financial return from each mill of tax it raised, and the extent to which wealthy districts could outspend poorer ones should be limited.[136] When his proposal took a bad beating in the state legislature, the governor sponsored a petition drive to get the financial reform measure on a referendum ballot for the elections in November 1972. The Michigan Education Association pledged $250,000 to the campaign, and the successful petition drive was also backed by civic and business groups like the League of Women Voters and the Michigan Chamber of Commerce.[137]

Milliken's proposal placed low constitutional ceilings on property taxes for public schools and instructed the state legislature to make up the difference in revenue from other, unspecified, sources. It was known that the governor favored raising the state income tax and creating a new value-added tax to fund the schools.[138]

Michigan voters soundly defeated Milliken's proposal.[139] Shifting from local to state financing would bring large increases in educational costs and in taxes. Recent court cases, in Michigan and elsewhere, implied that a shift to state financing would require reducing expenditure dispari-ties among districts within the state. Reducing expenditures in wealthy districts was out of the question, so expenditures in less-affluent communities would have to rise nearer to those of the big spenders. Governor Milliken estimated a shift to state financing would cost an added $45 million in Michigan. But the head of the Michigan Senate Taxation Committee put the figure between $114 million and $1.3 billion, depending upon the norm toward which all districts would be raised.[140] Tax resistance was already palpable in Michigan, so the prospect of further tax hikes virtually killed the reform proposals.

Suburbanites opposed the state financing of education because it would mean a decline in the autonomy and power of local districts. This concern was intertwined with suburban fears about metropolitan-wide bussing and with out-state sentiments that the reform proposals were designed to benefit Detroit's schools and not their own.[141]

The Michigan legislature finally managed to reach a compromise agreement, after a turbulent period of many months. The state came up with a new allocation formula that encouraged local school districts to raise their taxes, by tying the amount of state aid to the local tax rate. The state also made a modest effort to equalize spending among school districts by guaranteeing a floor below which local expenditures would not be allowed to fall. And Michigan implemented a property tax relief plan designed to help the elderly and low-income groups. These reforms combined incentives to increase the local tax effort with measures to blunt some of the harsher features of the fiscal system, and they brought Michigan a national reputation for progressive school finance.[142] Yet these reforms didn't really address the causes of the fiscal plight of Detroit, nor did they challenge the unequal structure of education in Michigan.

Metropolitan Governance

The school finance battle was just one attempt to try to equalize the financial status of local units of government. A far more ambitious—though unsuccessful—effort took place in the mid-1970s with the introduction of regional governance legislation into the Michigan House of Representatives. This did not succeed, but other crises in the region forced politicians to look at other options, most notably the reorganization of the Wayne County governmental structure. At the end of this period of proposals and reorganizations, the region's municipalities remained practically as isolationist as they had at the beginning.

William Ryan, chairman of the House Urban Affairs Committee, introduced legislation (HB 5527) establishing regional governance in southeast Michigan. Metropolitan Fund President Kent Mathewson had designed the proposal, which was backed by "good government" advocates within the state. Ryan's introduction of the bill, staff of the Metropolitan Fund later wrote, was "easily metro Detroit's most significant ... regional event in the mid-1970's."[143] The proposal called for the wholesale restructuring of the relatively weak SEMCOG, a voluntary association of local governments, into an agency responsible for both planning and implementation at the regional level. Designed to cover the entire seven-county SEMCOG area, the new agency would have been supported by mandatory dues levied upon all the municipalities in the region. Half of the representatives to the policy body would have been elected by direct vote and half indirectly by local governments, with a highly visible chairperson to be elected directly by the public. A bold proposal, it generated swift reaction. Although media editors, business leaders, and labor representatives endorsed the legislation, local government officials opposed. Members of SEMCOG were particularly vocal in their opposition.[144]

Although the legislation did not pass, a survey conducted by the Metropolitan Fund before the bill's introduction revealed opposition to increased regional cooperation was not as great as casual observers may have thought. The Metropolitan Fund commissioned a political science professor to supervise structured interviews of regional leaders. A total of 51 leaders interviewed in 1974 included 18 party officials, 8 county officials, 8 city or township officials, and 17 civic, business, and union leaders from a cross section of southeast Michigan counties. Examination of the leaders' reactions to the proposal revealed possibilities for cooperation as well as likely reasons that the legislation did not eventually pass.

Almost one-half of the respondents were in favor of a strong, central regional governance system. Although 11 thought that any form of regional government was "a mistake and 16 said that a voluntary association like SEMCOG was adequate, 24 were much bolder in their assessment, selecting the option of regional government as a "real answer to area problems [that] should be developed." The proponents of strong regional government generally gave one of two reasons for their position: that the growing urban area had generated the need for widespread pooling of resources and coordinated action or that the population was not evenly distributed across geographic space by age or income and that it would be better to deal with the region as a whole.

About half of the 51 leaders interviewed opposed regional governance. Their opinions clustered around three basic arguments. First the "prolocal government" group complained about big government and protested that regional government would destroy the power base of local politicians. Second the "no benefits" group, mainly from outlying counties, thought that regional government would give their communities few if any benefits. Third the "suspicious" group, largely from suburbs and outlying areas, feared that regional government would be a wing of Detroit city government and that the city's problems would be dumped upon the outlying areas. Although the interviewers reported that race was seldom mentioned as a factor by opponents, some respondents did specifically mention the widespread fear of bussing and of losing control of local schools, even though the proposal did not involve the educational system.

Interviewers also asked the 51 leaders about specific aspects of the proposal, such as the suggested funding system, election of delegates, district plan, and compulsory participation. Although polarization in responses to these questions was not as great as polarization over the whole question of regional governance, strong disagreement did arise over whether the system should be compulsory or voluntary, whether the elections to the assembly should be partisan, and which district plan should be chosen. Twenty-eight respondents opposed the popular election of the chairperson. If a chairperson had been elected, he or she would have been a powerful figure in state as well as regional politics, a fact not lost on respondents. Opponents thought the plan would lead to "name" candidates, chosen with powerful political or economic backing. Comments from both opponents and proponents are revealing: "A 'name' isn't a qualification and with a big area we would get 'name' candidates." "Election would give him an independent political club. He would dominate the assembly as he should. He [would be able to] communicate with the people as the governor would." "It [popular election] would ... create a chief executive, probably more powerful than the governor."[145]

After HB 5527 was introduced, the *Detroit Free Press* analyzed its chances of success. It claimed that the plan was "feared and despised" by white political suburban leaders, who would have to provide more support to the hub city of Detroit, as well as by Detroit's black political power structure, whose power base would be diluted. Mayor Coleman Young had freely commented in several interviews that he did not believe his white suburban colleagues would cooperate in such an effort, so neither would he. "Those people who fled to the suburbs to escape Detroit's problems in the first place aren't going to help support Detroit now," he said. "I might feel differently if there were some way we [Detroit] could get in on the tax base of the whole region"

At a seminar held on regionalism at Wayne State University, where many of these opinions were expressed, one black critic said that the measure had been "'spoon-fed'" to him by the influential white leadership of the Metropolitan Fund. Young enumerated for the seminar audience a long list of grievances, including the fact that the Detroit Zoo, the Detroit Art Institute, and the Detroit Free Library had been supported largely with Detroit money, even though the primary users were non-Detroiters. He noted that the city furnished half of the water in the state of Michigan, but others wanted to take control of the service. He said that Detroit's bus system was used and financed primarily by Detroit residents but was threatened with takeover by a regional body, the Southeast Michigan Transportation Authority (SEMTA). Young proclaimed, "Detroit's current fiscal problems stem from the fact that we furnish services to people who don't pay for them because of an unequal tax structure. We must achieve some equity before we'd be willing to go further or exchange any power. I'll tell you up front [that] I'm not willing to deal with people who have refused to deal fairly with me. I'm going to turn over my autonomy to people like that? I have to look askance at this whole proposal."[146]

The ironic thing about Young's statement is that he was presenting arguments that could be used for regional governance. Detroit had indeed carried an unfair burden; the plan proposed to remedy that. Metropolitan Fund's Kent Mathewson suggested that Young wanted equity in the financing of regional facilities and institutions but did not want commensurate equity on the boards that oversaw those facilities and institutions. In sum, Young wanted other municipalities' money, but he wanted to keep control in the hands of the city.

Young, of course, was not the only reluctant party; suburban leaders also balked. This was true even though other municipalities in the region, such as suburbs in the downriver area, also suffered from financial problems and low socioeconomic status. At no time did a viable coalition of poorer municipalities rise to press strongly for regionalism, in large part no doubt because of racial politics. When the proposed legislation failed, it had been the region's one big chance at meaningful regional governance.

Other efforts continued. SEMCOG survived and gained skill and influence as a regional planning agency. SEMTA, the regional transportation authority created in 1967, survived several structural changes to become a fairly powerful agency supported by federal transportation dollars, although conflicts between SEMTA and the city of Detroit's Department of Transportation continued well into the 1980s. Occasionally new proposals arose, such as Governor William Milliken's proposed tax-growth sharing plan, based on the Minneapolis/St. Paul, Minnesota program. The tax proposal fell before the wrath of suburban Detroit communities. By the early 1980s what had been a growing public awareness of regional issues had declined considerably.[147]

Regionalist thought plummeted to such depths that in 1980 the Citizens Research Council of Michigan wrote a report considering the policy implications of an actual separation of the city of Detroit and Wayne County, a proposal that certainly moved in the opposite direction from consolidation. Apparently inspired by the rising fiscal crisis of Wayne County, which ran an illegal deficit between $20 million and $22 million in fiscal year 1980, the proposal would have relieved Wayne County of the costs of serving the citizens of Detroit. Authors of the report indicated that Detroit residents provided $102 million in revenues for 1980 but required $148 million in county expenditures. Out-county residents more than paid their way with $179 million in revenue contributions and only $133 million required in expenditures.[148] Although this proposal died an early death, it illustrated the fact that those concerned with the declining economic status of Detroit's parent county were desperate for some changes in county governance.

The change that was finally chosen was simply to reorganize Wayne County's government. The Citizens Research Council of Michigan, which in past years had sponsored many regionalist proposals in cooperation with the Metropolitan Fund, spent much of the later part of 1981 refining proposals for a new Wayne County charter. The charter provision had many positive features and refined the governance of what had become an unwieldy, almost comically inept county government. The charter separated the powers of the executive and legislative branches. It reduced the awkwardly large county commission to a manageable size, cutting it from 27 members to 15. It required improved financial management. Most important, perhaps, it provided for the election of a chief executive officer, who would be able to appoint several executive branch officials and veto decisions of the commission.[149]

Wayne County voters eventually adopted the new charter but only after an extended battle over its terms. The charter commission, that body of citizens who had been charged with writing the new charter, was itself split between those who wanted drastic change and those who wanted to keep the *status quo.* A strong racial split developed on the charter commission as black members united in opposition to reducing the size of the 27-member board, fearing that

Detroit's power would be reduced. The black members were outvoted at the charter commission's adoption of the provision, and all 9 of them promised to work against the charter's ratification by county voters. Prominent local interracial and black organizations, including the 13th Congressional District Organization, the Detroit Urban League, and the interracial New Detroit, Inc., also expressed misgivings about the new county charter. Detroit's Mayor Young, who chose not to fight the charter revision, publicly expressed distaste for it, both because of the representation issue and because a county executive could emerge as a powerful rival to the mayor of the central city. In spite of these misgivings, county voters did adopt the new charter in November of 1981. Soon thereafter many of the fears of black politicians were calmed, after a county reapportionment committee—whose 5 members included at least 1 staunch political ally of Coleman Young—adopted a redistricting plan for the county commission that gave Detroit candidates from predominantly black districts a good chance to win 6 or 7 of the 15 seats. The redistricting would end the historic dominance of the Board of Commissioners by suburban white Democrats.[150]

When the voters elected Wayne County Sheriff William Lucas as the new Wayne County chief executive, they sent a strong signal about the future direction of the county. An elected chief executive could be much stronger than one appointed by the commission, since an appointed executive could hardly be expected to show strong opposition to any commission decisions. William Lucas had already earned a reputation in his position as Wayne County sheriff as a strong-headed, effective individual who did not hesitate to oppose, even defy, the Board of Commissioners. For example, when the commission, in an economy move, had ordered the sheriff to eliminate the road patrol, Lucas filed a suit to block the move and ordered his deputies to keep working. Lucas effectively doubled the costs of running the sheriff's office (in real dollars) during his tenure, yet this only gained him a strong law-and-order aura that doubtless increased his acceptability as a black candidate in conservative white voters' opinions.[151]

The decision to restructure Wayne County's government also meant that, for the time being, other regional governance proposals would not be practical. Those citizens in the region who might have pushed for stronger cooperation, as they had in 1975 for the seven-county governance plan, had put all of their efforts into either supporting or revising the new county charter and its reapportionment. In the process they created a stronger county government and placed at its helm a leader whom the press quickly dubbed the "governor of a small state," a man clearly unafraid to exercise power even in the gray areas of the new charter, where such power was not particularly clear.[152] It was hardly the time to discuss multicounty, multipurpose authorities.

By 1981 the regionalist Metropolitan Fund. Inc., had become the Metropolitan Affairs Corporation. For a few years it issued reports suggesting intergovernmental cooperative arrangements and regional economic development, but later it focused on improving local governmental performance.[153] Rather than promote regional thought and action, central-city and area county officials are seriously talking about dismantling one of the two primary regional organizations, the transportation authority, SEMTA. In mid-1985 the state legislature's passage of a regional hotel tax provided a mechanism for funding expansion of Detroit's Cobo Hall, but little else provided evidence of increased metropolitan cooperation.

CONCLUSION

In the final analysis, both suburbanites and central-city residents have been content to keep the council of governments, SEMCOG, as the primary vehicle for intergovernmental cooperation above the county level. SEMCOG's beneficial functions include regional economic development, promoting a successful ride-sharing program (to encourage commuters to share work trips), and regional planning data analysis. The annual budget of $3.5 million (fiscal year 1983) limits the activities of the agency, as do its bylaws, which state clearly that the purpose of SEMCOG is to foster "cooperative efforts to resolve problems, and to formulate policies and plans that are common and regional."[154]

Previous attempts to strengthen or replace this agency have failed because of the fears of both suburbanites and central-city residents. Suburbanites have been afraid of taking on the burden of a declining city with seemingly endless problems. Many central-city residents have been afraid of losing control to the very people who abandoned the city, thereby creating many central-city problems. Racial hostilities in the region, as evidenced by housing and school desegregation controversies, have made matters more difficult.

Given the history of black political development in the central city, the turf mentality of Detroit's black politicians is understandable. As the first part of this chapter explains, black political power did not come easily in the city. Many qualified black candidates lost elections over the years simply because white voters would not support them. Only careful coalition building and aggressive political organization enabled blacks to obtain local offices, and many black politicians, notably Coleman Young, overcame great personal obstacles to obtain political success. Even after Young's election and reelection, not many black candidates could draw a significant number of white votes. William Lucas accomplished this in Wayne County only by becoming a political conservative. Blacks more comfortable with the labor/liberal/black coalition feared that very liberal black candidates would not stand a chance in a district or region with no black majority. In this assessment they were probably right.

Likewise, given the history of racial flight and school desegregation battles, the turf mentality of suburbanites is also understandable. Racial and income segregation still exist to the extent that racial and class isolationism are accepted as a matter of course. It's barely conceivable that suburban politicians would actively work to promote true regionalist cooperation and responsibility, in spite of the fact that many might believe this is a viable option. To take the initiative to promote it could be political suicide.

Though Detroit's financial status remains uncertain and its school system has neared collapse, no regional tax base plan on anything other than a token scale has ever succeeded. It just never seemed to be the right time to implement regional governance schemes.

NOTES

1. August Meier and Elliot Rudwick, *Black Detroit and the Rise of the UAW* (New York: Oxford University Press, 1979), pp. 32–33.

2. *Detroit Free Press,* April 26, 1969; Wade H. McCree, Jr., "The Negro Renaissance in Michigan Politics," *Negro History Bulletin* 26 (October 1962), pp. 7–8; "Women in Politics: Negro Women Hold Ten Positions," *Ebony,* August 1956, p. 82.

3. McCree, "The Negro Renaissance," p. 8.

4. David Greenstone, *Report on the Politics of Detroit,* p. V-30.

5. Edward T. Clayton, *The Negro Politician* (Chicago: Johnson Publishing Company, Inc., 1964), pp. 86, 89.

6. *Ibid.*

7. McCree, "The Negro Renaissance," p. 8.

8. B. J. Widick, *Detroit: City of Race and Class Violence* (Chicago: Quadrangle Books, 1972), p. 155.

9. *Ibid.*

10. *Ibid.*

11. Denise J. Lewis, "Black Consciousness and the Voting Behavior of Blacks in Detroit: 1961–1968" (master's thesis, Wayne State University, Detroit, Mich., 1969), p. 29.

12. *Ibid.*

13. *Ibid.,* p. 88.

14. *Ibid.*

15. *Ibid.*

16. *Ibid.,* pp. 88–89.

17. *Ibid.,* p. 92.

18. *Michigan Chronicle,* October 31, 1934.

19. Albert B. Cleage, Jr., "Black Power—An Advocate Defines It," *Public Relations Journal* 24 (July 1968), p. 18.

20. *Ibid.*

21. *Michigan Chronicle,* November 22, 1969.

22. *Ibid.*

23. Remer Tyson, "Long Struggle Led to Firm Power Base," *Blacks in Detroit,* a reprint of articles from the *Detroit Free Press*, December, 1980, p. 40.

24. *Ibid.*

25. *Michigan Chronicle,* November 22, 1969; Tyson, "Long Struggle," p. 40; Widick, *Detroit,* p. 160.

26. Tyson, "Long Struggle," p. 40.

27. *Michigan Chronicle,* September 6, 1969.

28. *Detroit Free Press,* September 10, 1969.

29. *Ibid.; Detroit Free Press*, August 17, 1969; *Michigan Chronicle,* September 6, 1969.

30. *Detroit Free Press,* September 28, 1969.

31. *Detroit Free Press*, September 10, 1969.

32. *Michigan Chronicle,* September 20, 1969 and October 18, 1969.

33. *Michigan Chronicle,* November 1, 1969.

34. *Detroit Free Press,* November 1, 1969.

35. *Detroit Free Press,* September 11, 1969.

36. *Detroit Free Press,* November 2, 1969.

37. Quoted in *Detroit Free Press*, October 21, 1969.

38. *Detroit Free Press,* September 11, 1969 and September 19, 1969.

39. *Michigan Chronicle,* August 23, 1969.

40. *Michigan Chronicle,* September 23, 1969.

41. *Ibid.*

42. *Detroit Free Press,* November 5, 1969.

43. *Detroit Free Press,* November 9, 1969.

44. *Detroit Free Press,* January 4, 1976; Tyson, "Long Struggle," p. 39.

45. Philip S. Foner, *Organized Labor and the Black Worker, 1619–1981* (New York: International Publishers, 1981), p. 295.

46. *Detroit Free Press,* January 4, 1976.

47. *Ibid.; State Journal, September 26, 1968.*

48. *Detroit Free Press,* September 22, 1968.

49. *Detroit Free Press,* July 3, 1969.

50. Patrick James Ashton, "Race, Class and Black Politics: The Implications of the Election of a Black Mayor for the Police and Policing in Detroit" (Ph.D. diss., Michigan State University, East Lansing, Mich., 1981), p. 301.

51. *Detroit Free Press,* May 11, 1973.

52. Ashton, "Race, Class and Black Politics," p. 30.

53. *Ibid.,* p. 313.

54. *Ibid.,* pp. 3–4.

55. *Detroit Free Press,* November 8, 1973.

56. *Detroit Free Press,* January 3, 1974.

57. *Detroit Free Press,* January 4, 1974.

58. Ashton, "Race, Class and Black Politics," p. 369.

59. *Ibid.,* p. 368.

60. Tyson, "Long Struggle," p. 38.

61. *Ibid.*

62. *Detroit Free Press,* November 7, 1977.

63. *Detroit Free Press,* January 5, 1978.

64. *Lansing State Journal,* November 2, 1981; *Detroit Free Press,* January 1, 1984.

65. *Detroit Free Press,* January 1, 1984.

66. *Detroit Free Press,* January 7, 1984.

67. *Detroit Free Press,* January 2, 1984.

68. *Detroit News,* January 6, 1985.

69. *Detroit Free Press,* May 16, 1985.

70. *Detroit Free Press,* January 31, 1985.

71. *Detroit Free Press,* April 27, 1985.

72. *Detroit Free Press,* June 1, 1985.

73. *Michigan Chronicle,* March 14, 1953.

74. City of Detroit, Commission on Community Relations, *Annual Report,* 1960, p. 11; *Michigan Chronicle,* October 29, 1960.

75. Detroit Commission on Community Relations, *Annual Report,* 1960, p. 12.

76. Citizens Advisory Committee on Equal Educational Opportunities, *Findings and Recommendations* (Detroit, Mich.: Detroit Board of Education, 1962), p. v.

77. *Ibid.,* p. ix.

78. *Ibid.*

79. *Illustrated News,* March 19, 1962.

80. *Illustrated News,* February 5, 1962.

81. *Illustrated News,* March 19, 1962.

82. *Illustrated News,* February 26, 1962.

83. William R. Grant, "Community Control vs. School Integration in Detroit" *Public Interest,* Summer 1971, p. 63.

84. *Michigan Chronicle,* March 23, 1968.

85. *Michigan Chronicle,* February 24, 1968.

86. Grant, "Community Control," p. 63.

87. *Ibid.*

88. *Ibid.*

89. *Bradley v. Milliken* 433 F. Supp. 2d 897 (6th Circuit, 1970).

90. *Bradley v. Milliken* 338 F. Supp. 582 (1971).

91. *Ibid.,* p. 587.

92. *Ibid.,* pp. 588, 589.

93. *Swan v. Board of Education* 402 U.S. 1 (1971); *Monroe v. Board of Commissioners* 391 U.S. 450 (1968); *Green v. County School Board* 349 U.S. 294 (1955); *Brown v. Board of Education,* 347 U.S. 483 (1954).

94. *Bradley v. Milliken* 345 F. Supp. 914 (1972), p. 916.

95. *Ibid.*

96. *Bradley v. Milliken* 484 F. Supp. 2d 215 (1973), p. 249.

97. *Detroit Free Press,* June 15, 1972. p. 3a.

98. *Detroit Free Press,* June 21, 1972.

99. *Detroit Free Press,* June 16, 1972, p. 1.

100. Marianne R. Zepka and Stephen Franklin, "Races Are Still Apart in Detroit Schools," *Blacks in Detroit,* a reprint of articles from the *Detroit Free Press,* December, 1980, p. 52.

101. *Detroit Free Press,* June 24, 1972.

102. *Detroit Free Press,* June 17, 1972.

103. *Bradley v. Milliken* 484 F. Supp. 2d 215 (1973), pp. 250–251.

104. *Bradley v. Milliken* U.S. 418 (1974).

105. *Swan v. Charlotte Mecklenburg Board of Education* 402 U.S. 1 (1971).

106. *Bradley v. Milliken* U.S. 418 (1974), p. 757.

107. William R. Grant, "The Detroit School Case: An Historical Overview," *Wayne Farm Review*, October 1970, pp. 857–863.

108. *Detroit Free Press*, March 9, 1976.

109. George Metcalf, *From Little Rock to Boston: The History of School Desegregation* (Westport, Conn.: Greenwood Press, 1983), p. 131.

110. *Ibid.*

111. *Detroit Free Press,* May 13, 1984.

112. Metcalf, *From Little Rock to Boston,* p. 132.

113. *Detroit Free Press,* May 13, 1984.

114. *Detroit Free Press,* November 10, 1971 and July 23, 1972.

115. *Detroit Free Press,* November 21, 1971.

116. *Detroit Free Press,* November 21, 1971, July 23, 1972, and June 15, 1972.

117. *Detroit Free Press,* July 18, 1972.

118. *Detroit Free Press,* July 23, 1972.

119. Metropolitan Fund, Inc., *Regional Organization: Part One,* (summary of staff papers by the Citizens Research Council of Michigan, May 1965).

120. The 1965 data is from *Ibid.*; the 1982 data is from the U.S. Bureau of the Census, *1982 Census of Government* (Washington, D.C.: U.S. Government Printing Office).

121. Metropolitan Fund, Inc., *Regional Organization,* pp. 17, 35–50.

122. Citizens Research Council of Michigan, "Southeast Michigan Regionalism" (May 1972), in Kent Mathewson (ed.). *The Regionalist Papers*, 2d ed. (Southfield, Mich.: Metropolitan Fund, Inc., 1978), pp. 85–89.

123. York Wilbern, "Local Government Reorganization in Indianapolis," in Kent Mathewson (ed.), *The Regionalist Papers,* 2d ed. (Southfield, Mich.: Metropolitan Fund, Inc., 1978), pp. 48–49.

124. Ted Kolderie, "Regionalism in the Twin Cities of Minnesota," in Kent Mathewson (ed.), *The Regionalist Papers*, 2d ed. (Southfield, Mich.: Metropolitan Fund, Inc., 1978), pp. 26–47.

125. Citizens Research Council of Michigan, "Southeast Michigan" (1977 update), pp. 91–92.

126. See Citizens Research Council of Michigan, *Financial Problems in the Detroit School District,* Memorandum No. 222, Lansing, Mich., February 1972, pp. 7–9; Robert Reischauer and Robert Hartman, *Reforming School Finance* (Washington, D.C.: Brookings Institution, 1973), pp. 62–64; *Detroit Free Press,* July 2, 1974.

127. Citizens Research Council of Michigan, *Financial Problems in the Detroit School District,* Memorandum No. 222, Lansing, Mich., February 1972, pp. 3–4, 6; Detroit Board of Education, *Facts About Detroit Schools* Detroit, Mich., February 1, 1974, p. 14.

128. Detroit Board of Education, *Facts About Detroit Schools,* p. 3.

129. George Peterson (ed.), *Property Tax Reform* (Washington, D.C.: Urban Institute, 1973), p. 9. According to Peterson's research, suburban tax rates averaged 50 percent less than those in central cities in the early 1970s.

130. James Guthrie *et al. Schools and inequality* (Cambridge, Mass.: Massachusetts institute of Technology Press, 1971), pp. 119–121.

131. William B. Neenan, "Suburban-Central City Exploitation Thesis," *National Tax Journal,* June 1970, pp. 117–139. For a critical response to Neenan's thesis, cf. Peter Brown, "On Exploitation," *National Tax Journal,* March 1971, pp. 91–96.

132. Many public finance specialists argue that even though there are large differences in tax base among school districts, comparisons of differences in properly value per pupil may overstate fiscal inequalities. This is so, they argue, because within any labor market area it seems safe to assume that communities housing families with equal economic means will have equal fiscal capacities, whatever their per-pupil property tax base. If a district enjoys a tax advantage, families living elsewhere will move into the area and bid up housing prices. Families in the community they left pay higher taxes, but the rest of their housing costs are lower.

   As elegant as this deductive model may be, it suffers from one very faulty assumption: that families are free to move where they choose. Ignored are housing discrimination against minorities and exclusionary zoning and class pressures, which keep low-income families out of higher-income suburban areas.

133. *Detroit Free Press*, March 18, 1973.

134. State of Michigan, Department of Management and Budget, "Expiration of Detroit Board of Education Income Tax." Accounting Division Letter 81, November 5, 1973, Lansing, Mich.

135. Cf., for example, U.S. Advisory Commission on Intergovernmental Relations, *State Aid to Local Government* (Washington, D.C.: U.S. Government Printing Office, 1969); Committee for Economic Development, *Education for the Urban Disadvantaged: From Preschool to Employment* (New York: Committee for Economic Development, 1971).

136. *Detroit Free Press*, July 13, 1973.

137. *Detroit Free Press,* October 13, 1972.

138. *Michigan State News,* October 25, 1972.

139. Proposal C was defeated by a margin of 58 percent to 42 percent.

140. *Michigan State News,* October 25, 1972.

141. *Detroit Free Press,* October 16, 1971.

142. John Shannon, "The Property Tax: Reform or Relief?" in Peterson (ed.). *Property Tax Reform* (Washington, D.C.: The Brookings Institution, 1973), pp. 35–36.

143. Metropolitan Fund, Inc., "Regional Planning and Development Act; Regional Governance Opinion Survey; Regional Electoral Districting Study, 1974."

144. Citizens Research Council of Michigan, "Southeast Michigan" (1977 update), p. 93.

145. Metropolitan Fund, Inc., "Regional Planning." Quotes on p. 42. See also pp. 23–84.

146. *Detroit Free Press,* December 29, 1975, pp. 3a, 9a.

147. Citizens Research Council of Michigan, "Southeast Michigan" (1977 update), pp. 94–95.

148. Citizens Research Council of Michigan, "City-County Separation: Detroit and Wayne County" (a report to the Wayne County Efficiency Task Force, Detroit, Mich., March 1980), pp. i-v. See also *Detroit Free Press,* September 3, 1980.

149. Citizens Research Council of Michigan, "The Proposed Wayne County Charter," Report 275, September 1981, pp. iv-vi.

150. *Detroit Free Press,* April 26, 1981, June 17, 1981, September 4, 1981, October 12, 1981, and January 13, 1982.

151. *Detroit Free Press,* February 22, 1981.

152. *Detroit Free Press,* February 7, 1983.

153. See Metropolitan Affairs Corporation, *Annual Report, 1984;* and *Intergovernmental Cooperative Arrangements: Exploring Opportunities,* December 1982, which was prepared by the Southeast Michigan Council of Governments.

154. Southeast Michigan Council of Governments, *Annual Report, 1983* and *By-Laws.*

4

Urban Renewal and Detroit

EMILY SMITH

INTRODUCTION

Urban renewal planning in the United States started as early as the 1930s. What eventually became national urban renewal programs were first proposed in the early 1930s by Robert Moses, the enormously influential head of several governmental authorities and commissions in New York City. Renewal efforts continued to grow across major US cities during the interwar period, and they were aided by slum clearance and the establishment of public housing authorities. As the United States entered the post-WWII period, federal programs began to cater to the large masses of men returning from war in the pursuit of the suburban dream.

Suburbanization ballooned with federal policies: the Housing Act of 1934, GI Bills, the Housing Acts of 1949 and 1954, and the Federal Highway Act of 1956. American cities began to shift drastically in those years of experimental policies aimed at rebuilding the inner cities, which had suffered tremendously during the interwar and postwar deindustrialization periods. The paradoxical nature of urban renewal is that while it produced many successful outcomes in terms of commercially popular redevelopment in city districts, it also rebuilt American cities by destroying functional if lower-class neighborhoods and districts, leading to tragic and monumental problems.

As a national policy that fundamentally altered numerous postwar US cities, urban renewal remains controversial in its results nearly two generations after its implementation. The social and political upheaval it caused remains a focus of scholarly contention and debate. The large-scale urban renewal projects that took place in major US cities, made possible through federal programs, were implemented under the platform of reshaping American cities that faced decline in the era of postwar deindustrialization. These initiatives proved a wholly insufficient solution to the problem of decline in great American cities, introducing displacement, segregation, deindustrialization, and suburbanization—and disproportionately affecting African American populations, with Detroit serving as an exemplar of urban renewal's deleterious effects.

ROBERT MOSES AND URBAN RENEWAL

Robert Moses's extraordinary rise and consolidation of power in mid-twentieth-century New York City remains unprecedented for an unelected official in a major US city. In his nearly half a century of incumbency in various offices, he forever shaped the development patterns of the state and the city. Moses was appointed cochair to the State Emergency Public Works Commission of New York by Franklin D. Roosevelt during the onset of the Great Depression. Under the New Deal, Moses approved numerous public works projects, including parkways and housing projects. The underlying themes of urban renewal were observable in his vast highway expansion projects, connecting Manhattan to its neighboring boroughs, while also beginning the process of slum clearance and housing projects within Manhattan. According to Joel Schwartz (2005),

> Wearing both park and planning hats, Moses claimed that decent housing required nearby recreation space, a formula that convinced [Mayor] La Guardia to allow Moses to influence project decisions at the New York City Housing Authority. When La Guardia wanted a plan for postwar public works in 1943, Moses headed the commission that drew up the list of highways, slum clearance sites, public schools, and other projects. These kinds of politics were no stranger to the great American cities of the past, but his attitudes of control, expansion, and slum clearance espoused the goals and aspirations of the inner workings of the newly emerging urban renewal era sweeping the nation.

Chronopoulos (2013) details the masked subtleties of Moses's plans to eradicate blight across New York City: "During the 1950s in New York City, Robert Moses led the largest slum clearance program in the United States. Title I of the US Housing Act of 1949 provided subsidies for the clearance of areas designated as slums, so that private developers could rebuild them." In addition, Moses "used photographs and brochures to educate residents on the conditions of the blight within their community, justifying the acts of slum clearance," which continued to be made possible by the federal programs brought forth under the New Deal and the following Fair Deal politics.

SLUM CLEARANCE AND MODERNIZATION

There has been a long-standing mutual relationship between architecture and city order, historically in the realm of planning and architecture. The inherent reality that cities evolved both slums and wealthy districts seemed, according to Chronopoulos, to have sparked the connection between Moses's plans for rebuilding New York City and the rise of modernist architecture in the United States. Within his brochures and drawings, "Moses highlighted the chaos and hodgepodge of building structures that encompassed the blighted areas to be torn down, starkly contrasting them with the proposed ideas of orderly modernist architecture that would replace the disarray." Moses continued to use urban renewal, Chronopoulos reports, "as a tool to demolish countless buildings across the city, claiming them disorderly slums to be replaced by modernist architecture, parks, and the ideas of Le Corbusier." Further,

> Le Corbusier did not invent but combined many elements of architectural and planning theory that existed since the Renaissance to insist that visual order based on urban design was a major precondition of urban order. Architects have historically assumed a connection between order in architecture and order in society and have aimed to regulate and anticipate social relations through architectural design.
>
> These ideas and visions of the Swiss-born French architect resonated heavily with the US cities trying to transform themselves in the age of urban renewal, hoping to restore order and stability to their tarnished reputations. Moses was just one of many fans of Le Corbusier, as other architects and planners across the nation looked to implement modernism, a cheap and efficient way to achieve urban renewal with the immediate help of federal funding.

Chronopoulos (2013) describes the archetypical modernist city born from urban renewal:

> The gridiron street system was replaced with superblocks. Buildings and functions were separated from each other. Gardens surrounded buildings. Parking facilities were neatly integrated in the site. Playgrounds were placed within meaningful distance from the residential buildings and incorporated into the gardens. The streets surrounding the superblocks were widened so that automobile traffic could flow easier. Stores were limited to specific locations that were separate from the residential tower.

Moses's intricate rise to power, unwavering views of blight in the inner city, and visionary solutions to expand public works and expressways—along with the takeover of modernist architecture amid the wide-scale demolition of slums—proved to be an accurate anecdotal portrayal of the politics and viewpoints during the time of urban renewal. Still, it is important to understand the different federal programs that made his vision possible.

NATIONAL HOUSING ACT OF 1934

The National Housing Act of 1934, as part of the Roosevelt administration's New Deal, was an attempt to make housing purchases more affordable and to combat the rising number of home foreclosures. Additionally, the National Housing Act of 1934 created the Federal Housing Administration (FHA), the Federal Savings and Loan Insurance Corporation, and the United States Housing Authority. It is strongly associated with mass suburbanization in US cities. According to

Kevin Gotham (2016), "The FHA paved the way for post–World War II mass suburbanization by lowering home down payments from 30 percent to less than 10 percent, establishing minimum standards for home construction, and eliminating lending institutions' risk in providing mortgage financing." Not only did these policies prompt mass suburbanization, they also infused the housing and real-estate markets with racial bias and discriminatory practices. Institutional racism was visible through restrictive covenants and lending/real-estate practices. Thomas Sugrue details the discriminatory policies present within the National Housing Act of 1934 and the FHA, drawing a causal relationship with the decline of Detroit as a result of these policies. Sugrue (1996) notes, "The FHA perpetuated private industry's opposition to funding black residential development in or near white neighborhoods. The FHA regularly refused loans to black homebuilders while underwriting the construction of homes by whites of a similar economic status a few blocks away."

While the FHA accelerated white suburbanization, it also restricted blacks to inner-city slums, as FHA loans backed only new home construction and offered no loan guarantees for existing home renovation. This had the discriminatory effect of keeping blacks in the same substandard living conditions. In addition, such practices as redlining, restrictive covenants, and steering further segregated the white suburbs from the black inner city. When neighborhoods were redlined, black areas were identified as "hazardous risk" and received a D rating, which prevented them from receiving lending from banks and deterred whites from moving into the area. This was further instigated by realtors' use of steering to concentrate blacks into declining white neighborhoods. Concurrently, whites moved out at low costs and sold their homes to black families at a high cost, reinforcing housing segregation patterns. These patterns were exacerbated in white neighborhoods by property deed covenants that prohibited certain racial, ethnic, and religious groups from purchasing a home in that neighborhood. The Home Owners Loan Corporation (HOLC) sought to provide long-term amortized mortgages, but it continued discriminatory practices by justifying redlining under the National Housing Act of 1934. As Gotham (2016) explains, "the HOLC systemized appraisal methods throughout the nation by devising a neighborhood rating system in which physical condition of the property, characteristics of the neighborhood and location within the city, deed restrictions, and assorted land-use controls were evaluated to assess the credit-worthiness of the housing it financed."

Ultimately, the policies that resulted from the New Deal's National Housing Act of 1934 began the process of white flight and mass suburbanization as lending and housing became more expansive for the white population. The same policies excluded fair lending and housing practices for the black population, restricting them to the inner city. This was justified by the Housing Authority's creation of low-income dwellings in the "slums" of the inner city, creating a visible color line within the housing market and cities amid the process of urban renewal. Gotham attributes this to the causes and effects of the National Housing Act of 1934: "The preservation of racial discrimination and segregation in private housing and lending activities was a conscious goal of real estate and banking elites, and the political power of national organizations provided elites with direct access to this arena of policy making."

THE HOUSING ACTS OF 1949 AND 1954

The Housing Act of 1949, under President Harry Truman's Fair Deal, was a continuation of the slum clearance and urban renewal promoted during the National Housing Act of 1934. As Arnold Hirsch (2000) describes it, "The long-awaited passage of the Housing Act of 1949 provided a spark of optimism within the aging, decaying cities of postwar America." The legislation would increase the redevelopment programs and slum clearance provision of Title I, while also responding to the large influx of African Americans to northern cities that faced housing shortages rooted in the housing crisis of the Great Depression. The large African American population found themselves housed in the inner city, where conditions were less than desirable, as whites enjoyed the suburban lifestyle that expanded rapidly as a result of the National Housing Act of 1934. The slum clearance provisions targeted the inner-city dwellings and set out to replace them with affordable housing, but by doing so it displaced large populations of blacks, adding to the insurmountable color line in housing and the growing racial tension that was largely a product of urban renewal. Hirsch (2000) concludes, "The passage of the housing act in the summer of 1949 found a number of cities already engaged—under municipal and state laws—in slum clearance, redevelopment, and public housing programs. They expended special effort in trying to influence the implementation of the Housing Act of 1949. Painfully aware of the grave dangers to minorities inherent in the use of massive new powers to redevelop aging, postwar cities." This illustrated, yet again, the themes and results of power-hungry legislation. The process of urban renewal continued through the Truman administration to the Eisenhower administration, when the Housing Act of 1954 was made law. According to Hirsch (2000),

> The shift in focus from the slum clearance to the protection and rehabilitation of sound, but threatened neighborhoods—the shift from urban redevelopment to urban renewal—embodied in the 1949 and 1954 laws grew just as clearly from the massive movement of minority populations. Urban renewal continued to grow under the Housing Act of 1954 but this time focused on nonresidential development of non-slum areas, furthering the displacement and neglect of inner-city African American populations.... [W]hile the building boom was by and large backed by and initiated under the new federal administration, the policies began to seek a solution to the excessive displaced minority population. Public housing projects were on the rise in inner cities, aiming to provide low-income housing to the massive black population that previous legislation had eradicated.

Hirsch (2000) attributes the following to the success of the 1954 act,

> Three years after the passage of the Housing Act of 1949, perhaps a half-dozen slum clearance projects had started operations; only another 47 had been approved for final planning. Five years after the 1954 act, however, 877 towns had adopted "Workable plans" and, according to the U.S. Commission on Civil Rights, some 645 projects were being carried out in 386 localities.... [T]he progress between the New Deal, Fair Deal, and subsequent Housing Act of 1954, reveals the longstanding history of discrimination espoused within federal government policies, with the 1954 act as a symbol of transformation in inclusionary development via urban renewal.

While the Housing Act of 1954 was a hopeful stride forward in terms of project planning, the United States would continue urban renewal development and its attendant discriminatory practices. This would further detract from cohesive community building by constructing numerous high-rise projects that would be devoid of community needs.

FEDERAL HIGHWAY ACT OF 1956

While urban renewal initially grew out of housing policies, a major dimension of it was the 1956 Federal Aid Highway Act, which allocated federal funding of the interstate highway system, the most expensive public works project in history. As described in "The Interstate Highway System" (History.com Staff 2010):

> The Federal Highway Act was a response to the congested traffic and need for alternate routes, but it was also a precautionary measure against a potential atomic attack, providing evacuation routes away from target areas. The passage of the law warranted the construction of 41,000 miles of interstate highway, allocating $26 billion for the funding of the highway systems. While the act provided relief from traffic congestion for a short period of time, its long-lasting effects were visible in the displaced neighborhoods that the highways would cut through, adding to the destruction of the inner city and displacement of black communities that had already suffered greatly under previous legislation, while also furthering the accessibility of the suburbs to whites and aiding in the mass suburbanization.

Not only did it destroy inner-city communities and displace residents, it also disrupted the industries of large US cities. Sugrue (1996) writes that "federally funded highway construction after 1956, made central industrial location less necessary by facilitating the distribution of goods over longer distances." The results of the Federal Highway Act of 1956 are deeply embedded in the developmental history of Greater Detroit, including high levels of segregation and abandonment of the city proper.

JANE JACOBS'S CRITIQUE OF URBAN RENEWAL

Jane Jacobs's seminal book, The Death and Life of Great American Cities (1961), criticized Robert Moses's development plans for New York—and urban renewal generally. Jacobs intricately captures the failure of urban renewal:

> But look what we have built with the first several billions: Low-income projects that became worse centers of delinquency, vandalism and general social hopelessness than the slums they were supposed to replace. Middle-income housing projects which are truly marvels of dullness and regimentation, sealed against any buoyancy or vitality of city life…. Promenades that go from no place to nowhere and have no promenaders. Expressways that eviscerate great cities. This is not the rebuilding of cities. This is the sacking of cities.

URBAN RENEWAL: DETROIT

Detroit, colloquially known as "The Motor City," had always proved resilient to the forces of change, as evidenced by eighteenth-century shifts in occupation among Native Americans, the French, the British, and ultimately the United States, and nineteenth-century fires, race riots, and fundamental industrial transformation caused by the auto industry in the twentieth century. However, it is noteworthy that Detroit's decline, measured by capital and population loss, was concurrent with mid-1950s federal urban renewal policies. That said, it is important to point out that Detroit's segregated racial history has its antecedents in industrial history, irrespective of national urban renewal policies. Henry Ford's complicated past with Detroit and its black population aided in the mass suburbanization of whites and the legacy of the city. Ford was influential in that he broke the color line within the automobile industry and granted jobs to blacks who otherwise faced discrimination in the job market, even though the increased employment of blacks was largely a product of availability in the job market as white men left for war. Sugrue (1996) explains, "By 1940, nearly twelve percent of Ford workers were African American. Henry Ford's idiosyncratic paternalism toward black migrants, combined with the company's interest in finding workers willing to accept the dirtiest and most grueling jobs, led the Ford Motor Company to turn toward black migrants." Although Ford provided African Americans with employment, they were given the most dangerous jobs and were urged to abstain from unionizing. Tensions escalated as white men began to return from war to find their jobs had been taken, resulting in rebellion and mass suburbanization that was a result of the federal housing policies born at the time of urban renewal.

A race riot in the city in 1943 occurred because of the growing racial tensions and policies that defined the era in history. A fight between young blacks and whites broke out on a summer day on Belle Isle, drawing attention from neighboring communities that would soon sweep the entire city, sparking a deadly conflagration that lasted several days and resulted in 34 dead and hundreds wounded. Whites were furious that their jobs had been taken by blacks as they were returning from war, and blacks were sick and tired of the discrimination they had faced in housing, employment, government policies, and the criminal justice system. These escalating racial tensions would not stop. In fact, they would continue to erupt for years to come, and the increased segregation and massive white flight to the suburbs would only underscore the severity of Detroit's racial problems. At the same time, the political leadership pursued urban renewal policies in the city. Detroit's mayor in the early 1950s, Albert Cobo, was an advocate for highway expansion, and under the highway acts passed during that decade he was able to transform Detroit into one big highway-connected escape route to the suburbs. The massive construction of the new highway system would have costly effects on the majority-black Detroit population. As if they had not already faced enough turmoil, an expressway would now cut directly through their communities. Sugrue (1996) details the fear that black residents had during the highway-happy phase of Detroit's urban renewal:

> Poor residents of center-city neighborhoods, mainly renters, had to fend for themselves when relocated by highway construction because the state highway commission had no legal obligation to assist households that had been forced to move because of highway clearance. Blacks who lived along proposed freeway routes worried about the difficulty of finding rental housing in other parts of the city.

Sugrue goes on to quote Mayor Cobo's take on the expansive highway projects: "'Sure there have been some inconveniences in building our expressways and in our slum clearance programs, but in the long run more people benefit. That's the price of progress.'" The displacement of black families continued well into the 1950s, and these "inconveniences" would again manifest themselves into the extensive slum clearance that would wreak havoc across Detroit's inner city. As Sugrue (1996) tells it,

> The centerpiece of Detroit's postwar master plan was the clearance of "blighted areas" in the inner city for the construction of middle-class housing that it was believed would revitalize the urban economy. Like most postwar cities, Detroit had high hopes for slum removal. City officials expected that the eradication of "blight" would increase city tax revenue, revitalize the decaying urban core, and improve the living conditions of the poorest slum dwellers.
>
> One of the most notable redevelopment projects was the Gratiot Redevelopment site on Detroit's Lower East Side. Mentioned in the "Detroit Plan," the proposed project was to clear the Lower East Side slum and rebuild it with private housing. The plan was proposed under Mayor Edward Jeffries, funded by the 1949 Housing Act, and adopted and carried out under the Cobo administration. The Douglass Homes were another landmark of the major redevelopment projects taking place in Detroit under urban

renewal and would demolish the slums in the center of the city and erect new, high-rise public housing.... The most obvious problem with slum clearance was that it forced the households with the least resources to move at a time when the city's tight housing market could not accommodate them.

The election of a Democratic mayor in 1961 was achieved on the strength of a white and black coalition that coalesced around the young Irish American Jerome Cavanagh, who remained enormously popular throughout his first term, despite his continuation of urban renewal policies, and the city's designation as a national Model City. Economist Edward Glaeser, in *Triumph of the City* (2012), highlights Cavanagh's term:

> Cavanagh's fatal flaw was his penchant for razing slums and building tall structures with the help of federal urban-renewal dollars.... The city was shedding people and had plenty of houses. Why subsidize more building? Successful cities must build to accommodate the rising demand for space, but that doesn't mean that building *creates* success. While urban renewal in Detroit put up countless new buildings and made Cavanagh look like a city savior in the form of urban success, Detroit did not need new buildings—it needed human capital.

Glaeser suggests the greatest flaw of urban renewal:

> Investing in buildings instead of people in places where prices were already low may have been the biggest mistake of urban policy over the past sixty years.... Ironically, as Cavanagh set out to reform police brutality, it ended up being the tipping point of racial injustice within the city. The lack of crime reduction and police force reform resulted in insurmountable racial tensions, observable during the 1967 Social Rebellion. A white police force raided an after-hours black club, resulting in mob violence to combat police brutality, which would soon erupt in the form of social rebellion across the entire city.... Those riots and rising crime rates helped create the sense that civilization had fled the city. As a result, many of those who could leave Detroit did.... As Detroit continued to decline, so did the efforts of its political successors.... Detroit's fall has more to do with economics than politics, but the political response to the city's decline only made things worse.

In the early 1960s, the City of Detroit enacted a local income tax on residents and nonresidents who worked in the city, in order to raise the declining local revenues that had been lost to population outflow. According to Glaeser (2012), "Local income taxes illustrate the problem of trying to create a just society city by city. The direct effect of the income tax was to take money from the rich to fund services that helped the poor. The indirect effect of a local income tax is to encourage richer citizens and businesses to leave." The detrimental economics and politics of urban renewal continued throughout mayor Coleman A. Young's time in office (beginning in 1974) and were apparent in numerous development projects that were aimed at revitalizing the declining rust belt city. Glaeser (2012) writes:

> Today urban leaders love to pose at the opening of big buildings that seem to prove that their municipality has either arrived or come back. For decades, the federal government has only exacerbated this tendency by offering billions for structures and transportation and far less for schools and safety. Young's major development projects during his leadership, Joe Louis Arena, the People Mover, the Renaissance Center, and the use of eminent domain in Poletown, displacing a community for the construction of a new General Motors factory, highlight the millions of dollars thrown at building and infrastructure for a diminishing population that would not reap or produce the benefits of such construction.

CONCLUSION

The long history of urban renewal—aided by the countless federal programs and policies that led to slum removal—and widespread infrastructure and highway construction projects proved to have a detrimental effect on the city of Detroit, with the greatest negative impacts on its African American population. From the age of Henry Ford and the large black employment base of unskilled workers, to the growing racial tensions of the postwar era, and the massive white flight that erupted in unison with the decentralization of the Ford plant, and the federally funded highway system, it is undeniable that black Detroiters have felt the tremendous effects and turmoil of urban renewal.

Urban renewal, the investment in infrastructure with the lack of human capital, has taken its toll on American cities, and it continues to have long-lasting effects. The current revitalization process within Detroit will hopefully acknowledge the failure of the past and policies that have attempted to rebuild the city, but that have ultimately created more problems for the future. The resiliency of Detroit has undoubtedly been tested throughout the course of history. Detroit will strive to disconnect itself from the destructive legacy of urban renewal and create a hopeful and successful city of the future.

WORKS CITED

Chronopoulos, T. 2013. "Robert Moses and the Visual Dimension of Physical Disorder: Efforts to Demonstrate Urban Blight in the Age of Slum Clearance." *Journal of Planning History* 13 (3): 207–33. Accessed December 5, 2016. http://journals.sagepub.com/doi/pdf/10.1177/1538513213487149.

Glaeser, Edward L. 2012. *Triumph of the City: How Our Greatest Invention Makes Us Richer, Smarter, Greener, Healthier, and Happier.* New York: Penguin.

Gotham, Kevin Fox. 2016. "Racialization and the State: The Housing Act of 1934 and the Creation of the Federal Housing Administration." *Sociological Perspectives* 43 (2): 291–317. Accessed December 5, 2016. http://journals.sagepub.com/doi/abs/10.2307/1389798.

Hirsch, Arnold R. 2000. "Searching for a "Sound Negro Policy: A Racial Agenda for the Housing Acts of 1949 and 1954." *Housing Policy Debate* 11 (2): 393–441. Accessed November 28, 2016. https://www.innovations.harvard.edu/sites/default/files/hpd_1102_hirsch.pdf.

History.com Staff. 2010. "The Interstate Highway System." *History.com*. A&E Networks. Accessed December 5, 2016. http://www.history.com/topics/interstate-highway-system Jacobs, Jane. 1961. *The Death and Life of Great American Cities*. New York: Random House. Schwartz, Joel. 2005."Moses, Robert." In *Encyclopedia of New York State*. Edited by Peter R. Eisenstadt and Laura-Eve Moss, 1015+. Syracuse, NY: Syracuse University Press.

Sugrue, Thomas J. 1996. *The Origins of the Urban Crisis: Race and Inequality in Postwar Detroit*. Princeton, NJ: Princeton University Press.

5

Detroit Public Transit:
Past, Present, and Future

MARISSA MEWITZ

INTRODUCTION

Effective public transportation is crucial for functioning cities. The public transit system is often the framework for which the city is defined. Can you imagine New York without its subway system, Chicago without its elevated rail lines, or San Francisco without its iconic cable cars? These systems become part of the symbolism and spirit of American cities. In Detroit, public transit has—for better or worse—shaped how the city and the metropolitan area have developed. Our transportation systems have determined who could live where, who could work where, and who knew whom. In many ways, our transit systems are a microcosm of city, regional, and state politics and of economics and social norms.

Because of limited routes and necessary infrastructure investments, public transit chooses winners and losers, and ultimately it shapes the city spatially, socially, and politically. This essay seeks to examine Detroit's public transportation system through the lens of the past systems, current systems, and conceptual future systems of Detroit.

A Brief Timeline of Detroit Transit History

author: Marissa Mewitz
sources: (Brown 2016)
(Craig 2010)
(Fleming 2016)
(Hanifin et al 2013)
(RTA 2016)
(State of Michigan 2009)

1847 Horse-drawn Omnibus service begins along E. Jefferson Ave.

1863 first trip of Detroit City Railway Company Streetcars occurs

1886 first electric streetcar lines begin operating in Detroit.

1892 Detroit Citizens' Street Railway electrifies 50% of its lines in the city.

1899 Michigan Supreme Court decision renders municipally owned streetcar lines in Detroit illegal

1922 Department of Street Railways takes over operation of all streetcar lines within city limits.

1956 last streetcar line is replaced by bus service.

1987 The Detroit People Mover is built

1998 All former suburban DDOT lines are operated by SMART

2003 DARTA is formed by Wayne, Macomb & Oakland to create regional transit.

2009 MI Rail a private nonprofit entity is launched to establish lightrail along Woodward Avenue

2012 The RTA was created by the Michigan Legislature

2014 Construction begins on MI rail

2016 RTA millage ballot is blocked by Oakland and Macomb county officials.

1862 Common Council of Detroit passes ordinance for exclusive rights for Streetcar Lines

1865 Fort Street and Elmwood Avenue Railway Company streetcar service begins

1891 Transit workers strike of the Detroit Street Railway Co. and Grand River Railway Co.

1894 Mayor Pingree is instrumental in starting Detroit Railway Company is in order to offer a competing system to spur lower fares for riders.

1900 Detroit United Railway consolidates streetcar companies and begins offering service to surrounding suburbs

1937 First Streetcar line is replaced by a bus

1974 Department of Street Railways is replaced by Detroit Department of Transportation (DDOT)

1989 SMART bus operation is begun

1999 Construction of I-375 eliminates downtown passenger railway access.

2006 the Michigan Supreme Court dissolved the DARTA agreement between the metropolitan counties

2011 Bus Rapid Transit concept is introduced

2013 Detroit Future City Streategic Framework with Transit Oriented Development is released to the public

THE ERA OF HORSE-DRAWN STREETCARS (1863–1892)

Spatial Context

When Detroit's first public transit system, horse-drawn streetcars, was introduced on Jefferson Avenue, Detroit was a much smaller city than it is today. Though some street names have been changed, some new streets have been added, and others have been reconfigured, the boundaries of the city, shown in figure 5.2, followed roughly 25th Street to the west, the tracks of the Grand Trunk Railroad to the north, Mt. Elliot to the east, and the Detroit River to the south (Robinson 1873). The entire city was only 12.7 square miles at that time.

Figure 5.1: 1864 Map of Metro Detroit Area (Cornell 1864)

The 1864 metro area, shown in figure 5.1, was a collection of small communities along the Detroit and Rouge rivers. The communities included Huron, Trenton, Wyandotte, Ecorse, and Dearborn. It's notable that these communities are connected both by the Detroit River and its tributaries, and by the railroads. The Detroit, Monroe and Toledo Railroad lines connect Huron, Trenton, Wyandotte, and Ecorse to Detroit, and the Michigan Central Railroad connects Detroit to Dearborn (Cornell 1864).

Political Context

In 1863, when the first horse-drawn streetcars began operating in Detroit, Abraham Lincoln was president, the Emancipation Proclamation had just become law, and the United States was fighting a civil war. Harriet Tubman was still helping African Americans escape slavery via the Underground Railroad (OnThisDay Staff 2016).

The city of Detroit was in a time of transition as well. Construction began on the first streetcar line in June of 1863 (Craig 2010). Just a few months earlier, Detroit had experienced its second race riot, the first occurring In 1833.

From an account of this second incident in March of 1863, a man—who was thought by an angry mob to be African American, but was said to be white by several

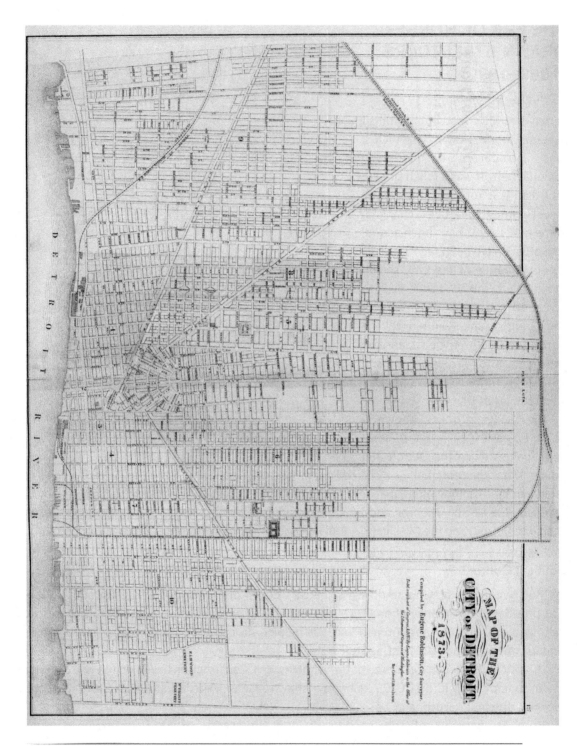

Figure 5.2: Detroit City Limits 1873 (Robinson 1873)

firsthand accounts of the incident—was accused of raping a young white girl and a young African American girl (A Thrilling Narrative 1863).

This, along with the institution of the draft for the civil war and general racism, sparked a riot by white men and boys: they stoned and beat African Americans, murdered two, looted their homes and shops, and committed arson on thirty-five buildings (Woodford 2001). This bloody day is depicted in the lithograph in figure 5.3. The riot resulted in the creation of the city's first full-time police force two years later (Hunter 2015).

For the next 30 years, while the horse-drawn streetcar was the pri-

Figure 5.3: 1863 Race Riot in Detroit

mary form of public transportation in Detroit, more social and political changes ensued. In 1870, African Americans were given the right to vote, and in the same year women were granted the same right in Michigan. The state began requiring school attendance, and the Detroit Federation of Labor was founded (Detroit Historical Society 2016). As this series of events shows, the state and city were becoming increasingly progressive.

Economic Context

Detroit's first streetcars were built during an important time in Detroit's economic history, when industry brought new wealth to the city from a variety of exports. The 1860 US Census ranked the city as the 18th largest in the country, with a population of 45,619 residents, and by 1890 Detroit's population reached 205,876, the fifteenth largest. This population boom was caused by rapid industrial development. Though the automobile had not yet transformed it into the "Motor City," Detroit was quickly becoming a manufacturing boom town (Woodford 2001). In these pre-automotive years, Detroit was the stove manufacturing capital of the world (Loomis 2015), and the Detroit Dry Dock was one of the first companies to produce steamships, and by the 1860s steam engines were one of Detroit's main exports (Watkins 2016). It was during this time that Detroit inventors brought the world the railroad refrigerator car, Vernor's ginger ale, and the automatic lubricating cup for steam locomotives, along with many other inventions that would be mass-produced in Detroit factories. The economy was diverse and growing. Much of this industrial work was dangerous, which inspired Richard Trevellick to form the Detroit Trades Assembly, the first union in the city to protect all these industrial workers' rights (Detroit

Historical Society). Later in this same era, Detroit would be the first city with individual telephone numbers, and the first city with asphalt roads. These all fueled greater business productivity and greater economic growth (Galster 2012). The first era of Detroit transit was marked by a diverse and growing economy.

Ownership and Funding

In 1862, the Detroit Common Council established guidelines for obtaining a thirty-year franchise, with exclusive rights to build and operate streetcar lines within the city. In January of 1863, a group of investors from Syracuse, New York, started the Detroit City Railway Company (DCRC). Unfortunately, the DCRC was not able to turn a profit, and in 1866, the DCRC leased all its routes to the owners of the former omnibus line. George Hendrie and Thomas Cox made the routes profitable (Dahlheimer 1951).

Early on, the DCRC forfeited its exclusive rights to build along other streets in the city that the Common Council resolution had allowed (Schramm 2006). Because of this, many other companies sought to build new streetcar lines to serve the residents of Detroit. The second company to build in Detroit was the Fort Street and Elmwood Avenue Railway Company, beginning in 1865. In 1868, the Grand River Street Railway began operating along Grand River Avenue. In 1873, the city's fourth street-rail company began running streetcars along Cass and Third Avenues, and its fifth street-rail company, Detroit and Grand Trunk Junction Street Railway, began operating. The following year, the Russell Street, St. Aubin and Detroit and Milwaukee Junction Street Railway began operating; there were now six independent street-rail companies operating within the city (Craig 2010).

In the 1880s, the DCRC, began buying out these smaller companies. By 1892, only three of the original six Detroit street-rail companies remained: the DCRC, Fort Wayne and Elmwood Railway, and the Grand River Street Railway (O'Geran 2012).

Who Was Served

With the introduction of the first streetcar line, working men and women could afford to use the lines—with 5 cent fares—for their daily commute (Dahlheimer 1951). As shown in figure 5.4, by 1874 the entire city limits was within a few blocks of a streetcar line that could take people to their manufacturing jobs along the rivers. By 1875, the four lines operated by the DCRC alone carried 2.9 million passengers per year (Schramm 2006).

Shortcomings

The horse-drawn streetcar system was popular, and it was certainly an improvement over the pre-transit private omnibus and cab, however, the system was far from ideal. At rail line switches, when cars had to pass one another, there were long waits, sometimes up to ten minutes, that made the rides annoying (Dahlheimer 1951). The rail cars were also slow, traveling a maximum of

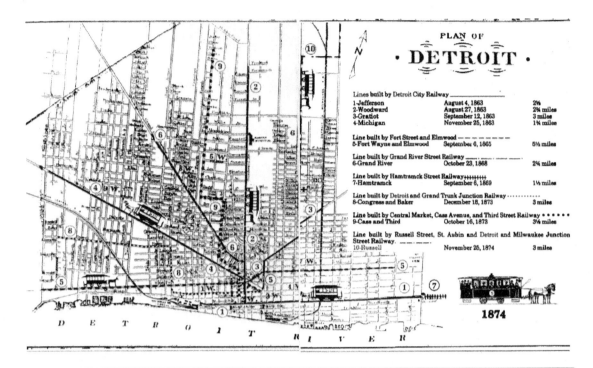

Figure 5.4: Map of Detroit's Horse-Drawn Street-Rails

six miles per hour. Additionally, due to the high level of ridership, ventilation was poor, and many riders considered the cars to be unsanitary (O'Geran 2012).

Additionally, horses required considerable care. Horses deposited several thousand pounds of manure and many gallons of urine onto the streets each day, creating an enormous public health hazard. Additionally, the hard work of pulling streetcars shortened the life of the animals, so dead horses were a common sight on Detroit streets in the late 1800s, as shown in figure 5.6 (Bak 2011).

Figure 5.5: Horse-Drawn Streetcar

Figure 5.6: Dead Horse on Fort Street

HORSES ARE REPLACED BY ELECTRIC STREETCARS (1892–1937)

Spatial Context

Detroit looked a lot different in the era of electric streetcars than it had looked at the beginning of the previous transit era. Detroit was quickly annexing the surrounding suburbs, as shown in figure 5.8, and by 1926 the boundaries of the city had expanded to roughly those of today: Eight Mile to the north; Alter, Mack, and Kelly to the east; the river to the south; and Telegraph to the west (Craig 2010).

The metro area was well along in separating into the many distinct municipalities that make up the system today. By 1915, a large portion of the metro area was connected by interurban street railways (Parsons et al. 1915).

Ownership and Funding

In 1890, Hazen Pingree was elected to his first term as mayor. He ran on a ticket of lowering streetcar fares for the working man. The following year, in 1891, local transit workers went on strike from the Detroit Street Railway Company and the Grand River Railway Company, to demand that the workday be shortened from twelve hours to ten. This resulted in a three-day riot (O'Geran 2012).

Later that same year, when the Detroit Street Railway Company applied for an extension of its franchise for another 30 years, Mayor Pingree fought them. It was Pingree's opinion that because the street railways created a natural monopoly, the city couldn't simply give away the rights to these franchises for free. He believed that the city itself should operate the street railways, and he refused to extend the franchise of the Detroit Street Railway Company. However, in December of 1891 a new company—Citizens' Street Railway—formed, and it bought the controlling interest of the DCRC.

Frustrated with trying to improve private transit services for the public, Mayor Pingree decided the municipal ownership route was the city's only true choice for addressing its transportation needs. In 1896, he was elected governor of Michigan. As governor, he ushered through the McLeod Act, which gave the City of Detroit the authority to operate its own street railway. However, the Michigan Supreme Court found this act unconstitutional (Schramm 2006), pushing Detroit municipal ownership of public transit off by a few years.

By the end of 1901, a new corporation, the Detroit United Railway (DUR), was formed. This company consolidated all the smaller streetcar companies in the city. However, the DUR was not allowed a franchise, and so it refused to upgrade the system. Instead, as lines' franchises ran out, the DUR was allowed to rent the lines for $3,000 per day. In 1913, the US Supreme Court ruling preventing municipal ownership of the street railway was overturned by constitutional amendment, finally allowing for municipal ownership of the street railway system (Dahlheimer 1951).

In 1920, mayor James Couzens was able to get voters to pass a $15 million tax appropriation to build a municipally owned street railway. In 1922, voters agreed to appropriate $19.8 million to buy the remaining DUR lines in the city. In May of that same year, the Department of Street Railways took over Detroit's entire transportation system (Craig 2010).

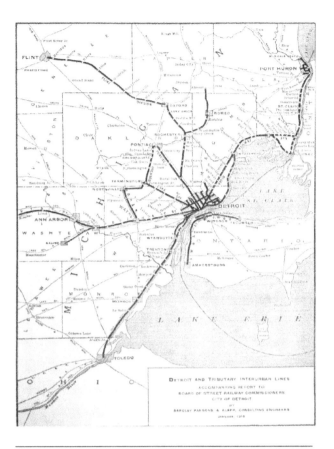

Figure 5.7: Interurban Street-Rail Map of Metro Detroit

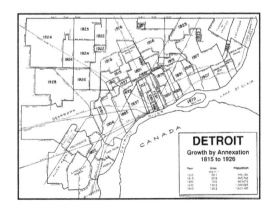

Figure 5.8: Detroit Growth by Annexation 1815–1926

Figure 5.9: Municipal Owned Electric Streetcar in Detroit

Ridership

Everyone rode the electric streetcar lines in Detroit. The cars were often overflowing with passengers. The Detroit streetcars connected to the interurban rail system, allowing streetcar users to easily travel to Port Huron, Flint, Pontiac, Ann Arbor, and Jackson, Michigan; to Toledo, Ohio; and to Windsor, Ontario, Canada. (Schramm 2006).

However, as the map in figure 5.10 shows, the outer neighborhoods of the city were far less well served than the inner core of the city. Residents in the outer areas would likely rely on the newly introduced Jitney autobuses (Dahlheimer 1951) or personal motor vehicles.

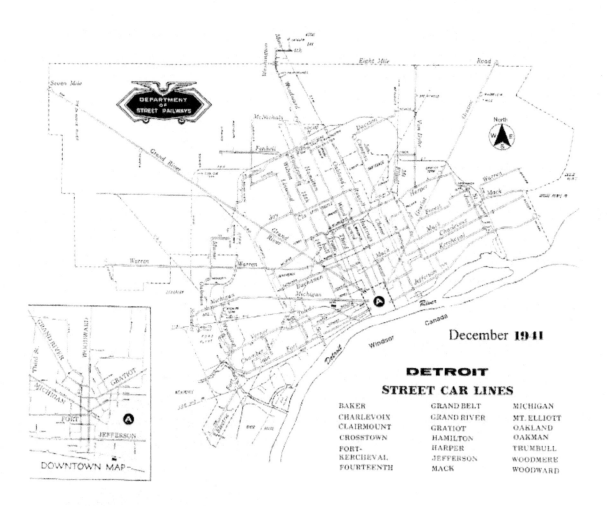

Figure 5.10: Map of Detroit Street Car Lines

Shortcomings

The electric streetcars in Detroit were not without their problems. The cars were overcrowded, and the equipment was quickly becoming outdated (Dahlheimer 1951). The city's population had grown so fast that service couldn't keep up with the volume of riders who wanted to use the rail line. The fares increased to six cents a day, even though the people felt that an affordable fare would be closer to three cents per day (Schramm).

Passengers would often press charges against DUR drivers for failing to stop a streetcar that had space for more passengers when patrons were waiting at a legal boarding zone (Craig 2010). The systems also became too expensive to replace and run. For these reasons and others, the streetcar system was converted to a bus service.

DETROIT MOVES TO BUS SERVICE (1937–PRESENT)

Spatial and Political Context

When Detroit began converting to bus service in 1937, the city boundaries had expanded to their present-day limits. The city streetcar lines covered the 140 square miles of the city, and interurban lines still covered much of the metro area.

During this time, the country was heading to war. World War II brought tremendous social change. It lifted the country out of the Great Depression, as factory work ramped up to supply military needs. Women entered the workforce in greater numbers than ever before. In Detroit, the racial strife and conflict that had begun long ago continued with increased ferocity. In 1943, Belle Isle was the site of a race riot; in the end, twenty-five black residents and nine white residents had been killed, and racial tensions were greater than ever.

After the war, racial tensions continued unabated. As soldiers returned from war, Detroit neighborhoods were burgeoning, and the areas where African Americans were sequestered were bursting at the seams (Sugrue 1996). Home Owners Loan Corporation (HOLC) maps from the federal housing authority reinforced underlying racism and gave credence to arguments for segregation. Combined with massive real-estate development in the suburbs, this led to white flight from the city (Galster 2012). In the post-war years, the suburbs became more and more divided from the city—culturally, racially, economically, and politically (Sugrue 1996).

Economic Context

In the early years of the conversion from streetcars to buses, Detroit was serving as the "Arsenal of Democracy," supplying tanks, aircraft, and other goods necessary for fighting the war in Europe and Japan. After the war, Detroit found itself in the beginning of a serious economic crisis, as the factories it depended on moved to the suburbs in pursuit of the larger amounts of land required for assembly-line technology and lower taxes. State and federal freeways were built that allowed suburbanites to quickly get in and out of the city in automobiles. The exodus to the suburbs accelerated income disparities among Metro Detroit residents, as well as causing an increase in segregation indices throughout the area.

Ownership and Funding

The city-controlled Department of Street Railways (DSR) owned the mass-transit system. When the DSR was set up, it was arranged as a separate entity. The system was expected to be financially self-supporting and self-managing, much like a corporation. The DSR also paid property taxes and school taxes to the City of Detroit and service charges to other city agencies, such as the water department (Schramm, 2006). In fact, it was mandated that all operating expenses for the system had to be paid exclusively from passenger fares. Consequently, no tax money went to the system.

Unfortunately, fewer and fewer people depended on mass transit in the area—because automobiles were becoming common and less expensive to own. This led to a steady decline in fares, which in the late 1970s nearly led to the bankruptcy of the DSR. In 1964, voters approved a City Charter amendment (Proposal G) that allowed the DSR to stop paying taxes to the city, allowed it to apply for grants, and allowed tax dollars from the General Fund to be spent to provide matching funds for federal grants for mass transportation (Craig 2010). In 1969, with the passage of Proposition A, the DSR came under the management of the Detroit Common Council. In 1974, with the passage of the 1974 Home Rule Charter, the DSR was dissolved and the Detroit Department of Transportation (DDOT) was formed. This system was and is fully owned and operated by the city and is funded mostly by tax dollars.

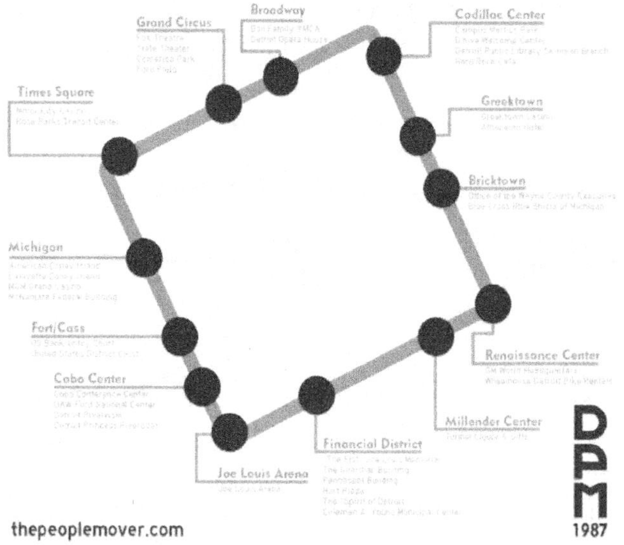

Figure 5.11: Area of Detroit People Mover Coverage (Hill 2013)

THE PEOPLE MOVER (1987 TO PRESENT)
Spatial Context

The Detroit People Mover (fig. 5.11), an elevated light rail system, was built in 1987 to connect the Downtown area with several tourist destinations. It has thirteen stops: Times Square, Grand Circus, Broadway, Cadillac Center, Greektown, Bricktown, Renaissance Center, Millender Center, Financial District, Joe Louis Arena, Cobo Center, Fort/Cass, and Michigan (Hill 2014). It is a 2.9-mile loop (Detroit People Mover 2015).

Ridership and Shortcomings

The People Mover is an underutilized system. Operating in an area with very little residential land use, and going to places where transit-dependent Detroiters generally don't need to go, it is a system built almost exclusively for tourists. In this writer's experience, it mainly serves tourists who are leaving Joe Louis Arena to go to the Greektown Casino. It has the potential to improve traffic flows in Downtown Detroit; but because the places it travels are a very short distance from each other, its practical use is closer to that of a short-haul tram than a comprehensive urban transit system. It is largely an expensive novelty piece for the city (Detroit People Mover 2015).

THE FUTURE OF DETROIT TRANSIT
The QLINE

As cars become less popular because of high costs of ownership and a trend toward walkable neighborhoods, a movement to bring streetcars back to the city has brought together Downtown institutions, local foundations, and city residents. The QLINE, originally known as M-1 Rail, is a modernized light rail transit system that will serve the Woodward Corridor between Downtown and the New Center area. It is the result of a public–private partnership involving local, state, and federal governments and major institutions and foundations. The line was completed in May 2017 (Railway-Technology Staff n.d.), and it holds promise as the first phase of Detroit's reincarnated streetcar transit system.

REFERENCES

Bak, R. 2011. "Detroit's Ride from Horse to Horsepower." *Hour Detroit*, December 30. Accessed August 2, 2016. http://www.hourdetroit.com/Hour-Detroit/January-2012/Galloping-to-the-Future/.

Cornell, S. S. 1864. Principal Cities of the United States [Map]. In David Rumsey *Historical Map Collection* (Ser. 9). New York: Appleton & Co. Accessed August 2, 2016. http://www.davidrumsey.com/luna/servlet/detail/RUMSEY~8~1~28043~1120183:Principal-cities-U-S-?sort=Pub_List_No_InitialSort,Pub_Date,Pub_List_No,Series_No&qvq=q:detroit;sort:Pub_List_No_InitialSort,Pub_Date,Pub_List_No,Series_No;lc:RUMSEY~8~1&mi=4&trs=425.

Craig, H. B., II. 2010. Detroit Transit History. Accessed July 31, 2016. http://www.detroittransithistory.info.

Dahlheimer, H. 1951. *Public Transportation in Detroit*. Detroit: Wayne University Press.

Detroit Historical Society. 2016. Industrial Detroit (1860–1900). Accessed August 2, 2016. http://detroithistorical.org/learn/timeline-detroit/industrial-detroit-1860–1900.

Detroit People Mover. 2015. Company Profile and Mission. Accessed July 31, 2016. http://www.thepeoplemover.com/about-dpm/overview/.

Fleming, L. N. 2016). "Plan for Metro Detroit Transit Millage Fails." *The Detroit News*, July 28. Accessed July 31, 2016. http://www.detroitnews.com/story/news/local/detroit-city/2016/07/28/rta-master-plan-metro-detroit-transit/87669370/.

Galster, G. C. 2012. *Driving Detroit: The Quest for Respect in the Motor City.* Philadelphia: University of Pennsylvania Press.

Hanifin, L., Anderson, S., Bernasconi, C., Dutta, U., Hoback, A. & Semple, L. (2014). Detroit Regional Transit Study: A Study of Factors that Enable and Inhibit Effective Regional Transit. Mineta National Transit Research Consortium, Report No. 12–22, pp. 48.

Hill, A. B. 2013. Minimalist Map of the Detroit People Mover. Accessed August 4, 2016. https://detroitography.com/2013/11/22/minimalist-map-of-the-detroit-people-mover/.

Hunter, G. 2015. "Detroit Police Department Marks Its 150th Anniversary." *The Detroit News*, February 28. Accessed August 2, 2016. http://www.detroitnews.com/story/news/local/wayne-county/2015/02/26/detroit-police-anniversary/24094399/.

Johnson, Lillian E. B. 1921. Report of the Detroit Branch of the NAACP. Rep. no. 256.00.00. Manuscript Division, Library of Congress. Washington, DC: NAACP Records.

Loomis, B. 2015. "When Stoves Were the Hot New Thing." *The Detroit News*, January 25. Accessed August 2, 2016. http://www.detroitnews.com/story/news/local/michigan-history/2015/01/24/stove-capital-detroit-history/22234051/.

O'Geran, G. 2012. *A History of the Detroit Street Railways.* Detroit: Conover Press.

OnThisDay Staff. 2016. What Happened in 1863. Accessed August 2, 2016. http://www.onthisday.com/date/1863.

Parsons, Brinckerhoff, Hogan, and Macdonald. 1915. Report on Detroit Street Railway Traffic and Proposed Subway, Made to Board of Street Railway Commissioners, City of Detroit. Tech. Detroit.

Railway-Technology Staff. n.d. Woodward Avenue Streetcar Project in Detroit. Railway-technology.com. Accessed August 04, 2016. http://www.railway-technology.com/projects/m-1-rail-woodward-avenue-streetcar-project-detroit/.

Robinson, E., and H. F. Walling. 1873. Map of the City of Detroit [Map]. In *Printed Maps of the Middle West to 1900* (Ser. 84, pp. 126–127). Detroit: R. M. & S. T. Tackabury. Accessed August 2, 2016. http://www.davidrumsey.com/luna/servlet/detail/RUMSEY~8~1~22421~740033:Map-of-the-City-of-Detroit-?sort=Pub_List_No_InitialSort,Pub_Date,Pub_List_No,Series_No&qvq=w4s:/where/Detroit+%2528Mich.%2529;q:detroit;sort:Pub_List_No_InitialSort,Pub_Date,Pub_List_No,Series_No;lc:RUMSEY~8~1&mi=5&trs=22#

RTA Staff. 2016. About RTA. Accessed July 31, 2016. http://www.rtamichigan.org/about/.

Schramm, J. E. 1978. *Detroit's Street Railways*, Vol. I: City Lines, 1863–1922 (CERA Bulletin 117). Chicago: Central Electric Railfans Assn.

Schramm, K. 2006. *Detroit's Street Railways.* Charleston, SC: Arcadia.

State of Michigan House Intergovernmental Committee 13. 2009. Transit History in the Detroit Region. Accessed July 31, 2016. https://legislature.mi.gov/documents/2009–2010/CommitteeDocuments/House/Intergovernmental and Regional Affairs/Testimony/Committee13-3-31-2009.pdf

A Thrilling Narrative From the Lips of the Sufferers of the Late Detroit Riot, March 6, 1863, with the Hair Breadth Escapes of Men, Women and Children, and Destruction of Colored Men's Property, Not Less Than $15,000. March 6, 1863. Accessed August 2, 2016. http://docsouth.unc.edu/neh/detroit/detroit.html.

Watkins, T. 2016. The History of the Economy of Detroit. Accessed August 2, 2016. http://www.sjsu.edu/faculty/watkins/detroit.htm.

Woodford, A. M. 2001. *This Is Detroit, 1701–2001*. Detroit: Wayne State University Press.

IMAGE CREDITS

- 5.1: S.S. Cornell. Copyright in the Public Domain.
- Fig. 5.2: Eugene Robinson and H. F. Walling. Copyright in the Public Domain.
- Fig. 5.3: https://commons.wikimedia.org/wiki/File:New_York_Draft_Riots_-_fighting.jpg. Copyright in the Public Domain.
- Fig. 5.4: Copyright in the Public Domain.
- Fig. 5.5: Copyright in the Public Domain.
- Fig. 5.6: Copyright in the Public Domain.
- Fig. 5.7: https://commons.wikimedia.org/wiki/File:Detroit_united_railway_map-1904.PNG. Copyright in the Public Domain.
- Fig. 5.8: Source: https://detroitography.com/2012/12/27/44/detannexmap-1815-1926/#image-attachment-anchor
- Fig. 5.9: Copyright in the Public Domain.
- Fig. 5.10: Copyright © Matth (CC by 4.0) at https://localwiki.org/detroit/Detroit_Streetcars/_files/DSR-map_railservice-1941.gif/_info/.
- Fig. 5.11: Copyright © 2014 by Alex B. Hill.

SECTION V

READINGS

REBUILDING
A LEGACY

INTRODUCTION

U nderstanding a city begins with understanding its people. **George Galster's** recent book includes a chapter that asks the question "What Drives Detroiters? That chapter is included here to better inform future policy decisions. **Victoria Kovari** explains the importance and history of faith-based organizing and community development in Detroit. The book closes with **Gary Sands'** original essay "Is Detroit America's Future City," which explores, with robust statistical evidence, the extent to which the city is recovering post-bankruptcy.

1

What Drives Detroiters?

GEORGE GALSTER

What you need, you know I got it ... What I need is just a little bit of respect, just a little bit ... just a little bit ...
—*"Respect," sung by Aretha Franklin in 1967*

RESOURCES OF RESPECT

People are people, and psychologists have observed some common behavioral and psychic characteristics that unite our species. What humans everywhere need are three basic sorts of resources: *physical* (like food, clothing, shelter, time, energy), *social* (like love, status, affirmation, community), and *psychological* (like identity, esteem, efficacy, and purpose). We all strive to obtain, retain, and expand resources of all three types, though the physical is more basic in terms of biological survival. When people have attained a sufficient amount of all three sorts of resources, they will have gained what I call in shorthand "respect." Given the crucial importance of the resources comprising respect, it is no wonder that their potential or actual loss creates psychological stress for humans. How people respond to such stress offers a provocative lens through which to perceive and better understand Greater Detroiters.

Psychologists have suggested that these motivations can extend beyond individuals to groups and organizations as well. They have advanced two principles. The first states that resource gains and losses are not symmetric; losses are much more damaging than similarly sized gains. This explains why so many organizations and cultures have frequent rituals and commemorative events attempting to restore resources lost in significant disasters.

The second principle states that people must invest resources if they want to expand their stockpiles or protect them against potential losses. For example, individuals must continu ally invest resources in interpersonal relationships if they want love to be maintained or grow.

Organizations must invest in developing the skills and behaviors of their employees if they wish to become more productive.

These two principles lead to a corollary with crucial implications for Greater Detroit. Those with only meager resources and those suffering repeated events where resources were lost will adopt a defensive posture to conserve remnants. Confronted with the terrifying prospect that their resources may fall below the minimum threshold of acceptability, people and groups behave conservatively. They practice cognitive denial and hoard resources in the short-term, while avoiding investing resources to create a more secure or expansive future. Thus, ironically, such folks often respond in the short term to stressful situations in ways that produce self-defeating long-term consequences.

Greater Detroiters are no different from other Americans in their motivations to secure respect: adequate physical, social, and psychological resources. What distinguishes them are the uniquely daunting obstacles they have faced in their search for respect. Greater Detroit creates these obstacles with its economic base and housing market, abetted by external media and federal government forces. Its economic base and housing market are "engines of anxiety": fundamentally corrosive of the physical, social, and psychological resources that people expect to reap from their places of work and residence. How Detroiters have tried individually to cope with and collectively adapt to these corrosive forces at the heart of their metropolis has taken extreme—and extremely dysfunctional—forms.

A good many men break down mentally and physically ... [under the strain of] continuous application to one line of work.
—Samuel Marquis, Ford Motor Company executive, 1918

A city which is built around a productive process ... is really a kind of hell ... Thousands in this town are really living in torment while the rest of us eat, drink and make merry.
—Reinhold Niebuhr, Detroit minister before moving to Union Theological Seminary in New York, 1929

It has been asserted that machine production kills the creative ability of the craftsman. This is not true.
—Henry Ford, 1929

Life in Detroit ... is empty as a dried gourd for the creatures of the assembly line. Empty and insecure.... It is a city of strangers.
—Forrest Davis, first director of the Detroit Urban League, 1936

THE ECONOMIC ENGINE OF ANXIETY

Greater Detroit's economy has been dominated by the automobile industry for over a century. Throughout these decades, it has tantalizingly offered a Faustian bargain to its people: you will gain immense physical resources relative to your skills, but you will need to sacrifice psychological resources to get them. Generations of Detroiters have willingly sealed the deal, with predictable and some unpredictable consequences for themselves and their metropolitan area. Like Faust, auto workers found that the devilish font of their physical resources extracted considerably more sacrifices of psychological resources than anticipated. Four core characteristics of the Detroit auto industry—assembly line production, draconian management, cyclical instability, and long-term employment declines—ally to forge an economic engine of anxiety. It is an engine that drives away fundamental psychological resources that workers might expect to gain from the workplace: self esteem, personal efficacy, security, pride of accomplishment, a modicum of appreciation and understanding from management.

The nature of production in the auto industry is especially degrading to its workers. Assembly line work is uncomfortable, monotonous, and completely beyond the control of the worker on the line. Not only what you do but how fast you do it is controlled by someone else. Karl Marx had it right—this kind of work makes the employee nothing more than a machine-like appendage to a machine, an appendage that, the more machine-like the tasks it performed, the more likely it would be amputated and replaced by an actual machine. Thus, the cruel, ironic capitalist maxim is true in Motown: as workplace dehumanization rises, so does job insecurity from automation.

Auto plant work is also notoriously dangerous, especially in the foundry, stamping, welding, and painting divisions. Cuts, bruises, burns, and punctures are normal; noxious inhalations, broken bones, and dismemberments are frequent; deaths are not uncommon. In 1916, Ford's Highland Park Model T plant alone recorded 192 severed fingers, 68,000 lacerations, 5,400 burns, and 2,600 puncture wounds. Though conditions improved with unionization, UAW records indicated over 15,000 serious industrial accidents in the notorious year of 1970.

As if the ambient conditions of the auto workplace's physical environment were not sufficiently challenging, a long tradition of demeaning management styles has infected the industry. As a Depression-era federal government report uncovered by Mary Stolberg put it, worker dissatisfaction in the first-generation auto plants arose from industry practices generating "insecurity, inequitable hiring methods, espionage, speedup and the displacement of workers at an extremely early age."

In the front line of management, foremen acted as petty tyrants, daily fomenting insecurity and stress for the hapless workers. In pre-UAW days, foreman were the workplace cops, judge, and jury, bullying and threatening workers and dispensing "justice" as they saw fit. Their powers even extended to rehiring workers (or not) after the weeks-long annual retooling process to accommodate the latest-model vehicle. Foremen corruption was rampant because no jobs were guaranteed through the retooling cycle. The UAW scored a major victory in 1936 when the Kelsey-Hayes strike was settled with a guarantee that foremen could not arbitrarily fire workers. Yet problems persisted even in unionized plants. Bigoted foremen remained catalysts for racial angst through the mid 1970s, generating an epidemic of workplace absenteeism, grievances, violence, wildcat strikes, and antiestablishment organizations like the Dodge Radical Union Movement.

Petty tyrants were the norm higher up the management food chain as well. Detroiter Philip Levine, 2011 poet laureate of the United States, has written poignantly about job applicants standing for hours in the cold rain outside an auto plant, only to be told eventually by some company official that "we're not hiring today" for any arbitrary reason he wanted.

In the top line of management, bosses' attitudes and policies showed a similar disrespect for working people. Ford Motor Company was exceptional is this regard. Ford's fabled 1914 announcement of the $5 a day wage immediately had its intended effect of reducing labor turnover and aiding recruitment. It was so spectacularly successful that a week later, on January 12, 10,000 men gathered on Manchester Avenue outside the Highland Park plant seeking work, despite the nine-degree temperature and howling winds. The company made no provision for an orderly application process. Instead, officials inside the plant repeatedly bellowed through a megaphone that Ford was not hiring today. The frustrated, freezing crowd refused to disperse unless they could apply. The company responded by calling out the Highland Park police and dousing the crowd with two of the plant's fire hoses. The outraged, ice-covered crowd responded by throwing stones at the plant, the public by fuming indignantly over Ford's callous behavior.

When it came to stripping workers' psychological resources of identity and self-esteem, the ultimate insult, however, was Ford's "Americanization Project." The "$5 a day plan" came with conditions: it was only available to workers who met certain standards. The first was to speak English. So Ford set up its own English School and required all non-English-speaking employees to enroll in its 72-session course. Between 1914 and 1917 over 14,000 did so. In this English course workers also learned "American-style" table manners, personal hygiene, punctuality, and prejudice. Other "American" behavioral standards were enforced by Ford's Sociological Department, a corps of investigators who visited workers' homes in off-hours to inspect, interrogate, and, if needed, educate. Grounds for disqualification from the $5 a day plan included gambling, drinking, taking in boarders, poor hygiene, buying on credit, or having a wife in the labor force. Because Ford thought that a woman's place was in the home, no women were ever eligible for the $5 a day plan unless they were the family's sole breadwinner.

James Johnson's case epitomizes the intense stress the auto plants created through inhumane working conditions and intolerable management practices. The twelve months preceding July 15, 1970, were particularly deadly for workers at Chrysler Corporation plants. Mamie Williams was forced back to work from her doctor-ordered sick leave under threat of dismissal, to die on the job soon thereafter. Rose Logan was struck by a motorized jitney in a factory and later died. Gary Thompson was ordered to load a five-ton pallet of steel into a railcar using a defective forklift he was not trained to operate; he was crushed to death in the attempt. These and other run-of-the-mill workplace atrocities spawned a series of wildcat strikes called by the Eldon Radical Union Movement (ELDRUM) at Chrysler's Eldon Avenue Gear and Axle plant. Yet, the capitalist cancer of disrespect could not be so easily excised; on July 15, James Johnson could not stand it any more.

Hampered by a weak education and a racially oppressive childhood in the South, Johnson had cycled from one bad job to another since moving to Detroit. Finally, he had found steady, decent-paying work at Eldon Avenue and was preparing to buy his family's first house. But there had been disputes with management over lost vacation days and arbitrary pay reductions where he was treated unfairly. So, on July 15, 1970, Johnson refused to participate in an assembly line speed up. When he was suspended from work, the accumulated disrespect crossed Johnson's tolerance threshold. He returned to the plant later that day, an M-I rifle camouflaged under his clothing, and shot to death two foremen and a machine-setter before quietly surrendering.

A few days later, ELDRUM published at leaflet entitled "Hail James Johnson." It recounted the events leading up to Johnson's outburst, blaming it on the plant's working conditions. It argued that Chrysler Corporation in effect pulled the trigger and that the indifferent UAW was an accessory after the fact. Kenneth Cockrel, Sr., fresh from his victory defending those charged in the New Bethel Church incident, used a similar strategy to defend Johnson. After the jury visited the Eldon Avenue assembly line and saw how alienating it was, their verdict—"not guilty by reason of insanity"—was a foregone conclusion.

Visibly outraged trial judge Robert Colombo, the Detroit Police Officers Association's former attorney, urged Ionia State Hospital to confine Johnson for life. It was not to be, because in 1974 the Michigan Supreme Court ruled that those acquitted for reasons of insanity could not be detained indefinitely unless their mental illness persisted. Johnson was released in 1975 since the Ionia psychiatrists never thought him clinically insane in the first place.

This proved a bittersweet victory for James Johnson, however. In May 1973, the Workman's Compensation Board had ordered Chrysler Corporation to pay him $75 per week for the rest of his life, retroactive to the day of the shootings, based on the putatively permanent psychological harm its workplace had caused. With these harms now apparently mitigated with his release from Ionia, the Workman's Compensation Appeals Board ruled in 1975 that compensation need only be paid for sixteen months.

> Please Mr. Foreman, slow down your assembly line.
> No, I don't mind workin', but I do mind dyin'.
> —"Please Mr. Foreman," written and sung by Joe L. Carter,
> a worker at the Rouge complex during the 1930s

THE ROLLER COASTER OF ANGST

Even with the most humane work processes governed by the most enlightened management practices imaginable, the auto industry would still be an engine of anxiety because of its cyclical instability, and its long-term trend of falling employment. Motor vehicles occupy a special niche in the world of goods: mass consumer, big-ticket durables. An inevitable (if uncertain duration) period of slumping sales and idle capacity, followed eventually by a sharp recovery, is the auto industry norm. From the auto workers' perspective, the result is cyclical layoffs, followed by potential callbacks after an indefinite period, followed by a potential period of overtime work with extra hourly pay. The livelihoods of nine times as many other Detroit region workers who directly or indirectly earn a living from the auto workers by selling *them* goods and services also become cyclically unstable. Thus, Greater Detroit's hyper boom-bust local economy has created a stressful way of life due to persistent economic insecurity. Just because insecurity is expected, however, does not make it psychologically easy. In the region's Second Great Depression from 1979 to 1983, for example, the suicide rate rose 20 percent and deaths from drug overdoses doubled.

Like a roller coaster, Greater Detroit's auto-based economy not only goes up and down, but it trends downward. Compared to forty years ago, there are relatively few auto industry jobs—white- and blue-collar alike—left in Greater Detroit due to the Big Three's constant cost-cutting pressures to automate and outsource overseas and to intensifying competition from foreign-based companies. This steady hemorrhaging of its economic base has affected the economic security of everyone in the region, not just those directly employed by the auto companies. This is reflected in a November 2009 Kaiser Family Foundation poll in Greater Detroit: a whopping 65 percent said that the current economic situation was a cause of stress.

The desperate stench of evaporating economic, social, and psychological resources fills the Greater Detroit air, even among the population segments for whom insecurity was previously unknown. Between 2006 and 2008, each of the Big Three firms announced that tens of thousands of their Detroit-area white-collar, salaried retirees would no longer get company-provided group health care benefits. As one Chevy white-collar retiree said in July 2008 after GM's surprise announcement, "We just feel betrayed." In May 2009 a Grosse Pointe career counselor described a palpable fear among her executive friends: "A few years ago, an executive from GM would never have asked me for advice [about reentering the job market]. People came to equate the company with stability. You had a job for life. It had 100 years of prosperity and suddenly that's all gone."

> Why do they always say: Don't look back.... Don't hold on to the past?
> Well, that's too much to ask.
> —"This Used to Be My Playground," sung by Madonna in 1995

*   *   *

It was all gone. Everywhere George Milton and Helen looked around the city where they were born and raised they saw empty spaces where memories used to reside. Helen's childhood home on Hurlbut near Ossian Sweet's house and George's childhood home on Moran near Acme Wire and Iron Company were weedy vacant lots. The social clubs where they had partied with their friends had vanished. Their original First English Lutheran Church on Mt. Elliot, where they met, married, and baptized their son, was boarded up awaiting the wrecking ball. Drug addicts camped under the main entrance portico. So, it was time for them to disappear too, never to set foot in Detroit again.

*   *   *

When they bring
a building down,
when they make
history absent,
when they implode
a cistern of memories
into a basement grave,
where do the ghosts go?

another landmark gone—
another space left behind,
another hole in a story,
another burial
to collect bones,
another place
from where
ghosts
are gone.

—"The Burial of a Building" by Melba Joyce Boyd

THE HOUSING ENGINE OF ANXIETY

In normal places, workers can put workplace stresses behind them when they reach their homes' front doors. But Greater Detroit is not a normal place. For over a century, its housing market stressed out residents who feared loss of physical, social, and psychological resources.

First, the stress on whites associated with threats of neighborhood racial invasion and transition began with the Great Migration during World War I. Whites were in constant fear of the next Ossian Sweet moving into their neighborhood. Not only would their property values plummet, but their local networks and social status would be compromised. The threat to their physical, social, and psychological resources was thus palpable. Hence, the origins of the "white protection racket" can be easily understood.

Second, the regional Housing Disassembly Line began in the 1960s to produce stress on all households living in older neighborhoods associated with threats of neighborhood decay and abandonment. Owners of homes, apartments, and stores in these areas faced stress over potential property devaluation. Residents faced distressing prospects of deteriorating quality of life or, if they could afford to, moving somewhere else until the decay caught up with them again. But the Housing Disassembly Line produced a loss of more than physical resources.

Neighborhood decay and abandonment also levied a heavy psychological tax on Greater Detroit residents, for both those who lived amid it and those who managed to escape. Those who must live with proximate decay suffer erosion of their self-respect. If all around one sees dilapidated homes, burned-out hulks, and vacant lots of dumped tires, what does that do to one's self-image? As Kenneth Clark summarizes the psychological impact, who of worth would live in an environment like this? Those who escape before the decay arrived suffer from erosion of their histories. They witness their sacred ground—homes and stores built, owned, and occupied by their forebears—deteriorate, become abandoned, and eventually demolished. The places of their past are erased, replaced by feelings of never being able to go home again, a peculiar rootlessness. Thus, the Housing Disassembly Line strips a sense of humanity both from those who have (temporarily) escaped the decay and those who have not.

The Housing Disassembly Line creates a space for *imagined memory.* Because so much of the built environment has disappeared or is present only in ruins or vestiges of former grandeur, Greater Detroiters have few tangible, legible mementos of their past. Like the film *Memento's* protagonist, they are condemned to live in a state of partial amnesia, informed only by faded photographs with mysterious captions. With amnesia, one has no context to make sense of a current event or assess the reality of someone else's historical assertion. Instead, the past must be perpetually reinvented by the amnesiac, and here is where imagination necessarily comes into play.

When imagination invents the past, a romantic nostalgia—filled with sanctified (if nonsensical) myths, heroes, and villains—has free rein. All these aspects of imagined memory are dysfunctional. Hypernostalgia leads Greater Detroiters to live in an invented past, which proves a huge barrier to investing bravely and creatively in the future. The future can never be as great as the glorious, albeit imagined, past. Besides, we now have so little that we cannot risk it on an uncertain future. So, like Madonna and her playground, Greater Detroiters cling to the past and leave the future to fate or divine intervention. Or, like George and Helen, stripped of much of their historic home, they see no reason not to leave the metropolitan area and start a home afresh.

> "You came all the way from London to Detroit on holiday?" the U.S. Customs official at the Big Mac airport terminal asks the two female U.K. visitors with first incredulity and then suspicion. "Was that a bad idea?" they enquire. "Well," he grunts, "I'd have gone to Chicago … I mean, why would you want to come to Detroit?"
> —As told by reporters Laura Barton and Amy Fleming
> of the *Guardian,* July 2004

Greater Detroit has long been overlooked as a site for major military installations. The one exception is Selfridge Air Force Base, opened in 1917 near the northeastern suburb of Mt. Clemens. Congress named the base after army lieutenant Thomas Selfridge, the first air passenger fatality in history. He died in a crash of a Wright Flyer aircraft piloted by Orville Wright at Fort Meyer,

Virginia, on September 17,1908. Isn't it just like Washington to give the region a memorial to a passive victim!

DISSING THE D

The region has been perpetually disrespected by the national media, as if its economy and housing market did not already provide enough barriers to its population's quest for psychological resources. It now seems as if the federal government has joined in gratuitously heaping on insults.

At no time did this become clearer than in fall 2008. Top executives from GM and Chrysler, supported by UAW officials, testified before Congress about the auto industry's dire conditions and their needs for short term federal financing. By the harshness of the congressional inquisitors' tones and their patronizing, accusatory lectures, observers might have thought they had magically time-traveled into a 1951 House Un-American Activities Committee hearing with Senator Joe McCarthy at the microphone. The contrast could not have been starker to Congress's deferential, kid-glove treatment of major financial institution representatives at similar hearings a few months earlier. Leo Gerard, president of United Steel workers union, had this take on the hearings, "Washington will bail out those who shower before work, but not those who shower afterwards." In the end, Congress gave nearly $1 trillion with no strings attached to the perpetrators whose risky and often illegal financial machinations brought the world economy down. GM and Chrysler, clearly victims of the credit crunch and resultant economic meltdown, got $14 billion conditional on subsequent hearings, draft plans to review and approve, and close federal oversight.

This and the other not-so-subtle messages have not been lost on Detroit's collective psyche. No wonder that eventually Greater Detroiters internalize this disrespect and are prone to display an inferiority complex. This seems to be true across the socioeconomic spectrum.

The inner-city crowds filling the pews on Sundays and weekday services, in grand cathedrals and storefront churches alike, testify to the aching need for the psychological resources of efficacy, dignity, and self- respect:

> Within the church the Negro porter or maid can assume responsibilities and authority not available to him elsewhere. Only there can he participate ... in decisions open to whites in many other aspects of their lives. Here the Negro domestic exchanges her uniform for a "high-fashion" dress and enjoys the admiration and envy of other friends.... The Negro has managed to salvage some self-esteem from his church, and until he achieves such self-esteem elsewhere he will not give up this, the last and only sanctuary.

Although originally written by Kenneth Clark about Harlem in 1965, this quotation equally applies to Detroit today. It is not coincidental that, if you are a good customer in a black-owned store in Detroit, you will be blessed farewell with the ultimate compliment: "With respect!"

Even the most successful Detroit capitalists have not been immune to an inferiority complex about their hometown. A legion of wealthy Detroiters have invested their philanthropic legacies in ways that met their drive for self-esteem but did not redound to the benefit of their home town. Railroad car magnate Charles Freer built a permanent gallery for his impressionist master-pieces, including James McNeill Whistler's *Peacock Room*, on the mall in Washington, D.C. Henry Ford established his foundation in New York, only a few blocks away from where Walter Chrysler built his iconic skyscraper. GM's Alfred P. Sloan endowed the business school at MIT and a foun-dation in New York. And, of course, Berry Gordy moved Motown Records to Los Angeles. All these captains of industry must have felt that the grandeur of their legacies would be tarnished if they were left to languish in a third-rate place like Detroit. The implicit message conveyed to the troops commanded by these captains is unmistakable.

And what about the average, white suburbanite? Unfortunately, there are no good psycho-logical surveys to tap on this point, but we can draw some inferences from their observed driving behaviors. Their penchant for large, American-nameplate vehicles, and their fascination with speed in excess of legal limits, is well documented. Oakland and Macomb County commuters also led the nation for the last quarter-century in the percentage driving single-occupancy vehicles. Put these facts together and you have the portrait of someone who desperately seeks personal efficacy.

> We curse
> congestion, honk
> and gesture, punch
> up all-news,
> all-sports, all
> oldies all-the time, cut
> each other off,
> whatever we can do
> to simulate control.
>
> —"Motor City Trilogy III," by Kristin Palm

Detroit is a new city. Here is the utmost in technology ... a city where nothing in sight existed yesterday; the last word among twentieth century communities, in which, one might suppose, the scientific spirit had swept aside such anachronisms as night riders. Detroit is bounded on the west by Fordissimus—by Ford's Rouge plant.... By Ford's company town ... by Ford's presence as a disguised feudal monarch. On the north, Detroit is bounded by the Reverend Charles E. Coughlin's pulpit—a triumph of that other modern engine, the microphone. In between these points of interest, Detroit's million and a half souls go through the gestures of moderns. Yet this brittle new town harbored the Black Legion [responsible for several gun and bombing murders of labor leaders from 1933 to 1935] The truth, it would appear, is that there are at least two

Detroits—Fordissimus and night riders, side by side. The marvels of industrial production on the one hand; on the other, reactionary night skulkers.... Two Detroits apparently far apart but not total strangers.

> —Forrest Davis, first director of the Detroit Urban League, 1936

COPING WITH STRESS, MOTOWN STYLE

Systemic forces of disrespect attack from many fronts in Greater Detroit, stripping physical, social, and psychological resources from its population and institutions. Disrespect attacks internally through its regional labor and housing markets and externally through the media and the federal government. These attacks motivate individual psychological coping mechanisms attempting to cushion the intense stresses that most face. These coping mechanisms have four distinctive qualities: fealty to hierarchy, forming oppositional identities, sanctifying intolerance, and creating scapegoats.

Greater Detroiters seemingly need a hierarchical social order. With a hierarchy, one can be reasonably sure of one's place in life and can take satisfaction in knowing there is almost always someone below one in the rankings. One's personal resource stock is evaluated relative to individuals in another group considered the *inferior other.* It is the opposite of *relative deprivation:* Greater Detroiters more often look down to feel satisfied than look up to feel dissatisfied.

Who Greater Detroiters *are* is typically defined by who they are *not.* Their identity is formed in opposition to the inferior other: "I am not poor, not black, not union, not *whatever."* The 2004 Detroit Area study of the University of Michigan revealed that many whites hold deep-seated feelings of superiority over blacks. High percentages thought that, compared to blacks, whites tend to be more intelligent (50 percent), prefer being self-supporting instead of living off welfare (47 percent), tend not to be involved with street crimes and gangs (58 percent), and do a good job supervising their children (53 percent).

Intolerance is the necessary consequence of oppositional identity formation. To "live and let live" is anathema to intergroup competition and establishing one's own superiority. The 2004 Detroit Area Survey also revealed that both whites and blacks think much more warmly of members of their own group than the other, but both think more warmly of the other than of Arab Americans. A 2006 Detroit Renaissance/Crain's *Detroit Business* survey of more than 350 executives, entrepreneurs, venture capitalists, real estate developers, and institutional board members found that 43 percent believed the region was unwelcoming for people of diverse backgrounds. Greater Detroiters of certain religious and ideological persuasions have turned this coping response of intolerance into a virtue: "the savior of society's true values." Most such absolutists would opt for Henry Ford's brand of "education" or Rev. Pat Buchanan's brand of "conversion." It is only a short intellectual walk, however, to the costume shops that so many intolerant Greater Detroiters have patronized over the years, where they purchase white robes of the Ku Klux Klan, black skull-and-bones hats of the Black Legion, and camouflage fatigues of the Michigan Militia. Given these individual coping mechanisms, the dualities of Greater Detroit are not as mystifying as Forrest Davis's observations imply.

HERDING THE SCAPEGOATS

Any real or prospective loss to an individual's resources cannot be perceived as the responsibility of that individual, given these coping reactions of hierarchy, opposition, and intolerance. Instead, the fault must lie in what some *other* person or group did or did not do. Given the region's chronic labor and housing market generated insecurities, Greater Detroiters have had a lot of practice blaming someone besides themselves. Usually, the scapegoating followed the fundamental dichotomies: blacks and whites blame each other; unionists and management blame each other.

The career of the Catholic "radio priest of Royal Oak," Father Charles Coughlin, iconically represents the region's gift for scapegoating. He blamed all the troubles of the 1930s world on the "twin secular manifestations of Satan": Wall Street and Communism. Conveniently, he saw Jewish conspirators at the heart of both evils. At the height of his popularity in the early 1930s, Father Coughlin's radio broadcast drew tens of millions of listeners, and his office received 80,000 letters of support weekly. These letters often contained coins and dollar bills, enough eventually to build the opulent Shrine of the Little Flower Church, which cannot be overlooked while driving by on Woodward Avenue.

White and black politicians alike over the years scored easy points with racial scapegoating based on imagined memory. Politicians added a pinch of historical fact and a generous helping of imagined memory in a recipe to convince their constituents that their turf was violated by the other: "It used to be wonderful, but *they* ruined it." Essentially, they tried to build a case of "space rape." This charge stuck readily because it constituted for both races a deeply felt and profoundly insulting loss of identity and spatial roots, for which the perpetrator must "pay."

White politicians make their space rape recipe by fingering black scapegoats for the decay, abandonment, and eventual demolition of their constituents' ancestral homes, the "loss" of their religious institutions to new users, and the pitiful decline of the once-magnificent city they loved. Black homeowners are blamed for "not keeping up their homes" and "letting the city go to hell." The City of Detroit's near bankruptcy is offered as proof of the incompetence and corruption of black public officials. Similarly, the 1967 riot showed that blacks are thieves and only want to tear up the place. The upsurge in gang violence associated with distributing the "new" 1970s drug—crack cocaine—made it clear that Mayor Young could not control the city. So, the space rape recipe white suburbanites are fed is essentially summarized, "Everything was fine for us in our wonderful city until *they* came in hordes, *they* rioted, and *they* took power."

Here's how black politicians make their equivalent recipe for space rape. Black Detroiters are encouraged to blame white suburbanites for "abandoning the city." By moving their residences, businesses, and patronage of retail and commercial establishments, whites have caused systematic deterioration of the building stock and erosion of the tax base. Even worse, whites are portrayed as aggressively destroying hallowed black turf, a now-idealized place with a vibrant black business-professional-entertainment district embedded in the heart of a thriving community. Here is how Councilwoman JoAnn Watson framed this imagined memory in September 2004:

> The famed "Black Bottom" and Paradise Valley were replete with black-owned hospitals, hotels, restaurants, grocery stores, pharmacies and entertainment clubs that provided an important network of commerce, social and family resources for Detroit's black community. Urban renewal programs supported by federal, state and local governments effectively dismantled the black businesses and disenfranchised the black owners and their customer base.

Though Watson never used the word "white," the scapegoating recipe of space rape worked fine without it.

> We want the river dragged
> for distraught souls.
> We want our homes rebuilt.
> We want the guilty
> to pay a greed tax
> for the living they stole.
> We want our city back.
>
> We want our streetlights on.
> We want our garbage gone.
> We want to be rid of smack and crack.
> We want to retire
> by the river.
> We want our ancestors
> to rest in peace.
> We are claiming our history,
> seizing the hour.
> Cause, we mean to take
> our city back.
>
> —"We Want Our City Back" by Melba Joyce Boyd

The scapegoating space rape game is not just a black-white thing. In 2004, Detroit City Council commissioned an economic development analysis by former Detroiter Claud Anderson at a cost of $112,000. The resulting report, "A Powernomics Economic Development Plan for Detroit's Under-Served Majority Population," concluded that immigrants from Mexico, Asia, and the Middle East were stealing the city's resources and a black-owned "Africantown" must be developed in response. In line with the report's recommendations, the Council passed two resolutions by 7–2 majorities in July that year. The first established an economic development agency supported by casino revenues that would authorize business loans and grants only to the "major underserved minority" in Detroit. The second resolution designated blacks as that "major underserved minority." One opponent, Council-woman Kay Everett, said with considerable psychological insight, "The rationale for this ill-conceived plan is rooted in victimhood justifications that scapegoat those of other ethnicities." On the bright side, it is perhaps a sign of growing multiculturalism that now the finger of blame is pointed in more than one direction.

The key correlate of scapegoating is *passivity.* Other than perhaps exacting retribution from the culprits, failure to take responsibility for one's own loss of resources fundamentally means that one does not need to change behavior or devise resource-strengthening strategies for the future.

SOME FOR ONE AND ONE FOR SOME

Like all humans, Greater Detroiters have responded to environmental stress not only through individual coping mechanisms but also through collective adaptations. All these adaptations can be characterized as "some for one and one for some": limited collectivities of perceived similar people whose actions try to thwart the aims of dissimilar others.

These adaptations took four primary forms: unionization, segregation, fragmentation, and identity politics. The first three need no further elaboration. Working-class Greater Detroiters relied on unionization as a collective vehicle for offsetting management power and thereby extracting their rightful share of physical and psychological resources from the workplace. Whites and economic elites used segregation of neighborhoods and schools by race and class to preserve their physical, social, and psychological resources. Political jurisdiction fragmentation offered new tools for furthering race and class segregation (like exclusionary zoning) and gave residents an enhanced sense of power over local decision making.

The fourth collective adaptation meshes neatly with the others. Identity politics means voting primarily on the basis of a candidate's "being like me," rather than policy proposals or competence. Greater Detroit has been the longtime playground of identity politics, for understandable reasons. What could be better for those desperately seeking self-esteem and a sense of efficacy than to have perceived alter-egos in power?

The power of identity politics was not lost on former Detroit Mayor Kwame Kilpatrick during his 2005 reelection campaign against H. Freman Hendrix. After running far behind Hendrix in the primary because of his numerous first-term scandals, Mayor Kilpatrick stooped to a bizarre, albeit effective, form of racial identity politics. Noting disapprovingly that Hendrix was the offspring of a union between a German woman and a black U.S. soldier, the mayor implied that his opponent was not a "real black man." To remind campaign crowds that Hendrix's identity was suspect, the mayor only referred to him by his heretofore-never-used first name, "Helmut." Kilpatrick won the general election handily but was later convicted of perjury, bribery, and obstructing justice; forced to resign; and imprisoned halfway into his second term. Apparently, there are some charges that identity politics cannot deflect, even in Detroit.

DENIAL IN THE D

Despite Greater Detroiters' individual coping mechanisms and collective adaptations, the regional economic and housing market engines of anxiety often extracted too many of their resources. More and more individuals and organizations fell below the lower threshold of respect—that modicum of economic, social, and psychological resources considered bare minimum. As a consequence, these individuals and organizations frequently adopted the two defensive responses psychologists would predict: denial and myopia. Both came at the expense of conceiving and investing in longer-term strategies for resource conservation and expansion.

Denial is rampant in Greater Detroit. In a 2003 televised public hearing, Detroit Councilman Alonzo Bates criticized a white developer who wanted to buy some vacant, city-owned parcels to build market-rate housing: "Now that the city is *worth something*, you want to take it back!" Bates bellowed. In 2006 Bates upstaged this remark by muttering "Ku Klux Klan" when a federal jury convicted him of corruption. In 2007, a year of record-high gasoline prices and record-low auto sales, a large billboard next to I-94 coming into Detroit from Metropolitan Airport showed a powerful, gas-guzzling car with caption "There's No Muscle like Detroit Muscle." In 2007, Deputy Police Chief Gary Brown and two other black police officers sued the City of Detroit for wrongful termination, claiming that, in the course of an investigation, they were about to expose a sexual affair between Mayor Kilpatrick and his chief of staff. In September, the Wayne County-based jury, eleven white and one black, found in favor of the three officers. After the city settled out of court for $8.4 million plus legal fees, Mayor Kilpatrick shrugged off the verdict, commenting, "I can't help it if 12 people—11 who don't live in Detroit and one who did—decided to decide this way." In February 2008, the *Detroit Free Press* revealed text messages showing that the two indeed were having an affair, proving that the mayor had lied under oath at the September trial when he denied this allegation. Nevertheless, the mayor re fused to step down because, as he said in a radio interview, "I believe I'm on an assignment from God in this position." It took the subsequent felony convictions for perjury, obstruction of justice, and corruption to make him face reality.

Statistical evidence shows that denial is more widespread in the region than these vignettes imply. A November 2005 *Detroit News* poll found shockingly low percentages of respondents from Greater Detroit who agreed with the statement "People who have a college education are usually better off than people who don't." Only 47 percent of black, 57 percent of Hispanic, and 68 percent of white respondents agreed. Despite the decade-long drubbing the region has taken, only a third of the Greater Detroit respondents in the Kaiser Family Foundation poll taken in November 2009 said that they were pessimistic about the future of the Detroit area, and only 22 percent expected that their standard of living would be lower in ten years. In the same poll, 22 percent said they would recommend a career in manufacturing to their children.

Greater Detroit once was a place of dynamic ingenuity and entrepreneurship. It was a place where multiple paths to opportunity beckoned, though the difficulty of the path depended on the current state of play in the power struggles between labor and capital, blacks and whites. It was once a place where many people with modest talent but oversized dreams could make decent lives for themselves, whether it be from baking chicken pies like Bruno and Helen, rolling cigars like Emma, or twisting wrought iron like George Jacob.

Today the old Germantown neighborhood where those opportunities were realized and lives lived—their former homes, social clubs, and church—has been swept away. The exception is Acme Wire and Iron Works—one of a handful of hundred-year-old companies still in operation in Detroit (see Figure 1.1). It is owned by a fourth-generation descendent of the founder. The factory would easily be recognized by George Jacob, for remarkably little has changed. The company still uses the original building to produce the identical wire mesh product with the original, leather belt-driven machinery installed in 1899. To walk inside Acme is to travel through time, or at least through Greenfield Village. It is a vestige of nineteenth-century technology improbably hanging on against all odds—as is its city. And like its host city, it is stubbornly unchanging, locked in the past as everything crumbles to dust around it, denying that tomorrow will come.

MYOPIA UP CLOSE AND PERSONAL

It is also easy to find instances in Greater Detroit where individuals behaved myopically, desperately grasping in the moment for some morsel of power or self-esteem, while ignoring negative longer-run implications. A few involved famous protagonists. In 1923 a few Klansmen thought that preserving their place in the social hierarchy warranted burning out a Catholic priest from his recently occupied northwest side home. The priest in question, Father McNichols, was then undertaking the nefarious task of building a new campus of the Jesuit-run University of Detroit on Six Mile Road. Fortunately, the priest was neither injured nor deterred, and new higher educational opportunities for both Catholics and Protestants (like George Milton) were created on the now-renamed McNichols Road.

Generic myopic acts are more frequent. For example, to "diss" someone in Detroit is to ask for a fight. Only in a world bereft of resources of all kinds would people be so willing to risk injury, death, or prison time for the immediate gratification of preserving shreds of self-respect through violence. One day in May 2010, a skinny, seventeen-year-old named Je'Rean Blake gave a dirty look to Chauncey Owens, age thirty-four, in a party store on Mack Avenue near St. Jean Street. A short while later, Owens returned to the store, shot Blake to death, and drove off in his SUV.

Soft Side of Hasting, Oakland Avenue,
Wilfred's Billiard Parlor jammed between
The Pig Bar-B-Q and the Echo Theatre.
Slick Herman chalks his cue with resolution,

Figure 1.1: Acme Wire and Iron Company factory amid the fields of the east side of Detroit.

blue powder whispers to the floor,
he misses an easy bank shot in the corner.

Safe Eddie would always leave you on the rail
or hidin' behind balls you didn't want to shoot.
And steady Jerome looks for nonbelievers.

Hasn't missed a bank shot in four days.
Silent Ambrose shoots 9 ball
with Ralph, the Merchant.
Ralph accuses Silent of moving his balls
for a better angle, calls Silent a name.

Silent flashes quicker-than-light
2 inches of switchblade to Merchant's jugular.
In the stop-stillness of the moment,
you could hear a rat piss on cotton,
Don't you ever call me that ... ever.

Silent wins the 9 ball game by forfeit.
Merchant can't find a cue
that will sit still in is hand.

—"8 Ball in Side Pocket" by Murray Jackson

Myopia in the face of organizational resource scarcity abounds in the City of Detroit. First, take the Detroit Public School Board. Frustrated by the lack of progress in improving student outcomes and financial accountability, in 1999 the Michigan State Legislature imposed a new governance structure on the DPS. Instead of being elected directly, now the Board would be appointed by the mayor of Detroit, except for one member appointed by the governor. Despite notable successes under the new appointed Board structure, it was met with fierce opposition when it came up for renewal in the Proposition E vote on the November 2004 ballot. Characterizing the new structure as "a takeover," opponents cynically capitalized on the populace's thirst for efficacy: "We believe that this extension of the takeover is being driven by people like the owner of [construction company] Barton Malow, who are current beneficiaries of contracts at DPS," contended Heaster Wheeler, executive director of the Detroit NAACP. Victor Marsh, coordinator of the Just Say No to Proposition E group, laid the core issue bare: "It's all about controlling the dollars.... [If Proposal E is passed] the [DPS] Chief Executive Officer would be nothing more than a puppet for the Detroit Regional Chamber of Commerce." Proposition E was soundly defeated. Detroiters needed control and the respect that came with it, and they needed it right away. To get it, they would willingly sacrifice a structure that insulated the DPS chief executive from the vagaries of a patronage-elected, micro-managing, preening, and often-corrupt School Board. Predictably, the resulting fiscal chaos led the State of Michigan to take over complete control of the finances of DPS in December 2008.

Robert Thompson made a fortune in the private sector and generously wanted to pay it forward. So, in 2003, he proposed donating $200 million to build charter schools in Detroit. Thompson had two big problems, however, that rendered his philanthropy suspect in resource-starved Detroit: he was white, and he lived in the suburb of Plymouth. The Rev. Wendell Anthony, former head of the

Detroit NAACP, publicly decried this initiative at a 2004 school summit by appealing to the need for self-respect. He rhetorically asked, "What would Grosse Pointers think if Oprah Winfrey approached them about building a school for *them?*" Thompson's largesse was refused. Short-run gains in psychological resources for adults again trumped potential long-term economic gains for children.

The DPS Board lags far behind Detroit City Council, however, in demonstrating resource-hoarding myopia. In the aforementioned 2004 controversy over the "Africantown" proposal, Council overrode a mayoral veto, defiantly reiterating their belief that blacks indeed were the city's "major under served minority" and that immigrant groups had unfairly acquired economic resources at their expense. This represents a textbook example of short-run resource hoarding with negative long-run consequences. This resolution discouraged desperately needed immigration that might provide a huge financial boost to primarily black owners of homes and businesses in this rapidly depopulating city. One Africantown opponent, Councilwoman Sheila Cockrel, saw this short-sightedness clearly: "[The proposal] advocates exclusionary classifications and illegal set asides [for blacks] that only serve to divide and polarize within the city and the region. And we have plenty of that already."

The Detroit City Council repeatedly demonstrated unwillingness to consider long-term benefits if it risked losing control in the short term. In 2003 the Michigan Legislature passed a bill facilitating the establishment of land banks: independent, nonprofit organizations whose job would be to assemble derelict properties and vacant land owned by local governments through the tax foreclosure process and speed their redevelopment. Despite its surplus of city-owned land, Detroit did not create a land bank, because it would only have the power to appoint a minority of seats on the land bank board. Council refused to cede control of city-owned land—worthless in all but symbolic terms—to a body that was not controlled exclusively by Detroit. Only in 2008, after the unique advantages of a land bank in acquiring foreclosed properties became irresistible, did the council relent and agree to establish one.

In another bizarre case, the City Council voted in March 2008 to withhold federal funds from Detroit-based charities, unless 51 percent of their board members were Detroit residents. One councilwoman defended her vote by caustically suggesting that non-Detroiters have a "slave-master mentality." Never mind that these suburban board members typically have the deepest pockets and the wealthiest networks that ultimately funnel more economic resources into Detroit. No, city control is more important; short-term psychological resources are more important than long-term physical resources.

Consider the Cobo Convention Center expansion controversy of February 2009. A $288 million deal to expand and upgrade the city-owned home of the internationally renowned North American Auto Show was painstakingly negotiated by representatives of Wayne, Oakland, and Macomb Counties, state legislators, and Detroit Interim Mayor Kenneth Cockrel, Jr. The proposal would give Detroit $20 million to retire debt incurred in building the Cobo parking garage and would relieve it of both an annual operating deficit of $15 million and deferred maintenance charges of $200 million. In return, Cobo would be put in the hands of a regional authority directed by a five-person board. Although only one board member would be appointed by the City of Detroit, each member would have veto power. The City Council turned this sweet deal down on a 5–3 vote. As if to underline the myopic response that psychologists would have predicted, Councilwoman JoAnn Watson said, "Detroiters have spoken loud and clear in opposition to giving away or transferring another Detroit asset."

Finally, the city fights changes in its water system as if it were a matter of life and death. Now, the city provides water for the entire region. Though paid for providing this service, Detroit must bear the financial burden of maintaining and updating the ancient system of pipes and complying with strict new federal water quality mandates. Many proposals have arisen over the years to create a regional water administration, sharing the responsibilities for delivering this vital service; all have been defeated by Detroit. The latest proposal was greeted with predictable public outcries as in March 2011; "Detroit is facing a hostile takeover from greedy suburban lawmakers for control of our water system!"

Detroit is a poster child for how threats to already meager resources are met with a defensive posture, a crouched position that inhibits seeing the future. Potential resource gains of all kinds are sacrificed on the blood stained altar of fragile civic ego. The city fairly shouts, "It's *OUR* land, it's *OUR* water, it's *OUR* schools, it's *OUR* convention center, and we are going to keep control of them whether it makes long-term sense or not! They all may be like an albatross around our neck, but at least it's *OUR* albatross!"

Detroit's suburbs are not, however, immune to myopia. Their myopic strain is different from the city's in that it focuses on conserving economic resources and social status in the short term, instead of ceding either to an "undeserving" city occupied by "the others.". The behavior of the suburbs fairly shouts, "It's *OUR* money; why should we share it with *them*?."

In 2005, Wayne and Oakland Counties voted on a proposed property tax assessment to be used for ongoing support of cultural institutions and recreation programs in the two counties. Though the proposal would raise the typical homeowner's taxes only $100 annually, it would provide a critical revenue stream for a myriad important institutions, mostly based in Detroit, such as the Institute of Arts, Symphony, Opera Theater, Historical Museum, and Museum of African American History. The Detroit Regional Chamber of Commerce provided a comprehensive rationale for how the added funding would redound to the benefit of everyone in the region and led an aggressive publicity campaign in support. The referendum passed in Wayne County but lost so heavily in Oakland County that the measure was defeated.

Suburban Detroiters must put up with an inefficient, fragmented bus system because they have steadfastly refused to vote taxes on themselves. As of 2005, fifty suburban communities had opted out of the Suburban Mobility Authority for Regional Transportation (SMART)—costing it a quarter of its budget. More perversely, this frugal shortsightedness imposes costs on the suburbs that do participate in SMART, by forcing convoluted bus routing that delays and discourages riders. Suburbanites have also been unwilling to fund the requisite local match for building a regional mass transit system, thereby failing to secure generous federal matching monies. Their first opportunity was in 1976; Detroit came up with its share of the local match but the suburbs did not. The result was that the city ended up building its downtown loop "People Mover," but the light rail transit lines de signed to feed suburban commuters into it never materialized.

Why would suburbanites respond in such a myopic way? Could it have anything to do with the fact that Coleman Young had become Detroit's mayor in 1974? Or perhaps because today over 80 percent of the region's bus ridership consists of black people? Why indeed should they support a decent transit system for *them*?

Rosa Parks died in Detroit on October 24, 2005, five weeks shy of the fiftieth anniversary of her famous act of civil disobedience on that Montgomery, Alabama, bus. To mark her passing, all Detroit Department of Transportation buses (which serve only the city) had one *front* seat cordoned off with a black ribbon until the day of her funeral. After lying in state in the Capitol Rotunda in Washington, Parks' remains returned to Detroit for a seven-hour funeral at the Greater Grace Temple. A horse-drawn cortege proceeded majestically from the church down Seven Mile Road to Woodward Avenue and interment in Woodlawn Cemetery. Thousands of mourners lined the miles-long route. Parks' coffin had been interred less than a week when Livonia, an inner-ring suburban municipality of 89,000 white and 3,000 black residents, voted to withdraw from the SMART bus system.

THE LAST CHICKEN

How markets in an American metropolitan area operate holds profound implications for the abilities of its populace to gain respect: fundamental physical, social, and psychological resources. In the case of Greater Detroit, century-long reliance on assembly-line manufacturing of a durable consumer good meant that economic opportunities were cyclically unstable and increasingly scarce over time. The workplace itself, potentially a core vehicle for human actualization, proved corrosive to self-esteem, efficacy, pride, and fulfillment in the auto industry context. It proved the Engine of Anxiety. Instead of a sanctuary from the workplace, the home was yet an other source of stress over threatened resource losses. This was guaranteed by rampant racial tipping and the inexorable degradation and devaluation of neighborhoods produced by the Housing Disassembly Line. The resulting abandonment and demolition of the city's physical history created a vast prairie of the imagined past where the weeds of rootlessness, mutual blame, and hypernostalgia sprout.

As abrasive as it has been to the human psyche and soma, Greater Detroit might more aptly be named Grater Detroit. It is a place that fundamentally and perpetually *disrespects* its citizens. Perhaps the deepest meaning symbolized by the Joe Louis *Fist* statue in downtown (see Figure 5) is the devastating punch in the gut this region gives its citizens as they quest for respect.

Greater Detroiters coped with and adapted to their disrespectful metropolis as best they could in an attempt to gain and preserve resources. Individually, they coped by glorifying hierarchy, emphasizing oppositional identity formation, and raising intolerance to a virtue. This led to epidemic-level scapegoating whenever resources were threatened or lost. Collectively, they adapted by forming unions, segregating themselves according to income and ethnic status, and creating tiny, homogeneous political jurisdictions that they could control and in which they could elect those "like themselves." These adaptations may seem rational and functional in the short term, the best choices in a bad situation. Denial and myopic hoarding, instead of investing resources in the future, are understandable responses of people who have suffered repeated and increasingly severe losses at the hands of the disrespectful metropolis called Motown. But, as psychology has shown, these are also desperate, conservative, ultimately self-defeating responses. And when aggregated to the metropolitan scale, these responses indeed have produced pernicious, unintended consequences in the long run.

Greater Detroiters fear they have only one chicken left in their coop after the seemingly endless raids by the foxes, so they hold on to it for dear life, strangling it in the process.

The Detroit Public Library stands regally on Woodward Avenue in the Cultural Center. Its second floor Grand Hall proudly displays the city's other great mural, *Man's Mobility*, painted by John S. Coppin. Though less famous than Diego Rivera's *Detroit Industry* in the Detroit Institute of Arts only 300 yards across the street, *Man's Mobility* offers a powerful lens through which to examine the ultimate concerns, aspirations, and myths of Greater Detroit. The mural is a triptych portraying the transportation technologies of three eras to which Detroit's industries have contributed mightily. The 1855 panel shows a steam locomotive and steamship figuratively passing a Conestoga wagon, ox cart, and sail-powered ship. The 1905 panel portrays a horse rider, bicyclist, and mother with baby pram frightened by a prototype horseless carriage as it careens past, belching smoke from its tailpipe. The 1965 panel has a group of white males gazing admiringly skyward as jets roar overhead and a rocket blasts off to outer space.

The caption next to *Man's Mobility* reads, "Man's will and his creative imagination have impelled him ever onward; thus has come new knowledge, understanding, peace, dignity, and fulfillment." Ah, if only this were true for Greater Detroit today.

Though Pilgrim Church is located near the MotorCity Casino in west-central Detroit, it caters to a distinctly different clientele. Every evening at Pilgrim Church, I Am My Brother's Keeper Ministries opens for business.

The group provides a place where some of Detroit's homeless people can get the most basic physical, social, and psychological resources: a warm meal, shelter, and some sympathetic human attention. These people are the ultimate victims of the region's degrading job and housing markets. Before eating, they are asked to repeat over and over, following the leader's chant: "I Am Somebody!"

2

Faith-Based Organizing for Metro Equity in Detroit

VICTORIA KOVARI

ONCE UPON A MEETING

The story of MOSES's Fix It First campaign began in October 2000 in a basement room in St. John's Parish Life Center in Plymouth, Michigan. Organizers from the faith-based organization MOSES (Metropolitan Organizing Strategy Enabling Strength) and from the Gamaliel Foundation gathered with several clergy and the three guests who would shake up our organizing forever: john powell from the University of Minnesota Institute of Race and Poverty; Myron Orfield, a lawyer and state senator from Minnesota; and David Rusk, a national urban policy expert from Washington, D.C. These experts had been brought to Michigan by the Gamaliel Foundation as "strategic partners" to help local organizations analyze and strategize about important emerging regional issues.

Most of the people in the room on that chilly October day did not have a clue about how to translate the concept of "metropolitan equity" into an actual organizing campaign. They barely understood what the term meant. Some could not even get past the word "metropolitan." We were deeply rooted in the City of Detroit and its problems. To look to the larger region seemed to be a betrayal.

After all, this is *Detroit*—at or near the bottom of every quality-of-life scale, and plagued by urban decay that seems to just never go away. Detroit's schoolchildren rank lower than those in rural Mississippi, Detroit's neighborhoods are home to more than ninety thousand abandoned properties, and Detroit's fiscal crisis is among the worst of any urban area.

Between 1950 and 2000, Detroit lost half its population—nearly one million people. Significantly, the half that stayed in the city was the older and poorer half. In the past twenty years, the flight of the black middle class to the suburbs has changed the landscape dramatically because the center of black economic power has been moving to the suburbs as well. Detroit's music topped the charts in the 1960s and 1970s; now the only chart that Detroit tops is the segregation index, ranking first as the most racially segregated region in the country.

At the center of the economic and racial segregation in Detroit is the automobile. Cars are the lifeline in metro Detroit, but in the world's car capital, nearly 383,000 people are without one. The average annual cost of owning a car in metro Detroit is more than $6,000. With one of the worst public transit systems in the country, it is no wonder that as of 2005, Detroit is the poorest large city in the United States.

The question that both organizers and leaders were forced to grapple with was how does a poor city like Detroit pay to repair its infrastructure when it cannot even keep up with emergency services like police, fire, and EMS? The answer was it can't. This meant that a regional perspective would be required. Yet, as MOSES sought regional solutions to some of Detroit's problems, it faced considerable criticism—both from those inside the city who saw regionalism as a power grab by the suburbs, and from suburbanites who saw regionalism as a grab by the city for their precious and more plentiful tax dollars.

The Gamaliel Foundation's national leadership training teaches that even the most well-intentioned people cannot solve their community's problems if they are alone and do not have power. Looking at the City of Detroit and its leaders, we see that the same principle applies: no matter how well-intentioned its leaders were, and no matter how much federal or state aid it received, Detroit could not solve its problems in isolation. To revitalize Detroit and other urban areas of the state, the flow of resources within southeast Michigan would need to be redirected.

In Michigan, policies that control the flow of resources are often determined at the state level. Inevitably, then, changing these policies would require learning how to work at the state level.

A POLITICAL WATERSHED

In October 2000 at the gathering of MOSES leaders, Rusk, powell, and Orfield put forward a scenario about a political watershed that was about to happen in the state of Michigan, about which most in the room were totally unaware. They hammered home the message that if MOSES was to have any impact on revitalizing Detroit and its older suburbs, it would be necessary to understand the political decisions being made at the state level, paying particular attention to the upcoming 2002 state elections.

In Michigan in 2002, term limits had set the stage for a nearly complete turnover in state government. Michigan was to elect a new governor, a new attorney general, a new secretary of state, two-thirds of the state senate, and half of the state representatives. This offered an unprecedented opportunity to put the MOSES agenda before a whole new slate of politicians.

The vehicle chosen to advance the MOSES agenda was a mass public meeting. MOSES's then-director, Bill O'Brien, decided that if the organization was ever going to undertake to organize the biggest mass meeting in its history, 2002 was the time to do it. Plans were launched for a meeting of five thousand, to which the candidates for governor would be invited. This would be the occasion to put forward the organization's first central organizing issue related to urban sprawl. However, the *particular* issue to be put forward had not yet been decided upon.

After a series of trainings beginning in 1998, the MOSES Metro Equity Task Force was formed. In December 2000, a group of leaders from MOSES attended the Gamaliel Foundation's National Leadership Assembly, an annual gathering of leaders and organizers from around the United States. One lesson became very clear: if you want to become a more powerful player in your region and begin to redirect the flow of resources in a more equitable way, then you better be ready to take on any regional institution that controls some of those resources.

This was the first time most people had heard the term *MPO* (metropolitan planning organization). Who knew that a single organization controlled a billion dollars of federal money flowing into southeast Michigan every year, and that this money was literally and figuratively driving urban sprawl? The federal money was for transportation—the biggest item in the federal budget after defense spending, and the process of spending it was filled with more pork than a piece of sausage.

MOSES leaders came back to Detroit and began to engage in a "power analysis," a comprehensive process of research, reading, and dialogue to determine who controlled what, and which pieces of the process or the pie could be changed. With the help of some students from the University of Michigan, the leaders discovered how transportation dollars flowed in and out of metro Detroit. They began attending meetings of the MPO and the Southeast Michigan Council of Governments (SEMCOG). They interviewed dozens of people inside SEMCOG and outside: suburban mayors, state bureaucrats, legislators, and business people. At the end of each session, the leaders asked, "Who else should we talk to?"

While the power analysis was under way, a deep sense of intimidation began to surface regarding all the experts and information. Some leaders began to question their own capacity for taking on such a campaign. After all, they hardly knew anything about transportation. The more they learned, the more they realized how much they didn't know, and the more paralyzed they became.

At this point, action—any action—was the best antidote to combat their fear. Having a victory, however small, would help them get over this hurdle.

GIVING BIRTH TO "FIX IT FIRST"

MOSES began to do a series of actions and gained several wins. Among the victories were getting a seat on the SEMCOG Transportation Advisory Committee, defeating an attempt in the state legislature to cut the budget for public transit by 50 percent; and getting the Big Three auto companies to issue a joint statement in support of regional mass transit. Several public meetings of 300 to 1,000 people were held, at which some of these victories were celebrated.

At one of these meetings, leaders announced the formation of a Metro Equity Allies table. One of the allies at the table was a statewide environmental group that had come up with the phrase "Fix It First" several years earlier. This phrase resonated with our own leaders because it evoked images of crumbling bridges, roads, sewer pipes—images that were all too familiar whenever we drove around the state of Michigan. The issue of metropolitan equity could be very complex and abstract, but "Fix It First" seemed to capture the essence of metro equity and is in a language most people understand. Most important, it offered the potential to put MOSES on the radar of the 2002 candidates for governor.

In the summer of 2002, MOSES's leaders and organizers visited dozens of congregations with a PowerPoint presentation to detail issues of urban sprawl. Additionally, the presentation addressed the need not only to repair and maintain existing roads, sewers, and schools before building new ones but also to invest in regional mass transit. The issues of mass transit and Fix It First seemed to resonate with nearly every congregation across the city and suburbs, cutting across the lines of race and class.

In the course of those presentations, MOSES evolved a three-part Fix It First platform:

1. Devote 90 percent of the money that the state spends on roads, sewers, and schools to fixing the existing infrastructure.
2. Appoint a smart growth commission to make recommendations on comprehensive land use reform in Michigan, and appoint a MOSES/ MY VOICE representative to that commission.
3. Commit to developing fiscal incentives that encourage regional cooperation across the state.

MOSES had finally decided on the issues to be featured at their blockbuster meeting!

¡SÍ SE PUEDE! YES, WE CAN!

On a beautiful Sunday afternoon in September 2002, five thousand people packed the newly built Greater Grace Temple on Detroit's northwest side. Dozens of state and local officials were in attendance, along with members of 120 congregations from across metro Detroit and 500 students from various high schools and universities. The two candidates for governor of Michigan came to the front of the church to sign on to the MOSES Fix It First platform. Democratic candidate Jennifer Granholm, who was ultimately elected governor, added: "I will make this a cornerstone of my campaign and one of the major focuses of my administration."

MOSES leaders and organizers were thrilled. More than one thousand members of the largely Spanish-speaking congregation began to break out into rounds of "¡Sí se puede!" Yes, we can! And we have.

In the two years following the 2002 public meeting, MOSES continued to win significant policy victories. Two months after taking the oath of office in February 2003, Governor Jennifer Granholm appointed a statewide commission called the Michigan Land Leadership Use Council. In May 2003, during a bitter budget process, the governor came out with a mandate to defer more than one billion dollars in funding for thirty-four new road projects across the state. She eventually prevailed on seventeen of these projects, including the largest ones, slated for metro Detroit. In September 2004, at a meeting of four thousand people, the governor reaffirmed her commitment to Fix It First.

Detroit and other urban areas across the state can sustain their revitalization efforts only when state lawmakers commit to rebuilding the aging infrastructure of Michigan's central cities and older suburbs.

LAYING A FOUNDATION FOR LASTING CHANGE

Campaigns organized around regional equity strategies are powerful tools for faith-based organizations to influence state policies—especially when coupled with a political analysis and an issues-based electoral strategy. This kind of organizing has enormous implications for faith-based and community organizations working together to shape our future.

Is Detroit America's Future City?

GARY SANDS

INTRODUCTION

In the early years of the twentieth century, Detroit was widely recognized for its rapid population growth and booming economy. As Detroit became the Motor City, it attracted large numbers of immigrants and migrants, developed a large blue-collar middle class, and boasted neighborhoods of owner-occupied single-family housing. A hundred years later, Detroit has become infamous for its massive population decline, widespread poverty, and abandoned housing. In 2013, this unprecedented decline led to the largest municipal bankruptcy in American history.

Should Detroit's recent history be taken as a harbinger of the future of older urban centers across America? Is Detroit ahead of the curve, the first urban area to encounter a set of challenges that all metro areas will, in time, have to confront? Or is Detroit an outlier, the victim of a unique conjunction of circumstances that are unlikely to occur elsewhere?

This essay examines where the city of Detroit fits in the array of America's legacy cities. Legacy cities are "older industrial urban areas that have experienced significant population and job loss" (Legacy Cities Partnership 2016). As a result, they often suffer from high rates of vacancy and abandonment, low incomes, and limited retail and commercial service opportunities (Mallach and Brachman 2013).

Nineteen other legacy cities, ranging in size from Gary, Indiana (79,000), to Chicago, Illinois (2,713,000), were selected for the comparisons; most are in the Midwest and the Northeast. Five are located in Ohio, and four are in upstate New York. In addition, these legacy cities are benchmarked against twenty US cities that have experienced substantial growth since 1990. These cities are all located in the Sunbelt and include six Texas cities. Such demographic and socioeconomic factors as race/ethnicity, educational attainment, employment, and housing values are examined, as are municipal financial indicators.

POPULATION

Since the end of the nineteenth century, Detroit's population has been in a constant state of rapid and substantial change. While much attention has been given to Detroit's population decline since 1950, the city's population growth during the first three decades of the twentieth century was larger and more rapid (Reese, Sands and Skidmore 2014).

Detroit's population trajectory over the last twenty-five years can be distinguished from the trends in other legacy cities in two respects (Table 3.1). First, the 36.8 percent decline in Detroit's population between 1990 and 2014 exceeded that of every other legacy city except Gary, Indiana, which also recorded a 36.8 percent decline. A second difference is that Detroit continues to lose population, while some other legacy cities have seen their populations stabilize or begin to increase. Between 2010 and 2014, Detroit's population fell by more than 35,000 (5 percent), while the aggregate population of the other legacy cities rose by 63,000.

Detroit in 2014 had fewer non-Hispanic white residents than any of the legacy or growing cities. Even much less populous legacy cities—such as Syracuse, Akron, and Dayton—have more non-Hispanic white residents. Segregation by race in Detroit is higher than in any other large city. In general, the dissimilarity index for legacy cities is higher than for the growing cities; Houston had the highest dissimilarity index among the growing cities, but less than 16 of the legacy cities.

Foreign-born residents constitute just 5.2 percent of Detroit's population; in 1910, the 156,000 foreign-born made up 33.6 percent of Detroit's population. While other legacy cities also have a low proportion of foreign-born residents, their white non-Hispanic population share is much closer to the comparable figure for the growing cities.

EDUCATIONAL ATTAINMENT

As manufacturing employment has declined across North America, it has been supplanted by New Economy jobs—particularly in technology, information, and higher-order services—that have become the economic base of many cities. Postsecondary education is often a prerequisite for these New Economy jobs. These high levels of educational attainment not only are an

Table 3.1 Demographic and Socio-Economic Characteristics 2014

	White, Non-Hispanic	Dissimilarity Index	Foreign-Born	College Graduate
Detroit	8.7%	86.7	5.2%	13.1%
Legacy	39.3%	76.7	7.3%	23.8%
Growth	42.8%	55.4	18.2%	33.8%

Source: American Community Survey

indicator of current economic health but also may indicate the presence of a pool of talented workers that may attract new firms, improving the resiliency of local economies (Florida 2002).

Among legacy cities, Detroit, along with Flint and Gary, had the lowest proportion of college graduates, less than 14 percent. The average proportion of adults with university credentials in the other legacy cities was a full ten percentage points higher. Pittsburgh and Chicago had the most college graduates at 37 percent and 35 percent, respectively. In growing cities, more than a third of the adults were college graduates; in six of the high-growth cities (Austin, Charleston, Charlotte, Denver, Raleigh, and San Diego), the proportion of college graduates was over 40 percent, more than three times that of Detroit.

EMPLOYMENT

The official definition of the labor force includes only those residents who are working or actively looking for work, excluding discouraged workers, students, homemakers, and the disabled. Detroit's labor force participation rate has been among the lowest. Moreover, for several decades the unemployment rate in Detroit has consistently been one of the highest in the United States. This combination of high unemployment and low labor force participation results in a significant deficit in the number of Detroiters with jobs, compared to the national average. How far behind the other cities is Detroit? If the labor force participation and unemployment rates in Detroit were equal to the national averages, the number of employed Detroiters would be over 311,000, rather than the 210,000 recorded in 2014. If Detroit had an employment rate equal to Milwaukee's, there would have been 95,000 more Detroiters with jobs. Only Flint has a lower resident employment total than Detroit. Detroit's jobs deficit is even larger when compared to growing cities like Austin (368,000 jobs) and Charlotte (346,500). Detroit lags behind most other legacy cities as well.

INCOME AND POVERTY

Given the low levels of educational attainment and employment, it is not surprising that incomes in Detroit are well below the national average. Income per capita in other legacy cities is 40 percent higher than in Detroit; one-third more Detroiters are living below the poverty level (Table 3.2). Detroiters are even more disadvantaged compared to the growing cities. Detroit's poverty rate is double that of growing cities, and its per capita income is just over half.

The income ratio provides an indication of income inequality by comparing household income at the ninety-fifth percentile with the income of a household at the twentieth percentile. The higher the ratio, the greater the gap between rich and poor households in each city. Among the forty cities in this study, Detroit was at the bottom of the list for twentieth percentile ($9,519) and ninety-fifth percentile ($103,547) income. In Detroit, even high incomes are relatively low. The resulting income ratio of 10.9 ranks fourteenth from the top among legacy cities.

Table 3.2 Income and Poverty Rates 2014

	Employed	Income per Capita	Income Ratio	Poverty Rate
Detroit	38.9%	$14,984	10.9	39.8%
Legacy	51.3%	$20,940	11.6	30.7%
Growing	61.5%	$28,112	9.6	19.2%

Source: American Community Survey

MUNICIPAL FINANCE INDICATORS

The widespread economic hardships of Detroiters are reflected in the fiscal conditions of local government. Data from the Lincoln Institute of Land Policy Fiscally Standardized database (Lincoln Institute of Land Policy 2016) provide an indication of the fiscal stress imposed on these central cities by the Great Recession of 2008–2009. The data have been standardized to reflect the aggregate of all overlying jurisdictions. This improves comparability by taking into account the differences in the services provided by the municipal government. Thus, they represent the burden on the taxpayers rather than the municipal balance sheet. To facilitate comparisons, the data presented here are per capita and are not adjusted for inflation.

Currently, this database extends only through Fiscal Year 2012. Although information is available for several years after the end of the Great Recession, recovery was still ongoing in many cities (Chernick and Reschovsky 2014). While many cities were showing signs of improving economies in 2011 and 2012, Detroit was continuing to move toward its bankruptcy filing in 2013. The turning point for Detroit did not occur until after the bankruptcy settlement, rather than the end of the Great Recession.

Table 3.3 presents the changes in General Fund Revenue per capita during the three years before and after the Great Recession. Before FY09, Detroit's per capita revenue increased by about 4.4 percent; in the post-Recession period, per capita income declined, despite increases in state and federal transfer payments. Also note that between 2006 and 2012, Detroit's population declined by 137,000; as a result, the absolute decline in total General Fund revenue was about 15.8 percent.

Table 3.3 Change in General Fund Revenue per Capita

	2006–09	2009–12	2006–12
Detroit	+$243	−$239	+$4
Legacy	+$580	+$121	+$701
Growing	+$71	−$23	+$48

Source: Lincoln Institute of Land Policy

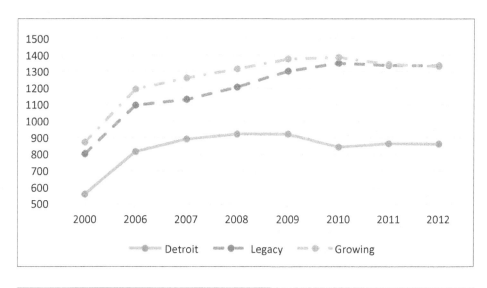

Figure 3.1: Property Tax Revenue per Capita

Source: Lincoln Institute of Land Policy

The data for the other legacy cities indicate a substantial (10.6 percent) increase in General Fund revenue between 2006 and 2009, followed by a smaller (2.0 percent) increase by 2012. General Fund revenue per capita was 13.0 percent higher in 2012 than in 2006. The pattern for the growing cities is actually similar to that of Detroit. A modest increase (8.6 percent) between 2006 and 2009 was followed by a decline of 1.0 percent between 2009 and 2012.

Property taxes and intergovernmental revenue are generally major sources of local government revenue.[1] Figures 3.1 and 3.2 show trends in these two revenue sources between 2006 and 2012. Despite having one of the highest property tax rates in the country, Detroit's per capita property tax revenue is consistently less than the comparable figures for other legacy and growing cities. Compared to these other cities, property in Detroit is relatively low-valued, and much of the tax base benefits from exemptions and abatements (Sands and Skidmore 2015). Applying a high rate to a small base yields a low return.

There is relatively little difference in the per capita revenue generated by property taxation in the growing and other legacy cities. Figure 3.1 shows that the trend lines are roughly parallel. Between 2000 and 2006, Detroit's per capita property tax revenue rose by 46 percent, compared with increases of about 37 percent for both the other legacy cities and the growing cities. Revenue per capita for these latter groups continued to increase until FY10, when the curve became much flatter and then declined slightly. Detroit property tax revenue began to decline in FY07, averaging $876 annually through FY12. Property tax revenue per capita in the other legacy cities and the growing cities averaged $1,252 and $1,316, respectively.

Between 2006 and 2012, intergovernmental revenue per capita in legacy cities leveled off at an average of $2,800. The high-growth cities, on the other hand, received an average of just $1,500 in

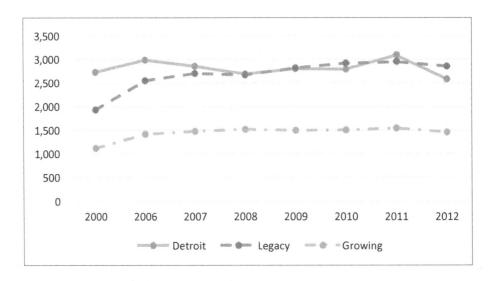

Figure 3.2: Intergovernmental Revenue per Capita
Source: Lincoln Institute of Land Policy

state and federal general fund revenue. For this group of cities, property taxes were a more important source of revenue.

Transfer payments from the federal and state governments are a much larger source of General Fund[2] revenue for Detroit and other legacy cities than is the property tax (Figure 3.2). Throughout this period, Detroit received an annual average of $2,800 per capita in federal and state transfer payments. This is more than three times the average revenue that the city derived from property taxes. Flint, the other Michigan legacy city included here, received an average of $2,950 per capita in annual funding from senior levels of government. For both Detroit and Flint, intergovernmental revenue per capita peaked in 2008; in most other cities included in the Lincoln Institute database, intergovernmental revenue peaked after the end of the Great Recession (Langley 2015).

Intergovernmental transfers per capita are much lower for the rapidly growing cities, averaging just over $1,500 between 2006 and 2012. Transfer payments to growing cities averaged less than $300 more than the comparable figure for property taxes; for Detroit, the difference is more than $1,900.

Detroit was in a class by itself with respect to bonded debt per capita (Figure 3.3). After a relatively stable period leading up to the Great Recession, Detroit's debt rose rapidly, from about $12,000 per capita in 2009 to almost $17,000 in 2012. The city with the next highest debt load in 2012 was Chicago at $14,000. Birmingham, Philadelphia, Pittsburgh, and Cleveland each had over $10,000 in debt per capita in 2012. For all nineteen legacy cities, per capita debt averaged $7,329 in 2012; the average debt in growing cities was slightly higher, averaging $8,432. Per

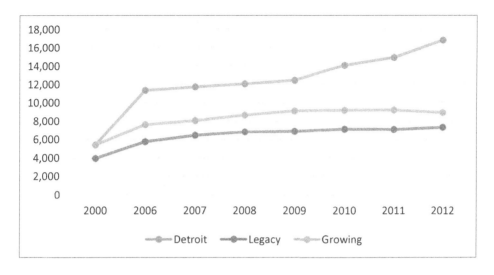

Figure 3.3: Bonded Debt per Capita

Source: Lincoln Institute of Land Policy

capita debt in Denver was just over $16,000 in 2012, close to the debt load in Detroit. Seven other growing cities had per capita debt of more than $10,000.

NEIGHBORHOOD PERSPECTIVE

Just as there are spatial differences across the metropolitan counties, Detroit's neighborhoods are far from homogenous. In Detroit, the Downtown/Midtown area has been leading Detroit's resurgence on a number of indicators (Hudson-Weber Foundation 2015). Is the rhetoric of positive change in Detroit matched by reality? Here, we examine trends in key indicators over the last five years. While the record is complex, two major conclusions stand out: (1) on a number of measures, Detroit continues to decline, and even when positive change has occurred, growth has been much less robust than many narratives would suggest. (2) Within the city, recovery has been highly uneven, resulting in increasing inequality, especially between the Downtown and Midtown areas and the city's residential neighborhoods (defined here as the balance of the city outside of the Downtown and Midtown).

Population: Between 2010 and 2014, the American Community Survey (ACS) estimates that Detroit's population fell by about 2.6 percent (Table 3.4). Downtown recorded a population gain of almost 15 percent, but this amounted to just 666 new residents. Midtown (–17 percent) and the balance of the city (–2 percent) lost population. While Detroit's population had a net decline of 18,340, the balance of the Metro area added just 14,737 to its population.

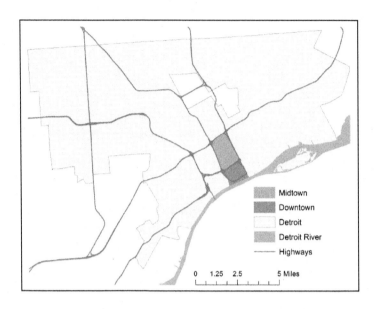

Figure 3.4: Midtown and Downtown Areas of Detroit

Table 3.4 Population, 2000–2014

	Central Business District	Midtown	CBD + Midtown	Balance Detroit	Total Detroit	MSA Balance
2000	3,822	33,512	37,334	913,936	951,270	3,501,287
2010	4,556	26,745	31,301	682,476	713,777	3,582,473
2014	5,222	20,860	26,082	669,355	695,437	3,597,210
Change 2010–2014	14.6%	−22.0%	−16.7%	−1.9%	−2.6%	2.7%

Source: Data Driven Detroit

Changes in the population in poverty between 2009 and 2014 for Downtown/Midtown and the balance of the city are shown in Table 3.5. Poverty in Midtown specifically is higher than the rest of the city, as is the Gini coefficient of income inequality.[3] It appears that as the "creative class" has moved into Midtown, income inequality has increased as suggested in previous critiques (see, for example, Peck 2005). Adding higher-income new residents to the area does not eradicate the legacy of poverty from the Cass Corridor days when substantial numbers of subsidized housing units were built in Midtown. While some of these have been demolished or converted to market-rate housing, many low-income housing units remain. The generally lower incomes of students in the Wayne State area are also a factor.

Table 3.5 Poverty and Income Disparity

		City of Detroit	ZIP Code		
			48226	48201	48202
2014	Gini Coefficient	0.50	0.55	0.58	0.52
2009	Poverty Rate	33.2%	32.4%	48.4%	43.0%
2014	Poverty Rate	39.8%	26.1%	49.7%	43.5%

Source: Data Driven Detroit

Table 3.6 Per Capita Income

	CBD	Midtown	CBD + Mid	Balance
1999	$30,846	$20,648	$22,620	$20,854
2014	$36,102	$17,638	$21,591	$14,735
Change	17.0%	−14.6%	−4.5%	−29.3%

Source: Data Driven Detroit

A similar pattern is evident in Table 3.6, which shows change in per capita income (in constant 2014 dollars) between 1999 and 2014 in Downtown/Midtown and the rest of the city. In this case, however, incomes in the Downtown area have risen while Midtown shows a decline; falling per capita incomes in the balance of the city are more severe.

Economic Indicators: According to ZIP code–level data from County Business Patterns, the number of business establishments in the city declined by about 6 percent between 2010 and 2013 (Table 3.7). Number jobs available at these firms increased by almost 4 percent, and annual payroll grew by almost 19 percent. In terms of employment and payroll, however, the record for Downtown is substantially better than the other areas of the city. In both Downtown and Midtown, average wages increased by over 17 percent, compared to a change of just 7 percent

Table 3.7 Change in Detroit Economic Indicators 2010–2013

	Establishments	Employees	Payroll	Average Wage
Detroit	−6.2%	3.7%	18.8%	13.9%
Downtown	−11.5%	21.7%	42.6%	17.2%
Midtown	−7.5%	−6.5%	9.8%	17.5%
Neighborhoods	−5.2%	−0.9%	8.1%	7.0%

Source: ZIP Code Business Patterns

Table 3.8 Employment 2007–2014

	City of Detroit	Central Business District	Midtown	CBD + Midtown	Detroit Balance
2007	245,230	73,365	48,428	121,793	123,437
2012	234,739	69,247	47,237	116,484	118,255
2014	234,552	72,618	45,296	117,914	116,638
Change 07–12	−4.3%	−5.6%	−2.5%	-4.4%	−4.2%
Change 07–14	−0.1%	4.9%	−4.1%	1.2%	−1.4%

Source: Data Driven Detroit

for neighborhood jobs. Although they represent just five percent of the city's area, the core included just over half of the job opportunities and more than 62 percent of payroll expenditures.

An important caveat in considering these employment and establishment trends is that data are currently available only through 2014. Media reports suggest that Downtown and particularly Midtown have seen significant numbers of new businesses, many relocating from the suburbs, opening in the past three years. While there have been new business openings in some neighborhoods, the gap persists. From 2007 to 2012, employment fell across Detroit, with the downturn most severe in the downtown Central Business District (Table 3.8). The increase in the number of jobs in the CBD between 2012 and 2014 nevertheless left downtown with 600 fewer jobs than in 2007. The rate of employment loss accelerated in Midtown between 2012 and 2014. The balance of Detroit showed a slowing of employment loss. In 2014, the majority of Detroit jobs were located in Downtown/Midtown.

However, even these employment gains do not hold much promise for the residents of Detroit. Table 3.9 shows the share of jobs in the city actually held by Detroiters. In all cases, the

Table 3.9 Jobs Held by Detroiters

	Central Business District			Midtown		
	Non-Detroiters	Detroiters	Total	Non-Detroiters	Detroiters	Total
2007	47,239	26,126	73,365	28,245	20,183	48,428
2012	51,664	17,583	69,247	33,187	14,050	47,237
2014	55,351	17,267	72,618	32,688	12,608	45,296
Change 2007–2014	8,112	−8,859	−747	4,443	−7,575	−3,132
Percent	17.2%	33.9%	−1.0%	15.7%	−37.5%	−6.5%

Source: Data Driven Detroit

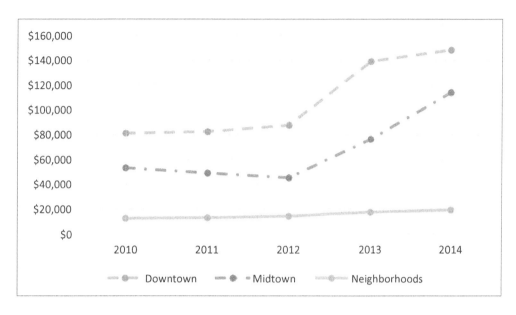

Figure 3.5: Average Residential Sales Prices Detroit 2010–2013

Source: Core Logic

percent of jobs held by residents has dropped over time, while those held by non-Detroiters has increased. In the CBD, for example, Detroiters held almost 36 percent of jobs in 2007, but just 23.7 percent in 2013; the comparable figures for Midtown are 42 percent and 28 percent. In short, any increases in jobs in the city appear to have benefited workers living in the suburbs. Returning to the map of the metropolitan distribution of race, it also seems clear that the bulk of these suburban workers are white.

There are a number of possible explanations for these trends. Many of the jobs added to Detroit's downtown core have been relocated from the suburbs; not all of the workers have chosen to change their place of residence along with their place of work. In the case of newly created jobs, Detroiters often lack the skills and education necessary to obtain some the new technology-related employment opportunities. Reduction in the number of public sector jobs, primarily with the city and Detroit Public Schools, has also been a factor.

Housing: These demographic and economic trends are reflected in the price and condition of housing in Detroit (Figure 3.5). Home prices in Downtown and Midtown are clearly much higher than in Detroit's neighborhoods, and they are increasing much more rapidly. In 2010, the average sales price of a home (most likely a condominium) in Downtown Detroit was six and a half times the average sales price in the neighborhoods; in 2014, the ratio had increased to 7.6. In 2014 the average sales price in Midtown had risen to 5.8 times the neighborhood figure, from 4.2 times in 2010. One contributing factor in the low neighborhood sales prices is the high proportion of foreclosure sales, which are often heavily discounted. Over 41 percent of the neighborhood sales in 2014 were short sales or real-estate-owned (REO) sales; the comparable figures for Downtown and Midtown were zero and 15 percent, respectively.

There are, of course, considerable differences in the housing markets in different Detroit neighborhoods. In 17 of the ZIP Code–defined neighborhoods, the average sales price increased by less than $10,000 between 2010 and 2014, while Downtown and Midtown sales prices rose by $67,000 and $60,800, respectively. In the neighborhood just west of Midtown, which includes the Woodbridge community, average sales prices increased by $72,500. Several other neighborhoods close to the core area recorded price increases in the $19,000 to $28,000 range. Recovery of the housing market in many neighborhoods has been inhibited by a lack of demand (too few households with adequate income and credit history) as well as a limited supply of housing that is in good condition. It continues to be difficult to secure financing for home purchases in many neighborhoods.

CONCLUSIONS

Returning to the question raised at the beginning of this essay: Does the Detroit narrative describe the destiny of central cities in general or even other legacy cities? There are certainly a number of commonalities between Detroit and other legacy cities. Deindustrialization, aging infrastructure, shrinking tax base, unfunded pension obligations, and growing income inequality are problems not limited only to Detroit. The question is not so much whether other legacy cities will confront problems similar to Detroit's, but rather whether they will be able to deal with them more successfully.

In terms of the municipal fiscal indicator variables considered in this essay, Detroit is far from the worst, generally ranking in the bottom half. The one exception is that, before the bankruptcy settlement, Detroit had the highest debt per capita. Detroit is also in the middle of the rankings on proportion of foreign-born and income ratio. For other demographic and socioeconomic variables, Detroit is consistently at the bottom of the rankings. Only Flint and Gary come close to matching Detroit's poor performance.

The geographic scale of the analysis makes a difference. Detroit compares unfavorably with its suburbs, particularly on income and employment-related measures; many other legacy cities have similar problems. But other legacy cities are recovering more rapidly than Detroit. While there have been tangible improvements in limited areas of Detroit, particularly Downtown/Midtown, the balance of the city's neighborhoods and population continue to struggle.

Based on the available evidence, it seems unlikely that many other legacy cities will experience declines as dramatic as Detroit's. While there may be few additional municipal bankruptcies at the scale of Detroit's, some changes seem inevitable. Reductions in municipal services through elimination, privatization, and regionalization are likely to impact most cities; over time, a new and more limited definition of *essential public services* is likely to emerge. Higher taxes and fees will be widespread.

Given the magnitude of its problems, would it be realistic to expect Detroit to reverse its decline as some other legacy cities have already done, or at least to achieve an equilibrium on its way to eventual improvement? Katz and Bradley argue that Detroit, in particular the Downtown and Midtown areas, is an example of an innovative city. They conclude that Detroiters recognize they are "on their own and must fend for themselves" (2013, 140). Detroit, the prime example of urban collapse, has become a model for other cities and metropolitan areas.

But the limited and uneven nature of Detroit's recovery to date suggests that citywide recovery is tenuous. The economic growth in Downtown/Midtown may be engulfed by the continued decline in the neighborhoods that make up 90 to 95 percent of the city's area, population, and economic activity. Without minimizing the impressive accomplishments in Downtown/Midtown in recent years, there has been only limited progress in some of the city's neighborhoods, and some continue to decline. Outside of the city center, few neighborhoods have the concentration of community assets that have been the basis for the Downtown/Midtown revival. The Midtown revitalization template may be a poor fit for Detroit's neighborhoods. Solving these problems is likely to require interventions that are regional and state-led, on a scale well beyond what has been seen to date. Whether this will occur and what the next hundred years will bring for Detroit is by no means clear.

NOTES

1. Detroit also receives substantial revenue from a municipal income tax and casino wagering taxes.
2. State and federal funds for specific functions, such as education and highways, are not included in these totals.
3. The larger the Gini coefficient, which can range from zero to one, the greater the inequality.

REFERENCES

Chernick, Howard, and Andrew Reschovsky. 2014. *The Fiscal Health of U.S. Cities.* Working Paper. Cambridge, MA: Lincoln Institute of Land Policy.

Florida, Richard. 2002. *The Rise of the Creative Class.* New York: Basic Books.

Hudson Weber Foundation. 2015. *7.2 Square Miles: A Report on Greater Downtown Detroit,* 2nd ed. http://detroitsevenpointtwo.com/resources/7.2SQ_MI_Book_FINAL_LoRes.pdf.

Katz, Bruce, and Jennifer Bradley. 2013. *The Metropolitan Revolution.* Washington, DC: Brookings Institution.

Langley, Adam. 2015. *Local Government Finances During and After the Great Recession.* Conference Paper. Cambridge, MA: Lincoln Institute of Land Policy. http://www.lincolninst.edu/publications/conference-papers/local-government-finances-during-after-great-recession.

Legacy Cities Partnership. 2016. *Working Together to Empower America's Legacy Cities.* http://www.legacycities.org/.

Lincoln Institute of Land Policy. 2016. *Fiscally Standardized Cities*. Cambridge, MA: Lincoln Institute of Land Policy. http://datatoolkits.lincolninst.edu/subcenters/fiscally-standardized-cities/explanation.

Mallach, Alan, and Lavea Brachman. 2013. *Regenerating America's Legacy Cities*. Policy Focus Report. Cambridge, MA: Lincoln Institute of Land Policy. http://www.lincolninst.edu/publications/policy-focus-reports/regenerating-americas-legacy-cities.

Peck, Jamie. 2005. "Struggling with the Creative Class." *International Journal of Urban and Regional Research* 29 (4): 740–770.

Reese, Laura, Gary Sands, and Mark Skidmore. 2014. "Memo from Motown: Is Austerity Here to Stay?" *Cambridge Journal of Regions, Economy and Society* 7 (1): 99–116.

Sands, Gary, and Mark Skidmore. 2015. *Detroit and the Property Tax*. Policy. Focus Report. Cambridge, MA: Lincoln Institute of Land Policy. http://www.lincolninst.edu/publications/policy-focus-reports/detroit-property-tax.

IMAGE CREDITS

- Tab. 3.1: U.S. Census Bureau, https://factfinder.census.gov/faces/nav/jsf/pages/searchresults.xhtml?refresh=t. Copyright in the Public Domain.
- Tab. 3.2: U.S. Census Bureau, https://factfinder.census.gov/faces/nav/jsf/pages/searchresults.xhtml?refresh=t. Copyright in the Public Domain.
- Tab. 3.3: Source: http://datatoolkits.lincolninst.edu/subcenters/fiscally-standardized-cities.
- Fig. 3.1: Source: http://datatoolkits.lincolninst.edu/subcenters/fiscally-standardized-cities.
- Fig. 3.2: Source: http://datatoolkits.lincolninst.edu/subcenters/fiscally-standardized-cities.
- Fig. 3.3: Source: http://datatoolkits.lincolninst.edu/subcenters/fiscally-standardized-cities.
- Tab. 3.4: Source: http://datatoolkits.lincolninst.edu/subcenters/fiscally-standardized-cities.
- Tab. 3.5: Source: http://datadrivendetroit.org/services/.
- Tab. 3.6: Source: http://datadrivendetroit.org/services/.
- Tab. 3.7: U.S. Census Bureau, http://www.census.gov/data/datasets/2013/econ/cbp/2013-cbp.html. Copyright in the Public Domain.
- Tab. 3.8: Source: http://datadrivendetroit.org/services/.
- Tab. 3.9: Source: http://datadrivendetroit.org/services/.
- Fig. 3.5: Source: http://www.corelogic.com/about-us/researchtrends/corelogic-home-price-insights.aspx#.WCSCl70rJPY.

Appendix Table 1
Select Legacy Cities

City	Population	Change 1990–2010	White non-Hispanic	Dissimilarity Index	Foreign Born	Income per capita	Income Ratio	Employment Rate	College Degree	Poverty Rate
Detroit	695,437	-31.7%	8.7%	86.7	5.2%	$14,984	10.9	38.9%	13.1%	39.8%
Akron	198,492	-10.4%	60.7%	69.7	4.6%	$20,245	8.4	53.5%	20.5%	26.7%
Baltimore	622,271	-16.9%	28.1%	71.8	4.7%	$25,052	11.5	53.4%	27.7%	24.2%
Birmingham	211,705	-20.8%	21.3%	77.4	3.4%	$19,640	9.6	50.4%	23.1%	31.0%
Buffalo	259,959	-21.0%	45.6%	80.4	8.6%	$20,726	11.7	52.2%	24.7%	30.9%
Chicago	2,712,608	-3.8%	32.2%	83.6	20.9%	$28,623	11.9	57.6%	34.9%	22.7%
Cincinnati	297,117	-19.8%	48.8%	78.0	5.1%	$25,256	15.7	56.2%	32.3%	30.9%
Cleveland	392,114	-22.4%	34.3%	79.7	4.7%	$17,436	11.6	47.5%	15.2%	35.9%
Dayton	141,527	-23.4%	51.5%	73.9	4.0%	$16,673	10.3	47.7%	16.7%	35.9%
Flint	100,569	-28.4%	36.9%	81.2	1.1%	$14,527	12.0	37.0%	11.3%	41.6%
Gary	79,165	-33.0%	10.6%	87.9	1.8%	$15,983	13.8	42.0%	13.1%	38.7%
Hartford	125,211	-9.6%	15.9%	69.5	22.2%	$16,813	11.5	49.5%	15.0%	34.4%
Milwaukee	598,078	-5.6%	36.6%	84.4	9.8%	$19,836	9.0	56.5%	22.8%	29.4%
New Orleans	368,471	-36.7%	30.7%	74.7	2.6%	$27,255	17.7	54.7%	34.4%	27.7%
Philadelphia	1,546,920	-5.8%	36.2%	76.9	12.5%	$22,543	11.8	50.4%	24.5%	26.7%
Pittsburgh	306,045	-18.6%	65.1%	72.5	1.0%	$27,435	11.5	56.1%	37.2%	22.8%
Rochester	210,461	-8.9%	36.6%	71.1	9.1%	$19,180	9.7	52.7%	24.4%	33.8%
St. Louis	318,727	-22.1%	42.8%	78.0	6.8%	$23,244	12.5	55.8%	30.4%	27.8%
Syracuse	144,648	-11.5%	51.8%	73.6	11.8%	$19,283	11.3	49.3%	26.0%	35.1%
Toledo	283,932	-14.3%	61.3%	72.9	3.4%	$18,113	9.2	52.7%	17.7%	27.7%

Source: American Community Survey

Appendix Tab. 1: U.S. Census Bureau, https://factfinder.census.gov/faces/nav/jsf/pages/searchresults.xhtml?refresh=t. Copyright in the Public Domain.

Appendix Table 2
Select Growing Cities

City	Population	Change 1990–2010	White non-Hispanic	Dissimilarity Index	Foreign Born	Income per capita	Income Ratio	Employment Rate	College Degree	Poverty Rate
Albuquerque	553,576	37.1%	41.3%	39.4	10.7%	$26,876	9.9	59.5%	33.2%	18.5%
Austin	864,218	55.0%	48.7%	57.1	18.4%	$32,672	9.3	68.2%	47.6%	19.0%
Charlotte	774,807	64.6%	43.9%	61.1	15.3%	$31,844	10.3	64.2%	40.7%	17.2%
Charleston	125,458	31.6%	69.7%	54.1	4.5%	$33,117	9.8	61.0%	49.2%	19.0%
Dallas	1,240,985	18.9%	29.3%	64.4	24.2%	$27,917	12.2	61.8%	32.0%	24.1%
Denver	633,777	23.4%	52.9%	66.2	16.0%	$34,423	10.6	65.4%	43.7%	18.3%
El Paso	669,771	24.4%	14.8%	41.1	24.9%	$20,050	8.9	53.3%	22.7%	21.5%
Ft. Worth	778,753	55.5%	40.9%	64.5	17.5%	$24,756	12.2	61.2%	26.9%	19.3%
Houston	2,167,988	23.1%	26.0%	71.8	28.4%	$27,938	11.6	62.0%	29.8%	22.9%
Jacksonville	837,533	22.2%	54.2%	59.3	9.7%	$25,496	8.5	56.9%	25.5%	17.8%
Las Vegas	597,353	119.2%	46.3%	47.4	21.3%	$25,555	7.9	55.6%	21.6%	17.7%
Oklahoma City	600,729	27.2%	55.7%	60.5	12.4%	$26,275	8.9	62.0%	30.9%	18.2%
Orlando	250,224	43.9%	39.8%	60.0	18.3%	$25,664	9.3	65.1%	33.4%	19.8%
Phoenix	1,490,758	42.9%	46.0%	49.1	20.2%	$24,057	9.3	59.2%	26.5%	23.2%
Portland	602,568	21.9%	71.8%	55.8	14.0%	$32,438	10.7	62.9%	34.1%	18.3%
Raleigh	423,287	73.8%	54.0%	52.7	13.3%	$31,169	8.9	64.8%	47.6%	16.3%
San Antonio	1,385,438	30.3%	26.3%	55.5	14.2%	$22,784	8.9	58.5%	24.9%	20.1%
San Diego	1,341,510	17.7%	20.2%	58.2	26.3%	$33,789	8.9	58.8%	42.3%	15.8%
San Jose	986,320	19.9%	27.5%	45.9	38.7%	$34,992	8.1	67.8%	38.2%	11.8%
Tucson	525,031	24.1%	46.3%	44.2	14.9%	$20,437	8.5	61.7%	24.9%	25.1%

Source: American Community Survey

Appendix Tab. 2: U.S. Census Bureau, https://factfinder.census.gov/faces/nav/jsf/pages/searchresults.xhtml?refresh=t. Copyright in the Public Domain.

AUTHOR BIOS

Lynn Bachelor is an associate professor in the Department of Political Science and Public Administration at the University of Toledo.

Joe T. Darden is a professor of geography at Michigan State University.

Hon. Sharon Tevis Finch was a Michigan civil rights commissioner, a judge on the Detroit Court of Common Pleas and later a judge on the Wayne County Circuit Court for 25 years.

Sidney Fine was emeritus professor of history at the University of Michigan.

George Galster is the distinguished professor and Clarence G. Hilberry Professor Emeritus of Urban Affairs at Wayne State University.

Richard Child Hill is emeritus professor of sociology at Michigan State University.

Melvin Holli was emeritus professor of history at the University of Illinois at Chicago.

Jeff Horner is a senior lecturer in urban studies and planning at Wayne State University.

Bryan Jones is professor and J.J. Pickle Regents Chair in Congressional Studies at the University of Texas at Austin.

Hon. Nathaniel R. Jones is a retired judge on the United States Court of Appeals for the Sixth Circuit.

Victoria Kovari is the executive director of the City of Detroit Mayor's Office of Neighborhoods.

Marissa Mewitz is a Masters of Urban Planning graduate at Wayne State University, and an urban planner, cyclist, and Detroiter.

Gary Sands is emeritus professor of urban studies and planning at Wayne State University.

Emily Smith is a recent graduate of the Urban Studies Program at Wayne State University.

Joel Stone is senior curator at the Detroit Historical Museum.

Thomas Sugrue is professor of social and cultural analysis and history at New York University.

June Thomas is Centennial Professor of Urban and Regional Planning at the University of Michigan Taubman College of Architecture and Urban Planning.

Richard Thomas is emeritus professor of history at Michigan State University.

Susan Villerot is an academic services officer in the Department of Anthropology at Wayne State University.

CPSIA information can be obtained
at www.ICGtesting.com
Printed in the USA
LVOW04s1928060917
547784LV00001B/2/P